BURT FRANKLIN: BIBLIOGRAPHY & REFERENCE SERIES 357

Privately Printed Books

FAC-SIMILE OF THE BINDING OF QUEEN ELIZABETH'S COPY
DE ANTIQUITATE ECCLESIÆ BRITANNICÆ.

PRIVATELY PRINTED BY ARCHBISHOP PARKER, MDLXXII.

BIBLIOGRAPHICAL CATALOGUE

OF

𝔓𝔯𝔦𝔳𝔞𝔱𝔢𝔩𝔶 𝔓𝔯𝔦𝔫𝔱𝔢𝔡 𝔅𝔬𝔬𝔨𝔰.

BY

JOHN MARTIN, F.S.A.,

LIBRARIAN, WOBURN ABBEY.

SECOND EDITION.

BURT FRANKLIN
NEW YORK

Published by BURT FRANKLIN
235 East 44th St., New York, N.Y. 10017
Originally Published: 1854
Reprinted: 1970
Printed in the U.S.A.

S.B.N. 22646
Library of Congress Card Catalog No.: 73-128844
Burt Franklin: Bibliography and Reference Series 357

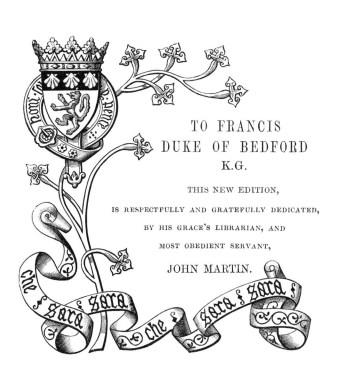

TO FRANCIS
DUKE OF BEDFORD
K.G.

THIS NEW EDITION,

IS RESPECTFULLY AND GRATEFULLY DEDICATED,

BY HIS GRACE'S LIBRARIAN, AND

MOST OBEDIENT SERVANT,

JOHN MARTIN.

PREFACE

(TO THE FIRST EDITION).*

THIS attempt to describe a peculiar class of books in the literature of our country has long engaged the Editor's attention; and although it comprises several works of little interest, except to the writers and to their immediate connections, it will be found to contain many of considerable value, highly worthy the attention of those who take an interest in the study of the history, antiquities, and topography of their country.

By privately-printed books, the Editor means to designate such only as were not intended by the writers for sale, and the circulation of which has been confined entirely to their friends and connections, or to those who took an interest in the matter contained in them. The difficulty of distinguishing such will be easily understood by those who have paid any attention to the collecting books of this kind; and amongst the number herein enumerated, it is very probable that some will be found with a doubtful claim to appear in this catalogue.

---

* A few slight additions have been made, distinguished by brackets.

Again, it is exceedingly difficult to distinguish between books *secretly* and *privately* printed ;—with the former, the Editor has not interfered, as they were, to all intents and purposes, printed for sale, and consequently foreign to the object he had in view. The earliest book which he has judged to be strictly entitled to this claim, will be seen in the instance of the rare volume on the English Church, by Archbishop Parker ; a work unquestionably printed for private circulation alone ; on the examination of which, much pains has been bestowed. Previous to the time of Parker, and on the change of Religion, which called forth so many controversial publications from the advocates of different opinions, many books were circulated without the printer or publisher's name : these, from this circumstance, have been frequently styled privately printed ; although there is little doubt they were secretly sold, the fear of prosecution preventing a more public sale. This was not the class of books which it came within the Editor's intention to describe ; nor is he aware that, if he had attempted it, he could have added much to the information which the labours of Strype, and others, have brought to light upon these books.

Although he has been long engaged in collecting the materials for this work, he is sensible that many articles have escaped his search; the peculiarity, under which these works have for the most part been printed, rendering the task the more difficult—this, however, is invariably the case with attempts of this kind ; and he could hardly have expected, had he longer delayed its appearance, to have rendered it much more perfect.

It was not within his design to include *Pamphlets;* the number of tracts which have been privately circulated in this shape is too great, and in most cases they are of too ephemeral and uninteresting a nature, to have permitted him to make so considerable and so useless an addition to his volume : a few exceptions have been made, which the subject, or the celebrity of the writer, seemed to justify.

The Editor has not felt himself at liberty to indulge in any remarks of a critical nature; the circumstances, under which these works have appeared, clearly preclude him from such a course : where notices of that nature appear, the source from which they have been derived is mentioned, and the opinion will be respected according to the value placed upon the authority. It was his intention to have added a catalogue of suppressed books; but the length to which this work has extended, as well as the delay which would have been incurred, have induced him to abandon the design : he had made some progress in collecting materials for that purpose, which, should the present attempt be favourably received, he may be induced to resume.*

The second portion of the work, consisting of an account of the publications from literary clubs, and private presses, will probably be found the more interesting : no pains have been spared to render it perfect, and the compiler's endeavours have been most liberally

---

* It is not very probable the Editor's intentions will ever be carried out; such materials as he had collected, he has transferred to his son, Under Librarian to the Honourable Society of the Inner Temple ; whether his duties will afford him leisure to continue it, is at present uncertain.

and kindly seconded by the different parties most able to give him information.

Private presses appear to have existed at a very early date in this country : a slight sketch is here attempted of those which have come under notice, in the researches for books connected with this undertaking. At the period of the Reformation, the advocates of the ancient faith were compelled, from the fear of prosecution, and the severe punishment entailed on the printer of seditious works, as these were then styled, to avail themselves of a foreign press for the dissemination of their opinions. The inconvenience and delay, thereby occasioned, natu-rally led to the establishment of a private press in this country. " The first appearance," says Johnson,* " of pamphlets amongst us, is generally thought to be at the new opposition raised against the errors and cor-ruptions of the church of Rome. Those who were first convinced of the reasonableness of the new learning, as it was then called, propagated their opinions in small pieces, which were cheaply printed ; and, what was then of great importance, easily concealed. These treatises were generally printed in foreign countries, and are not therefore always very correct. There was not that opportunity of printing in private ; for the number of printers was small, and the presses easily overlooked by the clergy, who spared no labour or vigilance for the sup-pression of heresy. There is, however, reason to suspect that some attempts were made to carry on the propagation of truth, by a secret press ; for one of the first treatises in

* Preface to Harleian Miscellany.

favour of the Reformation, is said, at the end, to be printed at *Greenwich, by permission of the Lord of Hosts."* *

Edward III. founded a convent at Greenwich, in 1376; but the record of its foundation is buried in much obscurity. In 1486, Henry VII. however, granted a charter to the Franciscan Friars there established. In the reign of his successor, Katharine of Arragon was a great protector of this order, and one of its members was her confessor; having taken up the cause of their illustrious patroness, when the divorce from her brutal husband was in agitation : that monarch, in revenge, suppressed the whole order throughout the kingdom. They assembled again on the accession of Queen Mary, but Elizabeth finally suppressed the establishment, in 1559.†

In the reign of Queen Mary, a small tract purports to be printed at Greenwich, entitled *A faythful Admonycion of a certain trewe pastor and prophete sent into the Germanes, &c., now translated into Inglyshe, &c."* At the end it is stated, *Imprynted at Greenwych, by Conrade Freeman,* in the month of May, 1554. Dr. Cotton, ‡ however, is of opinion, that it was executed in the Low Countries, or Switzerland : a copy of the tract is in the Bodleian Library.

In the reign of Edward VI., a press is said to have been in action in Devonshire, about the period when the insurrection in that county broke out against the royal authority. So great appears to have been the

---

* A volume formerly belonging to the Grey Friars of Greenwich, is in the Arundel collection of MSS. No. 71.

† Dugdale, Monasticon.

‡ Typographical Gazetteer, Second Edition.

annoyance which the existence of private and unlicensed
presses gave to the ruling powers, that it is reported to
have given rise, in the reign of Queen Mary, " to a
charter granted to certain freemen of London, in whose
fidelity no doubt she confided, entirely prohibiting *all*
presses but what should be licensed by them—which
charter is that by which the Company of Stationers in
London is at this time incorporated." *

In the reign of Queen Elizabeth, a private press was
erected at Wandsworth, where the Nonconformists established, in 1572, a presbytery, " the first born of all the
presbyteries in England."† The most active member of
this establishment was Thomas Cartwright, the brother-
in-law of Stubbs, who with Page, " had their right hands
cut off with a cleaver, driven through the wrist by the
force of a mallet, upon a scaffold in the market place at
Westminster,"‡ for being concerned in the publication
of a pamphlet against the projected match between
Queen Elizabeth and the Duke of Anjou ; styled in the
proclamation in 1579, as " a lewd seditious book, rashly
compiled and secretly printed." Herbert § mentions a
book entitled *Certain Articles, &c.,* || said to have been
privately printed at Wandsor [Wandsworth], near London, 8vo. 1572.

---

* Johnson; Preface to Harleian Miscellany.
† Fuller's Church History, Book viii.
‡ Camden, Annals of Elizabeth.
§ Ames, History of Printing, page 1632.
|| " Certaine Articles, collected and taken (as it is thought) by the Byshops
out of a little Boke, entitled an Admonition to the Parliament, wyth an answere
to the same, containing a confirmation of the sayde Booke in shorte notes."
A copy was in the Heber Catalogue, part 2. No. 1019.

" This junto," says Collier, * " published a great many venomous pamphlets, under the disguise of Martin Mar-Prelate."† The same authority says, " The Puritan libels were generally printed by one Walgrave; he had a travelling press for this purpose ; 't was removed from Moulsey, near Kingston upon Thames, to Fawsley, in Northamptonshire. The next stage was Norton; from Norton 'twas shifted to Coventry." ‡

The exertions of the ministers of Elizabeth at length broke up the press at Wandsworth. It is said to have been established again at Esher, and conducted in such secrecy, as to have defied all the efforts made to destroy it. From this press issued the pamphlets directed against Archbishop Whitgift ; and, when finally put down at Manchester, by the Earl of Derby, where the printer and press were both seized, it was employed upon the well-known pamphlet, called *More Work for a Cooper*. " Never," says Mr. D'Israeli, § " did sedition travel so fast, nor conceal itself so closely ; for they employed a movable press ; and as soon as it was surmised that Martin was in Surrey, it was found he had removed to Northamptonshire, while the next account came that

---

* Collier, Eccl. History, vol. ii.

† " Of these libels the most famous went under the name of Martin Mar-Prelate, a visored knight of those lists, behind whose shield a host of sturdy puritans were supposed to fight. These were printed at a moveable press, shifted to different parts of the country as the pursuit grew hot, and contained little serious argument, but the unwarrantable invectives of angry men, who stuck at no calumny to blacken their enemies."—*Hallam's Constitutional History of England*, vol. i. p. 277. 1839.

‡ Wood says, in the Life of Penry, " printed by stealth, partly in that nest of rigid puritans and schismatics, at Fawsley in Northamptonshire, and partly at Coventry, and elsewhere."—*Ath. Ox.*, by Bliss, vol. i. page 595.

§ Quarrels of Authors, vol. iii.

he was shewing his head in Warwickshire." These proceedings of this sect appear to have been finally extinguished by Elizabeth; and no more is heard of them until 1635, when Heylyn says,* they again made their appearance.

The reign of the peaceful James appears to have been little disturbed by the productions of private presses; although the work of Vorstius, *De Deo*, published on the Continent, which was publicly burnt here, gave him considerable uneasiness; and was the subject of a long diplomatic correspondence.† The reign of his unfortunate successor has been well styled by Johnson, the " Age of Pamphlets." The British Museum contains the celebrated collection of the tracts published on both sides of the then prevailing controversy, consisting of upwards of two thousand volumes.‡ This valuable series was presented to the nation by the munificence of George III. More than one hundred volumes in this collection were clandestinely printed at private presses, all traces of which are now obliterated.

---

* Ecclesia Vindicata.

† Mr. Trumbull was the agent of James at Brussels during this period. In the valuable manuscript collection of the Marquess of Downshire are several letters on this subject.

‡ " It consists of 30,000 tracts, bound in 2000 volumes ; 100, chiefly on the King's side were, printed, but never published. The whole was intended for Charles the First's use, carried about England as the Parliament army marched, kept in the collector's warehouses disguised as tables covered with canvas, and lodged last at Oxford, under the care of Dr. Barlow, till he was made bishop of Lincoln. They were offered to the library at Oxford, and at length bought for Charles II. by his stationer, Samuel Mearne, whose widow was afterwards obliged to dispose of them by leave of the said king, 1684 ; but it is believed they continued unsold till his present majesty (George III.) bought them of Mearne's representatives. In a printed letter it is said the collector refused 4000*l.* for them."—*Nichols' Anecdotes*, vol. iv. p. 103. Oldys' Dissertation.

During the puritanical reign of the usurper Cromwell, Rinuccini, the Pope's legate, established presses at Kilkenny and Waterford, for the purpose of disseminating those doctrines which he conceived to be essential to the interests of his master.* Dr. O'Conor styles them vile publications. †

In the reign of James II. Obadiah Walker " set up cases of letters and a press in the back part of his lodgings, belonging to him as Master of University College, where he printed the works of Ab. Woodhead, his quondam tutor, and would have printed many more (all, or most, against the Church of England), had King James II. continued longer on the throne." ‡

Among the tracts printed at this press was, *Some Reflections, by Thomas Deane,* Fellow of University College, an. 1688, 4*to.* Walker had a license granted to him by the King, dated May, 1686, for the exclusive sale of certain books for twenty-one years. The list of them is printed in the second volume of Gutch's Miscellanea Curiosa: they are all in favour of the Roman Catholic religion.

Dr. Lee, in a Memorial for the Bible Societies of Scotland, states that at Holyrood House several papers and works were printed, by the authority of James II. §

---

* Cotton, Typographical Gazetteer.

† *Columbanus,* Letter 11.

‡ Wood, Athenæ Oxonienses, by Bliss, vol. iv.: Bodleian Letters, i. p. 35.

§ Mr. Macaulay says, Lestrange was sent to Holyrood House by James, vol. ii. p. 124. See Wodrow, iii. x. 3.

An account of the Holyrood printing will be found in Cotton's Typographical Gazetteer, Second Edition, p. 126.

Few traces remain of private presses after this time; the necessity for establishing them having pretty well subsided, from the tranquillity consequent on the Revolution; politics and Religion, the two prime agents which supplied these secret presses, being generally allowed to state their claims and advance their arguments with tolerable freedom. The Rebellion in Scotland may perhaps have given rise to a temporary establishment of such a press. Dr. Cotton mentions, that a private press appears to have been once established at Ragland Castle, in Monmouthshire; from whence issued, *A Collection of Loyal Songs, Poems, &c.* said to be privately printed, in 1750.*

The purposes, to which the institution of private presses has been applied in later days, have differed considerably from those of former times. The more elegant branches of literature, poetry, and topography, have supplanted the controversies of the religious bigot and political partizan.

To the slight but imperfect sketch already given, there remains but little to add. The first that occurs, is that of a press established at Glynde, near Lewes in Sussex; † a seat belonging to the late Lord Hampden, which Dr. Cotton states to have been erected in the year 1770.

The Bodleian Library contains the first sheet only of a poem, called *The Summer Day, a Descriptive Pastoral,* 4*to.* Glynd, 1770. ‡

---

* Vide page 51.

† Typ. Gazetteer, 8vo. p. 108.

[‡ Dr. Hurdis, professor of poetry, Oxon, printed a volume of Lectures on Poetry. Printed at the author's own press, at Bishopstone, in Sussex. 1797. 8vo. pp. 330.—See Heber, pt. i. 3678.]

The celebrated John Wilkes had a press at his house, in Princes Court, Great George Street, Westminster, where he printed two works, mentioned in this volume.*

At Hafod, in Cardiganshire, its late owner, Mr. Johnes, established a press; from whence issued, as is well known, the Chronicles of Froissart, Monstrelet, and Joinville; works which, independent of their typographical excellence as the productions of a private press, have conferred a lasting benefit on the literature of the country.

At Hartwell, in Buckinghamshire, when occupied by the exiled Royal Family of France, it is said that a press was used for the purpose of printing proclamations, and other small pieces, in support of the claims of the House of Bourbon.

This imperfect account of private presses cannot better be closed than by the notice of that established at WINTER HARBOUR, off Melville Island, by Captain Parry and his enterprising companions, in 1819 and 1820, when the sound of the tympan and frisket was heard, for the first time, amid " a bleak expanse, shagged o'er with wavy rocks, cheerless and void," and the *North Georgia Gazette and Winter Chronicle* made its first appearance.†

[The Editor is indebted to the kindness of J. Winter Jones, Esq., F.S.A., of the British Museum, for the following account of the theatricals, and printing press,

---

* Vide pages 59, 61.   † Printed for sale, 1821.

b

in the Arctic Expedition of 1850-1, under the command of Captain Austin.

" A theatre was fitted up on board the ' Assistance,' and a corps of actors formed, under the management of Captain Ommanney. And on board the ' Resolute' and ' Intrepid' saloons were opened for masquerade balls, several of which took place with great success during the long Arctic night. A *printing-press* was given to the Expedition by the Admiralty, for printing balloon-papers. There were no printers in the squadron, but some of the officers soon learned the art ; and besides balloon-papers, play-bills, and announcements of fancy dress balls, were regularly sent to press. Several of the men, too, became adepts in the art of printing, and set up in type songs and other trifles, chiefly of their own composition. So great a passion, indeed, did printing become amongst them, that when at length their stock of paper was run out, they printed on chamois-leather, on shirts, and in one instance on a blanket."—Extract from the *Preface* to *Arctic Miscellanies*, by the Officers and Seamen of the Expedition. 1852.

In the British Museum are some specimens of this Arctic printing-press.

Two are play-bills, one printed on leather on both sides.

" Royal Arctic Theatre. H.M.S. Assistance. Last night for the season. Friday, 28th February, 1851. Historical Drama, in two Acts, of Charles XII. After which, grand Phantasmagorial Magical Figures. To conclude with the new Pantomime of Zero. Doors open at six o'clock, commence at 6.30.—*Griffith's Island Printing Office.*"

The second on pink paper, for January 9th, 1851. " The Farce of the Turned Head, Bombastes Furioso, and Zero. —*Griffith's Island Printing Office.*"

" The English Maiden's Song," sung in the Pantomime of " Zero," printed on yellow paper.

A specimen of the means adopted for dispersing intelligence by balloons, consisting of a message, printed on a slip of green silk.]

In the present volume will be found a more particular history of other private presses, the number and importance of their productions appearing to demand a more complete account.*

Nothing more now remains for the Editor, than that he should discharge one of the pleasantest parts of his duty; namely, that of acknowledging the great kindness and valuable assistance he has received.

To enumerate all the different parties who have taken an interest in his undertaking,—who have aided him by their advice, and furnished him with several valuable communications, he would have to record a list which, however gratifying to himself, would most probably weary the reader's patience, and appear like an endeavour to throw over his work an air of consequence and value far beyond its deserts. In the work itself will be found his acknowledgments to several friends, for particular assistance ;

---

* Will appear in the volume now in preparation.

but, although he refrains from swelling his list with the names of all to whose kindness he is indebted, he cannot content himself without particular mention of a few, whose assistance has been most material.

From the earliest announcement of his intentions, the Venerable Archdeacon Wrangham has constantly favoured him with numerous and important communications, drawn, for the most part, from his own valuable library, rich in books of the class herein described.*

The Venerable Archdeacon Cotton, whose bibliographical knowledge is too well appreciated to require the feeble tribute of his pen, the Editor has to thank for several curious communications, and for his readiness in answering inquiries, which he has had occasion to trouble him with.

To the Rev. Dr. Lamb, Master of Corpus Christi College, Cambridge, he begs to return his thanks for his condescension in examining Archbishop Parker's work, not only in the Library of his own College, but in other Libraries of that University.†

To the Rev. Dr. Bandinel, Keeper of the Bodleian Library, Oxford, and the Rev. John Lodge, Keeper of the Public Library, at Cambridge, his thanks are due, for the great kindness with which they forwarded his views, and facilitated his access, not only to the treasures entrusted to their peculiar care, but to the various other Libraries dispersed in the different Colleges of the two

---

* This excellent man died in 1844, and his valuable library was sold by Messrs. Sotheby. See page 344.

† Dr. Lamb died in 1849.

Universities; and fr<.n the Keepers of which he is bound, for the most part, to acknowledge the greatest attention to his wishes.

To the Rev. Dr. Bliss, his acknowledgments are due, for the very lively interest he has displayed in seconding his wishes during his visits to Oxford.

To Charles George Young, Esq., F.S.A., York Herald, * his thanks are pre-eminently due. The readiness, with which that gentleman renders his valuable assistance to any literary undertaking, is well known; and the present work has had the benefit of his suggestions, and been enriched by several of the most important and valuable books described in it.

To Mr. Thomas Moule, † he has to render his sincere thanks, not only for several interesting communications, but for the benefit of his correct taste, in many of the illustrations dispersed throughout the volume.

From the Shakspeare Press, several of the works herein described have issued; and to Mr. Nicol, the proprietor of that establishment, he is indebted for valuable hints with respect to the works printed by him, as well as for some very interesting information, which, without his kindness, he should have been unable to have obtained.

The Editor regrets that the expenses necessarily incurred in printing this work, have been so considerable as to make it necessary to fix a high price upon it; which he trusts will not be considered unreasonable, when it

---

* Since Garter.
† This diligent antiquary died June 14, 1851.

can be truly stated that the sale of all the copies will not pay the expenses. But he will feel amply rewarded for the labour this attempt has cost him, should it be found worthy a place among the few bibliographical works of this country; and, in the words of the Historian of the Aldine Press, "il conserve l'espoir qu'au moins par un petit nombre de personnes bien disposées en sa faveur, son livre ne sera point jugé *labor irritus et incassum.*"

Mount Street,
January, 1834.

Several years have elapsed since the first edition of this attempt to describe works printed for private circulation, appeared.

In the interval numerous additions have accumulated, and the book having become scarce, the Editor has been induced to reprint it. Little alteration has been made, but the additions added comprise nearly twenty years. Some pamphlets of temporary interest have been omitted, and a few volumes which were discovered to have been printed for general circulation.

The present edition contains Books only; to have included, as in the first, the account of private presses and clubs would have increased the size of the volume, already too large, to an inconvenient bulk. If life and leisure are granted, this portion, including literary clubs which have been formed since, will be proceeded with.

To have enumerated the names of the *various* friends
to whom the Editor is indebted for information and assistance, would have exhibited an array, which, however
gratifying to himself, would have savoured of affectation
or vanity. In several instances they are recorded in the
works described by their aid.

He cannot, however, suffer it to go forth without
mentioning a few to whom his thanks are especially due.

The assistance derived from the learned bibliographer,
Archdeacon Cotton, has been invaluable ; with a kindness
and patience, the Editor cannot sufficiently acknowledge,
he suggested numerous corrections and improvements,
beside contributing some very curious information relative
to Irish works, which it is to be regretted was not received in time to insert in their proper order. They will
be found in the Addenda.

To His Excellency M. Sylvain Van de Weyer, he
owes the knowledge of several works, which, without his
aid, would most probably have escaped notice. M. Van
de Weyer's library is rich in volumes of this class.

To James Maidment, Esq., he is indebted for the communication of several works connected with Scottish
history and poetry, freely communicated from the valuable collection he possesses in this class of literature.

To David Laing, Esq., he is also under great obligations for some interesting notes, relative to books privately printed in Scotland.

To John Gough Nichols, Esq., he owes much information relative to various works, many of which have appeared from the time-honoured press of Sylvanus Urban.

To Henry Foss, Esq., whose retirement—a matter of

regret to all literary collectors—from a pursuit he so zea-
lously and ably followed, and almost the last of learned
booksellers, he has to return his thanks for the patience
with which he answered the numerous inquiries the Editor
was under the necessity of making. *

---

* However gratifying it is to observe the increased circulation and demand
for books, which swarm at the railroad station, always excepting the reprint of
trashy English novels, and French translations, it is impossible not to witness
without a sigh, the passing away of those eminent booksellers, of the past and
present day, to whose choice collections the scholar and the student alike resorted
for the objects of their particular pursuit ; by whose zeal, industry, and knowledge, the private and public libraries of our country were enriched with the
treasures of ancient and modern literature, happily preserved in the fine libraries
at Althorp, Chatsworth, and Woburn, and numerous others, and rendered accessible to the inquirer in the noble repositories of our national libraries.[1] A cur-
sory mention of a few who have passed away, almost all in our own time, may
not be considered out of place here, more especially as we fear they have hardly
left successors who tread the same path, or administer to the same wants.

Robson, who brought the celebrated Pinelli collection into this country;
Edwards, tracking the French revolutionary armies in their career, and securing
the valuable literary plunder of ancient monastic or public libraries ; Cuthell and
Priestley, whose valuable collection of the classics was so important to the student
when the Continent was shut against importation ; Thorpe, whose energy was so
remarkable; Rodd, whose acquaintance with English history was so great; and,
lastly, the honoured descendants of " Honest Tom Payne," have yielded to the
change, and retired to enjoy the literary leisure those labours for others so justly
entitle them to.

In what has been said, it is hoped it will not be imagined there is any intention of disparaging the activity which administers to the great demand for books
in the rapid appearance of small catalogues now so generally prevalent ; nor still
more that the Editor is unmindful of what remains of the olden days—but it
would be invidious to speak of the present ; and he must content himself with
alluding only to one collection of the present times in theology, the value of
which, and the knowledge of its proprietor, will be readily admitted by all who
resort to it.

---

[1] The Bodleian, Cambridge, Dublin, and Edinburgh.

Nor can he forget the assistance he derived from his friend and neighbour, Mr. Benjamin Wiffen, whose eager search after rare early-printed Spanish books, of a peculiar class, frequently brought under his notice several privately-printed works dispersed in the numerous catalogues which he consulted.

He desires to return thanks to all, but for the reasons already mentioned, should have been glad to name them specifically; but he must not omit to thank his old and valued friend the publisher, (whose publications, by the most eminent writers in natural history, have contributed so much to assist its cultivation, and whose embellishments owe so much to his liberal expenditure and good taste,) for permitting the Editor to tax his kindness and patience in riding his hobby at a pace, which hardly any other publisher would have permitted.

The Editor is well aware, that, notwithstanding the aid of his friends and his own exertions, many books will have escaped notice; and several, from the inability to see them, are probably not correctly described.

These are results to which all such works are liable; he shall be content in having laid a foundation, which, if thought worthy, others can complete.

JOHN MARTIN.

Woburn Abbey,
May, 1854.

PRIVATELY PRINTED BOOKS.

M.D.LXXII.

E ANTIQUITATE
BRITANNICÆ ECCLESIÆ
ET PRIUILIGIIS
ECCLESIÆ CANTUARIENSIS,
CUM ARCHIEPISCOPIS EIUSDEM. 70. AN: DOM: 1572. *folio.*

Absentem qui rodit amicum,
Qui non defendit alio culpante, solutos dicavis, (*sic*)
Qui captat risus hominum, famamq;
Fingere qui non visa potest, commissa tacere
Qui nequit, hic niger est, hunc tu Romane caueto.

IT is not easy to ascertain, at this remote period, whether many of the works which are called privately printed, are strictly entitled to that distinction. The absence of a publisher's name is by no means a certain indication; many of the volumes were written on points of religious or political controversy, and, being obnoxious to the prevailing system, were naturally put forth in a manner that might not

B

draw down the arm of the law upon the printer ; but that they were distributed secretly, and might be purchased by the members of the sect whose opinions they supported, there can be little doubt ; many were imported from abroad : a list of them may be seen in Strype's Life of Parker,*—these bearing no place or publisher's name, are frequently designated as privately printed ; an erroneous conclusion, as it was simply from fear of prosecution that these marks are found wanting.

The rare and curious volume now under consideration may, however, justly be entitled a privately printed volume. The copy which Archbishop Parker sent to the Lord Treasurer Burghley was accompanied by a letter † in which he states :—

" The reason of his employing himself in this study, was to make compensation for his not preaching oftener. For neither his health nor quiet would suffer him to be a common preacher ; yet he thought it not unfit for him to be otherwise occupied in some points of religion, for his meaning was by that his *poor collection*, thus caused to be *printed* and *yet reserved to himself*, to note at what time Augustin, his first predecessor, came into England, &c." The work was printed at Lambeth, by John Day : the archbishop states in another part of the same letter, "that he had within his house in wages, drawers [of pictures], and cutters [that is, engravers], painters, limners, writers, and bookbinders."

The archbishop's share in this compilation has been a matter of considerable dispute. In the letter above mentioned, he states it to have been the amusement of his leisure hours ; and Dr. Drake, in the preface to his edition, is of opinion that Parker was himself the author. The fair conclusion, however, will I think be that the archbishop received considerable assistance from Dr. Ackworth ‡ and Josselyn, his secretary. In the copy in the Lambeth library, there are several manuscript papers, letters, and notes ; among them will

---

* Vol. ii. p. 392.

† Strype's Life of Parker, vol. ii. pp. 244–5.

‡ Dr. George Ackworth had been orator of the University of Cambridge, and became an inmate of Parker's house about 1570 ; which, Strype observes, " was a kind of common receptacle for learned and ingenious men."

be found some proofs that Ackworth and Josselyn had a considerable share in the compilation. At the beginning of the Life of St. Augustine,* we find this note : "These 24 pages of St. Augustine's Life were thus begun by George Ackworth, Dr. of laws, at the appointment of Mathew Parker, Archbishop of Canterbury, and the lives of all the Archbishops should have in this course been perfected— (some words not intelligible)—but deth prevented it." Dr. Ackworth was living in 1576, but how long after is not known. In the title-page of the History, in the same copy, is the following note : "This historie was collected and penned by John Josselyn, one of the sons of Sir Thomas Josselyn, Knight, by the appointment and oversight of Mathew Parker, Archbishop of Cant. ; the said John being entertained in the said Archb. house, as one of his antiquaries, to whom, besides the allowance afforded to hym in his house, he gave to hym the parsonage of Hollinbourn, in Kent, &c." There can be little doubt that the plan of the work was laid down by the archbishop ; and although he received considerable assistance in its progress, the materials were chiefly supplied from his own collections of ecclesiastical history.

The number of copies printed must have been very small. In the letter already quoted, the author states, "he had not given to FOUR men in the whole realm; and peradventure, it shall never come to sight abroad, though some men, smelling of the printing it, were very desirous cravers of the same." Dr. Drake states, at the period he was preparing his new edition, that he had met with twenty-one copies. I have taken some pains to trace out those existing at the present time, the list of which is as follows :—

1. The British Museum, Queen Elizabeth's copy.

2. In the same library, Lord Arundel's copy.

3. Lambeth library.

4. Cambridge Public Library, Bishop Moore's copy, and formed one of the collection presented to that University by George I.

---

* This is the Life of St. Augustine, mentioned in the description of the copy in the Lambeth Library. No. 3—which see.

5. Cambridge Public Library : with this is bound "Annales Witichendi Monachi Corbiensis." Franc. 1577.

6. Cambridge, Peter House, ex dono Andreæ Perne, olim huius Coll. et Decani Cath. Eccl. Eliensis (circa 1589,) master of Peter House· He built the library, and left this among other volumes, amounting to 300. A letter from Perne, then Vice-Chancellor, to Parker, thanking him for his donation of books to the library at Cambridge, is printed in Strype.

7. Oxford. Bodleian. Lord Oxford's copy, afterwards Rawlinson's. In this copy is this note :—   *5to Januarii*, 1593.

" Hunc Librum dono dedit Richardo Cosin Johannes Parker armgr. filius primogenitus Matthei Parker, nuper Cantuariensis Archiepī, cuius auspiciis et sumptibus liber iste et collectus et impressus est proprijs in ædibus Lamethæ positis."

8. Oxford, Bodleian ; also Rawlinson's, and the copy mentioned in Strype's Life of Parker, as then in the library at Ely.

9. Oxford. Merton College.

10. Oxford. Magdalen College, "dono Richardi Boughton ejus. Coll. Socii."

11. Earl Spencer.

12. Mr. Grenville (now in the British Museum).

13. The Rev. T. Russell : formerly Mr. Bindley's, afterwards Mr. W. Taylor's, then Mr. Dent's, and purchased at the sale of his library.

14. Library of the Dean and Chapter of Westminster.

15. Corpus Christi College, Cambridge. Presented by Baker the antiquary. By a memorandum in the book, he appears to have purchased it at York, for 1*l*. 11*s*. 6*d*.; it is the copy mentioned in Strype's Life, as being Mr. Baker's intention to have presented to St. John's College; in the copy of Strype's Life in that library, there is a note in Baker's hand-writing, "So intended by me, but I found reason to alter my intentions, and disposed of my three copies otherwise ; viz. two to the Archbishop of Cant., and one to Bene't College." Baker mentions a copy of this work, with various notes in the hand-writing of Sir John Parker (the archbishop's son), and adds, " This copy is now in the possession of Lord Sunderland."

16. Eton College Library. This copy, which is one of the books presented by Storer, was formerly Mr. Tutet's, who purchased it at West's sale, with the rare portrait by Hogenberg, for 2*l*. 2*s*. The portrait has been taken out, and placed in the illustrated Granger in that library. The following note is in Rawlinson's hand-writing, " Collated, and according to my best thoughts, this edition perfect." It has a few illustrations added to it, and has a modern blue morocco binding, but the binder has played sad work with the margin.

17. Miss Currer, in her library at Eshton Hall, formerly Sir M. Sykes's ; it has the rare portrait by Hogenberg, for which Miss Currer paid 13*l*., she describes it as a most beautiful impression.

18. The Earl of Leicester, at Holkham, with the portrait.

19. Christ Church. Oxford.

20. Christ Church. Oxford.

21. Mr. Heber ; now in the library of the late William Henry Miller, Esq.

These are all the copies I have been enabled, after considerable inquiry, to discover. Whether the splendid copy sent to the Lord Treasurer, which Parker states " that he had bound it costly, and laid in colours the arms of the Church of Canterbury, empaled with his own paternal coat," still remains in the library of his descendant, I have been unable to ascertain.

It has been observed that no two copies of this work have been found alike ; and I can bear witness to the truth of the assertion in those I have collated. For this there is perhaps a *primâ facie* reason in Parker's own words : who says—" For the present he purposed to keep it by him, while he lived, *to add and mend* as occasion should serve him, or utterly to suppress it, and to bren it." The variations are however so singular, that long as this account already is, the rarity of the volume will perhaps excuse giving an account of them as they occur in the copies enumerated above.

The collation of Nos. 1 and 2 will be found in Lowndes's Bibliographical Manual, and I apprehend these to be the earliest copies that issued from Parker's press. Queen Elizabeth's is bound in green velvet ; the title-pages with the arms of the bishoprics are illuminated and on vellum. The volume is ruled throughout. Lord Arundel's copy "Ex dono Mathei Cantuariensis Archiepiscopi," has no vellum leaves; but the arms of the bishoprics, with some of the capital letters, are illuminated. These two copies, with the one presented to Lord Burghley, most probably form part of the *four* the archbishop states as having been presented by him; since it is pretty certain that he would present his royal Mistress and her principal officers with the first that issued from the press. In page 4 (of these two copies)—Augustine, the lines commencing "adde quod" are printed in two columns, and in italics; at page 95, the enumeration of bishops and abbots, after the bishop of London, ends thus—" cum multis aliis episcopis et abbatis ut in Archiuis patet;" this distinction prevails also in Nos. 4 and 10.

In all the other copies (with the exception of Mr. Grenville's, which was most probably printed subsequently,) the verses will be found not in double columns, but in long lines, and in Roman characters. The "multis aliis" are enumerated, occupying nearly half a page; with these copies also the Life of Parker,* printed in 1576, will frequently be found; which is not the case with those which are considered the earlier ones.

I proceed to notice the variations from the copies No. 1 and 2.

No. 3.—Lambeth copy : contains in addition a single leaf, entitled "Cantriæ status ab adventu Cæsaris," signed B. C., who is stated to be Barth. Clerk,† postea Decanus de Arcub. Lond. Life of Parker,

---

* " For it is to be known, that our archbishop's life was written in elegant Latin, and ready for the printing, under the title of Matthæus; and though it came not forth with the rest of the Lives in the aforesaid book, yet it got into the press afterwards, and, as it seems, in the archbishop's life-time, and with his privity. Those (and they very few) that were printed, were kept carefully undispersed (I believe) in the archbishop's own possession till his death."—*Strype*, vol. ii. p. 246.

† Dr. Bartholomew Clerk was a member of the University of Cambridge, and admitted in King's College in 1554 ; he was a very good scholar, and had an excellent Latin style ; through the interest of Parker and Burghley, he was made, after much opposition on the part of Elizabeth, Dean of the Arches.

pp. 1—23. On the last leaf is the rare portrait of the archbishop. Two copies of the leaf of the wood-cut of the Public Schools, with Elizabeth at the back of *one* only. De Scholarum Collegiorumque; *two* leaves paged at the bottom, 27, 8, 9, 30. Catalogus Cancellm, &c.; the arms of the colleges at the back, those of St. Peter and the University are as *now* borne: see remark on this, page 9. No vellum leaves in this copy: the title is *written,* and not printed: Scholarum Pub. Extructio is wanting. It contains also the Life of St. Augustine; A—c in fours, printed in three columns, the text in the centre, and a commentary on both sides, of which Drake, who has reprinted it in his edition, says—"Fusior Augustini historia; opus rarum, ac nisi *quatuor* in exemplaribus frustra quærendum." It will be found in the Bodleian, No. 8; in the Chapter library of Westminster, No. 14; and in the Eton copy, No. 16.

No. 4.—Cambridge; De Scholarum, &c., *two* leaves—the title-pages and the arms of the bishops are on vellum and emblazoned; the volume is ruled throughout with red lines; the capitals are illuminated. The single leaf "ac præter," the "list of books," "Scholarum publicarum extructio," and errata, are wanting in this copy, which contains several marginal notes in the hand-writing of Parker.

No. 5.—Cambridge. This copy contains the Life of Parker, pp. 1—18 (17, a single leaf, printed on one side only), 19, 20, 21, 22 (23 not paged); the arms of Peter House and Cambridge correct.

No. 6.—Peter House. This copy contains the Life of Parker—but is very imperfect—it wants the title, last leaf of the preface, and pages 247, 8, 9, 50.

No. 7.—Bodleian. This copy contains the Life of Parker. Catalog. Canc.: the wood-cut with the arms of Peter House and Cambridge, incorrect. Another leaf, the same, with the arms correct. Two copies of the wood-cuts of the schools as in No. 3.

No. 8.—Bodleian. The wood-cut of Peter House and Cambridge, incorrect. It contains the History of Augustinus.

No. 9.—Merton College. This copy contains the Life of Parker and two leaves of the wood-cut of the schools as in No. 7. The title is wanting, it is supplied by a leaf with a wood-cut from some other volume; pp. 311, 12, 13, 14, are supplied by MSS.

No. 10.—Magdalen College. This copy is very imperfect. The arms of the bishops, from Lanfrancus, p. 93, to Baldwinus, 127, have been cut out and pasted over the initial letter. The lines, "adde quod," and the archbishops, &c., as Nos. 1 and 2.

No. 11.—Lord Spencer's. This copy contains the Life of Parker ; the title-page is on vellum ; the leaf of the arms of the archbishops on vellum, illuminated ; and the Catalog. Cancel. with the arms of colleges on vellum, the arms only illuminated ; the leaf of the public schools, with Elizabeth, on vellum, the title illuminated. The arms of Peter House and Cambridge incorrect. This copy wants, in "De Vetustate," pp. 57, 58, 63, 64. It contains the rare portrait.

No. 12.—Mr. Grenville's. This copy contains the Life of Parker ; with the rare portrait, and Woodburn's copy of it :* but it is very imperfect : there is a variation in this copy found in no other. The lines at p. 4, of Augustine, are not in columns, but in long line ; and the enumeration of the abbots and bishops ends with the bishop of London, &c. "ut in Archiuis patet." In all other copies, when the lines have been printed in this manner, the bishops have always been enumerated at length.

No. 13.—The Rev. T. Russell's copy, unfortunately wants several of the addenda, viz. the Catalogus Canc. ; the wood-cut of the public schools ; Catalogus, sixteen pages, &c. : but, to compensate in some degree for these defects, it contains a very fine impression of the portrait of the archbishop in its genuine state—and the volume is most admirably bound in blue morocco, by C. Lewis.

No. 14.—In the library of the Dean and Chapter of Westminster. This copy, although very incomplete, is remarkable for containing the History of Augustine, mentioned in No. 3, but which has evidently been inserted after it had been bound.

---

* The distinctions between the original and copy in Mr. Grenville's are these: In the inscription round the portrait, in the original, there is a mark of abbreviation over "mudus," not in the copy. The figures are 70 in the original, 69 in the copy ; the date 1573 in the original, 1572 in the copy: the same variations prevail in Mr. Russell's impression of the portrait, in the copy at Eton, the Duke of Buckingham's (sold at the sale of the "Stow Granger," No. 224),

No. 15.—Corpus Christi College. This copy wants the title-page. The arms of Peter House and Cambridge are incorrect. It is rather singular, that, although Parker was so great a benefactor to this college, it did not possess a copy of his work, until Baker presented it.

No. 16.—Eton College. This copy, which is certainly a very complete one, has the title-page and the cut of the public schools on vellum ; the life of Parker, and the rare " History of Augustine." The list of books given by Parker to his college is in MS. : there are several marginal notes ; and a letter from Dr. Drake, who consulted it for the purpose of the new edition.

No. 17.—Miss Currer.

No. 18.—The Earl of Leicester. The following collation was made by the late Earl Spenser, and given to me by Dr. Dibdin.

A MS. leaf with a quotation from Seneca, and another from Ecclesiasticus.

A list of Bishops of London, from Richard Clifford, 1407, to Thomas Kempe, 1449.

A note, as follows :—" Great St. Marie Church in Camb. was begun 18. E. 4. finished 19. H. 8. quib' int'iectis annis Academia ad ædificac'onem ei'dem contulit 795*l*. 2*s*. 1*d*. Int' qs, D^r. Barrow, Rotulorum Custos, Archidiaconus Cœlcestriæ, ac Aulæ Regiæ soci' dedit 240*l*."

The Title follows, printed on vellum and illuminated, with Sir Edward Coke's autograph, stating that he received it from Sir John Parker, Kn^t, son to the Archbishop, as a present.

A Preface, consisting of four leaves, unpaged with a large illuminated capital on the first page. Signatures ¶ j to ¶ iij, the fourth without signature, finishing with 14 lines on recto-verso blank.

De Vetustate Britannicæ Ecclesiæ testimonia. 45 pages, of which

---

that at Lambeth, and in Messrs. Colnaghi's. Mr. Woodburn says, that his was taken from an impression with the mark and figures exactly as he has copied them, but he has no recollection where that impression is at this time. It is remarkable that all the original impressions have evidently had the dates corrected since the engraving was executed ; impressions therefore of the portrait in the state of Mr. Woodburn's copy, must be very early, and very rare ; the original copper-plate is supposed to be in existence.

page 15 is double, being marked 15a, 15b ; and page 16 is quadruple 16a, 16b, 16c, 16d. The reverse of page 45 blank.

An illuminated Title, on vellum, "De Archiep'is Ecclesie Cantuarien' Septuaginta."

Three leaves, unpaged, of Tables ; the first with sign. ¶ ij, the two last 𝕂☞ i and ij.

The Lives of the Archbishops, beginning with St. Augustine. 424 pages numbered, of which page 4 is quadruple, page 91 blank on the reverse, page 122 octuple from 122a to 122h (being the life of Thomas à Becket), page 254 repeated by mistake, there being no 255, page 294 double, 315 misprinted 351.

A leaf, with the very rare Portrait of Archbishop Parker ; inscription round it Ætatis suæ Anno 69, Die Mensis Augusti sexto+ Mūdus transit et concupiscētia ejus. Anno Domini 1572. 4 Coats of Arms at the corners R. Berg f.

The Life of the Archbishop, entitled Matthæus. 12 leaves without numbers of pages, but the nine first numbered at the bottom from 1 to 18.

A blank leaf. Then 3 more leaves, the two first numbered in like manner from 19 to 22, the last without a No. with the Arms illuminated after the Colophon. The reverse of this leaf blank.

An Index, consisting of 7 leaves, in three columns each, pages not numbered ; signatures irregular.

A Title, illuminated and printed on vellum, "Catalogus Cancellariū" &c. Arms blazoned on the reverse.

Another Title, illuminated and printed on vellum, a q' recto Area scholar' Cantebrigion sium (sic), &c. On the reverse an illuminated Portrait of Queen Elizabeth, with Justice and Mercie supporting her Crown. Texts in Latin, above and below.

A paper-leaf, containing a MS. List of Chancellors of the Univ. of Cambridge, from A.D. 1263 to 1498.

A printed Table of 16 pages, numbered at the bottom, of the Officers of the University, from 1500 to 1573 (the two last filled up in MS.)

A leaf, containing a List of Bishops from the Univ. of Cambridge, from 1501 to 1555 ; and ending with four Irish Bishops, from 1535 to 1561.

A blank leaf.

Four leaves, paged at bottom, from 17 to 24, (the last, MS.), containing a Table of Statutes and other memoranda relating to Cambridge.

One leaf, on the recto of which is an Inventory of Articles delivered to M. Bedell and Pearson, taxators, from Cosin and Bojet, the former taxators. The reverse blank.

One leaf, containing a List of other articles, the property of the University.

One leaf, " De Scholarum, Collegiorumq : in Acad. Cantab. Patronis atque fundatoribus.

Two leaves, containing a List of Books given to the custody of the University by Archbishop Parker, describing the No. of pages in each.

The two first Articles are the Nuremburg Chronicle 1493, and Montanus' Polyglott. Nothing else that appears of any great interest.

Two leaves, entitled " Scholarum publicarum Extructio."

Nine leaves, paged at bottom, from 31 to 47 (the last page unnumbered), containing an Account of Halls and Colleges in Cambridge.

One leaf, containing a page and a quarter of Errata.

One leaf MS., containing a Copy of a Letter from Melanchthon to Frederic Miconius.

Another leaf, MS., containing a List of Books. The reverse blank.

The whole of this volume is in most beautiful and perfect condition ; and the impression of the Portrait remarkably good.

No. 19 and 20.—Christ Church. These copies formerly belonged to Mr. Baker, the " Socius ejectus" of St. John's College, Cambridge. The first has this note " Ex dono Joannis Colbatch Theologiæ practicæ professoris," and contains in the " Hæc monumenta" after the catch-word, M. Bedel, on page 24, a leaf, commencing " M. Bedel et Pierson taxatores" and ending " Cantabridgia :" this leaf is generally deficient ; although the catch-word indicates it as wanting, and Drake has reprinted it in this manner. It contains the life of Parker, and is altogether a very complete copy, in beautiful condition, bound in russia, and containing numerous manuscript notes, written in a very beautiful hand. The arms of Peter House and Cambridge are wrong ; the enumeration of the abbots and bishops, at page 95 of the life of Augustine, at full length.

The other copy, formerly belonging to Sir Christopher Hatton, and said to have been bought at the sale of Falconbridge's library, is by no means so complete ; but it contains, in the life of Parker, the following variation ; page 19 of the life of the Archbishop, in all the other copies, is printed but on one side, and only on half the page. This copy contains the apparent deficient matter, three leaves not paged, the first the half-filled page 19, and two other leaves besides ; and then follows, as has been the case in the copies containing the life, page 20, commencing, "Jam de interiori," &c. In Dr. Drake's edition of this work, he has re-printed this matter ; it begins at the fourteenth line from the top of page 553 of his edition, with the words, "Tum duodecimo Aprilis," and ends at page 588, "in hoc observantur."

This copy, in all probability, is the only one that contains these leaves, the copies in the libraries of Cambridge do not contain them, nor do those in the Bodleian, the British Museum, nor that in the library of Earl Spencer.

In the copies in the British Museum, on the leaf with the catch-word, M. Bedel, in *hæc omnia Monumenta*, at line 17, from the top, these words have been re-printed and pasted over others, "Nicholaus Cātelowe sive Cantelepus." The two copies in the Bodleian Library have not this castration, nor has Lord Spencer's ; and the words stand thus :

"Hugonis de Cātilupo Archidiacono Glouerniæ."

The correction would appear to be, therefore, the substitution of Nicholaus for Hugo. One of the copies in the Bodleian has the leaf, following the catch-word M. Bedel, commencing, "M. Bedel and Peerson Taxatores." The other copy wants this leaf, and Lord Spencer's also.

No. 21.—Mr. Heber, now in the library of the late Wm. Henry Miller, Esq.

Title page on vellum.

Arms of Colleges 1 leaf.

Plan of College 1 leaf.

Preface 4 leaves.

De Vetustate, as in Lowndes.

Arms of Bishopricks 1 leaf.

Episcopi, &c., 1 leaf.

De Regum, &c., 2 leaves.

Then the Lives p. 1—122 122 a—h 123—294 294 a—b 295—358.

Pages 359-60-61-62 wanting.

Pages 357-8 363-4 bis.

Then p. 363.—424.

Index 7 leaves.

At page 95 Bishops enumerated at length.

The lines "adde quod," in single lines.

In those copies originally issued by Parker, the two following variations will be observed from what I consider to be those issued subsequently, viz.—on the wood-cut leaf, "Catalogus Cancellm.," with the arms of the colleges at the back, the armorial bearings of Peter House will be found on a shield gules, charged with two keys saltierwise ; the arms of the University, a bridge, with the waves issuing through three arches ; above this device is an interior of a room, with a doctor seated and capped, between two priests standing in robes.

In the later copies, the arms of Peter House will be found as now borne, viz.—Paly, or and gules, on a border of the second, an orle of crowns ;—and of the University, gules, on a cross ermine between four lions passant guardant or, a Bible clasped and garnished.

The arms of Cambridge, as now borne, were granted in 1575 ; and from Parker being so closely connected with Cambridge, and perhaps being consulted on the grant, he very naturally had the erroneous bearings altered.   In the copies No. 1 and 2, now in the British Museum, the corrected arms of Cambridge will be found pasted over the others, but those of Peter House remain incorrect.

The edition of Hanau, folio, 1605, has been reprinted from one of the early copies, as the bishops and abbots end with " Archiuis patet ; " in Dr. Drake's edition, 1729, although they are enumerated, yet the arms of Peter House and Cambridge are printed with the wrong armorial bearings.

It is impossible to conclude this account without bearing testimony to the noble example which this eminent prelate held forth in the encouragement of learning and learned men, which is shewn not only in the publication and embellishment of this singular volume, but in the collection of curious and rare books which his library contained, now in Bene't College.

The wood-cut here given is taken from his work, and is supposed to represent the archbishop preaching.

SCHOLA THAMENSIS EX FVNDATIONE IOHANNIS WILLIAMS MILITIS, DOMINI WILLIAMS DE THAME. GOD SAUE THE QUEENE. *folio.* 1575.

The collation of this rare volume will be found in Mr. Upcott's English Topography, p. 1074, from the copy in the Royal Library, in the British Museum. There is one in the Bodleian Library, but unfortunately imperfect. There is also a copy in the possession of the warden and fellows of New College, who are trustees of the school ; but I was unable, as well as Mr. Upcott, to obtain a sight of it.

In Mr. Grenville's library is a copy on vellum, from which the following note is taken. "Only three copies of this book are known, and all of them on paper, and all imperfect: one in the Bodleian library, one in the British Museum, and one in New College, Oxon." This copy, as far as I know, is the only one perfect, and the only one on vellum. The New College copy wants all the appendixes.

A BRIEF TREATISE OF OATHES EXACTED BY ORDINARIES AND ECCLESIASTICAL JUDGES, TO ANSWER GENERALLY TO ALL SUCH ARTICLES, OR INTERROGATORIES, AS PLEASETH THEM TO PROPOUND, AND OF THEIR FORCED OR CONSTRAINED OATHES EX OFFICIO, WHEREIN IS PROVED THAT THE SAME ARE UNLAWFUL.

Circa 1582. 4*to*. pp. 58.

This rare pamphlet was communicated to me by Sir Charles George Young, Garter.

SONNETS TO THE FAIREST CÆLIA.
(BY WILLIAM PERCY.)
London: printed by Adam Islip, for W. P. 1594. 4*to*.

A copy of this volume, "probably unique," is mentioned in the Bibliotheca Anglo-Poetica, No. 570, and valued at 45*l*.

A copy was in Heber's Sale Catalogue, part IV., No. 1806, with the following note, it is believed, from the pen of the best authority, on all matters connected with early English Poetry (Mr. Payne Collier).

"Only one other copy of this work seems to be known. The scarcity is perhaps to be accounted for by the fact, that it was *privately* printed for the author; see the imprint." Since this note was written, Mr. Collier says, "Percy's Sonnets are not worth much in themselves." When I said, 'only one other copy seems to be known,' this was my belief when I wrote; I have since seen two other copies."

ΒΑΣΙΛΙΚΟΝ ΔΩΡΟΝ.

DIVIDED INTO THREE BOOKES.

Edinburgh : Printed by Robert Walde-graue, Printer to the King's Majestie. 1599. 4*to.* pp. 159.

Dedication, a sonet, 1 leaf ; Argument, a sonet, do.; "To Henrie my dearest Sonne," 2 leaves.

"This is the first edition of the work which has been supposed to have contributed more than any other to smooth James's accession to the Crown. Its rarity and literary value will be appreciated by the following extracts from M'Crie's Life of Melville. " Fond of seeing this work in print, and yet conscious that it would give great offence, James was anxious to keep it from the knowledge of his native subjects until circumstances should enable him to publish it with safety. ' With this view, the Printer being first sworn to secrecy,' says he, ' I only permitted seven of them to be printed, and these seven I dispersed among some of my trustiest servants to be kept close by them.'" "I have now," says M'Crie, "before me, a copy of the first edition, and I have no doubt that it is one of the *seven* copies (perhaps the only one now existing), to which that edition was limited. It is beautifully printed in a large Italic letter. Prefixed to it are two Sonnets, the first of which, entitled, ' The Dedication of the Booke,' is not to be found in the subsequent editions."

The same note is in the " Grenville Catalogue," Vol. 1, page 366, and in " Heber's Catalogue," Pt. I., No. 3709 ; from the extreme rarity of the work, Mr. Heber's copy most probably came into Mr. Grenville's possession.

M.DC.XLVI.

AGNÆ BRITANNIÆ AUSTER IKNO-
GRAPHICUS, AD I. VICECOMITEM SCUD-
AMOREM, MAGNÆ BRITANNIÆ REGIS
APUD REGEM FRANCORUM LEGATUM.
F. Charrier. 1637. 4*to*.

This book is said by Lowndes to be privately printed.

———

THE GENERALL JUNTO; OR, THE COUNCELL OF UNION,
CHOSEN EQUALLY OUT OF ENGLAND, SCOTLAND AND IRE-
LAND, FOR THE BETTER COMPACTING OF THREE NATIONS
INTO ONE MONARCHY. Anno Dom. 1642.

By Henry Parker, who signs his initials at the end of the preface.
"But fifty of them printed at the charge of Sir John Davers, not
intended to be sold, but given away to particular friends." MS. note
in the British Museum copy.

———

CHARACTERS AND ELEGIES. BY FRANCIS WORTLEY,
KNIGHT AND BARONET.
Printed in the yeare CIƆIƆCXLVI. 4*to*. pp. 98.

This book has usually been called privately printed, for which reason it is retained here, though I think it very doubtful. The reason

given in the Censura Literaria,* in the account of this book—that because no bookseller's name appears in the title-page it was most probably so—is a very unsatisfactory one. The elegies are, for the most part, on the Royalists who lost their lives in the civil war.

Anne, daughter and heir of Sir Francis, married the Honorable Sidney Montagu, second son of the first Earl of Sandwich, who took the name of Wortley; from whom is descended the present John Stuart Wortley, second Baron Wharncliffe. There is an extremely rare portrait of Sir F. Wortley in armour, engraved by Hertocks, in small folio. It was sold at Sir M. Sykes' sale for 42*l*. An account of Sir F. Wortley and his works will be found in Wood's Athenæ, by Bliss, vol. iii. 391.

<hr/>

Otia Sacra.

Optima Fides. Deus Nobis hæc Otia Fecit.

London : Printed by Richard Cotes, 1648. 4*to*. pp. 174.

This is the title prefixed to the rare volume of poetry by Mildmay Fane, Earl of Westmoreland, engraved by Marshall.

That this volume was printed only for private distribution, is pretty clear from the following lines in the last page :

> "And what alone to friends he would impart,
> Hath not at all to do with fair or mart."

An account of this volume will be found in the Bibliotheca Anglo-poetica, p. 405, where a copy is marked 21*l*. ; and in Brydges' Restituta, vol. ii. p. 96. There is a copy in Emmanuel College, Cambridge, where the author was educated ; but although inserted in the Catalogue, it could not be found when the editor inquired for it. Mr. Malone's is in the Bodleian Library, with the very curious dramatic collection formerly in his possession ; and there is one in the Grenville library.

<hr/>

* Vol. ii.

ENCHIRIDIUM EPIGRAMMATUM, LATINO-ANGLICUM.
AN EPITOME OF ESSAYS ENGLISHED OUT OF LATIN,
WITHOUT ELUCIDAT. EXPLANATORY, CONTAINING SIX
CLASSES OR CENTURIES :
I. OF THEOLOGICALS ; II. HISTORICALS ; III. HETE-
RÆOGENALS ; IV. BRYTO-ANGLICALS ; V. MISCELLA-
NEALS ; VI. MUTUALETEALS : BESIDES A FARDEL OF 76
FRAGMENTS. Lond. 1654. 12*mo.*

The author of this work was Robert Vilvain. In the preface he
says that it was printed purposely to bestow on his friends.
" The folio volumes announced in the preface, were never printed.
There is full enough of R. Vilvain in this volume. Longman has
blundered in his Bib.-Poet., p. 369. This volume is complete in 191
(not 404) pages." Note by Mr. Grenville in his copy.

FOUR TREATISES.
I. The *Sufferings* of the *Saints :* Most Comfortable.
II. The *Burning* of *Sodom,* and the *City* called *Sodom,*
Revel. xi. 8. Preached about a Moneth before the Burn-
ing of London : Exceeding Lamentable.
III. The *Fruitfull* Fasting : Very Profitable.
IV. The *Judgement* of the *World :* Most Considerable.
WHEREUNTO IS ADDED
A small Part of the great Wickedness, and Sacrilegious
Dealings of the Assistants of the great Anti-Christ, in
the Diocese of *Ossory.*
AND
A Sermon Preached at *Cork House, Dublin,* before Mr.
Henry Cromwell, then Governor of Ireland. By *Griffith*
Lord Bishop of *Ossory.*

c 2

London: Printed for the Author, to be Bestowed upon his Friends. 1666. *4to.*

Sufferings, pp. 245. Petition, Dedication to the King, to the Reader, 9 leaves. Fruitful Fasting, pp. 24. Judgment of the World, pp. 35. Great Wickedness, pp. 59. Sermon, pp. 31.

A copy of this work is in the Grenville Library, with the following note :

"This book, as the title-page shows, was privately printed, and is so rare as to be little known. It contains much curious historical matter relating to the county of Kilkenny and diocese of Ossory, of which Ledwich and the other topographical writers were quite ignorant."

An account of Griffith Williams and his works will be found in Wood's Athenæ, by Bliss, vol. iv. p. 952, where the date of this one is given 1667.

FIESTAS DE ARANJUEZ, TRANSLATED FROM THE SPA-
NISH OF ANTONIO DE MENDOZA, IN CELEBRATION OF
THE BIRTHDAY OF PHILIP IV. IN 1621. *4to.* 1670.

PRIVATELY PRINTED, as presentations to the translator's friends. In the notice preceding the prologue, Sir Richard Fanshawe particularly refers to the suffering it to be printed, " to distribute amongst those who ask for it, for I have not the presumption to offer it to any. No friends persuade me to publish it, for I have none so vain. I rather think that their opinion would obstruct me in this resolution, finding in it those defects which are hidden from the proper author ; for in the things of other men, it is easie to be more wise ; and without denying the defects of mine, I have been very willing to content with some copies as many as seek them, deceived with that which was ow'd to so splendid an occasion."

A notice of this work will be found in the preface to the "Memoirs of Lady Fanshawe." *8vo.* Lond. 1839, p. iv.

The Mother's Legacy to her Unborn Child, By Elizabeth Ioceline.

Oxford : Printed at the Theatre, for the satisfaction of the Person of Quality herein concerned. Ann: Dom : 1684. *12mo.* pp. 119.

"Written by the grand-daughter of William Chaderton, successively bishop of Chester and Lincoln. Collation : title, approbation by Thomas Good, five leaves ; letter of the authoress to her husband, Tourell Iocelin, nine leaves ; the legacy, pp. 119."—*Lowndes.*

This work was reprinted in 1852, by Blackwood, with a biographical and historical introduction. There is an earlier edition than that above mentioned. See "Notes and Queries," vol. iv. p. 410.

———

Succinct Genealogies of the Noble and Ancient Houses of Alno or de Alceto, Broc of Shephale, Latimer of Duntish, Drayton of Drayton, Mauduit of Werminster, Greene of Drayton, Vere of Addington, Fitz-Lewes of West-Hornedon, Howard of Effingham, and Mordaunt of Turvey :

Justified by Publick Records, Ancient and Extant Charters, Histories and other Authentic Proofs, and enriched with divers Sculptures of Tombs, Images, Seals, and other Curiosities. By Robert Halstead.

London: Printed in the Year of our Lord M.DC.LXXXV.
folio. pp. 702.

The collation of this volume will be found in Moule's Bibliotheca Heraldica, and in Upcott's Topography.

It is well known that the name of the author was fictitious : "it was compiled," says Gough, "by Henry, second Earl of Peterborough, and the Rev. Mr. Rans, his chaplain, rector of Turvey, in Bedford-

shire. The number was very limited. Gen. Mordaunt in a letter *
to Earl Spencer, writes, " I always understood about *twenty only* were
printed, for the use of the family and private donations." They have
never, however, been stated to exceed twenty-four. Copies are in the
following libraries : King's Library, British Museum ; Duke of Devonshire ; Marquess of Ailesbury ; Earl Spencer, formerly General Mordaunt's ; Mr. Poyntz ; Cambridge Public Library ; Bodleian Library;
Heralds' College ; Mr. Botfield ;† the late Sir S. Taylor (bought at the
sale of his library by Mr. Bohn) ; Marquess of Bath ;‡ Mr. Grenville ;
Sir J. Thorold ; Sir T. Phillips (this copy is imperfect) ; Henry Drummond, Esq. M.P. (bought by Mr. Pickering, at Lord Berwick's sale for
93*l.*) In Lord Spencer's library, is a MS. copy of the heraldic and
genealogical portion of this work on vellum.

Mr. Macaulay frequently refers to this work in his valuable History of England ; and in the interesting chapter on the habits and
customs of our nation, at the close of Charles II.'s reign, mentions
that he had found in it much useful information on the subject of
Coffee-Houses.

EPISTOLA ARCHIMEDIS AD REGEM GELONEM,
ALBÆ GRÆCÆ REPERTA.
Anno Æræ Christianæ, 1688. 12*mo*, pp. 48.

" Not published ; this copy given to Dr. Mead by the Editor Pitcairn." Note in the copy in the Grenville Library.

---

* Ædes Althorpianæ, p. 188.

† Formerly in the Benedictine monastery of Landspring ; a present from the
Earl of Peterborough.

‡ A gift to the first Lord Weymouth, by Sir John Jermayne, Bart.

A SHORT MEMORIAL OF THE SUFFERINGS AND GRIE-
VANCES PAST AND PRESENT OF THE PRESBYTERIANS OF
SCOTLAND, PARTICULARLY OF THOSE OF THEM CALLED BY
NICK NAME CAMERONIANS.

Printed in the year 1690.

4*to* pp. 56, title and preface pp. 6.

Privately circulated; of great interest and rarity. Communicated
by James Maidment, Esq., to whom the editor is indebted for notices
of several privately printed books.

ADVICE TO A PARSON, ON THE TRUE ART OF PREACH-
ING, IN OPPOSITION TO MODERN PRACTICE.

Written by a Person of Honour, to Dr. S—, his late
Chaplain, made publick, chiefly for the Edification of
Universities.

Printed in the year 1691. 8*vo.* pp. 89.

A poetical tract, in four cantos, which has usually been considered
privately printed : it is rather doubtful. There is a copy in the British Museum.

OFFICE FOR PENITENTS; OR, A FORM OF PRAYER FIT
TO BE USED IN SINFUL AND DISTRACTED TIMES.

1691. 8*vo.*

Privately printed. Prefixed is a portrait of John Ashton.—*Lowndes.*
A John Ashton was executed for high treason in January, 1691 ;
an account of him will be found in Burnet, and Rapin. There are
two portraits of him; one in folio, painted by J. Ryley, and engraved
by R. White; another in 12mo. a copy of the former : whether he was
the author of this book, I have been unable to ascertain.
See *Burnet's History of his Own Times,* vol. iii. p. 121.

M.DCC.

ISERY is Virtue's Whet-stone.
Reliquiæ Gethinianæ ;
or, Some Remains of the most
ingenious and excellent lady,
Grace Lady Gethin, lately deceased.
Being a Collection of choice Discourses, pleasant Apo-
thegmes, and witty Sentences ; written by her for the
most part, by way of essay, and at spare hours. Published by her nearest Relations, to preserve her memory,
and digested for method's sake under proper heads.

Prov. xxxi. 31.

" Let her own works praise her in the gate."

The Second Edition : * to which is added a Funeral
Sermon by Dr. Birch, with the Inscription on her Monument.

Printed by D. Edwards, in Fetter Lane. 1700.

4to. pp. 90. Sermon, pp. 28.

Grace Lady Gethin, was the wife of Sir Richard Gethin, of Gethin
Court in Ireland, daughter of Sir George Norton, of Abbots-Leigh in
Somersetshire. She was buried in Westminster Abbey. In the
south aisle of the choir is a mural monument, executed with different
coloured marbles ; in the centre is a statue of the deceased kneeling
between two angels. A sermon is still preached to perpetuate her
memory every Ash-Wednesday, followed by a dole of bread.

---

* A copy of the First Edition was in Mr. Bright's sale, 2442 ; said to be privately printed.

The book is principally a compilation from the works of Lord Bacon. In the preface it is stated, "They are not designed for every one's publick view, a few copies being only intended to be printed, enough to preserve her memory, and for the *private* use of some persons who were personally acquainted with her." Prefixed is a portrait painted by Dickson, engraved by Faithorne, jun.; there is another portrait, representing Lady Gethin in bed, with two females in attendance ; a figure of Death in the back-ground ; a coffin in front; over the tester of the bed, an inscription, "Lady Get," a 4to. print. There is an engraving, in mezzotint, of the monument in Westminster Abbey, small folio. Copies of the book with the two portraits are rarely seen. Although her monument is at Westminster, she is buried, says Mr. Chalmers, at Hollingbourne in Kent.

In Mr. Grenville's library is a copy, third edition, printed for John Graves, in 1703 : as there is no mention in this edition of its being printed " only for her friends," it was most likely sold. This copy, formerly Dr. Farmer's, has an additional print of Lady Gethin, very rarely to be found.

The most excellent Maria, in a Brief Character of her incomparable Virtues and Goodness, by her eternal Honourer, Sir Edward Dering, Knight. London: Printed by R. Roberts, for the author. 1701. 8vo. pp. 261. Carmen sepulchrale, five leaves.

In the epistle dedicatory to Madam Anne Edwin, of Hereford, the author states that he has caused a *few* copies to be printed, and in the address to the reader he states it was never designed for public view. It is an affectionate tribute to an excellent woman. The portrait is very rare, painted by Mollinarotto, engraved by R. White. It was sold for 8*l.* 10*s.* 6*d.* at Mr. Bindley's sale. Mr. Grenville's copy of this work is on larger and thicker paper than the ordinary copies, and a note states that "this is the only one he ever saw on large paper, and that the head, when a fine impression like this, is sold for 8*l.*"

CURIA MILITARIS ; OR, A TREATISE OF THE COURT
OF CHIVALRY, IN THREE BOOKS.

1. Concerning the Court itself, its Judges and Officers.
2. Of its Jurisdiction, and Causes there determinable.
3. Of the Process and Proceeding therein.

WITH AN INTRODUCTION,

Containing some Animadversions on two posthumous
Discourses concerning the Etymology, Antiquity, and
Office of the Earl Marshall of England, ascribed to Mr.
CAMDEN, and published in the last edition of the Bri-
tannia.

BY JOHN ANSTIS, ESQ., OF THE MIDDLE TEMPLE.

Etenim quod dicere supervacaneum est prodest cognoscere.
Sen. lib. iv. c. 1. de Benef.

London : Printed by T. Mead, in Giltspur Street, near
the back gate of St. Sepulchre's Church. 1702.

8*vo.*—Introduction, five leaves. Contents, pp. xli.

This treatise was printed, but not published,* and was most probably issued as a prospectus of the remainder of the work, which was
never printed; and although it has been stated by Noble, that it was
printed for the use of friends, it is doubtful whether its sale was not
general. It, however, affords an opportunity of stating that the curious manuscript collections made by Mr. Anstis for this purpose, are
now deposited in the British Museum, having been purchased by the
trustees, at the sale of Sir G. Nayler's library and manuscripts, in
1832 : they were sold at Mr. Anstis's sale, in 1769, to Mr. Edmonson,
for 2*l.* 5*s.* A copy of this work with corrections by Peter Le Neve
in the sale of Dawson Turner's library; Sotheby's, March, 1853.

---

* Moule, Bibliotheca Heraldica, p. 259.

A JOURNAL OR ACCOUNT OF WILLIAM DANIEL HIS
LATE EXPEDITION OR UNDERTAKING TO GO
FROM LONDON TO SURRAT IN INDIA.

Giving a short but impartial relation of the Dangers,
Distresses, Fatigues, and Hindrances, happening to him
during the said Expedition, till his return to England.
London, printed in the year M.D.CCII.   8*vo.*   (1702).

After the title, dedication to the Governor of the East India Company, a leaf of preface, and pp. 94, printed on thick paper—evidently
for presents.

————

RELIQUIÆ GETHINIANÆ. THE THIRD EDITION, WITH
A COPY OF VERSES WRITTEN BY MR. CONGREVE.

London : Printed for John Graves, at the Bible, in
Salisbury-street, in the Strand.   1703.   4*to.*

The full title of this work is not repeated here, as it has already
been given in the edition of 1700 : the copy in the King's library,
formerly Dr. Farmer's, has the portrait by Dickson, and print of the
monument.

————

THE CASE; OR AN ABSTRACT OF THE CUSTOMS OF THE
MANNOR OF MERDON, IN THE PARISH OF HURSELEY
(HURSLEY), IN THE COUNTY OF SOUTHAMPTON,

Which are to be observed and performed by the Lord
and Customary Tenants of the said Mannor, their Heirs
and Successors for ever.   As they were taken out of a
Decree, made and inrolled in the Honourable Court of

Chancery. Together with some remarkable Passages, Suits at Law and in Equity, and the great differences and expenses therein.

By Mathew Imber, Gent.

London: Printed Anno Dom: 1707. *small 8vo.* pp. 93.

"Printed for private use. The suit about the manor of Merdon began in 1691, when O. Cromwell, Esq. was lord (who, with about twenty of the tenants, died during the interval), and the decree was made in 1698, ratifying certain articles made in 1650, between Richard Major, then lord, and the tenants ; and an authenticated copy of it is preserved in Hursley church."—*Gough.*

Private Devotions for several Occasions Ordinary and Extraordinary.

London: Printed for F. Pawlett, 1709.   *8vo.*

Institutiones Geometricæ,

impressæ, sed non editæ, a Aldrich.   1709.

8vo.

The Life of Mr. Anthony a Wood, Historiographer of the most famous University of Oxford. With an Account of his Nativity, Education, Works, etc.

London, Printed for the Author.   1711.   *8vo.*, pp. 18.

This is an unpublished work, privately printed, and very rare in small paper ; see Hearne's Lives of Leland, Hearne and Wood.

"This is the only copy on large paper, being the Presentation copy from the Author to his brother T. Rawlinson. It was sold at Dent's sale for 9*l*. 19*s*. 6*d*."—Note in Mr. Grenville's copy.

Prefixed is a portrait of Wood by Burgher.

———

DE VALENTINIANORUM HÆRESI CONJECTURÆ, QUIBUS ILLIUS ORIGO EX ÆGYPTIACA THEOLOGIA DEDUCITUR. Londini: Sumptibus Auctoris, typis G. Bowyer. 1711. *4to.*

Dedication to J. Ernest Grabe, one page; text, pp. 3—27. One plate, between pp. 4, 5.

———

LETTER TRULY ADDRESSED TO MR. JOS. WILSON, REPRESENTING A MATRIMONIAL CASE, BY J. SHINKE, 1711.   *8vo.*

A curious volume of Family History, it contains an inventory of the goods and chattels, &c., of Sir John Williams, late of Langibby Castle, in the county of Monmouth, *whose lady appears to have been a party in the present case;* there are letters and affidavits also from Eliz. Pritchard, Benjamin Perkins, J. Sutliff, Mary Nuby, J. Cave, T. Baden, R. Rowe, Eleanor Morgan, &c.

This note is from one of the catalogues of the late Mr. Thorpe.

———

SPACCIO DELLA BESTIA TRIONFANTE; OR, THE EXPULSION OF THE TRIUMPHANT BEAST. TRANSLATED FROM THE ITALIAN OF JORDANO BRUNO. London: Printed in the year 1713.   *8vo.* pp. 280.

In a note in Mr. Bindley's copy, sold at Lord Guildford's sale, Part I. No. 41, he says, that "the first copies of this edition were put forth with a manuscript title, and that the printed title was an afterthought." This translation is commonly attributed to Toland ; but was really made by William Morehead, Esq., for the private use of Mr. Collins, and was never intended to be printed; though shortly afterwards taken out of Mr. Collins' library by Toland, as he believed, and sent to the press.—*Vide* West's Catalogue, p. 44. Fifty copies only are said to have been printed. The original edition, Parigi, 1584, is stated to have been printed in London, and not at Paris ; and the impression limited to twenty copies only.

Copy of a Decree of Chancery, between the Lord and Tenants of the Mannour of Ford, *alias* Fordshome, in the County of Salop.
Shrewsbury, 1717.

The Covenant to be the Lord's People, and to walk after the Lord; signed by the Church of Christ, under the Pastoral care of Joseph Jacob, a Servant of Christ Crucify'd.
Deut. xxix. 1, with 2 Chron. xxiii. 16, and xxiv. 31.
These are the Words of the Covenant, which the Lord commanded, &c.
London: Printed for the use of the Church, 1721.
8*vo.* pp. 32.

This society seems to have lasted somewhat more than five years, and never to have numbered more than twenty males and twenty-five females. The copy before me is the only one, probably, now in existence ; and it is the same in which the several parties signed their names on becoming members. This " Church of Christ," in many particulars, resembled the Society of Friends. They covenant to discharge their several social and moral duties ; to abstain from all excess, both in apparel and manner of living ; not to use profane, or even idle language ; and to contribute liberally to the support of their church. But they appoint a special minister, enjoin baptism, and allow of swearing by the name of God. Of Jacob and his followers, I have not yet discovered any particulars.

For the communication of this rare volume, and the interesting note which accompanies it, the Editor is indebted to the learned Dr. Bliss, ever as ready as able to afford information on all matters connected with English literature.

THE FIRST PART OF EARL CONINGSBY'S CASE
RELATIVE TO THE VICARIDGE OF LEMPSTER
IN HEREFORDSHIRE ;

Wherein is contained a full account of all the Tricks which the Lawyers Ecclesiastical and Temporal have made use of to deprive the said Earl of his undoubted right to present to the said Church of Lempster (not worth Twenty Pounds per annum), from the year 1712 to the last Summer Assizes at Hereford, when the present Lord Chancellor, on pretence that it was his Majesty's right to present to the said Vicaridge of Lempster, though there is no such Vicaridge in the King's Books ; with Mr. Kettleby, Recorder of Ludlow [confirmed in that place by his Lordship's interest], for his council, and Sir George Caswall, the Cashier of the South Sea Company [made by his Lordship a Justice of the Peace for that purpose], for his assistants ; Thomas Price, the Earl of Oxford's

Steward of his Courts, for his attorney; and Thomas
Rodd, the vilest of all attornies, for Price his coadjutor,
prosecuted a *quare impedit* against the said Earl, at the
said Summer Assizes, with success; but how that success
was obtained, the Second Part of this Case will shew.

London: Printed in the year 1721.   *folio.*   pp. 27.

————

PROOFS TO MAKE GOOD THE ASSERTIONS IN THE
TITLE-PAGE OF MY CASE
RELATING TO THE VICARIDGE OF LEMPSTER.

folio. pp. 24.   No title-page.

————

AN ABSTRACT OF EARL CONINGSBY'S TITLE TO ROYAL
FRANCHISES WITHIN HIS LIBERTY OF LEOMINSTER, IN
THE COUNTY OF HEREFORD, WITH REFERENCES TO THE
SEVERAL GRANTS.   *folio.*   No title-page.

Mr. Allen says,* "these pamphlets were privately printed in London, by order of Earl Coningsby, and a few copies were distributed
amongst his friends, but the greater number were probably destroyed."

Copies of these last three works are in Mr. Gough's topographical
library in the Bodleian.

————

* Bibliotheca Herefordiensis.

COLLECTIONS CONCERNING THE MANOR OF MARDEN,
IN THE COUNTY OF HEREFORD.   1722-1727.

small folio.

The collation of this very rare volume, will be found in Mr. Upcott's work on English Topography. The original copies have no title page; the scarcity of the index induced the Rev. Morgan Cove, prebendary of Hereford, to reprint, in 1813, at his own expense, twelve copies, being sheets Xxxxxxxx to Ddddddddd ; in all 28 pages. Dr. Cove also printed the same number of copies of a title page, and r brief historical descent of the manor of Marden, 2 pages, from Duncomb's Herefordshire. These reprints were all executed by Thomas Davies, printer, Hereford, and are nearly fac-similes of the type of the original volume.

These collections contain authentic extracts and transcripts of injunctions, records, &c., the originals of which were difficult of access, and many, in all probability, no longer exist. Thomas, Earl of Coningsby, who compiled this laborious work, and printed it at his own cost (probably in London), attempted to establish, by the documents he had collected together, claims on private property in Marden, Amberley, and other places in the vicinity, which he conceived ought to have belonged to him in right of his title of lord of the manor of Marden, which manor was purchased by him in 1717.

" In the old tower at Hampton Court* there were some perfect and imperfect copies ; but it is supposed these rare volumes were by mistake considered useless, and probably shared the fate of other waste paper." †

---

* Hampton Court, in Herefordshire, was sold by George, Fifth Earl of Essex (who inherited the property by right of his mother), to Richard Arkwright, Esq., in the year 1809. Stukeley, in his Itinerary, gives a description of the house. In the " Gentleman's Magazine " of April, 1825, there is an account of the publications of Earl Coningsby. A copy was sold in 1851, by Sotheby, a note to which says, " Certainly one of the rarest books connected with county history ; at the Townley sale it produced 48*l.* 6*s.* 0*d.*, and at Mr. Bindley's 24*l.* 3*s.* 0*d.*"

† Allen, Bib. Herefordiensis, p. 56.

The noble compiler of this volume was the first Earl of Coningsby, so created in 1719, and died in 1729 : his daughter Margaret was created Viscountess Coningsby of Hampton Court, but the title became extinct on her death in 1761. A large collection of MS. documents relating to this family is in the British Museum.*

Copies of this rare volume are in the following libraries, viz.—the British Museum, Bodleian, Marquis of Bath, Marquis of Bute, and Sir R. C. Hoare, Bart. : this last is illustrated.

THE CASE OF THE RIGHT HONOURABLE THOMAS, EARL OF CONINGSBY, IN RELATION TO THE FIVE HUNDREDS OF KINGTON, BODENHAM, BURGHILL, SHETFORD, AND CORVARN, IN THE COUNTY OF HEREFORD. 1723.   *folio.* pp. 88.

" This case of the Five Hundreds is not, to my knowledge, noticed by any collector or bibliographer. In a long course of collecting for Herefordshire, I have never met with any other copy of this book, which is, perhaps, the most rare of any of the strange publications of this most eccentric and irritable nobleman." †

DE FIDE ET OFFICIIS CHRISTIANORUM LIBER, AUCTORE THOMA BURNETIO, S.T.P.
Londini, 1722.   *4to.* pp. 223.

" Dono dedit prænobilis Comes de Macclesfield, Magnæ Britanniæ Cancellarius, cujus jussu et sumptibus quinquaginta tantum exemplaria excusa fuerunt."—Note in copy at Ingestre, the seat of Earl Talbot.

---

* Additional MSS. 6693.   † Allen, Bib. Herefordiensis.

De Statu Mortuorum et Resurgentium Liber.
Accesserunt Epistolæ duæ circa libellum de
Archæologiis Philosophicis.

Auctore Toma Burnetio, S.T.P.

Londini: 1723.   4to. pp. 327. Epistola, pp. 58.

In the preface to this volume it is stated, "Adhibita tamen est
cautela ne in vulgus emanaret."

The Statutes of the Most Honourable Order
of the Bath.

London: Printed in the year 1725.   4to.

These statutes were reprinted in the year 1772, pp. 69, with the star
of the order engraved on the title page; and again in 1812, pp. 77.

Short Preliminary Discourse to the History of
Ireland to be Published by Anthony Raymond.

1725.

Privately printed. Lowndes, p. 1544.

De Fide Mortuorum et Resurgentium Liber.
Accesserunt Epistolæ duæ circa libellum de
Archæologiis Philosophicis.

Auctore Toma Burnetio, S.T.P.

Londini: 1726.   8vo. pp. 302.

MEMOIRS OF THE LIFE AND WRITINGS OF THE LATE
CHARLES O'CONOR, OF BELANAGARE, ESQ.,
BY THE REV. CHARLES O'CONOR.
Dublin, 1726.   8vo.

"This memoir of the O'Connor Family was never published. The
author (the late Dr. O'Connor) destroyed the impression, after having
given away a very few copies." *Heber, Catalogue*, part iv. 1270.

DE FIDE ET OFFICIIS CHRISTIANORUM LIBER.
AUTHORE THOMA BURNETIO, S.T.P.
Londini : 1727.   8vo. pp. 190.

" Non ut in vulgus ederentur (ne forte auctoris defuncti proposito
fraus fieret), sed ut selectorum quorundam fidei, quasi depositum
quoddam concredita, tam a publicatione quam ab interitu tuta con-
servarentur."—*Preface.*

" Dr. Thomas Burnet had written a treatise, ' De Statu Mortuorum
et Resurgentium,' of which he had a *few* copies printed for the use
of himself and his friends. One of these, after the author's death,
happened to fall into Dr. Mead's hands ; who not knowing the author,
but liking the book, had *twenty-five* copies handsomely printed in
quarto. Maittaire revising the press, who made many blunders, by
inserting manuscript notes and additions from the author's interleaved copy into improper places of the text, Mr. Wilkinson, of Lincoln's Inn, who was executor to Dr. Burnet, lent Dr. Mead afterwards
a corrected copy, of which Dr. Mead was at the expense of printing
fifty copies, with a caution prefixed, to those chosen few on whom the
book was bestowed, not to suffer it to be translated, or reprinted and
published ; but this did not prevent a bad translation and a spurious
edition soon after getting abroad. So, to do justice to the author's
memory, Mr. Wilkinson himself caused an octavo edition to be printed
and published, as well of this book as of another, entitled ' De Fide

et Officiis Christianorum,' of which Lord Chancellor Macclesfield had prevailed on him to suffer as many copies to be printed, and in the same size, as Dr. Mead's edition of the 'De Statu Mortuorum et Resurgentium.' These gentlemen, with Maittaire, are the three persons whom Wilkinson means, but does not name, in the preface to his octavo edition of these two books in 1727."*

The author of this work was Master of the Charter House in 1685; he is said to have missed the see of Canterbury on the death of Tillotson, on account of his work entitled "Archæologiæ Philoso_phicæ." He died in 1715.

A brief ENQUIRY RELATING TO THE RIGHT OF HIS MAJESTY'S ROYAL CHAPEL, AND THE PRIVILEGES OF HIS SERVANTS WITHIN THE TOWER,

In a Memorial addressed to the Right Hon. the LORD VISCOUNT LONSDALE, Constable of his Majesty's Tower of London. 1728. *folio.*

" Signed H. Haynes, privately dispersed, and now become, from that circumstance, extremely scarce.

" Hopton Haynes was assay-master of the Mint, and principal tally-writer of the Exchequer."†

DE BENEDICTIONE PATRIARCHÆ JACOBI GENES. XLIX. CONJECTURÆ.

Oxonii, Theatro Sheldoniano. 1728. *4to.*

Lectori Præfatio, pp. i—viii ; Text, pp. 1—53.

---

* Nichols, Literary Anecdotes, vol. vi. p. 222.
† Nichols, Literary Anecdotes, vol. ii. p. 141.

In the preface, it is stated that these conjectures were by G. Hooper, Bishop of Bath and Wells; who printed, for friends only, one hundred copies, or fewer. The latter tract was edited, after the author's death, by Dr. Hunt, professor of Hebrew in Oxford, who signs the preface. The title-page contains a small copper engraving, which, it appears, was expressly designed by the Bishop for this work.

Devonshire Gems; or, Engravings from a portion of the Collection of Gems in the possession of his Grace the Duke of Devonshire. 1730. 4*to*.

" This Collection of Gems was begun to be formed by William the third Duke of Devonshire, and enlarged by William the fourth Duke, who was desirous of having the whole series engraved. He wished the engravings to be the precise representations of the originals. In his search, therefore, he was anxious to obtain an artist whose abilities were equal to the copying of the antique, and yet so much under command as not to improve any imperfection of the more moderate, or to fling on the more beautiful a cast of style, however admirable in itself, which the gem did not justify. It is not surprising, therefore, that some time elapsed before the Duke's inquiries met with success.

" At length, about the year 1724, M. Gosmond, a Frenchman, was recommended as well qualified to answer his Grace's expectations.

" The Duke, as was natural for a liberal man, evinced his satisfaction by many offices of generosity. But these unfortunately met with no grateful return: perhaps they were even the very cause of ingratitude. For M. Gosmond, conceiving that he had so strong a hold of his patron's good opinion as to establish himself in the family, relaxed in his attention, and by degrees entered into dissipation. The work now went on slowly, and objects of expense continued to increase on him. His calls on the Duke, therefore, were more frequent, while his claims for patronage were diminishing; and thus every day forfeiting the esteem of his noble employer, the Duke was under the necessity of declaring to him, when ninety-nine plates were finished, that he had already paid considerably more than the stipulated sum for the whole work, and with the hope of obliging him to be more attentive, re-^fused to answer any further demands till the work should proceed less negligently.

"Meeting with this unexpected refusal, and fearing the impatience of his creditors, M. Gosmond secretly left the kingdom, and carried many of the plates with him. What became of him after his return to the Continent is uncertain: inquiries were made, but they proved ineffectual.

" From this unlucky accident the Duke was frustrated in his purpose ; nor was he enabled to make up a few sets for his friends of what even were done. For, either impressions from several of the plates were not taken, or, if they were, they had been carried away by M. Gosmond. It does not appear what the number of plates left in the possession of the Duke amounted to. The Rev. C. M. Cracherode, whose taste and munificence are well known, could never obtain, though he made it an object, more than one hundred and one.

" The following account is from Mr. West's Catalogue of Books, No. 2790—

" 'The Duke of Devonshire's Cabinet of Gems, by Gosmond, 39 plates, being all that were engraved. M. Gosmond, a Frenchman, was employed by the old Duke of Devonshire to engrave his cabinet of gems, but when he had gone through the few here collected, he ran away, leaving some plates behind, and carrying the rest with him. What plates came into the Duke's hands he favoured me with proofs from : another parcel was purchased in France by the Hon. B. Bathurst, and presented to me by him. A.D. 1730.' "*

From the preceding note, it will easily be understood that copies of this work are extremely rare. Dr. Dibdin,† in his account of it, states that only four copies are known—viz. in the libraries of the Duke of Devonshire, the late Mr. Cracherode (now in the British

---

* Note in Lord Spencer's copy.   † Ædes Althorpianæ.

Museum, 101 plates), Earl of Besborough, * and Earl Spencer: in addition to these, the editor has ascertained that there are copies in the following libraries:—the Duke of Bedford (100 plates); Hunterian Museum, Glasgow; Sir J. Thorold, Mr. Botfield, Mr. Fountaine, and Sir A. Johnstone [formerly Mrs. Damer's]; this last has ninety-eight plates.

The original gems are in his Grace's mansion in Piccadilly.

THE TOAST: AN EPIC POEM, IN FOUR BOOKS.
Dublin: Printed in the year 1732.   8*vo.*   pp. 96.

The late Archdeacon Wrangham, to whom the editor of this volume was under the greatest obligation for much curious information, said there were only *two* books printed. The satire is stated by Dr. Warton, to have been principally aimed at the Countess of Newburgh.

" Swift is said to have declared to a lady, if he had read the Toast when he was twenty years of age, he would never have written a satire."—See *Moore's Journal,* vol. ii. p. 240.

CATALOGUS LIBRORUM BIBLIOTHECÆ
HONORABILIS SOCIETATIS MEDII TEMPLI LONDINI.
ORDINE DICTIONARII DISPOSITUS.
Impress: Anno Domini 1734, Carolo Worsley, Armigero, Thesaurio existente.

A quarto volume of 584 pages.

---

* This copy wants plates 9, 19, 24, 26, 28, 31, 34, 36, 44, 45, 46, 47, 49, 52, 71, 76, 78, 86, and 89.

An Account of the Funeral Ceremonies
perform'd at Rome, in honour of the Princess
Clementine Sobieski.
Translated from the Roman Journal of Jan. 29, 1735.
No. 2729.
Printed in the year 1735.   8*vo*. pp. 16.

For the communication of this scarce volume, the editor is
indebted to James Maidment, Esq., to whose kind and liberal
assistance this work will owe much of its value. The bibliographical
note that follows, is also from the same gentleman. " I never saw
another copy than the one in my library, which is sumptuously
bound in old red Morocco. At the end occurs a MS. 'Letter from a
Gentleman to his friend, copy'd May, 1735,' giving an account of the
Old Pretender. I need hardly remark that it is very much in his
favour. The printed tract was evidently intended for the exclusive
use of the Jacobite nobility and gentry."

The Toast : an Heroick Poem, in Four Books.
Written originally by Frederick Scheffer : now
done into English, and illustrated with Notes
and Observations, By Peregrine O'Donald, Esq.
Dublin, printed.   London, reprinted in the year 1736.
4*to*.   pp. 232.

The following key to this poem is taken from a copy formerly in
the possession of the editor.
Page 2.—Myra. Lady Frances Brudenell, sister to the Earl of Car-
digan; married first to Count Newburgh, afterwards to
Lord Bellew, and last to Sir Thomas Smith, Dr. King's
uncle, but this match was not owned.
    3.—.* *.   Walpole.

Page 5.—Volcan. Captain John Pratt, Deputy Vice-Treasurer of Ireland.

    7.—Mars Chevalier. Sir Thomas Smith.

    8.—Mrs. D—. Mrs. Denton.

   16.—Hortensius. Dr. Hort, Archbishop of Tuam.

   17.—Milo. Butler, a Lieutenant of the Yeomen of the Guards.

   20.—Trulla. A —— that he kept.

   27.—Lord A——. Lord Viscount Allen.

   37.—Ottor. Dr. Trotter, a Master in Chancery.

   40.—Jocco. Robert Jocelyn, Esq., Attorney General, afterwards Lord Chancellor of Ireland.

   49.—Little Ali. Lady Allen, wife of Lord Allen.

   84.—Piercy. Sir Edward Pierce, Surveyor General of Ireland.

   86.—Lord Pam. Dr. Hort, Archbishop of Tuam.

 *89.—A—p. Herring.

 *91.—H—. Sir Richard Hoare.

 *91.—G—n. Gideon. G. Gore.

 *92.—P—s. Pelhams. S. Pulteney.

 107.—Altes. Lady Allen.

       Maccar. One Mr. Macarty.

 113.—Curculio. Capt. Cayley.

*113.—Bocca. Bowes, Lord Chief Baron.

       C—r. The Chancellor. (Lord Talbot.)

*114.—Miracides. Lord Bellew, Myra's son.

 115.—P—r. Peter Daily.

 125.—* *. Walpole.

 126.—Cacus. Sir Edward Crofton ; he was executor to Sir Edward Pierce.

 146.—* * *. Little Allen. Vir. Lady Allen.

       Traulus. Lord Allen.

       * *. Jocelyn. *. Bowes.

       E—wood. Ellwood —. King.

 147.—E—pal. Episcopal. * *. Hoadly. *. Hort.

       Juseus. Judge Ward.

 149.—Dill. Counsellor Dillon.

 150.—Mac. Macarty.

Page 157.—Ondell and Jocco.   Dillon and Jocelyn.,

    158.—Surveyor.   Charles Withers, brother-in-law to Dr. King.

    168.—* * * *.   Duke of Grafton.

        S—l—gan.   Skylagan; a seat of Lord Allen's.

    193.—Ld. J——s.   Lord Allen.

    156.—In the note is the account of the usage of Dr. King.

The author of this poem was the son of the Rev. Peregrine King, born at Stepney in 1685, and was entered of Baliol College, Oxford, in 1701; he went to Ireland in 1727, when he wrote this Satire. He was author of various other works, a list of which will be found in Mr. Chalmers' life of him;* he died in 1763, and was buried at Ealing, but the inscription to his memory is at St. Mary Hall, Oxford. An edition of his works was printed in 1754, which see.

'Dr. King's picture is just put up in the Picture Gallery, and placed by his desire, next to Butler's. His heart is to be lodged in the chapel at St. Mary Hall, with an inscription, which he drew up himself. The most remarkable part of it is this: 'Permultos habui amicos, at veros, stabiles, gratos (quæ fortasse est gentis culpa), perpaucissimos. Plures habui inimicos, sed invidos, sed improbos, sed inhumanos.' This, and the whole of it, might, I think, very well have been omitted. I don't hear that he has left anything to be published. He printed, some years ago, a poem, in four books, called 'The Toast.' That edition was never published, but some copies of it given to his friends. The rest of the impression lay in his lodgings, and is now ordered to be burnt. It was a dirty subject, and it did not become the Doctor to spend so much time as he did in raking into it."—Letter of the Rev. Charles Godwyn, in Nichols' Anecdotes, vol. viii. p. 241.

Reed's copy, with a manuscript key, was purchased by the late Mr. Malone for 10l. 10s.

---

* Biographical Dictionary, vol. xix. p. 378.

THE HONOUR OF THE SEALS ; OR, MEMOIRS OF
THE NOBLE FAMILY OF TALBOT ;
WITH THE LIFE OF LORD CHANCELLOR TALBOT.
Printed in the year 1737. *8vo.*

"Dr. Johnston, of Pontefract, wrote a history of the Talbot family, from their Norman ancestor Richard Talbot, to the Lord Edward Talbot, last Earl of Shrewsbury, of the house of Sheffield."*

CARMEN EPISCENIUM AUGUSTISSIMÆ RUSSORUM
IMPERATRICI SACRUM. 1737.

A small poem, by Mr. Maittaire, printed only for private use."†

POEMS UPON VARIOUS OCCASIONS,
WRITTEN FOR THE ENTERTAINMENT OF THE AUTHOR,
AND PRINTED FOR THE AMUSEMENT OF A FEW
FRIENDS, PREJUDIC'D IN HIS FAVOUR.
Oxford : Printed by Leon Lichfield, near East Gate,
1737. *8vo.* pp. 78.

By William Shenstone. " Some copies have, and some have not, the author's name on the title-page." Lowndes. Shenstone bestowed uncommon pains to suppress this book, by collecting and destroying copies, wherever he met with them.

" Nothing but the extreme rarity of this, the first printed production of Shenstone, would entitle the writings of so recent an author

---

* Gough, British Topography, p. 545.
† Nichols, Anecdotes, vol. ii. p. 104.

to a place in this collection. Our pastoral poet seems to have evinced his riper judgment by this attempt at suppression, as these early pieces give no great promise that the author would hereafter obtain a niche in the temple of poetic fame: but it is matter of exultation that he did not recover all the copies, as it must ever be a desirable exercise to compare the first effusions of an ingenious writer with his more finished productions."

Mr. Park has given a minute account of these juvenile poems in the Censura Literaria, vol. i. p. 238, with a criticism upon each, and some short extracts.* The copy in the catalogue, from which this extract is taken, was priced at 15*l*.

The Question of the Precedency of the Peers of Ireland in England fairly stated in a Letter to an English Lord, by a Nobleman of the other Kingdom.
Dublin: Printed in the year 1739.   8*vo*.

" Written and printed for private circulation only, by John Perceval Earl of Egmont, upon occasion of a memorial presented by his Lordship to his Majesty, 2nd November, 1733, respecting the precedency of the Irish peers in the ceremonial of the marriage of the Princess Royal with the Prince of Orange. It was reprinted, and published in 1761."†

" Lord Egmont had, as is well known, excellent talents, and well adapted to the discharge of the highest public duties; but they embraced a variety of objects; and in the genealogy of several British or Irish families, he was as particularly conversant as Atticus is stated to have been in that of the great Roman houses, the Marcelli, the Claudii, and others. His heraldic knowledge was also singularly

---

* Bibliotheca Anglo-Poetica, p. 344.
† Moule, Bibliotheca Heraldica, p. 356.

minute and circumstantial; and on points of precedence, or adjusting the slow and solemn steps of exalted personages at public ceremonials, neither Mowbray nor Lancaster heralds, Blue Mantle or Rouge Dragon, could venture to approach his lordship."*

A GENEALOGICAL ACCOUNT OF THE BARCLAYS OF URIE, FORMERLY OF MATHER; EXTRACTED FROM ANCIENT REGISTERS, AND AUTHENTIC DOCUMENTS. Together with Memoirs of the Life of Colonel DAVID BARCLAY of Urie, and of his eldest son, the late Robert Barclay of Urie. Collected for the Information and use of their Posterity.

Aberdeen : Printed by James Chalmers, Printer to the Town and University. 1740. 8vo. pp. 61.

" Written by Robert Barclay, the son of the Apologist, and printed chiefly for distribution amongst his relations and friends: reprinted in 1821."†

ATHENIAN LETTERS :
OR, THE EPISTOLARY CORRESPONDENCE OF AN AGENT OF THE KING OF PERSIA RESIDING AT ATHENS DURING THE PELOPONNESIAN WAR.
London : 1741—3. 4 vols. 8vo.

Twelve copies only were printed of this edition. The following are

---

* Hardy, Life of Lord Charlemont, vol. i. p. 124.
† Moule, Bibliotheca Heraldica, p. 358.

the writers of the letters, taken from Nichols's Literary Illustrations of the Eighteenth Century, vol. i. p. 33:—

P.—Hon. Philip Yorke, afterwards Earl of Hardwicke.

C.—Hon. Charles Yorke.

R.—Rev. Dr. G. H. Rooke, Master of Christ's College.

G.—Dr. Green, Bishop of Lincoln.

W.—Daniel Wray.

H.—Rev. John Heaton, of Bene't College.

E.—Dr. Heberden.

O.—Henry Coventry.

L.—Rev. Mr. Lawry, Prebendary of Rochester.

T.—Mrs. Catherine Talbot.

B.—Rev. Dr. Birch.*

S.—Dr. Salter, Master of the Charter House.

The preface to this edition was written by Mr. Charles Yorke, that to 1781 by Mr. Heaton. Mr. Grenville says in a note to his copy, " it contains some letters not to be found in the subsequent editions."

Miscellanies in Prose and Verse.
London: Printed in the year M.DCC.XLI.

By Thomas Lord Paget, son of Henry first Earl of Uxbridge: he died at Drayton, near Uxbridge, January, 1742.

This volume was printed a year before his death; and in the advertisement it is stated, " that, for avoiding a general publication, he was brought to permit that a few books should be printed for the private use of himself and his intimate friends."

He was M.P. for Stafford 1714 and 1722. Lord of the Bed-chamber to the Prince of Wales; and on his accession to the throne as George II., was continued in the same office. He was author of "An

---

* In the MSS. in the British Museum will be found a considerable correspondence between the Yorke family and Dr. Birch relative to this work.

Essay on Human Life," in verse, 1734, 8vo., " Reflections upon the Administration of the Government," 1740.*

A copy was in Bindley's Catalogue, part ii. 2242.

———

A CATALOGUE OF THE LIBRARY OF THE FACULTY OF ADVOCATES, EDINBURGH. PART THE FIRST.

Edinburgh: Printed by Thomas, Walter and Thomas Ruddiman. M.DCC.XLII.   *folio.* pp. 1—649.

PART SECOND.

Edinburgh: Printed by Balfour and Smellie.

M.DCC.LXXVI.   pp. 1—598.

APPENDIX TO THE CATALOGUE OF THE ADVOCATES' LIBRARY.

Edinburgh: Printed by William Smellie.

folio. pp. 1—138.

An alphabetical catalogue; the first part was compiled by Thomas Ruddiman and Walter Goodall, keepers of the library. The second part and the appendix by Alexander Brown, librarian. A sketch of its history and contents is in Horne's "Introduction to Bibliography," vol. ii. p. 635.

———

AN ACCOUNT OF THE CONDUCT OF THE DOWAGER DUCHESS OF MARLBOROUGH, FROM HER FIRST COMING TO COURT, TO THE YEAR 1710: IN A LETTER FROM HERSELF TO MY LORD———.

London: Printed in the year M.DCC.XLII.

roy. 8vo. pp. 362.

———

* Nichols, Anecdotes, vol. ii. p. 115.

This volume was compiled by Hooke, the historian; it was a work which attracted great notice at the period of its publication*—a few cotemporary criticisms are subjoined.

"Your friend, the Duchess of Marlborough, has, in your absence, employed me as your substitute; and I have brought Mr. Hooke† and her together, and having done that will leave the rest to them, not caring to meddle myself with an affair, which, I am sure, will not turn out at last to her satisfaction, though I hope and believe it will to his advantage."‡

"This favourite Duchess, who, like the proud Duke of Epernon, lived to brave the successors in a Court where she had domineered, wound up her capricious life, where, it seems, she had begun it, with an apology for her conduct. The piece, though weakened by the prudence of those who were to correct it, though maimed by her Grace's own corrections, and though great part of it is rather the annals of a wardrobe than of a reign, yet has still curious anecdotes, and a few of those sallies of wit, which fourscore years of arrogance could not fail to produce in so fantastical an understanding." §

"She had no true wisdom or greatness of mind, and was, in truth, a very weak, passionate woman. She spoke ill, and her Memoirs are very mean."‖

"The spirit, humour, and language of this extraordinary piece proclaim it genuine. All that vivacity and contempt of dignities, which distinguish her from all other ladies, shine with such lustre in the book as to set it beyond comparison, except with Lord Clarendon's History, which I conceive to be like it, for this reason—he wrote it to shew that throughout his whole life he was ever in the *right*, and her ladyship has the goodness to publish her conduct, to shew that she *was never once in the wrong*."¶

---

* Another edition was printed for public sale in the same year. London. Printed by James Bettenham, for George Hawkins, at Milton's Head, between the two Temple gates. 8vo. pp. 316.

† The Duchess left Mr. Hooke 5000l.

‡ Earl of Chesterfield to Lord Marchmont—Marchmont Papers, vol. ii. p. 251.

§ Walpole, Noble Authors, by Park, vol. iv. p. 91.

‖ Speaker Onslow's Note in Burnet's Own Time, vol. v. p. 326.

¶ Gentleman's Magazine, 1742. p. 204.

E

This is an extract from a long review of this work, said to have been written by Dr. Johnson.

———

CATALOGUS LIBRORUM BIBLIOTHECÆ ECCLESIÆ
CHRISTI CANTUARIENSIS.
Cantuariæ: typis Jacobi Obree. M.DCC.XLIII. *8vo.*

An alphabetical catalogue, without dates.

———

THE TOAST : AN HEROICK POEM, IN FOUR BOOKS.
WRITTEN ORIGINALLY IN LATIN, BY FREDERICK
SCHEFFER : NOW DONE INTO ENGLISH, AND ILLUS-
TRATED WITH NOTES AND OBSERVATIONS, BY PERE-
GRINE O'DONALD, ESQ.
Dublin, printed. London, reprinted in the year 1747.
4to. pp. 232.

———

THE HISTORY OF THE BIBLE. TRANSLATED FROM THE
FRENCH, BY R. G. JUN., IN 1746.
London: Printed [by James Waugh] in the year 1747.
folio. pp. 612. Table, two leaves ; at the end of which
is printed, " Done at twelve years and a half old."

This was a juvenile production of the eminent antiquary, the late
Mr. Gough; no more than twenty-five copies were printed. Mr.
Bowyer Nichols possesses one.

THE CASE OF THE FREE SCRIVENERS OF LONDON :
Set forth in a Report from a Committee of the Court
of Assistants of the Company of Scriveners, London, to
the Master, Wardens, and Assistants of the Company, at
their Court, holden the 23rd day of June, 1748.

London : Printed in the year 1749.   4*to*. pp. 88.

"The Scriveners of London have been time out of mind a Society,
or Company by prescription, and were originally called Common
Scriveners, or Writers of the Court Letter of the City of London."

———

A MODEST ENQUIRY HOW FAR CATHOLICS ARE GUILTY
OF THE HORRID TENETS LAID TO THEIR CHARGE, BY S.B.
8*vo*. 1749.

From a bookseller's catalogue, who calls it privately printed.

———

THE CUSTOMS OF THE ISRAELITES.   TRANSLATED
FROM THE FRENCH OF THE ABBOT FLEURY, BY R. G.
1750. 8*vo*.

Another juvenile production of the late Mr. Gough.

———

A COLLECTION OF LOYAL SONGS, POEMS, ETC.
Printed in the year 1750.   8*vo*. pp. 72.

A collection of Jacobite poems; stated to be privately, most probably printed for sale; although, from the nature of the collection,
very cautiously.

E 2

LIFE OF SIR JOHN LEAKE, BART., ADMIRAL OF THE FLEET, ETC. BY STEPHEN MARTIN LEAKE.
London: Printed by Bowyer. 1750. 8*vo.* pp. 464.

It is stated, in the preface, that fifty copies only were printed for the use of the family and friends.

———

COLLECTANEA CANTABRIDGIENSIA; OR, COLLECTIONS RELATING TO CAMBRIDGE UNIVERSITY, TOWN AND COUNTY:
Containing the Monumental Inscriptions in all the Chapels of the several Colleges, &c., and Parish Churches in the Town, and in several others in the County; with a list of the Mayors; the most ancient Charters of the Town, and other historical Memoirs of several Colleges, &c.

BY FRANCIS BLOMEFIELD, late of Caius College, now Rector of Tenfield and Brockdesh, Norfolk, and Minister of St. Mary-in-Costany, in the city of Norwich.

Printed for the Author, at his house, in St. Giles' Parish, in the city of Norwich, in the year of our Lord 1750.   4*to.* pp. 268.

———

OPERA GUL. KING, LL.D. AULÆ B.M.V. APUD OXONIENSIS. OLIM. PRINCIP.

"———— at qui
Primores populi arripuit populumque tributim,
Scilicet uni æquus virtuti atque ejus amicis."

M.DCC.LIV. 4*to.* Preface, pp. viii. Opera, pp. 239.

" This volume is said never to have been published; but on the death of the author the whole of the impression, except sixty copies, were destroyed by the author's executors."

" The Toast " will be found in this volume, which contains a few vignettes.*

Fragments of a Prospect from a Hill in Fife.
Edinburgh. 4*to*. pp. 38.

No author's name or date, but written by George Wallace, Esq., Advocate, and forty copies printed for private distribution in the year 1754.

The work was printed with the author's name at Edinburgh, in 1796, 8vo.; and a second edition, with additions. Edinburgh, 1800, 8vo.

The author was son of the Rev. Dr. Wallace, one of the Ministers of Edinburgh, born in 1730; admitted Advocate in 1754, and died in 1805.

History of the Noble Family of Carteret, existing before the Reign of William the Conqueror, with the most memorable Actions and Achievements of the principal Persons thereof.
1756. 8*vo*.

" Privately printed; no other copy of this book can be discovered in any catalogue, either of public or private collections, nor does it appear to exist in the British Museum. It seems to be equally unknown to writers who have written expressly on the same subject, and to bibliographers, as it is not mentioned in the copious account of works of heraldry and genealogy by Moule."—*Thorpe's Catalogue*, 1825.

---

* Reed's Catalogue, No. 2204.

A copy was in Mr. Dent's library, No. 532. It is, most probably, only a portion of Collins' Peerage taken off separately, for the gratification of the family to whose history it relates : an edition (the 3rd) of that work was published in the same year.

LETTERS FROM AND TO SIR DUDLEY CARLETON, KNT., DURING HIS EMBASSY IN HOLLAND, FROM JANUARY, 1615-16, TO DECEMBER, 1620. London : Printed in the year 1757. *4to.*

Preface, pp. 111. Letters, pp. 510. Index, 11 leaves.

Only twenty copies were printed of this edition, which was edited by the Earl of Hardwicke.

"His negociations have been lately presented to the public ; it was not the fault of the minister or of the editor, that these transactions turned chiefly on the Synod of Dort." *

"These letters, if some allowances be made for party violences and prejudices, contain more clear, accurate, and interesting accounts of that remarkable period of Dutch history to which they relate, than are anywhere extant." †

BIBLIOTHECÆ COLLEGII REGALIS MEDICORUM LONDINENSIS CATALOGUS. Londini. M.DCC.LVII. *royal 8vo.* pp. 349.

Alphabetically arranged, and most probably compiled by Edwards the naturalist, who was then librarian. The library was founded by the Marquis of Dorchester in 1650, and has been considerably augmented by subsequent donations : no continuation of it has been published.

---

* Walpole, Noble Authors, by Park, vol. ii. p. 262.
† Chalmers, Biographical Dict. vol. viii. p. 254.

A State of Facts in Defence of His Majesty's
Right to certain Fee-Farm Rents in the
County of Norfolk.

London: Printed in the year M.DCC.LVIII. 4*to.* pp. 88.

By Philip Carteret Webb; called by Horace Walpole a dirty wretch,
from a supposed error in his evidence on the trial in the Court of
Common Pleas, and for which he was afterwards indicted for per-
jury, but acquitted. A copy is in Mr. Gough's library in the Bodleian.

———

Catalogus Librorum A. C. D. A.
[Archib. Campbell, Ducis Argatheliæ.]
Glasguæ, in ædibus Academicis, excudebant Robertus
et Andreas Foulis, Academiæ Typographi. 1758. 4*to.*
pp. 304.

In a note in a copy formerly Isaac Reed's, he says, "This Catalogue is perfect, though the word '*Finis*' is not printed. The library,
soon after the beginning of the present king's reign [George III.]
was purchased by the Earl of Bute."

"Archibald Campbell, Duke of Argyle, died April 15th, 1751: he
had a great thirst for books, a head admirably turned to mechanics,
was a patron of ingenious men, a promoter of discoveries, and one
of the first great encouragers of planting in England."*

———

Poems, together with a Latin Oration.
[By Sir James Marriott].
Printed by James Bettenham. 1760. 8*vo.* pp. 156.

———

* Walpole, Memoirs of George II. vol. i. p. 242.

Second Title.

POEMS, WRITTEN CHIEFLY AT THE UNIVERSITY OF
CAMBRIDGE, TOGETHER WITH A LATIN ORATION UPON
THE HISTORY AND GENIUS OF THE ROMAN AND CANON
LAWS, WITH A COMPARISON OF THE LAWS OF ENGLAND.
Spoken in the Chapel, at Trinity Hall, Cambridge,
December 21, 1756.

The author, in the conclusion to the preface, p. viii. intimates that
the printing of this volume was with the view of obviating the
opinion of there being other productions of his than are herein contained ; and also a desire of making to a few particular friends a
present, in an academical way, which it is not in their power to
purchase—" a circumstance which of itself gives value to trifles."

Sir James Marriott was Advocate-General, and afterwards Judge of
the Admiralty Court. He died April, 1803.

––––––––

SOME ACCOUNT OF BROWNE WILLIS, ESQ., LL.D.,
LATE SENIOR FELLOW OF THE SOCIETY OF ANTIQUARIES
OF LONDON.
Read before the Society of Antiquaries of London,
May and June, 1760.
London. 1760.   *4to.*

A small tract of eight pages, to which is added a list of his works.
Cole calls it " a paltry sketch." *

––––––––––––––––––

* MSS. vol. xliii. p. 56.

CATALOGUE DES PIERRES GRAVEES TANT EN RELIEF QU'EN CREUX, DE MY LORD COMTE DE BESSBOROUGH, PAIR D'ANGLETERRE ET D'IRLANDE, ETC.

Dressé par LAURENT NATTER, Graveur en pierres-fines et Médailleur, Membre de la Société-Royale des Arts et Sciences, et de celle des Antiquaires de Londres, aussi bien que de l'Académie Etrusque.

A Londres, de l'Imprimerie de J. Haberkorn, dans Grafton Street, Soho, M.DCC.LXI.   4to.

Title, 2 leaves (of address to Lord Bessborough, and Advertisement), and pp. 28. Also 7 engraved plates, three of which Natter states had been engraved for a work to be entitled "Museum Britannicum," but which he was forced to abandon for want of encouragement.

———

DE GRÆCORUM QUINTA DECLINATIONE IMPARISYLLA-BICA, ET INDE FORMATA LATINORUM TERTIA QUÆSTIO GRAMMATICA.

Adjiciuntur loca aliquot ex auctoribus Græcis et Latinis explicata.

Londini.   Anno 1761.   4to.   pp. 93.

By Jeremiah Markland. Forty copies only were printed, at the expense of William Hall, Esq., of the Temple. It was afterwards reprinted, with the edition of Euripides' Supplices Mulieres, 1763. Dr. Burney's copy, with some notes, is in the British Museum. Mr. Markland died July 7, 1776, and was buried in the church of Dorking, Surrey.

PHILEMON.

Printed for the Author.   1761.   *8vo.*   pp. 35.

The copy in the British Museum has been successively in possession of Cole, Bishop of Ely (Dampier), Dr. Lort, and Mr. Bindley ;
a note in Cole's writing says :—" This little tract was given to me in
1765, by Mr. Phillips, the writer of it, and of the life of Cardinal
Pole.   It is supposed to be a sketch of the chief incidents of his
own life : there were very few printed, and it is very difficult to get
one, as the writer afterwards suppressed it.   He had been entered
among the Jesuits, but quitted them and was afterwards one of the
Canons of Songres.

LIFE OF JOHN DOLLOND, F.R.S.   BY JOHN KELLY, LL.D. RECTOR OF COPFORD, ESSEX.
Circa 1762.

" This life was printed for private distribution, by Messrs. Dol-
lond.   Besides the life, there is an appendix of various important
papers relating to the discovery and uses of the achromatic te-
lescope." *

AN ESSAY ON WOMAN, IN THREE EPISTLES.
London : Printed for the Author, and sold by Mr.
Gretton, in Bond Street, and Mr. Pottinger, in Pater-
noster Row.   1763.   *8vo.*   pp. 40.

There is a title-page in French.

This infamous poem was by the celebrated John Wilkes ;† his
biographer says twelve copies only were printed.   " The Essay on

---

* Chalmers, Biog Dict. vol. xii. p. 216.
† Almon, Life of Wilkes, vol. i. p. 140.

Woman," says Kidgell, * " is a parody on Mr. Pope's Essay on Man, almost line for line, printed in red. The frontispiece, engraved curiously on copper, contains the title of the poem ; the title is succeeded by a few pages entitled Advertisement and Design." The notes are said by Almon to have been principally contributed by Mr. Potter. On the title-page is an obscene print, under which is an inscription in Greek, signifying the Saviour of the world. There is a long account of this work in the Gentleman's Magazine.†

" This was an obscene poem which he printed at his private press, but can scarcely be said to have published it, as he printed only a very small number of copies (about twelve) to give away to certain friends."‡

This infamous production originated at Medmenham Abbey ; the scene of impious buffooneries of Wilkes and his companions.

Horace Walpole § says:—"Fourteen copies only were printed ; one of which the ministry had bribed the printer to give up. Mr. Kidgell, a clergyman, had obtained from the printer a copy of the Essay on Woman, which he felt it his duty to denounce. His own personal character turned out far from being respectable."

" Ce poème infame est une parodie, presque vers pour vers, de l'Essai sur l'Homme de Pope. Le frontispiece, gravé en taille douve, renferme le titre du poème, avec une figure obscène, au-dessous de laquelle se lit une inscription en Grec, signifiant *le Sauveur du monde*. Les notes ont été en grande partie fournies par M. Potter." —*Brunet.*

The North Briton. By J. Wilkes. Vol. III.

" A few copies of a *third* volume of the North Briton were printed at his own private press, but were never published." In the Gen-

---

* Kidgell, Narrative of a Libel, Essay on Woman. 4to. Lond. 1763.
† Almon, Life of Wilkes, vol. i. p. 12.
‡ Chalmers, Life of Wilkes.
§ Letters to Lord Hertford.

tleman's Magazine* it is said,—" Mr. Wilkes has caused a printing press to be set up under his own direction, and has advertized the proceedings of the administration, with all the original papers, at the price of a guinea. The North Briton has again made its appearance."

SOME OBSERVATIONS ON THE LATE DETERMINATION FOR DISCHARGING MR. WILKES FROM HIS COMMITMENT TO THE TOWER OF LONDON, FOR BEING THE AUTHOR AND PUBLISHER OF A SEDITIOUS LIBEL, CALLED THE TRUE BRITON, No. 45, BY A MEMBER OF THE HOUSE OF COMMONS (PHI. CARTERET WEBB).

Printed in the year 1763.   4to.

COPIES TAKEN FROM THE RECORDS OF THE C. OF K.B.
4to.   1763.

A copy of this book was in Wilkes' Catalogue, No. 395; a note in it says that it was printed by P. C. Webb, one of the solicitors to the Treasury, but never published. He was solicitor during the period of the prosecution against Wilkes.

Philip Carteret Webb, a distinguished antiquary, born in 1700, was bred to the Law, chosen Member for Haslemere in 1754, and again in 1761: he was appointed Secretary of Bankrupts under Lord Chancellor Hardwicke, and in 1765 one of the joint Solicitors of the Treasury. He died at Busbridge, June 22, 1770, aged 70. His library was sold Feb. 25, 1771, and sixteen following days.

Nichols' Anecdotes, vol. ii. p. 280, where there is a list of his works.

---

* 1763. p. 256.

ANECDOTES AND OBSERVATIONS RELATING TO
OLIVER CROMWELL AND HIS FAMILY ;
Serving to rectify several Errors concerning him, pub-
lished by Nicolaus Comnenus Papadapoli, in his "His-
toria Gymnasii Patavini."
London : Printed in the year 1763. *4to.*

" This was printed for private circulation by James Burrow, Esq.,
Master of the Crown Office, who died in 1782. A portion of the
work was printed in the Gentleman's Magazine for 1767." *

RECHERCHES SUR L'ORIGINE DU DESPOTISME ORIENTAL.
OUVRAGE POSTHUME DE M. BOULANGER.

"Monstrum horrendum, informe, ingens——"

A Londres. 1763. *12mo.* pp. *239.*

" Printed at Wilkes' private press, in George-street, Westminster,
by Thomas Farmer, who also printed the Essay on Woman. He
was first employed by Horace Walpole at Strawberry Hill. This
was Wilkes' own copy, and has his autograph."†

MEMORIAL OF CHARLES HOWARD, ESQ., OF GREY-
STOCK, AND MISS FRANCES HOWARD, OF THE FAMILY OF
NORFOLK IN ENGLAND.

(1763.) *4to.* pp. *28.*

" Privately printed." Grenville Library.

---

* Moule, Bibliotheca Heraldica, p. 398.
† Extract from a note in a copy (No. 428) in the sale of the library of a
distinguished collector (M. Aime), March 11, 1829.

THE SECOND PART OF A LITERARY CORRESPOND-
ENCE BETWEEN THE BISHOP OF GLOUCESTER AND A
LATE PROFESSOR OF OXFORD.

Accurately printed from an authentic copy; to which
are added, the notes of the first Editor, with Notes upon
Notes, and Remarks upon the Letters.

8vo. pp. 50. 1765.

This work is a part of the appendix to Mr. Towne's Remarks
upon Dr. Lowth's Letter to Bishop Warburton, reprinted by Dr.
Lowth, for distribution among his friends; only seventy-five copies
were printed. Dr. Parr calls him the friend and advocate of Warburton, and the author of several acute and learned works. " I
should tell you that a pamphlet written by Towne, in answer to
Lowth, has some things which are very well approved of. In the
affair of punishing idolatry with death, he is thought to have the
advantage."

Rev. Charles Godwyn. Nichols' Anecdotes, vol. viii. p. 244.

OBSERVATIONS TOUCHING THE ANTIQUITY AND DIG-
NITY OF THE DECREE OF SERGEANT-AT-LAW.

With Reasons against laying open the Court of Common Pleas, as was proposed at the time of printing these
Observations.

Ordo amplissimus : et ordo is, qui est et Publici
Concilii et omnium conciliorum auctor.
Cicero de Provin. Consular.

London. 1765. *8vo.* pp. 167: Table of Contents,
three leaves; Index, five leaves; Errata, one leaf.

The author was Mr. Wynne, who says in the preface,—" a few
copies for the entertainment of a friend or two."

The History of the late Minority;
Exhibiting the Conduct, Principles, and Views of that
Party, during the years 1762, 1763, 1764, and 1765.
London : Printed in the year 1765.   *8vo.*

It was reprinted, with some additions, in 1766. *8vo.* pp. 332.

Of the original edition *twelve* copies only are said to have been
printed. The Monthly Review styles it, " an inflammatory piece of
party-work, which hath engrossed a much greater share of the public
attention than it seems to have merited."

———

An Apology for the Life of General Wolff,
by J. Mauduit.
London.   *8vo.*   1765.

A copy was in Mr. Heber's catalogue, pt. 3, No. 4888, where it is
said only twenty-five copies were printed ; this copy had MS. corrections by the author.

———

Catalogus continens Libros qui Bibliothecæ Honorabilis Societatis Medii Templi Londini additi
fuerunt, ab anno 1734 ad hoc tempus.

Ordine dictionarii dispositus.

Impress : Anno Domini 1766.   Prehonorabile Thoma
Sewell, Milite, Scriniorum sacrorum Magistro, Thesaurio existente.   *4to.* pp. 17.

This catalogue is alphabetically arranged.   Another catalogue, in
two *8vo.* volumes, arranged in classes and also alphabetically, was
compiled by the present librarian, the Rev. J. H. Rowlett, and
printed in 1845.   In this collection are thirty-seven volumes of

MSS., chiefly parliamentary and juridical. See an account of them in the first report of the Public Records, p. 375. There was a former catalogue of this library printed in 1700, 8*vo*, under the direction, and at the expense of Sir Bartholomew Shower. A copy of it is in the British Museum.*

THE STATUTES OF THE MOST NOBLE ORDER
OF THE GARTER.
London : Printed in the year 1766.   4*to.*

These statutes were reprinted by J. Hayes in 1786, but with the date 1766 on the title, making 60 pp. ; to which the additional statutes of 1805 were subsequently added, making 63 pp. ; reprinted again in 1814, 78 pp., and additional statutes added in 1816, making 80 pp. ; reprinted 1825, 84 pp., to which edition the additional statutes of 1831 were added, making 92 pp.

These statutes are printed solely for the use of the knights of the order ; the impression is limited according to circumstances.

FOSSILIA HANTONIENSIA COLLECTA, ET IN MUSÆO BRITANNICO DEPOSITA, A GUSTAVO BRANDER, R.S., ET S.A.S., MUS. BRIT. CUR.
Londini. 1766. 4*to.* pp. 43. With nine plates, drawn and engraved by Green.

The text for this work was written by Dr. Solander.

---

* Horne. Bibliography, vol. ii. p. 624.

A Short View of the principal Seats and Gardens in and about Twickenham.

London: Printed in the year 1767.   8*vo.*   pp. 36.

By Mrs. Pye, sister to H. J. Pye, poet laureate in the reign of George III.

Poems, by a Lady.

London: Printed in the year M.DCC.LXVII.   12*mo.*
pp. 36.

By Mrs. Pye, author of the previous volume.

" The Peep into the Gardens at Twickenham is a silly little book, of which a few little copies were printed some years ago for presents, and which now sets itself up as a vendible book. It is a most inaccurate, superficial, blundering account of Twickenham and other places, drawn up by a Jewess, who has married twice, and turned Christian, poetess, and authoress. She has printed her poems, too, and one complimentary copy of mine, which in good breeding I could not help sending her, in return for violent compliments in verse from her." *

A copy in Garrick's library, 1958: afterwards in Heber, pt. iv. 1922.

Relation des Mesures qui furent prises dans les Annees 1711, 1712, et 1713, pour introduire la Liturgie Anglicane dans le Roiaume de Prusse et dans l'Electorat de Hannover. Eclaircie par des Lettres et autres Pieces originales relatives a ce Projet.

---

* Walpole to Cole, Letters, vol. iv. p. 14.

F

Le tout extrait d'un Manuscrit qui n'est pas encore rendu public, contenant des Mémoires de la Vie du Docteur Jean Sharp, Archvêque d'York, traduit de l'Anglois, par J. T. Muysson, Ministre de la Chapelle Françoise du Palais de St. James et de l'Eglise de la Savoie, à Londres.

A Londres, imprimé par W. Richardson, dans Fleet Street. 1767.   4*to.* pp. 117.

Printed for the use of Mr. Sharp's friends.

***

CATALOGUS VETERIS ÆVI VARII GENERIS MONUMENTORUM QUÆ CIMELIARCHIO LYDE BROWNE, ARM. ANT. SOC. SOC. APUD WIMBLEDON ASSERVANTUR.
1768. 8*vo.*

Privately printed. A copy is in the British Museum.

***

AN ESSAY ON THE ORIGINAL GENIUS OF HOMER. BY ROBERT WOOD, ESQ.
London. Bowyer. 1769.   8*vo.*

" Of this literary curiosity no more than *seven* copies were taken off; one copy was retained by Mr. Bowyer, the printer. Amongst other curiosities in my small library at Canonbury, is the copy which Mr. Bowyer kept, enriched by a few of his own notes; and, what may be more curious to those who have had the mortification of deciphering my miserably bad hand-writing, the margin contains every addition and variation made afterwards by Mr. Wood, fairly transcribed, *jubente Bowyero manu pueri mei Ioannis Nichols.*" * Mr.

***

* Nichols, Literary Anecdotes, vol. iii. p. 85.

Wood was the travelling tutor of the celebrated Earl of Bridgewater. Several of his letters to the Duke of Bedford, his guardian, during their tour, are among the MSS. at Woburn Abbey. Mr. Wood was the well-known author of the " Ruins of Balbec and Palmyra ;" he was Under Secretary of State, and died in 1771.

The work was reprinted in 1775.

Some Account of the late Peter Collinson, Fellow of the Royal Society, and of the Society of Antiquarians, London: in a Letter to a Friend. London: Printed in the year 1770. 4*to*. pp. 18.

Prefixed is a portrait, engraved by Miller.

The Regulations and Establishment of the Household of Henry Algernon Percy, the Fifth Earl of Northumberland, at his Castles of Wresill and Lekingfield, in Yorkshire.

Begun Anno Domini 1512.

London: Printed 1770. 8*vo*. pp. 467: preceded by the Preface, pp. xxvi; Kalendar, pp. x.

" The following pages are copied from an ancient manuscript in the possession of the Duke and Duchess of Northumberland, who conceiving that so singular a curiosity might afford the same amusement and pleasure to others which it hath given to themselves, have caused a small impression to be taken off, merely to bestow in presents to their friends."—*Preface.*

Hume,* who has given an interesting abstract of the contents of

---

* Note Z, on the reign of Henry VII.

this volume, remarks, that it " gives a true picture of ancient manners, and is one of the most singular monuments that English antiquity affords us."

A new edition of this curious volume was published in 1827.

JOHN FREE, THE POLITICAL SONGSTER.

Birmingham. 1771.   8*vo.*

Privately printed, at Baskerville's press.*

CATALOGUS LIBRORUM IN BIBLIOTHECA AULÆ DIVÆ CATHERINÆ, CANTABRIDGIÆ.

Cantabridgiæ : Excudebat J. Archdeacon, Academiæ typographus. M.DCC.LXXI.   4*to.* pp. 94.

An alphabetical catalogue, compiled by Mr. Prescott, son of a former master of the college. This is the only printed catalogue of the College libraries, with the exception of that of Queen's, compiled by the Rev. T. Horne, in 2 vols. 8vo., which is printed for sale. Bishop Sherlock bequeathed his valuable library to this college, and a salary of 20*l.* per annum to the librarian.

CATALOGUS LIBRORUM IN BIBLIOTHECA OSTERLEIENSI.

ANNO 1771.   4*to.* pp. 116.

"Bibliotheca hæc olim fuit honorabilis viri Bryan Fairfax, cujus ab hæredibus pretio 2000 librarum redemit eam, Samuel Child

---

* Lowndes, Bib. Manual.

armiger, de Osterley Park. Catalogum curavit Thomas Morrell, S.T.P. cujus *viginti quinque* exemplaria in suum et amicorum usum imprimenda voluit dignissimus possessor. 1771."—*Note by Dr. Lort, in Mr. Gough's copy, now in the Bodleian Library.* There is a copy in the royal library at the British Museum. A MS. note in Isaac Reed's copy says *there were only twelve* printed. This library contains the finest copy of Coverdale's Bible, and some of the productions of Caxton's press. The catalogue was sold at Watson Taylor's sale for 5*l*. 7*s*. 6*d*., at Mr. Heber's, pt. ii. 1163, for 2*l*. 18*s*. 0*d*.

MINUTES OF THE PROCEEDINGS BEFORE THE LORDS' COMMITTEE FOR PRIVILEGE, ON THE " CLAIM TO THE TITLE OF THE EARL OF ANGLESEY."
London : Printed in the year 1771. 8*vo*. pp. 64.

MEMOIRS RELATING TO THE QUEEN OF BOHEMIA. BY ONE OF HER LADIES.
No place, date, or printer's name. Circa 1772. 8*vo*.
pp. 162.

This is evidently a private production, addressed " to my granddaughter," and never completed. In a copy of the volume, which is a kind of historical novel, in the possession of Charles K. Sharpe, Esq., he has written the following note :—

" The authoress of this book was Lady Frances Erskine, daughter of John, eleventh Earl of Mar. She was niece to Lady Mary Wortley Montagu, and married her cousin James Erskine, son of Lord Grange. She died at London, 20th of June, 1776. The information as to this work I obtained from her descendants, the Hon. David Erskine and his son. This copy was formerly in the possession of Archibald, Earl of Eglintoune." The editor is indebted to David Laing, Esq., librarian to the Signet Library, Edinburgh, for the account of this work.

SIGILLA ANTIQUA NORFOLCIENSIA.
Impressit Iohannes Ives, S.A.S. Anno M.DCC.LXXII.
12*mo.*

" This work consists of nine plates, engraved on wood, of old Norfolk seals; prefixed is a portrait on copper of Mr. Martin, since prefixed to the History of Thetford."* Mr. Martin was Suffolk herald extraordinary, an office revived in his favour by the Earl of Suffolk; a list of his works, chiefly on antiquarian subjects, will be found in his Life by Chalmers; he died June 9, 1776.

POEMS, BY MICHAEL WODHULL, ESQ.
London. 1772. 8*vo.* With a portrait of the author.

One hundred and fifty copies were printed, says Mr. Nichols, of this edition. The plates, says Reed, were designed by Sterne.

STATUTA AULÆ REGIÆ ET COLLEGII DE BRAZENOSE IN OXONIO.
Subjiciuntur excerpta ex compositionibus, et Testamentis Benefactorum, et alia quædam notatu digna ad idem Collegium pertinentia.

A.D. M.DCC.LXXII. 8*vo.* pp. 108 : variæ lectiones, &c. pp. 4; abstracts of compositions, &c. pp. lxii; contents, two leaves; index, two leaves.

---

* Nichols, Anecdotes, vol. iii. p. 199.

"This book was printed solely for the private use of the members of that particular society to which it relates, and cannot be interesting to any others. When, therefore, it shall have answered the owner's purpose, and can be no longer of service to him, it is hoped and expected that he or his heirs will cause it either to be destroyed or returned to the College, and not permit it to fall into the hands of a bookseller, and be sold to any accidental purchaser."—*Note prefixed to the copy in the possession of the present President of Brazen Nose,* by whose permission the editor was allowed to extract it. The statutes of New College are in the Hargrave MS. Collection, British Museum, No. 337.

Principles of Money, applied to the present State of Bengal. By Sir James Stewart.

1772. 4*to.*

Many documents connected with the East India Company are printed only for circulation among the proprietors; but though not published for sale, can scarcely be called privately printed. Perhaps this work was one so circulated.

Tables of English Silver and Gold Coins; with Autographical Descriptions.

London. 1772. 4*to.*

An Account of Ireland, by a late Chief Secretary.

Printed in 1773. 8*vo.*

By Lord Macartney. See his Life, by Sir John Barrow, Bart. A copy is in the library of Lord Clifden.

A Catalogue of the Antiquities, Houses, Parks, Plantations, Scenes, and Situations in England and Wales.

Arranged according to the alphabetical order of the several Counties. (By Thomas Gray.)

12*mo*.   1773.

Printed for private distribution by the friend of the poet, Mr. Mason. Vide Upcott's Topography, vol. i. p. 25.

––––––

Letters to the Right Honourable Lord Mansfield, from Andrew Stuart, Esq.

London : Printed in the month of January, 1773.   4*to*.

This edition was not printed for sale.   " We talked of Mr. Andrew Stuart's elegant and plausible letters to Lord Mansfield, a copy of which had been sent by the author to Dr. Johnson." *Johnson.*— " They have not answered the end. They have not been talked of. I have never heard of them. This is owing to their not being *sold*. People seldom read a book which is given to them, and few are given." *

" Have you heard of Mr. Andrew Stuart's letters to Lord Mansfield ? They will inform you how abominable abuse is, and how you may tear a man limb from limb with the greatest good breeding." †

––––––––––

* Boswell's Life of Johnson, by Croker, vol. ii. p. 218.
† H. Walpole to Mason, Letters, vol. i. p. 51.

An Abridgment of the Book of Common Prayer.
8vo. 1773.

Printed at the expense of the late Lord Despencer, at West Wycombe, Bucks: abridged by the late Sir Francis Dashwood, Bart. Dr. Dibdin, from whom this information was derived, said the late Earl of Bute shewed this abridgment to him, in his library, at Petersham. It is not in the British Museum, nor in the Bodleian Library.*

A Journal of a Summer's Excursion, by the Road of Montecasino to Naples, and from thence over all the Southern Parts of Italy, Sicily, and Malta, in the Year 1772.
Circa 1774.   12mo. pp. 141.

Only twenty copies of this work were printed, with one in small 4to. A copy was in the library of the Duke of Buckingham, with many drawings and additional MS. notes of the author, by whom it was presented to the Marquess of Buckingham in 1787.—"This journal, without addition or emendation, is printed from the copy-book I always carried in my pocket, and took my notes in. William Young, Delaforde near Uxbridge, April 24, 1774."

The editor is indebted to Mr. Smith, formerly librarian to the Duke of Buckingham, and editor of the Grenville Papers, for this and other valuable information.

Floræ Anglicæ, specimen, [imperfectum et ineditum].
Anno 1774, inchoatum.   8vo. pp. 104.

" By Sir Thomas Gery Cullum, Bart., an assiduous collector of

---

English plants, and a considerable contributor to English botany: he died in 1831. This work was suppressed on the appearance of the second edition of Hudson's Flora Anglica, and goes no further than the genus *Daucus*, a *few* copies only having been distributed gratuitously by the highly estimable author amongst his friends."[*]

There is a copy in the library of the Linnæan Society.

A Genealogical Account of the Family of Lutrell, Lotterel, or Luttrell.

Milborne Port.   1774.   4*to*.

Privately printed: Lowndes. A copy was in Mr. Nassau's sale, part i. 2570.

The Siege of Jerusalem.

1774.   8*vo*.

" Of this piece, which was the production of Lady Strathmore, a few copies only were printed, to be given away. It has not been published."[†] The author of this drama was daughter and heiress of George Bowes, Esq., of Gibside, and married to John, ninth Earl of Strathmore. She died at Christchurch, Hants, April 28, 1800; and was buried in Westminster Abbey.

Letters.

[1774].   8*vo*.   pp. 55.

(No title-page it is believed was printed.)

---

[*] Smith, Eng. Flora, vol. i. p. 15.
[†] Biographia Dramatica, vol. i. p. 272.

Containing forty-two Letters between Bishop Warburton and Mr. Bowyer.

At the end is this postscript :—

" **** *Twelve copies only* of these Letters are printed, from the originals. The three which were *not sent,* might perhaps have been thought exceptionable. The concluding Letter *was* sent ; and finished the correspondence, in a manner which, it is hoped, could not offend." To this Mr. Nichols has added with a pen, the initials, "W. B. 1774." On the first page he has also written, "Printed by W. Bowyer. Only twelve copies ; and most of these were *destroyed.*"

The Letters are reprinted in Nichols' Literary Anecdotes.

———

LETTERS TO AND FROM SIR DUDLEY CARLETON, KNT., DURING HIS EMBASSY IN HOLLAND, FROM JANUARY 16$\frac{15}{16}$, TO DECEMBER 1620.

The Second Edition, with large Additions to the Historical Preface.

London. M.DCC.LXXV. *4to.* pp. 510. Index 11 leaves.

" Of this edition, published by Lord Hardwicke, only *fifty* copies were printed." *

"Lord Hardwicke has indeed reprinted his heavy volume of Sir Dudley Carleton's dispatches, and says I was in the wrong to despise it. I never met with any body that thought otherwise." †

———

* Nichols, Anecdotes.
† Walpole to Cole. Correspondence, vol. iv. p. 34.

A SHORT TOUR MADE IN THE YEAR ONE THOUSAND SEVEN HUNDRED AND SEVENTY-ONE. London: Printed in the year M.DCC.LXXV. 8vo. pp. 89.

It is believed the writer was connected with the noble family of Percy.

———

A DESCRIPTION OF THE LIBRARY AT MERLY HOUSE, IN DORSETSHIRE, THE SEAT OF RALPH WILLETT, ESQ. 1776.

"Of this little pamphlet, 200 copies were printed for the use of Mr. Willet's friends before he conceived the design, which in 1785 he put in execution, of having the whole engraved and published in superb folio." *

———

THE HISTORY OF THE ANCIENT EARLS OF WARREN AND SURREY AND THEIR DESCENDANTS TO THE PRESENT TIME. BY THE REV. JOHN WATSON, M.A., F.A.S., AND RECTOR OF STOCKPORT IN CHESHIRE.

"His name shall live from generation to generation."—Eccl. xxxix. 9.

Warrington: Printed by William Eyres. 1776. 4to. pp. 437.

"Only *six* copies of this impression were issued, for the purpose of obtaining information and correction. The book was afterwards

———

* Nichols, Anecdotes, vol. viii. p. 2.

published, in 1782." * The object of the work was to prove the late Sir George Warren entitled to the ancient Earldom of Surrey; but the attempt did not succeed. Mr. Astle's copy is in the library of the Royal Institution, with numerous manuscript notes in the handwriting of the author.

NEEDWOOD FOREST.
[BY FRANCIS NOEL CLARKE MUNDY.]
Litchfield: Printed by John Jackson. 1776. 4*to.*
pp. 52.

Mr. Mundy, of Marston, was a correspondent of Miss Seward's.

ROBERTI SIMSON, M.D. MATHESEOS NUPER IN ACADEMIA GLASGUENSI PROFESSORIS, OPERA QUÆDAM RELIQUA, SCILICET.

I. Apollonii Pergæi de sectione determinata, Libri 11. restituti, duobus insuper libris aucti.—II. Porismatum liber, quo doctrinam hanc veterum Geometrarum et oblivione vindicare, et ad captum hodiernorum adumbrare constitutum est.—III. De Logarithmis liber.—IV. De limitibus quantitatum et rationum, Fragmentum. — V. Appendix pauca continens problemata ad illustrandum præcipue veterum geometrarum analysin; nunc primum post auctoris mortem in lucem edita, impensis Philippi Comitis Stanhope, cura vero Jacobi Clow in eadem Academia Philosophiæ Professoris, cui, auctor omnia sua manuscripta testamento legaverat. Gratum, ut speratur,

---

* Moule, Bibliotheca Heraldica, p. 427.

Geometris munus futurum nec Scriptoris, jam clarissimi, famæ offerturum.

Glasguæ: In ædibus academicis, excudebant Robertus et Andreas Foulis, academiæ typographi. 1776. 4*to*. pp. 594: de Logarithmis, pp. 34; de Limitibus, pp. 33; Appendix, pp. 23.

" A large volume, in the year 1776, was at Lord Stanhope's sole expense handsomely printed, under the care of Mr. Clow, and liberally distributed." *

EUGENIA, A TRAGEDY.
By SAMUEL HAYES AND ROBERT CARR.
London: Printed for the Author. 1776. 8*vo*. pp. 79.

" This play, which appears to have been never acted, was written by the Rev. Samuel Hayes, author of several of the Seatonian prize poems, and who was at one time usher in Westminster School. Robert Carr, who assisted him in writing it, appears to have been one of the Westminster Scholars about 1766, but I am unable to give any further account of him." †

BYE-LAWS, RULES, ORDERS, AND DIRECTIONS, FOR THE BETTER GOVERNMENT OF HIS MAJESTY'S ROYAL HOSPITAL FOR SEAMEN, AT GREENWICH.

Made and confirmed at Three General Courts of the Commissioners and Governors of the said Hospital, held

---

* Trail, Life of Simson. 4*to*. Bath. 1812.
† Notes and Queries. March 5, 1853.

at the Admiralty Office, on the 16th and 18th of December, 1775, and 16th of February, 1776.

London : Printed by J. Harrison and S. Brooke, in Warwick Lane. M.DCC.LXXVI. 4to. pp. 131.

OCCASIONAL ATTEMPTS IN VERSE. BY W. C.

" Meanwhile the rural ditties were not mute."
Milton's Lycidas.

Printed only for the writer's particular acquaintance (by W. Pennington of Kendal), M.DCC.LXXVI. 8vo. pp. 127. Preface pp. xiv.

The author was W. Cocken : a copy was in Thorpe's catalogue, 1835. No. 509, and another in the sale catalogue of Madison's library.

THE CHAPTER, BY NAUTICUS. VOL. I.
London : Printed by the Printer. 1777. 8vo. pp. 75.

ANECDOTES, BIOGRAPHICAL AND LITERARY,
OF THE LATE MR. WILLIAM BOWYER, PRINTER,
COMPILED FOR PRIVATE USE.

London : Printed in the year M.DCC.LXXVIII. 8vo. pp. 32.

" Of this pamphlet, now swelled into fourteen volumes," Mr. Nichols says, " only *twenty* copies were printed." * If Cole could

---

* Literary Anecdotes, vol. iii. p. 294.

speak in the following terms of this small volume, what language would he have used, had he lived to see it dilated into its present most entertaining and useful form?—"You will be much pleased with it,* and I cannot live without it. It is full of anecdotes of Johnian and other Cantabridgians."

A Tragi-Coomodie, called The Witch;
Long since acted by his Maties at the Black-Friers. Written by Tho. Middleton.
[London] : Printed by J. Nichols. 1778. 4to. pp. 111.

Reprinted at the expense of the late Isaac Reed. In the second volume of the Variorum Shakspeare, will be found an account of this tragedy, in the dissertation upon Macbeth.

A Continuation of Hudibras, in Two Cantos,
Written in the time of the unhappy Contest between Great Britain and America, in 1777 and 1778. [By S. Peart.]
London : Printed in the year 1778. 8vo. pp. 76.

An Historical Account of the Privileges of the College of Justice.
No imprint or date, but circa 1778. 4to. pp. 129.

The author was Walter Ross, writer to the Signet, whose lectures

---

* Cole to Lort, MSS. vol. xxiv. p. 164.

on the practice of the law in Scotland, were published after his death. Edin., 1792, 2 vols. 4*to.*

A List of various Editions of the Bible, and Parts thereof, in English, from the Year 1526 to 1776.

A manuscript List of English Bibles, copied from one compiled by the late Mr. Joseph Ames, presented to the Lambeth Library by Dr. Gifford, hath furnished some part of this publication : late discoveries of several learned Gentlemen have supplied the rest.

London. 1778. 8*vo.* pp. 73.

" Compiled by Dr. Ducarel." * Archbishop Sutton's presentation copy to Mr. Grenville is in his library.

The True Loyalist ; or, Chevalier's Favourite ;

Being a collection of elegant Songs never before printed : also several other Loyal Compositions, wrote by eminent Hands.

Printed in the year M.DCC.LXXIX. 12*mo.* pp. 144.

In this very rare and uncommon work is included a Tragi-Comedy, without any name. Scene I. commences as follows :—

Scene draws, and discovers Lady Polly Wemyss sitting in a mournful posture, with a Prayer Book in one hand, and leaning with her head on the other.

---

* Catalogue of the Royal Library, Brit. Museum, vol. ii. p. 371.

Enter Duke of Perth and Lord Elcho.

Lady Polly.

> Welcome, sweet Perth, thou 'rt to my soul most dear ;
> Say, where 's the P——ce ?   Thy dismal tale I 'll hear.

Duke of Perth.

> The P——ce is safe, and I no terror feel,
> While thus before thy lovely form I kneel.

Lady Polly then proposes to kneel herself beside his Grace, and to offer thanks for the Prince's escape. She becomes very energetic; and, after soliloquizing some time, concludes with observing—

> " Why do I speak ?—Your Grace I 'd rather hear."

The Duke commences with a description of the defeat of the Jacobites at Culloden ; and, after a long recital, calls upon his friend Elcho to finish the story, which he does, concluding as follows :—

> He left the field with a majestic grace,
> And threw his sword with vigour in their face.

The Duke of Cumberland, General Hawley, and Captain Lockhart, appear in the next scene, rejoicing over the discomfiture of the Prince ; and the last and concluding scene is placed in Dunbarton Castle, where the Duke of Athol and the Prince's valet, with Drumnykill, are brought in prisoners, and received by the Laird of Kier, who had previously been captured. This absurd production ends with the rejoicing of Kier upon the announcement of the escape of his son and the Laird of Craigbarrel.

Many of the songs are very clever.

———

CATALOGUE OF MR. CAPELL'S SHAKESPERIANA ;
Presented by him to Trinity College, Cambridge, and printed from an exact Copy of his own MSS.

1779.   8*vo.*   pp. 20.

In the copy presented by Steevens to Dr. Lort was the following letter :—

" Dear Sir,

" As some friends have been desirous to borrow Mr. Capell's Catalogue, to save trouble I have printed a few copies, and intreat your acceptance of one of them. Let me beg you will keep it from the sight of any bookseller, or otherwise it may prove the means of raising *Shakesperiana* above 100 per cent.

" I am, most faithfully yours,

" *Hampstead Heath,*   " G. STEEVENS."

" *Jan.* 1780."

In Farmer's copy was the following extract of a letter from Steevens :—" I was so plagued for transcripts of Capell's Catalogue, that I have printed thirty copies of it to give away."

LATIN VERSES,
BY THE LATE NICHOLAS HARDINGE, ESQ.

London. 1780.   *8vo.* pp. 124.

All copies of this work are deficient in pages 56—69. It was reprinted for sale in 1818.* Mr. Bindley's copy in Heber, part 2, 2390, was complete.

CATALOGUE OF ROMAN COINS. BY ROGER GALE.
London. 1780.   *4to.*

Of this Catalogue *twenty* copies only were printed in *4to.* by J. Nichols, for the use of particular friends. The coins are in the Public Library, Cambridge.† This celebrated antiquary died June 25, 1744.

---

* Nichols, Literary Anecdotes, vol. iii. p. 206.   † Ibid.,   iv. p. 548.

FRANCI NICHOLSII, M.D., GEORGII SECUNDI MAGNÆ BRITANNIÆ REGIS MEDICI ORDINARII VITA : CUM CONJECTURIS EJUSDEM DE NATURA ET USU PARTIUM HUMANI CORPORIS SIMILIARUM.

Scriptore Thoma Lawrence, M.D., e Collegio Sanctæ Trinitatis, Oxon., et Collegii Medicorum Londinensis Socio.

Londini. M.DCC.LXXX. 4*to*. pp. 106. Errata, one leaf.

With a portrait engraved by Hall.

————

THE DECREE, DEED OF USES, AND WILL OF HENRY SMITH, ESQ., BY WHICH DIVERS ESTATES ARE SETTLED TO CHARITABLE USES.

[London] : Printed by order of the Trustees. 1781. 8*vo*. pp. 40.

They relate to charitable estates left by Mr. Smith in the county of Surrey.

————

COPY OF MR. JOHN STOCKS' WILL AND CODICILS. 1781. 8*vo*. pp. 88.

No title-page; a copy in Mr. Hibbert's Catalogue, No. 7618.

GEMMARUM ANTIQUARUM DELECTUS ;

EX PRÆSTANTIORIBUS, DESUMPTUS, QUÆ IN DACTYLIO-
THECIS DUCIS MARLBURIENSIS CONSERVANTUR.

London.   1781-1790.   2 vols.   *folio.*

Prefixed to the title-page of Vol. I. is an engraving by Bartolozzi, from a drawing by Cipriani.* The title-page is in Latin and French. On the recto of the leaf following the title, "Gemmarum Antiquarum Delectus—Choix de Pierres Antiques Gravées." On the reverse commences the first description, in Latin. After the plate of the gem, is a French translation of the description : this prevails throughout the work.

PLATES—VOL. I.

  I. Publii Scipionis Africani caput juvenile.

  II. Lucii Cornelii Syllæ caput.

 III. Julii Cæsaris caput laureatum.

 IV. Marci Junii Bruti caput.

  V. Marci Junii Bruti caput, cum caduceo et testudine.

 VI. Lepidi caput, cum lituo.

 VII. Augusti caput, cum coronâ radiatâ.

VIII. Augusti Pontificis Maximi caput, cum pectore.

 IX. Marcelli, Octaviæ filii, caput.

  X. Liviæ Protome, cum capite laureato et velato pectore.

 XI. Tiberii caput juvenile.

 XII. Germanici Togati Protome, cum capite laureato.

XIII. Agrippinæ Majoris, uxoris Germanici, caput laureatum.

XIV. Ejusdem Agrippinæ, sub effigie Cereris.

 XV. Galbæ caput laureatum.

 XVI. Ejusdem Galbæ caput.

XVII. Nervæ Togati Protome, cum capite laureato.

XVIII. Ejusdem Nervæ caput.

---

* The original drawing was in Sir M. Sykes' copy, now in the library of Sir John Thorold.

XIX. Marcianæ, Trajani sororis, caput.

XX. Sabinæ, Hadriani uxoris, caput.

XXI. Antinoi caput, cum pectore velato.

XXII. Caracallæ Togati Protome.

XXIII. Caracallæ caput laureatum.

XXIV. Juliæ, Severi uxoris, caput, cum pectore velato.

XXV. Laocoontis caput.

XXVI. Semiramidis caput, cum pectore.

XXVII. Minervæ Alcidæ caput galeatum.

XXVIII. Phocionis caput.

XXIX. Jovis et Junonis capita jugata.

XXX. Veneris caput.

XXXI. Bacchæ caput.

XXXII. Hercules bibax, stans.

XXXIII. Bacchus stans.

XXXIV. Faunus, Tigridis pelli insidens.

XXXV. Athleta stans.

XXXVI. Mercurius stans.

XXXVII. Mars stans.

XXXVIII. Miles de rupe descendens.

XXXIX. Diomedes cum Ulysse contendit.

XL. Dei marini natantes.

XLI. Miles vulneratus a militibus duobus sustentatur.

XLII. Miles militi vulnerato opitulatur.

XLIII. Mulier stolata cum Virgine.

XLIV. Faunus pelle vestitus.

XLV. Alexandri Magni effigies.

XLVI. Æneas a Diomede saxo percussus.

XLVII. Pompæ ob Victoriam.

XLVIII. Amazon Amazontem morientem sustinet.

XLIX. Fragmen Gemmæ.

L. Nuptiæ Psyches et Cupidinis.

     Tail-piece, engraved and drawn by Basire.

PLATES—VOL. II.

Frontispiece drawn by Cipriani, engraved by Bartolozzi; "Genius arresting the hand of Time;" the arms of the Marlborough family in the back ground. In the first state of this plate, the letter t, at the end of the word "droit," in the motto of the Spencer family, is left out.

XXX. Antinöus.

XXXI. Caput ignotum, Antonini junioris forsan.

XXXII. Lucilla.

XXXIII. Didius Julianus Augustus, et Manlia Scantilla Augusta.

XXXIV. Caput Sirii Canis.

XXXV. Vaccæ.

XXXVI. Equi.

XXXVII. Taurus a leone interfectus.

XXXVIII. Mercurii Templum.

XXXIX. Imperator hostem prosternens.

XL. Coronis.

XLI. Cupidines.

XLII. Ganymedes.

XLIII. Ganymedes et Aquila.

XLIV. Hercules Λεοντοφονος.

XLV. Faunus.

XLVI. Omphale incedens.

XLVII. Triumphus.

XLVIII. Biga.

XLIX. Biga.

L. Silenus, Tigris, &c.

A tail-piece by Bartolozzi.

After the tail-piece, a single leaf of errata.

The Latin of the first volume of this work was the composition of the late Jacob Bryant; and that of the second volume, of the late Rev. Dr. Cole, Prebendary of Westminster. The translation into French of the first volume was by Dr. Maty,* and that of the second by Dr. Dutens. One hundred copies only are said to have been struck off, for presents. The gems were originally engraved with the inscription, "Ex Dactyliotheca Ducis Marlburiensis," on each, but this was subsequently erased, and the number of the plate inserted instead, above the subject; but no complete copies with the

---

* For which he was paid one hundred pounds. Nichols, Anecdotes, vol. iii. p. 261.

inscription are known. The plates are sometimes found without the inscription or number; these are, of course, engravers' proofs. Mr. Wodehouse and Sir Mark Sykes had collected the largest number of impressions in both these states, which were dispersed at the sale of their prints, at very high prices. Other collectors have made the same attempt, with more or less success, as to number; yet, to the collector, impressions in both states are very desirable, as the appearance of the ordinary copies is very inferior, owing to the person (said to have been a woman) employed being unaccustomed to copper-plate printing. Mr. Cracherode's copy, in the British Museum, contains a letter from the Duke of Marlborough, in which he says, "he has picked out some of the best impressions for him." Vol. I. contains duplicates of the following plates, with the *inscription*, viz. Plates II, X, XVII, XXII, XXIV, XXVIII, XXIX, XXXVI, XL, XLIII, XLIV, XLVII, L, all printed in red ink: but this is not the case with all the copies with the inscription; as they are printed sometimes in this colour, and sometimes in black.

The original gems are at Blenheim. The present Duke of Marlborough has recently printed a new edition.

LETTERS AND PARAGRAPHS,

Printed in the "Coventry Mercury," in the Years 1780 and 1781, relating to Captain John Donellan, convicted of the Murder of Sir Theodosius Edward Allesley Boughton, Bart., at the Assizes held at Warwick, Friday, 30th of March.

1781.   8*vo*.   pp. 32.

With a view of the house as it was.

" The total impression of this volume, privately printed at the press of John Merridew, residing at 27, Lower Parade, in the parish of Leamington Priors, in the county of Warwick, for, and at the expense of Joseph Walter King Eyton, F.S.A. Lond. and Scot., of

Elgin Villa, in the parish and county aforesaid, Esquire, consists of twelve copies upon drawing paper."

Elgin Villa, Leamington, Warwickshire, February, 1845.

A copy is in the library of John Sheepshanks, Esq., to whom the editor is indebted for several interesting additions.

ATHENIAN LETTERS; OR, THE EPISTOLARY CORRESPONDENCE OF AN AGENT OF THE KING OF PERSIA RESIDING AT ATHENS DURING THE PELOPONNESIAN WAR: Containing the History of the Times, in Dispatches to Ministers of State at the Persian Court; besides Letters on various Subjects between him and his Friends. London: Printed 1781. 4*to.* pp. 473. Frontispiece from a design by Stuart.

One *hundred* copies only were printed.*

METRICA QUÆDAM.

1781. 4*to.*

By the late Bishop of Hereford (Huntingford). The late Rev. P. Hall, to whom I owe this notice, informed me there were only *twenty* copies printed. Another edition was printed in 1782, in 8*vo.*

---

* Nichols, Literary Anecdotes, vol. i. p. 33.

Specimen of a History of Oxfordshire; being the History and Antiquities of Kiddington. By the Rev. Thomas Warton, B.D.

1782. *4to.*

Twenty copies only were printed of this edition. It was reprinted for sale, 1783, and again in 1815 : " It is certainly better than what an ordinary hand could produce, yet not equal to what might have been expected from such a master."

Dramatic Dialogues.

London. 1782. *8vo.*

" By Thomas Tyers, Esq., of the Inner Temple : printed, but I believe never dispersed: about 130 pages."* Mr. Tyers was the Tom Restless of Johnson's Idler, No. 48; he died at Ashted, Surrey, Feb. 1, 1787.

An Historical Essay on Mr. Addison.

London. 1783. *8vo.*

By the author of the previous work. " This Essay is not," says the writer in his preface, " for the world at large, but only for the little world of the writer's acquaintance." " *Fifty* copies only were printed."† The author of these works was the son of Jonathan Tyers, the founder of Vauxhall: he published a biographical sketch of Dr. Johnson, of which Boswell affects to speak slightingly; the recent editor of that entertaining work thinks better of it.‡

---

* Nichols, Literary Anecdotes, vol. viii. p. 80, 688.

† Ibid., vol. viii. p. 125.

‡ Boswell's Johnson, by Croker, vol. i. p. 314.

EMMÆ ANGLORUM REGINÆ, RICHARDI I. DUCIS
NORMANNORUM FILIÆ, ENCOMIUM;
Incerto Auctore sed coetaneo : item Gesta Gulielmi
II. Ducis Normannorum, Regis Anglorum I.
London : Printed for B. White. 1783. *4to.* pp. 380.

" This book was printed, I believe, for private distribution only,
with that disinterested love of literature, which, through a long life,
has adorned and dignified the various and profound studies of Baron
Maseres. The text is selected from the numerous pages of Du-
chesne's Scriptores Normanni, and illustrated with very ample and
curious English notes, and marginal abstracts of the contents, by
the present editor." *   There is some doubt whether this work was
printed for private circulation.   It was reprinted in 1807.

WALPOLIANA ; OR, A FEW ANECDOTES OF
SIR ROBERT WALPOLE.
London.   1783.   *4to.*

" Lord Hardwicke has printed what he calls ' Walpoliana ;' not
many copies are printed, and these distributed to only particular
people." †
" I do not in the least guess or imagine what you mean by Lord
Hardwicke's publication of a *Walpoliana*.   Naturally it should mean
a collection of sayings or anecdotes of my father, according to the
French *Anas*, which began, I think, with those of Menage.   Or, is it
a collection of letters and state papers during his administration ?
I own I am curious to know at least what this piece contains.   I had
not heard a word of it ; and, were it not for the name, I should
have very little inquisitiveness about it : for nothing upon earth

---

* Censura Literaria, vol. iv. p. 149.
† Dr. Lort to Cole, Restitutæ, vol. iv. p. 370.

ever was duller than the three heavy tomes his lordship printed, of *Sir Dudley Carleton's Negociations.*" *

THE FATHER'S REVENGE,
A TRAGEDY, BY THE EARL OF CARLISLE.
London: Printed by H. Hughes. 1783.   4*to.* pp. 81.

First edition of the tragedy, reprinted by Bulmer in 1800. "Johnson praised the Earl of Carlisle's poems, which his lordship had published with his name, as not disdaining to be a candidate for literary fame." Mr. Croker, in a note on this passage, says, "Lord Carlisle was not indeed a *great* poet, but he was superior to many whom Mr. Boswell was ready enough to admit into the 'sacred choir.'" His verses have good sense, sweetness, and elegance. It should be added, in justice to both Lord Carlisle and Lord Byron, that the latter very much regretted the flippant and unjust sarcasms he had uttered against his noble friend and relation. †

DREAMS, WAKING THOUGHTS, AND INCIDENTS;
In a series of Letters from various Parts of Europe.
London: Printed for J. Johnson, St. Paul's Church-yard, and P. Elmsley, in the Strand.   M.DCC.LXXXIII.
4*to.*   pp. 334 : Summary of Contents, seven leaves.

Frontispiece drawn by Cipriani, engraved by Bartolozzi, representing an incident connected with the history of a Prince of Carafa, in which the lady he was attached to appears as throwing

---

* Walpole to Cole, Letters, vol. iv. p. 245.
† Boswell's Johnson, by Croker, vol. iv. p. 485, in the same work, vol. v. p. 136, a letter by Johnson to Mrs. Chapone on this tragedy.

herself from a rock: another plate, prefixed to the letter on the Grande Chartreuse, represents St. Bruno, kneeling in adoration, by the same artists. This volume is the production of the late Mr. Beckford. Lord Spencer and Mr. Rogers have copies. This work was suppressed at the request of Lord Grantham, as it contained some severe reflections on the Dutch, a nation which it was then the policy of the English Government to conciliate. Mr. Beckford reprinted the substance in 1834, 2 vols. 8vo.

———

DESCENT OF THE CROWN OF ENGLAND.

Table I. The true Hereditary Succession, from Egbert the Great, King of Wessex, the Saxon Monarch of all England:

Table II. The true Hereditary Succession from William the Conqueror (supposing a Title in him by Conquest):

Table III. The *de facto* Succession from Edmund Ironside. 1783.

This is a reprint of the same work, which was completed by the Ritsons, and originally printed in 1778, an account of which will be found in Mr. Moule's work. Of this edition *fifty* copies only are said to have been printed.

———

THE POLE CAT; OR, CHARLES JENNINGS, THE RENEGADO SCHOOLMASTER OF PARSONS GREEN, DETECTED. Printed 1783.

" A very severe satire, written by Dr. Shebbeare, and privately printed."—Lowndes, 1020.

A copy in Sir M. Sykes' library, part iii. No. 17.

PEDIGREE OF SCOTT OF STOKOE, IN THE PARISH OF SYMONDBURN, AND COUNTY OF NORTHUMBERLAND, AND LATE OF TODERICK, SELKIRKSHIRE, NORTH BRITAIN: COMPILED BY WILLIAM SCOTT, M.B.

Newcastle: Printed by T. Angus. Anno 1783. 8vo. pp. 27.

A very scarce tract, printed at the expense of the editor.

———

IPHIGENIA, A TRAGEDY, IN FOUR ACTS.

——In Rege tamen Pater est.—OVID.

1783. 8vo. pp. 49.

" By John Yorke, of Gourthwaite, Esq., Yorkshire." MS. note by Mr. Napier, communicated by Mr. Maidment.

———

SUNDAY EVENING. BY SIR HERBERT CROFT.

8vo. 1784.

"These are all which the author is at the expense of printing for private perusal. H. C. Holywell, Oxford, June, 1784."*

———

CONVERSATIONS, POLITICAL AND FAMILIAR.

London. 1784. 2 vols. 8vo.

" By Mr. Tyers, and an enlargement of the Dramatic Dialogues printed in 1782. No more than *twenty-five* copies were printed, and

---

* Gent.'s Mag. 1816, p. 487.

which he sparingly distributed among his friends."* A copy was in Heber's Catalogue, part ii. 6069.

A Theologico-Controversialistical Conference, held at the Hague, the 2nd of June, 1785, between an English Lutheran, a Scotch Calvinist, and a Dutch Rabeen;
In which the Sects of each are explained in so familiar a style that they become immediately comprehensible to the most illiterate and limited understanding.
London: Printed for the Author. 1785. 2 vols. 8vo.

Doubtful if privately printed.

Botanical Tables,
Containing the different Families of British Plants, distinguished by a few obvious parts of Fructification, ranged into a Synoptical method.
London: [circa 1785]. 9 vols. 4to.

This rare work is said to have cost Lord Bute, at whose expense it was engraved and printed, 12,000l. The late Dr. Dutens, who was on very intimate terms with that nobleman, gives the following account of it:—

" L'etude favorite de Lord Bute etoit la botanique; il excelloit tellement dans cette science, que les plus grands maitres en Europe le consultoient et recherchoient sa correspondance; il avoit ecrit sur ce sujet un ouvrage en 9 vol. in 4to., qu'il fit imprimer a grands

---

* Nichols, Literary Anecdotes, vol. viii. p. 80.

frais. Il l'avoit composé pour la Reine d'Angleterre, et ne voulait jamais le publier, tant il etoit éloigné de tirer vanité de ses lumières. Il en fit tirer 16 *exemplaires*, dont il me donna un."*

Twelve copies were all that were ever printed; the plates said to be destroyed;† and by a note in Sir Joseph Banks' copy, now in the British Museum, the following was the original disposition of them:—

Lord Bute	2
The Queen	1
Empress of Russia	1
Sir Joseph Banks	1
M. de Buffon	1
Lady Betty Mackenzie (now in the possession of W. Stuart, Esq.)	1
Lady Ruthven	1
Lady Macartney	1
Duchess of Portland	1
Mrs. Barrington	1
M. Dutens (now the Marquis of Bute's)	1
	12

One of Lord Bute's copies came into the possession of Mr. Tighe, and was sold at the sale of his library, in March, 1798, for 120*l*., supposed to have been bought by the late Lord Gainsborough, and was resold at the sale of that nobleman's library, to the late Sir Richard Borough, Bart., for 82*l*. 19*s*.; the late Queen Charlotte's copy was sold at the sale of her library, in 1819, for 117*l*., and purchased for the King's private library, where it now remains; Buffon's copy is in the Bibliothèque Royale, at Paris; the Duchess of Portland's copy came into the possession of the late Dowager Marchioness of Bath; Lady Macartney's copy is in the possession of Lord Wharncliffe; Dr. Duten's copy was not in the sale catalogue

---

* Mémoires d'un Voyageur qui se Repose, vol. ii. p. 252.
† Gentleman's Magazine, 1792, p. 285.

H

of his library. An accurate collation of the contents of this work will be found in Dryander's Catalogue,* who does not speak in very flattering terms of its value: "Operis hujus, splendidi magis quam utilis, *duodecim* tantum exemplaria impressa sunt."

" Were some new Horace Walpole to amuse himself with making a catalogue of 'Royal and Noble Botanists,' one of the first places in it, if not the very first, would unquestionably be assigned to the nobleman here mentioned, John, the third Earl of Bute, the friend and favourite, and for a short time the Prime Minister of George III. To him botany is indebted for a very extraordinary work, entitled 'Botanical Tables,' &c.: another unpublished work, called 'The Tabular Distribution of British Plants,' in two parts; the first containing the genera, the second the species, printed by Davis, 1787, is also said to be by Lord Bute. Of this there is a copy in my library; but I nowhere find it mentioned. His Lordship died in 1792, aged 79." — Extract from Richardson's Correspondence, edited by D. Turner, 8vo. p. 406.

ANCIENT ERSE POEMS,
Collected among the Scottish Highlands, in order to illustrate the Ossian of Mr. Macpherson. By Thomas Ford Hill, Esq. 1785. pp. 34.

"This interesting pamphlet, consisting of thirty-four closely-printed pages, was not intended for sale; but printed solely for presents to the ingenious compiler's friends."† Mr. Hill died in Italy, July 16, 1795.

---

* Vol. iii. p. 133.
† Nichols, Literary Anecdotes, vol. viii. p. 154.

STATUTA ACADEMIÆ CANTABRIDGIENSIS.
Cantabridgiæ : Typis academicis excudebat J. Archdeacon. 1785. *4to.* pp. 600.

DESCRIPTION OF THE LIBRARY AT MERLY.
1785. *folio.*

This catalogue contains engravings of the interior ornaments designed by Mr. Willett.

NARRATIVE AND PROOFS OF THOMAS LORD CAMELFORD.
London: Printed in the Year 1785. *4to.* pp. 92. Appendix, pp. ciii.

This relates to a trial brought by a Mr. Smith against the executor of Mr. Wilkinson, whose daughter he married; she was sister to Lady Camelford: a copy was in Mr. Hibbert's Catalogue, No. 1792.

A SHORT GENEALOGY OF THE FAMILY OF MAITLAND, EARL OF LAUDERDALE.
Edinburgh. M.DCC.LXXXV. *Small 4to, oblong size.* pp. 24.

The following note is written at the beginning of the copy, which belonged to the late Mr. Archibald Constable:—

"This account of the Lauderdale family was drawn up, as I have been informed, by the late Professor Dalzel, who was preceptor of James Earl of Lauderdale. It was only printed for the use of the family, and is extremely rarely met with. A. C. June, 1821."

AN ACCOUNT OF THE REMAINS OF THE WORSHIP OF
PRIAPUS, LATELY EXISTING AT ISERNIA, IN THE KING-
DOM OF NAPLES.

In two letters ; one from Sir William Hamilton, K.B.,
and the other from a person residing at Isernia : to which
is added

A DISCOURSE ON THE WORSHIP OF PRIAPUS,

And its connection with the Mystic Theology of the
Ancients.   By R. P. Knight, Esq.

London : Printed by T. Spilsbury, Snowhill. 4*to.* pp.
195.   Eighteen plates, including frontispiece and those
printed on the text.   Page 47, an ancient *ex voto* in
silver, said in Mr. Hanrott's copy to be frequently
wanting.

" Never printed for sale, though copiously distributed."*

" The existence of this festival and fair, and the attendant ceremonies, became partially known to my countrymen in 1786, when a
learned dissertation on the worship of Priapus was printed by
R. Payne Knight, Esq., and delivered to each member of the Dilettanti Society, in the number of whom I was afterwards included.
A letter, written by Sir William Hamilton, from Naples, in 1781,
describing the fair of Isernia and its ceremonies, seems to have
given rise to this ingenious disquisition.   It has been treated
with unmerited asperity by the author of the Pursuits of Literature ; who, in his zeal for delicacy, forgot that equal objections, if
not greater, might be made to books of anatomy, which are generally sold, whereas the treatise in question was never published,
but distributed privately to the members of a very limited society."†

The fair, with its ceremonies, was abolished in 1780.

---

* Nichols' Anecdotes, vol. ix. p. 115.
† Sir R. Hoare's Tour through Italy, 4to. p. 172.

The Revenge of Guendolen.
(1786)? 8vo. pp. 92.

" This poem is the production of Lord Carysfort. Dr. Watson, Bishop of Landaff, told me, in 1786, that twelve copies of it only were printed."—Note in Reed's copy. There is no title-page. Heber, Part iv., No. 1860.

Malvina. A Tragedy.
Glasgow: Printed for Andrew Foulis. 1786. 8vo.
pp. 65.

A MS. note in Mr. Maidment's copy states the author was Mr. John Reddel, surgeon, Glasgow. A pamphlet on Fever was published in 1788, at Glasgow, most probably by the author of this tragedy.

The Memoir of Sir Hugh Cholmley, Knt. and Bart. Addressed to his two Sons:

In which he gives some Account of his Family, and the distress they underwent in the Civil Wars, and how far he himself was engaged in them; taken from an original manuscript in his own handwriting, now in the possession of Nathaniel Cholmley, of Whitby and Howsham, in the county of York, Esq. 1487.   4to.   1787.

" Only one hundred copies were printed."* " This book, printed for private use by the present worthy representative of the family, is one of those many curious family histories which we have reason to believe were compiled during the 18th, and perhaps preceding

---

* Nichols, Literary Anecdotes, vol. ix. p. 43.

century: a regular deduction of private life for six generations, from Sir Roger Cholmley of Flamborough, knighted by Henry VIII."*

AN ACCOUNT OF TANGIER.
BY SIR HUGH CHOLMLEY, BART.;
With some Account of himself, and his Journey through France and Spain to that place, where he was engaged in building the Mole, in the time of King Charles II.; and a Journal of the Work carrying on, and also some of his Speeches in Parliament, taken from manuscripts now in the possession of Nathaniel Cholmley, of Whitby and Howsham, in the county of York, Esq.

1787. 4*to.* pp. 320.

THE WHOLE PROCEEDINGS IN THE TRIAL OF AN EJECTMENT, BETWEEN RICHARD GOODRIGHT ON THE DEMISE OF MARY DONE, WIDOW, AGAINST DAVID ACKERLEY, GENTLEMAN;
At the Portmote Court of the city of Chester, on Monday the 27th day, and Tuesday, the 28th day of August, 1787.

Chester: Printed by J. Fletcher. 1788. 8*vo.*

A copy of this Trial was in Mr. Hibbert's Catalogue, No. 8084, and a note in it stated, "a few copies printed, for parties interested."

---

* Gentleman's Magazine, vol. lviii. p. 613.

An Unfinished Letter to the Right Honourable William Pitt, concerning the New Dictionary of the English Language. By the Rev. Herbert Croft, LL.B.

London: Printed in March, 1788. 8*vo*. pp. 44. Postscript, 4 leaves.

The author states, " of these pages I have had a few copies pulled for my particular friends." He died at Paris, April 27, 1816; after a residence of fifteen years in that city. Johnson adopted his Memoir of Young, for his Lives of the Poets.

Caius Valerius Catullus,
recensuit Ioannes Wilkes, Anglvs.
Londini: 1788. Typis Ioannis Nichols. 4*to*. pp. 124.

" The whole impression consisted only of *three* copies on vellum, and *one hundred* on a beautiful writing paper; all of which have been bestowed in presents to characters of the first eminence."* " Immaculate! not a stop misplaced or omitted."† Lord Spencer possesses one of the copies upon vellum.

Life of Antony Ashley Cooper, First Earl of Shaftesbury.

4*to*.

This rare volume has no title. The following account is taken from a catalogue by Mr. Evans, who sold a copy in June, 1830.

---

* Nichols, Literary Anecdotes, vol. ix. p. 50.   † Ibid. p. 466.

" This is one of the rarest biographical volumes in the English language. When the first Lord Shaftesbury fled into Holland, he gave Locke a Memoir of his Life, which that celebrated man destroyed, being alarmed at the fate of Algernon Sydney. About the year 1732, the then Earl of Shaftesbury placed the family papers and a manuscript memoir of his ancestor, written by Stringer (who had been clerk of the presentations to Lord Shaftesbury) in the hands of Benjamin Martyn, who drew up this memoir; but the Earl did not esteem it sufficiently finished for publication. Dr. Gregory Sharpe, Master of the Temple, commenced its revision, but relinquished it. The late Earl finally committed it to the care of Dr. Kippis, and gave him five hundred pounds for his trouble. After the book and introduction by Kippis had been printed, a difference arose between the Earl of Shaftesbury and the Doctor, and Lord Shaftesbury caused the impression to be destroyed. The late Duke of Grafton obtained a copy which Dr. Kippis had preserved, and it is believed no other copy was ever sold."

This copy was purchased by Mr. Singer. Dr. Kippis died in 1795; and it was at the sale of his library that the Duke of Grafton obtained the copy mentioned by Mr. Evans; this volume was most probably printed some time between the years 1789 and 1795.

MEMORIAL RELATIVE TO THE OFFICE OF THE LORD CLERK REGISTER, AND THE PRESENT STATE OF THE PUBLIC RECORDS OF SCOTLAND.

Edinburgh (April 10, 1788).   4to.   pp. 43.

Drawn up by William Robertson, Esq., Keeper of the Records.

Rules and Regulations
of the Hainault Foresters (Co. Essex).
1789. 18mo. pp. 22.

This work was brought under the editor's notice by the late Mr. Upcott; who stated that a copy is in the British Museum.

Thoughts on the Early Ages of the Irish Nation and History, and on the Ancient Establishment of the Milesian Families in that Kingdom; with a particular Reference to the Descendants of Heber, the eldest Son of Milesius.
1789. 4to. pp. 50.

" Of this curious work, never intended for sale, two editions of *one hundred* copies each were printed, under the superintendence of Richard Joseph Sullivan, Esq., assisted by Mr. Barak Longmate, with a copious genealogical plate engraved by him; entitled, a genealogical history of the Family of O'Sullivan More from Duach Donn, monarch of Ireland. Anno Mundi 3912."*

Symptoms of Advice to the O*****rs of an Amphibious Corps, with Notes of Naval Character.

" Qui capit ille facit."
Anglice,
When the cap fits, wear it.

By a Quondam Sub.
London : Printed in the Year 1789, pp. 96.

---

* Nichols, Literary Anecdotes, vol. ix. p. 51.

Cursory Remarks on some of the Ancient English Poets, particularly Milton.
London, M.DCC.LXXXIX.   8vo.   pp. 146.

This work was written by P. Neve : in a copy presented by him to Dr. Farmer, it is stated *two hundred* copies were printed. The authors noticed besides Milton, are Chaucer, Skelton, Earl of Surrey, Spenser, Overbury, Jonson, Drummond, Denham, Waller, Butler, Wycherley, Otway, Lee, and Dryden.

Eaton Chronicle ; or, The Salt Box.
1789.   *Royal 8vo.*   pp. 165.

At tu Eatonis lepidos sale tinge libellos
    Agnoscat mores quisque legatque suos :
    Angustâ cantare licet videaris avenâ,
      Dum tua multorum vincat avena tubas.

This volume was edited by the late William Gifford, editor of Massinger, and the first editor of the Quarterly Review, and is inscribed to the noble originator, Earl Grosvenor, the father of the present Marquess of Westminster: the following is a copy of the address to the reader, dated Eaton Hall, 1789,—

" In the summer of 1788, Lord Grosvenor, invited a numerous party of his relations, friends and acquaintance, to Eaton Hall, to celebrate the birthday of Lord Belgrave, who came of age in the spring of that year. As they met before the arrival of the period peculiarly set apart for the festival, his Lordship proposed in a sportive moment, that a little journal should be kept of their proceedings, and produced every morning at breakfast. As this could not occupy a large space, he further proposed to admit any little piece of prose or verse, whose subject might not be entirely foreign from the company: and it was hoped by these means that a sheet might be served up every morning with the tea. The paper took its name from a Salt-box, which was appointed to receive the contributions. This was examined every evening; and the contents arranged and transcribed by the writer of this introduction, who had the honour of being appointed EDITOR."

Archdeacon Wrangham possessed two copies of this volume.

SELECTIONS FROM " LES RECHERCHES PHILOSOPHIQUES SUR LES AMERICAINS," OF M. PAINE.
BY M. W. BATH.

1789.   8vo.

Edited by John Wilks. With copious notes. In the notice to the reader he says, " Care will be taken, it is hoped, that this copy may not fall into the hands of a publisher, as but few have been printed for the author's friends."

HISTORY OF THE LATE REVOLUTION IN THE DUTCH REPUBLIC.

1789.   4to.

By *George* ELLIS, the editor of " Specimens of the Early English Poets, Romances," &c.

AULII FLACCI PERSII SATYRÆ, WITH BREWSTER'S TRANSLATION.

London: 1790.   4to.   pp. 112.

There is no title-page to this edition, which was never completed —it was edited by Mr. Heber, and printed by Mr. Bulmer; two hundred and fifty copies were printed, which are in Mr. Nicols' possession.

BIOGRAPHIA SCOTICA ; OR, AN ATTEMPT TOWARDS A
HISTORY OF THE LIVES AND WRITINGS OF EMINENT
MEN OF SCOTLAND.
By SIR DAVID DALRYMPLE, LORD HAILES.
1790.   4to. with portraits.

From Heber's Catalogue, part ii., 1651, formerly Mr. Bindley's,
where it is said to be "privately printed." It is not enumerated by
Lowndes in his list of this author's works, but he mentions, as pri-
vately printed, " A Specimen of Notes on the Statute Law of
Scotland, with Specimen of a Glossary (1768)," 8vo. pp. 37. The
" Biographia" contains lives of John Barclay, Mark Alexander
Boyd, John Hamilton, Sir James Ramsay, George Lesley.

————

THE LIFE OF SIR FRANCIS BERNARD, BARONET,
LATE GOVERNOR OF MASSACHUSETS' BAY.
London.   1790.   8vo.   pp. 211.

By his son, the late Sir Thomas Bernard, at one time Treasurer
of the Foundling Hospital.

————

CASE OF THE BARONY OF LISLE.
folio.   1790.

This case, which, with the introduction, consists of seventeen
folio pages, was drawn up by Hume Campbell, Esq. Its object was
to show that the Barony of Lisle was a Barony by tenure, and
resting that assertion upon the recital in certain letters patent,
granted in the 22nd of King Henry VI. " declaring that the pos-
sessors of the Manor and Lordship of Kingston Lisle, had, by reason
of that possession, been Barons and Lords of Lisle; and by that
name had place and seat in parliament from time immemorial, and

conferring that right to the person who then possessed it, Sir John Talbot, and his heirs and *assigns* for ever." It then proceeds to state, that Sir John Dudley, the heir of Sir John Talbot, in the 29th of King Henry VIII., assigned the said Manor and Lordship to William Hyde, Esq., whose heir in 1749 assigned it to Abraham Atkins, Esq., in whom it was then vested, and being so vested, carried with it a right to the Barony annexed to the possession of the lands. The case was printed for *private* use only, and it does not appear that Mr. Atkins pursued this object by any formal claim to the Crown.

In 1824, Sir John Shelley Sidney made a claim, as one of the co-heirs to this dignity (he being heir-general of the same Sir John Dudley); but upon the ground of its being a Barony originating by *writ*, and not by *tenure ;* After a hearing of this case in the House of Lords, it was in 1826,

" *Resolved*, That there did not appear sufficient ground to advise his Majesty to allow the claim of the petitioner." The claim of Sir John Sidney was considered to have failed from the circumstance of his not being able to *prove* that Warin de Lisle, the ancestor of Sir John Dudley, although summoned, from the 43rd of Edward III. to the 6th of Richard II., ever *sat* in Parliament—a sitting consequent upon a writ being a point indispensably necessary to be proved, by the records of parliament, according to the rules laid down and rigidly observed by the House.

One or two articles relating to claims of Peerage have been noticed in this work, but the editor is well aware, that very many of value and interest upon that subject are omitted, and which have been printed for private circulation, an account of which would have been a very desirable addition to his catalogue; but he found it, until too late, exceedingly difficult to procure anything like an accurate list or series, of the numerous printed Cases on claims to the various honours of the Peerage: many have been preferred which have never proceeded beyond the report of his Majesty's Attorney-General, to whom the consideration of such petitions is in the first instance referred, though the statements of the cases pre-pared, and sometimes printed for private use and more convenient reference, are exceedingly curious. In instances where the claims are carried to the House of Lords, most elaborate cases have been prepared and printed, which abound in legal argument and recondite learning, deeply interesting to the lawyer, the historian, and the antiquary.

As there is no inheritance more splendid than the dignity of the Peerage, it is to be lamented that no well-digested report of the numerous claims to such honours exists. The law of Dignities has never been discussed in that comprehensive form, which the importance of the subject demands. Few indeed are the reports of cases decided even during the last two centuries. The indefatigable Collins, in his Precedents of Baronies by Writ, supplied many cases, opinions, and judgments. Mr. Cruise, in his Treatise on Dignities, considering how little had been done before, did very much for the subject, wherein will be found a brief systematic arrangement of the law respecting dignities or titles of honour, supported and illustrated by a short statement of cases and claims to Peerages, that have been referred, either to Commissioners or the House of Peers, from the time of Elizabeth.

The first work which can be called a *Report* of a claim of Peerage illustrating the subject with cases, was the admirable report of the Gardner claim, by Denis Le Marchant, now Sir Denis Le Marchant, Bart, where the point at issue was, the legitimacy of the counter claimant: that work exhibits a curious and learned display of cases elucidatory of the law of legitimacy; and where a particular and full account of the arguments urged in the Lords' Committees for Privileges, upon the final discussion and decision of the Banbury, case in 1813, will be found. This report has been followed by two others, those of the Lisle and Devon Peerage cases, by the late Sir Nicholas H. Nicholas: the former involving the question of a writ of summons, and the necessity of proving a sitting under it to constitute a descendible Peerage—and the latter referring to the construction of the words of limitation in the patent of creation. A subsequent work by that author on "Adulterine Bastardy," embraces much valuable matter, and discusses at length the Banbury case.

In the library of Lincoln's Inn, there is a collection of printed cases upon this subject, formerly belonging to Sergeant Hill; and in the library of Sir Charles George Young, Garter, is a very valuable collection of similar cases, in several folio volumes; and also an extensive collection, containing the Minutes of Evidence taken before the House of Lords upon the hearing of claims, forming in the whole between thirty and forty folio volumes. Of the value and extent of this collection, the Editor was not aware, until the work had nearly passed the press, when the use of the collection was offered to him. Its extent precluded the practicability of availing himself of it at that time, but he indulged the hope of availing himself of these collections at a future period. Upon the present occasion they were still open to him, and he seriously entertained a hope of introducing much new matter upon their subject. On referring, however, again to these volumes, he finds the lapse of twenty years has added so extensively to the collections, that no account which could do any justice to the subject, could be compressed within the limits to which this work could afford space. In fact the subject is one for a separate volume; and considering, after reflection, that very many of the printed *cases* in question, though of a *private* nature, are not strictly to be comprehended under the designation of privately-printed books or works, the author has reluctantly yielded to the necessity of exclusion, rather than put forth an imperfect and unsatisfactory account of claims involving points of great legal and historical interest. The materials are no less ample for, than the subject is worthy of, a separate Catalogue.

CATALOGUE OF THE BOOKS IN THE LIBRARY OF RALPH WILLETT, ESQ., AT MERLY, IN THE COUNTY OF DORSET. London: Printed in the Year 1790. 8vo. pp. 176.

A classed catalogue. Mr. Willett was sheriff of the county of Dorset in 1760. A view of the house, engraved at his expense, is in Hutchins's "History of the County," vol. ii. p. 108.

THE RIGHT OF THE ELDEST SONS OF THE PEERS OF
SCOTLAND, TO REPRESENT THE COMMONS OF THAT PART
OF GREAT BRITAIN IN PARLIAMENT, CONSIDERED.
Printed in the year 1790.   4*to.*   pp. 44.

Privately printed by Lord Daer. This production originated in a
rule which prevailed in Scotland, that the eldest sons of Scotch
Peers were not eligible to sit in Parliament. Prior to the Union,
there was some sort of principle for the thing; for as the Lords and
Commons sat together, the introduction of the heir apparent of a
Peer might materially add to the power of the Peerage. After the
Union, their sitting could hardly be dangerous, as the Peers and
Commons were separated, and the expediency of altering the rule
was the subject of a work now somewhat scarce, from the pen of
Alexander Lord Setoun, who adds to his designation " Advocate,"
from his being a member of the Scotch bar; entitled, " Thoughts
on the Disqualification of the eldest Sons of the Peers of Scotland,
to elect or be elected from that country to Parliament, with an Appendix." London, 1788, 8vo. Lord Daer, the eldest son of the
Earl of Selkirk, went farther. He tried the right before the Court
of Session and House of Peers, but unsuccessfully. He was a most
acoomplished and talented young nobleman, but he died in 1794,
before the earldom opened to him. He was buried in the Cathedral
of Exeter. The Editor is indebted to James Maidment, Esq., not
only for this note, but for numerous valuable communications which
are dispersed through the volume, more especially relating to the
history and literature of Scotland, and without which assistance
this catalogue would have been very incomplete.

———

ΘΕΟΦΡΑΣΤΟΥ · ΚΑΡΑΚΤΗΡΕΣ · ΗΘΙΚΟΙ.
JOHANNES WILKES, ANGLUS, RECENSUIT.
Londini : typis Joannis Nichols.   1790.   4*to.*

" Of this volume only *one hundred* and *twenty* were printed, and
four on vellum : one to Count Reviczky, one to Lord Spencer, one to

Mr. Bindley; the destination of the fourth I do not recollect."* A vellum copy was sold in Sir M. Sykes' sale, for 7l. 2s. 6d.; and one in the Rev. T. Williams', for 8l. 12s. This volume, as well as the Catullus, was intended only for presents.

———

CATALOGUE OF THE
LIBRARY OF DANIEL WRAY, ESQ., F.R. AND A.SS.;
Given by his Widow, agreeably to his wish, for the use of the Charter House, in the year 1785; and also of those Books which have been presented since that period.
London: Printed in the Year M.DCC.XC. 8vo. pp. 176.

Arranged alphabetically; the tracts are catalogued separately.

———

MEMOIRS OF A LATE EMINENT BOOKSELLER.

"Ubi lapsus? Quid feci."—*Lord Courtenay's Motto.*

London: Printed in the Year M.DCC.XC. 8vo. pp. 262.

This is a Memoir of John Almon, Bookseller, of Piccadilly.
(On the back of Title.)
"The original of the several Letters here printed will for three months be put into the hands of the publisher, for the satisfaction of any gentleman who may doubt their authority."—*Feb. 14th,* 1791.
I do not recollect the authority for this being considered private. Almon died in 1805, and there is no mention of the work in a well-drawn up Memoir of him in the *Gentleman's Magazine,* 1805, p. 1179.

———

* Nichols, Literary Anecdotes, vol. ix. p. 69.—It is in the Duke of Bedford's Library at Woburn Abbey.—ED.

I

FRAGMENTS OF THE HISTORY OF JOHN BULL.
BY SIR H. POLESWORTH.
1791.   *8vo.*

PANOPTICON :

Postscript, Part I., containing further Particulars and Alterations relative to the Plan of construction originally proposed; principally adapted to the purpose of a Panopticon Penitentiary House. By JEREMY BENTHAM, of Lincoln's Inn, Esq.

London: Printed for T. Payne, at the Mews-gate. 1791.
12*mo.* pp. 239.

Part II.   1791.   12*mo.*   pp. 232.

At the sale of the late Sir James Mackintosh's library was a copy, with this note: " Unpublished; given to me by the author, when I dined *tête-à-tête* at his hermitage, Queen Square, Westminster, in January, 1804.

"*Bombay, 7th July,* 1804.   J. MACKINTOSH."

HASTY PRODUCTIONS.
BY HORACE WALPOLE, EARL OF ORFORD.
Norwich, 1791.   *4to.*

" Only 25 copies were printed, some of which were burnt by his executrix, Mrs. Damer. They might all have gone to the fire, for they are sad trash."—*Note in Mr. Grenville's copy.*

Mr. Grenville's authority on Bibliography is so great, that it is almost presumptuous to dispute it; but I cannot help thinking that these "productions" were the work of his eccentric nephew, George Earl of Orford, who died in 1791.

GRÆCÆ LINGUÆ CONJUGATIONES,
IN USUM ORNATISSIMÆ FŒM. ANNÆ DAMER.
4*to.* 1791.

" This was composed by the celebrated scholar, Livie; published for presents only."—*Bookseller's Catalogue.*

NOMINA VILLARUM OF THE COUNTY OF SOUTHAMPTON ;
Or, a List of Divisions, Boroughs, Hundreds, Liberties, Parishes and Tythings, within the said County, with the Quota each pays to the County Rate.
Romsey. 1791.

From a bookseller's catalogue; it was unknown to Upcott, and is not in Gough's Catalogue of Topography.

ESSAY ON POLITICAL TACTICS,
Containing Six of the principal Rules proper to be observed by a Political Assembly in the process of forming a Decision ; with the Reasons on which they are grounded, and a comparative application of them to British and French practice : being a fragment of a larger work, a sketch of which is subjoined.
BY JEREMY BENTHAM, OF LINCOLN'S INN, ESQ.
London : Printed for T. Payne, at the Mews-gate.
M.DCC.XCI. 4*to.* pp. 66.

At the end of the volume is a large table, entitled " Heads treated of in a work never published."

I 2

Lusus Poetici, ex ludo literario apud Ædes
Carthusianas, Londini:
Quibus accessere Orationes binæ in Suttoni laudem in
ædibus Carthusianis habitæ.

1791.   8vo.   pp. 147.

"Unpublished; a very few copies printed for presents."—*Grenville Catalogue*, p. 420.

Catalogus impressorum librorum in Bibliotheca
Universitatis Glasguensis, Secundum literarum
ordinem dispositus.
Impensis Academiæ, labore et studio Archibaldi
Arthur, A.M., Philosophiæ Moralis Professoris.
Folio. Glasguæ: in ædibus academicis excudebat
Andreas Foulis, Academiæ Typographus, 1791.

pp. 496.

An alphabetical catalogue of works in general literature, in which
the titles are given in full, and printed in double columns.

Catalogus impressorum librorum in Bibliotheca
Universitatis Glasguensis, secundum literarum
ordinem dispositus, etc.

This volume, though bearing the same title and date as the above,
is strictly a press catalogue, in which the titles of every book and
pamphlet are given, in the order they stand in the shelves; it is
printed in double columns, and extends to 390 pages, folio.

A Supplement to the Catalogue of Books in the
University Library, Glasgow.
Glasgow: Printed by Andrew and John M. Duncan,
printers to the University, 1825.   8vo.   pp. 520.

A Second Supplement to the Catalogue of Books in the University Library, Glasgow.

Glasgow : Printed at the University press, by Edward Khull, 65, Virginia Street. 1836. pp. 800. 8*vo*.

Eleven Annual Appendices to the Catalogue, each bearing Titles similar to the following :—

Catalogue of Books bought, from August 20th, 1847, till August 20th, 1848, for the University Library, out of the Compensation Fund, allowed by Government on abolition of privilege under the Copyright Act.

Glasgow : George Richardson, Printer to the University. pp. 120. 8*vo*.

Three Annual Appendices to the Catalogue, with Title similar to the following :—

Twelfth Appendix to the Glasgow University Library Catalogue, 1849–50.

Glasgow : George Richardson, Printer to the University. pp. 58. 8*vo*.

The titles in the two Supplements and Appendices are arranged under the authors' names, and all treat of general literature.

It appeared better to keep the Catalogues of the Library of Glasgow College together, instead of arranging them under the different dates. They are not sold, but each professor is entitled to a copy. For this account the Editor is indebted to the Librarian, N. Jones, Esq.

MEMORIAL, TO SHEW THAT THE ELDEST SON OF THE
KING HAS RIGHT BY HIS BIRTH, TO THE PRINCIPALITY
AND GREAT STEWARDSHIP OF SCOTLAND, AND IS A PEER
OF THAT KINGDOM, BY THE STYLE AND TITLES OF DUKE
OF ROTHESAY, EARL OF CARRICK, BARON OF RENFREW,
AND LORD OF THE ISLES.
Printed in the Year M.DCC.XCI.   4to.

THE LIFE AND ADVENTURES OF JOSEPH EMIN,
AN ARMENIAN.   WRITTEN IN ENGLISH BY HIMSELF.
London : Printed in the Year 1792.   8vo. pp. 640.

Joseph Emin was an Armenian Christian, born in Persia in the
year 1726.   In 1731 he arrived in London from Calcutta; and after
undergoing various hardships, obtained the patronage of the Duke of
Northumberland, by whose interest he acquired a military education
at Woolwich.

" His character bears a strong resemblance to the ancient Christian knights of romance.   Virtuous, pious, and enthusiastic; to
raise the cross, and depress the crescent, seems to have been his
chief aim: brave and hardy; he formed a good and noble purpose,
and pursued it with unremitted ardour.   A lascar sailor, a London
porter, a volunteer on the continent of Europe, or a welcome guest
at the greatest tables in Europe, he never lost sight of his first
design."*

" His life is probably very little known.   The style of it is harsh
and dry, half Oriental and half English, very obscure and unsatisfactory, but bearing evident marks of truth and genuineness.   The
author affects to throw a veil of mystery over his ancestry; but it is

---

* Life of Sir William Jones, p. 278, 4to.

easy to discover that he thinks himself, or wishes to be thought, a descendant from the former sovereigns of Armenia.*

Alexander's Expedition down the Hydaspes and the Indus to the Indian Ocean.

London.   4to.   1792.

With the copy sent to Dr. Parr was the following account of this publication, by Mr. William Anstice:

" The late Dr. Beddoes must be known to Dr. Parr by character, if he was not personally: in any case, the literary fragment which accompanies this, cannot prove uninteresting. It owes its origin to a conversation which took place at the table of the late Mr. William Reynolds, in which some men of taste and genius contended that the poetic effusions of Darwin were inimitable. Dr. Beddoes maintained a contrary opinion; and to try the point, produced to the same party a short time afterwards, a manuscript of the present piece, as from his friend Darwin, and sent to him for his inspection, previous to publication: the advocates for Darwin's style were deceived, and the Doctor triumphed. Mr. Reynolds had it printed at his own expense, but for obvious reasons it was not published, and therefore may never have met Dr. Parr's eye. It was printed in Madeley; the types were set by a woman, and the engravings made on wood by the then and present clerk of this parish.

" *Madeley Wood, Oct.* 9, 1819."

---

* Preface to Mrs. Carter's Letters, vol. i. p. xix.

M.DCC.XCII.

POEMS TO THESPIA :
TO WHICH ARE ADDED SONNETS, ETC.

Oh, true name of Love,
Tender affection ! genuine source of bliss
Immaculate and pure ! the transient blaze
Of passion soon subsides ; thy steadier fire
Time but increases. Soft, coercive band,
Connecting souls ! without thee what is life !

Exeter : Printed by R. Trewman and Son, M.DCC.XCII.
By H. Downman, M.D.
8vo. pp. 210.

How poor, how basely frivolous the times
In which I print, but *publish not* my rhymes.
—Page 169.

The author was a physician at Exeter ; died in 1809. He appears
to have changed his mind about not publishing, as an edition of
these poems is stated to have been printed in 1804. He wrote
several other works, all poetical.

———

OBSERVATIONS ON THE REGIAM MAJESTATEM, AND
REMARKS ON SOME OF THE EDITIONS OF THE PARLIA-
MENTS OF SCOTLAND. BY JOHN DAVIDSON.
Not printed for sale.
Edinburgh. 8vo. 1792.

" Mr. John Davidson, the first figure in the division entitled ' Conversation,'* was the son of a bookseller in Edinburgh, and followed
the calling of a writer to the Signet. During the greater part of his
life he enjoyed, perhaps, the most lucrative and respectable business

———

* Kaye's Edinburgh Portraits, vol. i. p. 243.

in Edinburgh. He was a man of superior abilities, and of great industry. His literary acquirements were highly estimated by his friends, to whom he frequently rendered valuable assistance. For many years Mr. Davidson was agent for the Crown. He died at Edinburgh, 29th December, 1797."—From the information of David Laing, Esq., librarian to the library of the writers to the Signet, to whom the Editor is indebted for much valuable assistance.

CONTEMPLATIO PHILOSOPHICA ;

A Posthumous Work of the late Brook Taylor, LL.D., F.R.S., some time Secretary to the Royal Society. To which is added, a Life of the Author, by his Grandson, Sir William Young, F.R.S., A.SS. With an Appendix, containing sundry Original Papers, Letters from the Count Raymond de Montmort, Lord Bolingbroke, Marcilly de Villette, Bernouilli, &c.

London : Printed by William Bulmer and Co., Shakespeare Printing Office. 1793. 8vo. pp. 150.

Prefixed is a mezzotinto portrait of Brook Taylor, engraved by Earlom.

In the copy formerly in the Stowe library is the following note by Horace Walpole :

Berkeley Square, Feb. 15, 1793.

" Lord Orford is extremely obliged to Mr. Seward for the valuable present of Mr. B. Taylor's Life : the preface is particularly good, and the account of biography of learned men admirably drawn and expressed.

" Lord Orford will thank Mr. Seward much for a duplicate print of the head of Mr. Taylor, for his collection of English portraits."

Mr. Hallam says of this work:—" It bespeaks the clear and acute understanding of this celebrated philosopher, and appears to me an entire refutation of the scholastic argument of Descartes; one more fit for the Anselms, and such dealers in words, from whom it came, than for himself."—*Literature of Europe*, vol. ii. p. 441.

————

POEMS,

BY JOHN FREDERIC SACKVILLE, ON VARIOUS SUBJECTS.

> " Whoever thinks a faultless piece to see,
> Thinks what ne'er was, ne'er is, nor e'er will be."
>
> POPE.

London : Printed in the Year M.DCC.XCIII. 12*mo*. pp. 59.

Juvenile poems, written by the third Duke of Dorset, when Mr. Sackville. A very limited number was printed.

————

A CORRESPONDENCE BETWEEN MR. FOULKES, WHO MARRIED MISS PHILIPPA TROTTER, AND EDWARD BROWN, ESQ., OF BARN-HILL, STAMFORD, ONE OF THE EXECUTORS OF THE LAST WILL AND TESTAMENT OF THE LATE REV. BROWNLOW TOLLER, OF BILLINGBOROUGH, IN THE COUNTY OF LINCOLN, RESPECTING THE WILL, AND OTHER MATTERS.

Vir bonus est quis ?

1793.   8*vo*.   pp. 124.

THE LIFE OF THOMAS EGERTON, LORD CHANCELLOR
OF ENGLAND.
[Circa 1793.] *folio.* pp. 59.

"The Life of the Lord Chancellor, in the first edition of the Biographia Britannica, consists of only between three and four pages. It was first altered and enlarged by his descendant the Rev. Francis Henry Egerton, brother of the present Earl of Bridgewater, so as to make twenty pages printed in the manner of the Biographia Britannica. Mr. H. F. Egerton made a present to me of the much enlarged Life in August, 1793. He afterwards made further enlargement and alterations; and this volume, containing fifty-nine pages, exclusive of the life of his father Dr. Egerton, Bishop of Durham, was the result. 21 December, 1805."*

It is believed that the following is a complete list of the books written and edited by the late Francis, eighth Earl of Bridgewater.

1. The Life of Thomas Egerton, Lord Chancellor of England. Paris: *royal 4to.* pp. 508. Neither title-page, nor termination.

2. Another edition of the same Memoir: printed at Paris, by Didot l'Ainé. 1812. *imperial folio.* pp. 64.

3. Four Letters from Spa, to John William Egerton, Earl of Bridgewater. Printed by Thomas Davison, Whitefriars, London. *8vo.* pp. 11.

4. A Letter to the Parisians and French Nation, upon Inland Navigation : in English and French. *folio.*

4*. The First Part of a Letter to the Parisians and the French Nation, upon Inland Navigation ; containing a Defence of the Public Character of his Grace Francis Egerton, late Duke of Bridgewater, &c. By the Honourable Francis Henry Egerton, &c.; and including some Notices and Anecdotes concerning Mr. James Brindley. *8vo.* pp. 155.

5. Aperçu Historique et Généalogique. Paris. 1827. *8vo.*

6. A Fragment of an Ode of Sappho, from Longinus ; also an Ode of Sappho, from Dionysius Halicarn. pp. 26. Paris. 1815. *8vo.*

---

* Note in Mr. Hargrave's copy, in the British Museum.

7. Letters to John William, Earl of Bridgewater, in 1820-21. Printed by Thomas Davison, London. 8*vo.* pp. 16.

8. A Literal Translation of Milton's Paradise Lost: in Italian and French. Paris: Didot. 4*to.* pp. 85.

9. Family Anecdotes. Paris: Didot. 4*to.* and 8*vo.*

10. The Life of John Egerton, Bishop of Durham. Paris. *folio.* There is an 8*vo.* edition, from the press of Davison, distributed by Mr. Woodifield in the county of Durham, at Newcastle, and in Northumberland.

11. Description du Plan Incliné Souterain, executé entre les deux biefs des Canaux Souterains, dans les Houillieres de Walkden-Moor en Angleterre, par le Duc de Bridgewater. Par L'Hon. François Henry Egerton. A. Paris. An XI (1803). 8*vo.* pp. 19, and a long Plan.

The editor has heard of a catalogue of the different publications of this eccentric nobleman, in 4*to.* pp. 65; an account of the edition of Euripides, will be found under the date 1796.

The Earl of Bridgewater died at Paris, April, 1829; by his will he bequeathed 8000*l.* to the President of the Royal Society, for a work "On the Power, Wisdom, and Goodness of God," which legacy was distributed among the different writers of the well-known "Bridgewater Treatises." He bequeathed his manuscripts and autographs to the British Museum, with 5000*l.* to augment the collection of MSS., and the interest of 7000*l.* to the librarians who have charge of them.

In addition to the works mentioned above, his Lordship is said * to have printed "Lettre inédité de la Seigneurie de Florence au Pape Sixte IV., 21 Juillet, 1478." 4*to.* Paris. 1814. And in 1826, "Family Anecdotes," some extracts from which are in the "Literary Gazette," 1827. pp. 121, 153.

---

* Gentleman's Magazine, June, 1829.

Claudiani Opera.

[London.]   1793—6.   *small 8vo.*

This work was printed by Bulmer, and edited by the late Richard Heber, editor of the Persius mentioned in p. 107. Dr. Dibdin[*] states that one copy was taken off on vellum, for the late Mr. Edwards, the bookseller; and that this edition was printed with a view of completing the deficiencies in the series of Classics published by Barbou; the design was, however, abandoned.

———

Tracts. I. On the Right of Citizens. II. Political Government, and Political Liberty. III. The State of the Parochial Clergy of the Church of Ireland.

By William Hales, D.D.

Dublin: Printed by George Grierson, Parliament Street. 1794.   *8vo.*

I am unable to ascertain where the title of this work was obtained, and on applying to the learned librarian of Trinity College, Dublin, Dr. Todd, that gentleman states it is not in that library, and at the same time expressed great doubt as to its having been written by Dr. Hales; and refers to the publication called "Anthologia Hibernica," published at the end of the last century, where a work with the above title was published anonymously in 1791. The Editor of the "Anthologia" speaks of the author as generally known, but unfortunately does not name him, although he publishes a letter to him from Edmund Burke. Further notices of the work will be found in the "Anthologia," with a statement that the author

———

[*] Bibliographical Decameron, vol. ii. p. 384.

126   M.DCC.XCIV.

had prepared a second edition. The reputed author was a Fellow of Trinity College, Dublin; had the living of Kellesandra in 1787; and died at an advanced age in 1831.

***

CATALOGUE OF THE MANUSCRIPTS IN THE POSSESSION OF THE EARL OF HARDWICKE.
1794. 4*to.* pp. 91.

Compiled by the late Archdeacon Coxe, to whom the MSS. were of great use in the compilation of his various historical works.

***

MUSEUM WORSLEYANUM:
Or, a Collection of Antique Basso-Relievos, Bustoes, Statues, and Gems. With Views of Places in the Levant, taken on the spot in the years M.DCC.LXXXV. VI. VII.
London. M.DCC.XCIV.   *2 vols. folio.*

Sir Richard Worsley is said* to have expended upwards of 27,000*l.* in collecting the materials for this work, of which two hundred and fifty copies were printed. An analysis of the contents of the volumes will be found in Savage's Librarian.† In the year 1823 a new edition was announced by Mr. Prowett, the bookseller, which intention having been communicated to Lord Yarborough, his lordship threatened to move for an injunction, on the ground that the copper-plates had been improperly obtained: but on Mr. Prowett undertaking that no more than two hundred and fifty copies should be printed, the publication was allowed to proceed. After these

***

* Bibliographica Decameron, vol. ii. p. 387.   † Vol. i. p. 97.

copies had been printed, of which twenty-five were on India paper, the copper-plates were destroyed, in the presence of Lord Yarborough's solicitor.

That the copper-plates had been abstracted from the late Sir Richard Worsley in an improper manner, there can be little doubt. They were purchased by an eminent printseller at a pawnbroker's sale, and by him resold to Mr. Prowett, for 400*l.* The following plates were missing, which the publisher was under the necessity of re-engraving for his new edition, viz. :—

Portrait of Sir Richard Worsley   -   -   -   Vol. I.
Death of General Wolfe -   -   -   -   -   Vol. I.
Two plates of antique Greek gems, nine subjects on each   Vol. I.
The large folding plate of the basso-relievo of the Parthenon   Vol. II.

Soon after these had been executed, a person called upon the publisher, offering him the original plates for 150*l.*; the offer was declined. These plates, it is presumed, are now in existence.

Sir Richard Worsley is said to have distributed no more than twenty-seven copies of the original edition; and to have given 200*l.* to the executors of a gentleman to whom he had presented one. It is scarcely possible, although the *text* for two hundred and fifty copies was printed, that that number of the original edition was ever completed: in all probability the text is either in existence, or has been condemned as waste paper. Mr. Townley's copy of the original edition was sold for 96*l.* 12*s.* Copies are in the British Museum, and in the library of the Society of Antiquaries. The drawings were sold by auction, at Stewart and Wheatley's, Piccadilly, for fifty guineas; and were purchased for Lord Yarborough.

Persius's Sixth Satire imitated.   Squire's tale from Chaucer.

1794.   8*vo.*

Privately printed at the press of the late John Penn, Esq., at Stoke Park, Bucks, now the seat of Mr. Labouchere.

POEMS IN ENGLISH, SCOTCH, AND LATIN.

Majores majora sonent ; mihi parva locuto
Sufficit in vestras sæpe redire manus.—MART.

Paisley : Printed by J. Nelson for the Author. 1794.
pp. 140.   8vo.

By James Grahame, Esq., Advocate. Considerable professional influence induced Mr. Grahame to come to the Scotch bar, where he practised a few years. Ultimately his disinclination for legal avocations induced him to forsake a profession that might have been profitable, and to take holy orders.

ALTER ET IDEM, A NEW REVIEW, No. I. FOR A
SUMMER MONTH IN 1794.
Printed (but not for publication) by Smart and Cowslade, Reading, Berks.   1794.   4to.   pp. 119.

By Robert P. Deverell. A presentation copy, with autograph, was in Mr. Eyton's library, No. 466.

Mr. Deverell was author of several other works printed for sale. His work on Hieroglyphics will be found in a subsequent page.

DISCOURSE, BY WAY OF GENERAL PREFACE TO THE
QUARTO EDITION OF BISHOP WARBURTON'S WORKS ;
Containing some account of the Life, Writings, and Character of the Author.
London : Printed by John Nichols.   1794.   4to.

"Not printed for general sale; no more than 250 copies having been taken off, to supply that number which had been printed of the Bishop's works."—*Nichols' Anecdotes*, vol. v. p. 641.

" Privately printed and sparingly distributed."—*J. Bindly.*

PLEASANT PASSETIME FOR CHRISTMAS EVENINGS ; OR,
THE PREDICTIONS OF COSMOPOLITUS OCCULTARIUS, ETC.
London.   1795.   12mo.

By Lady Craven, Margravine of Anspach, youngest daughter of
Augustus, fourth Earl of Berkeley.   Privately printed.   A copy on
vellum, at the sale of the Mac Carthy library, brought 63 francs.   In
the autobiography of this lady, published in 1826, 2 vols. 8vo., there
is no mention of this, nor indeed any other of her published works.

A SHORT ACCOUNT OF THE PARISH OF WATERBEACH,
IN THE DIOCESE OF ELY.   BY A LATE VICAR.
1795.   8vo.   pp. 56.

A frontispiece, the remains of Denny Abbey.   Mr. Bindley, in a
note in his copy, says, " Of this book, written by the late Mr.
Masters, formerly fellow and tutor of Ben'et College, Cambridge,
there were only *five and twenty* copies printed, which the author
gave among his friends."
" This tract is among the scarcest on the subject of Topography.
It was written by the Rev. Thomas Martin (query, Masters), and was
never published.   He caused the impression to be destroyed, except
five or six copies, which, at his death, were sold with his effects in
Bow Street, Covent Garden."—*Upcott's English Topography.*

DECLARATIO PARLIAMENTI, UBI JOHANNES, PRIMOGE-
NITUS ROBERTI, HABET SUCCEDERE IN REGNUM, 1371.
1795.   *folio.*   pp. 7.

With a fac-simile of the document and the seals : printed at the
expense of the late Lord Frederick Campbell.

K

Observations on the Bequest of Henry Flood, Esq., to Trinity College, Dublin, with a Defence of the Ancient History of Ireland.
    By Sir Lawrence Parsons, Bart.
Dublin : Bonham, printer, 1795.   8*vo.*

Said, in Mr. Grenville's catalogue, to be "privately printed."

La Pucelle ; or, the Maid of Orleans.
A Poem in xxi. Cantos. From the French of M. de Voltaire; with the Author's Preface, and Original Notes.
London.   1796-7.   *2 vols.*   8*vo.*

This translation was made by the late Lady Charleville, and was never published. *Fifty* copies on small paper, and *five* on large paper, were distributed: the remainder of the impression was destroyed.

The following printed note was obtained from a work, the name of which has escaped the Editor's memory.

"This translation was made by Lady C——, and was never published. About fifty copies only were distributed, and the remainder destroyed by a relation of that lady.

"The Rev. Mr. B—— (the translator of D——), who was chaplain to the family, declared that he would instantly leave the house, if the work was published. The whole of the remaining copies were burnt at Lord C——'s seat."

Supplement to the Miscellaneous Works of Mr. Gibbon.
London.   1796.   4*to.*

"By the celebrated John Wilkes, which, though without his name, and not printed for sale, was avowed in the presents which he made of it to his friends."* This Supplement appeared in the "Observer," 1780.

A CATALOGUE OF DICTIONARIES, VOCABULARIES, GRAMMARS, AND ALPHABETS.
In Two Parts.—Part I. Alphabetic Catalogue of Authors : Part II. Chronological Catalogue of Works in each Class of Language.
BY WILLIAM MARSDEN, F.R.S.
London. 1796. 4*to.* pp. 154.

" Ce Catalogue, dans lequel il n'est question que des langues les moins connues, n'a été tiré qu'à un petit nombre d'exemplaires, et il n'a pas été mis dans le commerce."—*Brunet.*

Mr. Marsden published for sale other Philological works, and a History of Sumatra. 4*to.*

VIEW OF THE EVIDENCE FOR PROVING THAT THE PRESENT EARL OF GALLOWAY IS THE LINEAL HEIR MALE AND LAWFUL REPRESENTATIVE OF SIR WILLIAM STUART, OF JEDWORTH, SO FREQUENTLY MENTIONED IN HISTORY FROM THE YEAR 1385 TO THE YEAR 1429.
1796. 4*to.*

"Printed for private distribution by the Earl of Galloway. It was drawn up by the Rev. E. Williams, his lordship's chaplain."†

---

* Nichols, Literary Anecdotes, vol. ix. p. 476.
† Moule, Bibliotheca Heraldica, p. 481.

Euripidis Hippolytus Stephanephoros, Gr. et Lat., var. Lect., Valckenari Notis integris, ac selectis aliorum, quibus suas adjunxit F. H. Egerton. Oxon. 1796.   4to.

Privately printed for presents, at the Clarendon press, by Francis, eighth Earl of Bridgewater; a very few copies were struck off.

The noble editor printed at Paris, in 1813, the following supplement :—

"Numbers IX, X, XI, XII, XIII, of Addenda and Corrigenda to the edition of the Hippolytus Stephanephoros of Euripides, by the Honourable Francis Henry Egerton, &c., &c., &c. 1796." 4to. pp. 243.

————

Remarks on several Parts of France, Italy, etc., in the Years 1783, 1784, and 1785. By Benjamin Hobhouse, Barrister at Law. Bath : Printed by R. Cruttwell.   m.dcc.xcvi.   8vo. pp. 340.   Corrigenda, one leaf.

By the late Sir Benjamin Hobhouse, Bart., father of Lord Broughton.

"The following collection of Letters, written when I was between twenty-six and twenty-eight years of age, is not intended to be published. It is printed with the hope of affording an hour's amusement to my friends, many of whom had requested me to furnish them with copies."—*Preface.*

"*Hartnam House, Jan.* 8, 1796."

A Short Memoir, critically illustrating the Histories of Tracy and Courtenay, exhibiting likewise the ancient Usage or Variation of Coat Armour in that of Tracy.

Canterbury : Printed 1796.   8vo.   pp. 63.

Dedicated to Henry Lord Viscount Tracy and Hemlife, Reginald Courtenay, Bishop of Bristol, descendant in the male line, although bearing different surnames, from Reginald Courtenay.

By John Tracy, Brompton, in Gillingham, Kent.—March 6, 1796.

———

State of the Evidence produced for proving the claim of William Hamilton, of Wishaw, to be served nearest and lawful Heir Male of the deceased, James, last Lord Belhaven.

December, 1796.   4to.   pp. 21.

Prepared by the late Robert Hamilton, Esq., Sheriff of Lanark, one of the Principal Clerks of Session. The claim was successful. Mr. Hamilton died 31st Dec. 1831. He was a very able genealogist.

———

Review of the Events and Treaties which established the Balance of Power in Europe, and the Balance of Trade in favor of Great Britain.

London: 1796.   8vo.   pp. 181, with a sketch showing the ports of the Netherlands from which France may attack Britain and distress its trade.

By John Bruce.

M.DCC.XCVII.

POETICAL ESSAYS;

WRITTEN CHIEFLY IN THE WEST INDIES.

Printed for the Author by R. Cruttwell. Bath. 1796.

4*to.* pp. 43.

The author was Bryan Edwards.

The copy in Heber, part ii. No. 1943, had several MS. additions.

———

A WORD OR TWO IN VINDICATION OF THE UNIVER-
SITY OF OXFORD, AND OF MAGDALEN COLLEGE IN PAR-
TICULAR, FROM THE POSTHUMOUS ASPERSIONS OF MR.
GIBBON.

[Circa 1796]. 4*to.* pp. 44.

This was published soon after the appearance of the Miscellaneous
Works of Gibbon. Written by the late Mr. Hurdis.

———

POEMS; WITH A PREFACE BY THE EDITOR.

Consisting of some Anecdotes of Mr. Monck Berkeley,
and several of his Friends.

London: Nichols. 1797. 4*to.*

" Edited by his Mother. Privately printed. With a portrait of
the author, from a painting by the Rev. W. Peters; Bindley, part i.
737. 1*l.* 3*s.*"—*Lowndes.*

The author died in 1793. Mr. Berkeley published " Literary
Relics; containing original Letters from Charles II., James II., &c."
8*vo.* Lond. 1790.

Debates of the House of Lords, on the Evidence of Hastings' Trial.

1797. *4to.*

" A large volume in *4to.*, consisting of letters and papers concerning Mr. Hastings, written and printed under his own direction, for the use of his friends, but which was never published."* It was in the catalogue of the library of Wilkes, sold by Sotheby, No. 573.

Musæus. The Loves of Hero and Leander.

London : Printed by W. Bulmer and Co. M.DCC.XCVII.

4to. pp. 53.

Translated by the late Grosvenor Bedford, friend and correspondent of Southey.

Genealogical and Historical Table of the Families of Heron : verified throughout by Records, and other authentic Documents.

Printed in the year 1797. *folio.*

" A few copies of this thin folio were printed by the late Sir Richard Heron, Bart., for private distribution ; it is abundant in references to escheat rolls, and other records."† The author of this work was uncle to Sir Robert Heron, whose "Notes," severely noticed in the Quarterly Review, Vol. XC. p. 206, are said in that journal to have been privately printed some years since.

---

* Almon, Wilkes' Correspondence, vol. vi. p. 190
† Moule, Bibliotheca Heraldica, p. 483.

EXCERPTA ANTIQUA; OR, A COLLECTION
OF ORIGINAL MANUSCRIPTS. BY JOHN CROFTS.
York : Printed by William Blanchard. 1797. (Privately.) *8vo.*

This book is in Miss Currer's Catalogue, p. 248 ; and in Heber's, part i. No. 1854.

CATALOGUE OF THE LIBRARY OF THE RIGHT HONOURABLE LORD MENDIP : TOGETHER WITH A CATALOGUE OF THE BOOKS OF THE RIGHT HONOURABLE LORD MENDIP AT TWICKENHAM.
London. 1797. *4to.*

An alphabetical catalogue : the library is now in the possession of Viscount Clifden.

EPIGRAMMATA, EPITAPHIA, ETC., EX VETERIBUS GRÆCIS ET GNOMICIS POETIS SELECTA.
Londoni : Typis mandatum expensis R. Faulder. 1797.

Printed on vellum.

Thorpe, in his Catalogue, 1836, No. 940, speaks of this as " A privately-printed volume of 120 pages, probably unique, as it is evidently unknown to all bibliographers."

NOTES OF A JOURNEY FROM BERNE TO ENGLAND THROUGH FRANCE. MADE IN THE YEAR 1796. BY A. D. London: Printed by W. Blackader, No. 10, Took's court, Chancery-lane. 1797. *8vo.* Part I. pp. 101; Part II. pp. 56.

The first part contains the notes of Mr. A. Douglas, which were printed for the private perusal of his intimate friends; which he expresses his wish, in a letter prefixed, addressed to Mrs. Douglas, p. vii., may be considered " as a family dinner, not as a public entertainment." The second part, entitled "Notes of a Journey from Berne to England, through France, made in the Year 1796, by M. D.," contains the observations of Mrs. Douglas, made during the same tour.

———

COURS ELEMENTAIRE D'HISTOIRE ANCIENNE, A L'USAGE DE LL. AA. ROYALES MESDAMES LES PRINCESSES D'ANGLETERRE. PAR CH. DE GUIFFARDIERE, MINISTRE DE LA CHAPELLE FRANCOISE DU ROI ET PREBENDIER DE SALISBURY. Imprimé à Windsor, chez C. Knight, Imprimeur et Libraire. 1798. *2 vols.* 8vo.

The copy in the Royal Library in the British Museum contains a map, *Veteris Orbis elimata ex Strabone,* drawn by her Royal Highness the Princess Sophia. The author died January, 1810, aged 70.

———

STATE OF IRELAND. BY ARTHUR O'CONNOR. *8vo.* pp. 174.

No place or date, but most likely printed in Dublin; a pencil note in the Grenville copy says, " Never published; the Manifesto intended for the Rebellion."

The Equality of Mankind, a Poem.
By Michael Woodhull, Esq.
Revised and corrected, with Additions.
London. 1798. 8vo. pp. 38.

It is uncertain whether this was printed for private circulation only : an edition appeared in 1766. The author, a native of Northamptonshire, died in 1816. He translated Euripides, and published other poems.

The Ancient History of Ireland, proved from the Sanscrit Books of the Bramins of India.
By Charles Vallancey.
Dublin. 1797. 8vo. pp. 30. Title and plate.

" Privately printed, and distributed among the author's friends."
—*Lowndes*.

This is inserted on the above authority; but Dr. Todd, the librarian of Trinity College, Dublin, kindly informed the Editor that a copy in that library has no indication that it was privately printed. It is not in the British Museum with the author's other works, and is not mentioned by Watt, in the "Bibliotheca Britannica."

Report on the Arrangements which were made, for the internal Defence of these Kingdoms, when Spain, by its Armada, projected the Invasion and Conquest of England. By John Bruce.
1798. 8vo.

" Privately printed for the use of Ministers at the time of Bonaparte's threatened invasion."—*Lowndes*.

Odes, English and Latin.
By Thomas James Mathias.
Reprinted 1798.   [Not published.]   12*mo.*   pp. 75.

The Florentines own he came nearer their poetry than any other foreigner had done, but that still he was *but* a foreigner at it.*

––––––––

Summary and Free Reflections,
In which the great Outline only and Principal Features of several Interesting Subjects are impartially traced, and candidly examined.

Printed in the year 1798.   8*vo.*

The author of this was Henry Constantine Jennings, generally known by the name of Dog Jennings, from the celebrated antique statue, now in the possession of Lord Feversham.

––––––––

Julia, or Last Follies.

–––––– Franguntur Calami.

London : Printed by W. Bulmer and Co.   1798.   4*to.*
pp. 41.

By the late Rev. William Beloe, translator of Herodotus ; author of the Bibliographical work, "Anecdotes of Literature and Scarce Books," 6 vols. 8*vo.*, and other works.

––––––––

* Moore, Journal, edited by Lord John Russell, vol. ii. p. 205.   1853.

TABLES GENEALOGIQUES DES HEROS DES ROMANS, AVEC UN CATALOGUE DES PRINCIPAUX OUVRAGES EN CE GENRE.
A Londres : Chez M. Edwards, Pall Mall. 1798. 4*to*.
pp. 91.

This volume, not printed for general circulation, but for presentation to the author's friends, contains a list of the romances referred to by Cervantes, in Don Quixote.

CATALOGUE OF THE PORTRAITS AND PICTURES IN THE DIFFERENT HOUSES BELONGING TO THE EARL OF FIFE. 1798. 4*to*. pp. 71.

FIDELITY, OR LOVE AT FIRST SIGHT, A TALE : WITH OTHER POEMS. BY WILLIAM PARSONS.
London : Printed (not for sale) by Savage and Easingwold, James-street, Buckingham-gate. 1798. 4*to*.
pp. 92.

PROCEEDINGS AT KILLALLA, DURING THE FRENCH INVASION, AND THE SUBSEQUENT REBELLION, FROM AUGUST 22ND TO OCTOBER 27TH, 1798 :
In Letters from the Right Reverend Joseph, Lord Bishop of Killalla, to his Brother, Mr. Stephen Stock, of Dame-street, Dublin, and others.
Bath : Printed by R. Cruttwell. 1799. 8*vo*. pp. 91.

" These original Letters were never published. They were presented to me by my friend Dr. Joseph Stock, Bishop of Killalla, who printed a few copies of them at Bath, in September, 1799, for the use of his friends. To prevent their being made public, he framed from them the 'Narrative of the French Invasion,' which was published in Dublin in February, 1800, and in London in March, in the same year. " E. MALONE."

Note in a copy at the sale of Mr. Savill's library, by Evans, in January, 1833.

LETTERS FROM THE
CARDINAL BORGIA AND THE CARDINAL OF YORK.
London : Printed by W. Bulmer and Co. M.DCC.XCIX. -M.DCCC. *4to.*

Published by the late Sir John Coxe Hippisley, Bart. They relate to the distresses to which the Cardinal of York was reduced by the invasion of Italy by the French. The copy in the British Museum contains some MS. additions, and a letter from Lord Minto, announcing that his Majesty George III. had remitted 2000*l.* for the use of the Cardinal.

VALUATION ROLL OF THE STEWARTRY OF KIRKCUD-
BRIGHT, AS MADE UP BY THE COMMISSIONERS OF LAND
TAX, FOR THE SAID STEWARTRY, 14TH JUNE, 1799.
Dumfries : Printed by R. Jackson. *folio.* Forty leaves. (1799.)

Printed for the use of the Commissioners of Supply of the Stewartry.

Cupid and Psyche. A Mythological Tale from the Golden Ass of Apuleius.

London. 1799. *8vo.*

Translated by Mr. Hudson Gurney, who reprinted it in 1844.

Report on the Events and Circumstances which produced the Union of the Kingdoms of England and Scotland;

On the Effects of this great National Event on the reciprocal Interests of both Kingdoms; and on the Political and Commercial Influence of Great Britain in the Balance of Power in Europe. Vol. I. pp. 403.

Appendix to the Report.

Vol. II. pp. dxciii.

[London. 1799.] *2 vols. 8vo.*

These papers were collected by the desire of the fourth Duke of Portland, then Secretary of State, by Mr. Bruce, Keeper of the State Papers.

In the copy in the British Museum is the following letter :—

" The Duke of Portland presents his compliments to Mr. Planta, and requests he will offer for the acceptance of the Trustees of the British Museum, a Report on the Union between England and Scotland, and the Appendix, containing the original papers upon which the Report is founded.

" When the question of Union between Great Britain and Ireland came under the consideration of his Majesty's ministers, the Duke of Portland employed Mr. Bruce, the Keeper of the State Papers, to collect in his office the precedents in the history of the Union between England and Scotland, which might illustrate the subject, for the purpose of bringing, in aid of the intended arrangement with Ireland, the wisdom and experience of former times; by which investigation it will appear, that many of the arguments which were brought against the Union with Scotland, and which time has completely refuted, are the same with those on which the opponents of an Union with Ireland at present rely.

" *Whitehall*, 15 *Feb.* 1799."

Memorandums of the Face of the Country in Switzerland.

> " ——— To short absence I could yield,
> For solitude sometimes is best society,
> And short retirement urges sweet return."
>
> *Paradise Lost.*

London: Printed by Cooper and Graham. M.DCC.XCIX. 12*mo.*   pp. 103.

By Georgiana, Duchess of Devonshire. A copy was in Mr. Hibbert's Catalogue, No. 2346.

Wallace, a Tragedy. By James Grahame.
1799.   8*vo.*

Not printed for sale; and it is said that not more than *six* copies were printed. A copy was in the catalogue of Constable's library, sold by Sotheby, January, 1817.

This tragedy is by the author of the " Sabbath," a poem. The same author wrote, but never completed, " Fragments of a Tour through the Universe," 8*vo.*, pp. 176. It is believed the only copy of this work is in the possession of Mr. Maidment, who gave the Editor this information. It was suppressed, on account of its democratic tendency. It severely satirized George III. It will be remembered that that period was one of great political excitement.

A CATALOGUE OF THE LIBRARY AT BAMBURGH CASTLE, IN THE COUNTY OF NORTHUMBERLAND; DIVIDED INTO THREE ALPHABETICAL PARTS.

I. English: II. Latin, and other ancient Languages: III. French, and other modern Languages. With a Table of References to each. Published by order of the Trustees of the Estates of the Right Hon. Nathanael, late Lord Crewe, and Lord Bishop of Durham.

Durham: Printed by L. Pennington. [1799.] 4*to*. 60 leaves, not paged.

This Catalogue comprises the most valuable part of the library of Dr. John Sharp, Archbishop of York, formed at the latter end of the seventeenth, and the commencement of the eighteenth century; among other books, it comprehends a very curious assemblage of tracts and pamphlets, chiefly historical and controversial, during a period of more than thirty years. On the death of the Archbishop, in 1714, the principal part of his library descended to his son, Dr. Thomas Sharp, Prebendary of Durham; and at his decease, in 1758, to his grandson, the late Dr. John Sharp; during which succession it was, from time to time, enriched by valuable additions: and at the death of the last possessor, the library came into the possession of the Trustees of this splendid establishment, where

> " —— Charity hath fixed her chosen seat,
>   And Pity, at the dark and stormy hour
>   Of midnight, when the moon is hid on high,
>   Keeps her lone watch upon the topmost tower,
> And turns her ear to each up-rising cry,
>   Blest if her aid some fainting wretch might save,
>   And snatch him, cold and sleepless, from the grave."
>   BOWLES.

M.DCCC.

 OLLECTIONS RELATING TO HENRY SMITH, ESQ., SOME TIME ALDERMAN OF LONDON: THE ESTATES BY HIM GIVEN TO CHARITABLE USES, AND THE TRUSTEES APPOINTED BY HIM.

London: Printed by John Nichols, Red-Lion-passage, Fleet-street. 1800.   *8vo.* pp. 182.

Edited by the late William Bray, Esq. A frontispiece, represents the monument of Smith in Wandsworth church, from a drawing by Carter; and at p. 16, his autograph and seal.

———

RETURN FROM THE SOCIETY OF LINCOLN'S INN TO THE COMMITTEE OF THE HOUSE OF COMMONS, APPOINTED TO INQUIRE INTO THE STATE OF THE PUBLIC RECORDS OF THE KINGDOM.

1800.

This return was drawn up by the late Lord Glenbervie, and not printed for sale. It was reprinted in the Record Commissioners' Reports.

The Beauties of the Press; with an Appendix, containing the Speech of Arthur O'Connor, on the Catholic Question, in the House of Commons in Ireland, on Monday, May 4, 1795: also his Letter to Lord Castlereagh. London: Printed 1800. pp. 602. Speech, pp. 48. 8vo.

This book was never published, but privately printed, and most of the copies were seized before they could be circulated.

———

Plays, by Benjamin Stillingfleet. [1800]. 8vo.

"Never either finished or published; the only copy Mr. Reed ever saw."*

"Mr. Stillingfleet, some time before his death, printed a few copies of the following dramas, for his particular friends:—Joseph; Moses and Zipporah; David and Bathsheba; Medea; all intended for Oratorios."†

The author was an eminent Naturalist and poet. His works were collected and published by Archdeacon Coxe, in 3 vols. 8vo. Lond. 1811. He died in 1771, and was buried in St. James's Church, Piccadilly, where a monument to his memory has been erected by his great nephew, the late Edward Hawke Locker, Esq. The date given to the plays is no doubt erroneous; most probably they were printed before his death.

———

* Reed's Catalogue, No. 8561.   † Biographia Dramatica.

ORIENTAL MANUSCRIPTS,
Purchased in Turkey.
London. 1800. 4*to*.

Formerly in the possession of the late Sir William Ouseley, brother of the late Sir Gore Ouseley, Bart., whom he accompanied on
his Mission to Persia; he published an account of his travels in the
East in three volumes quarto, and several other works.

The Manuscripts are now in the Bodleian library.

The collection of MSS. belonging to Sir Gore Ouseley, Bart., were
purchased by an East India civilian, who sent them to India—but
the name of the Presidency, to which they were sent, as well as of
the liberal donor, are unknown to the Editor.

———

SKETCH OF A GENEALOGICAL AND HISTORICAL AC-
COUNT OF THE FAMILY OF VAUX, VANS, OR DE VAL-
LIBUS;
Now represented in Scotland by Vans Agnew, of
Barnbarrow, &c. in the County of Wigton, Scotland.
Pembroke: Printed by W. E. Wilmot. 1800. pp.
36. 4*to*.

"A few copies of this genealogical tract were printed, to gratify
the curiosity of some relations. A copy is in the library of the
Royal Institution." *

———

* Moule, Bibliotheca Heraldica, p. 491.

The Father's Revenge; with other Poems.
By Frederick, Earl of Carlisle.
London: Printed by W. Bulmer and Co. 1800. 4*to*.
pp. 163.

This edition is embellished with six engravings, from drawings by
by Richard Westall, R.A. Johnson's critique on this tragedy, in a
letter to Mrs. Chapone, is printed in Boswell's Life, edited by Mr.
Croker, vol. v. p. 136. 8*vo*.

A North Countrie Garland.
Edinburgh. 1800. 12*mo*. pp. 57.

Thirty copies only were printed, for the gratification of a few of
the friends of the editor, James Maidment, Esq.

Compilation of various Authentic Evidences
and Historical Authorities, tending to Illus-
trate the Life and Character of Thomas Eger-
ton, Lord Ellesmere, Viscount Brackley, Lord
Chancellor of England, etc. etc. etc., and the
nature of the Times in which he was Lord
Keeper and Lord High Chancellor; also a
Sketch of the Lives of John Egerton, Bishop of
Durham, and of Francis Egerton, third Duke of
Bridgewater. By Francis Henry Egerton.
London: Printed by Henry Reynell. 1801. *folio*.
pp. 91.

The Life of the Duke of Bridgewater is not in this volume. A
new edition of this compilation, with the same title, was printed at
Paris by Didot. 1812.

Memoirs of the Administration of the Board of Admiralty, under the Presidency of the Earl of St. Vincent.

> ——— Diram qui contudit Hydram,
> Notaque fatali portenta labore subegit,
> Comperit INVIDIAM, supremo fine domari.

London: [Circa]. 8vo. pp. 134.

Archdeacon Wrangham possessed, it is believed, the only copy in existence of this work; the remainder of the impression having been destroyed. No mention of this work is to be found in the Lives of Lord St. Vincent, by Capt. Brenton, or Mr. Tucker. Dr. Parr, in speaking of him, says, "Lord St. Vincent was a great man, and the ablest naval officer which the country has produced. He was the master and instructor of Nelson, who was a great hero, but with less grasp of mind than Lord St. Vincent, and more relaxed in his morals than I could tolerate, though I allow great latitude to gentlemen of your profession. St. Vincent, I say, was the tutor of Nelson: he taught and formed him; mark me, he formed him; he made him a greater man than himself, and then did not envy him." —*Life by Tucker*, vol. ii. p. 253.

Report on the Arrangements which have been adopted in former periods, when France threatened Invasions of Britain or Ireland, to frustrate the Designs of the Enemy by Attacks on his Foreign Possessions or European Ports, by annoying his Coasts, and by destroying his Equipments.

[London. 1801]. 8vo. pp. 120.

"The accompanying Report, though printed for facilitating perusal, is neither published, nor intended for publication, and it is

therefore requested that it may not be left open to common inspection, HENRY DUNDAS."

INVESTIGATION INTO PRINCIPLES, ETC.,
IN ENGLISH AND ITALIAN.
London: [1801]. 4to. pp. 720.

This ponderous mystical volume was written by the late Mr.
George Baldwin, who was Consul-General in Egypt. Two-thirds of
it are written in Italian. It has the following colophon : "Ales-
sandria d'Egitto, nell parelello di 31 gradi al nord, fatti e finiti quest'
opere. Lodrino Eddio ! Della Stamperia di Gul. Bulmer & Co.,
Cleveland-row, St. James'."

" It may be necessary to put the reader in possession of some historical facts concerning the birth of this extraordinary volume. . .
. . The fact is, that it is born of the magnetic sleep. . . . . That
man should be affected by a spirit whose whole soul is spirit, whose
body is no body, any longer than he is moved by it, is not so far
from sense and nature ; but I could no more in the beginning
believe in all the wonderful effects attributed to magnetism than
the reader perhaps at this moment." The author, then in Alexandria, is visited by an itinerant Italian poet. " The poet was
pleased with the accounts of my exploits. . . . . Excepting a little
treatise of my own upon the soul and its prerogatives, the substance
of the whole volume was written by him."—See pp. 88-93.

THE FESTIVAL OF THE ROSE, WITH OTHER POEMS.
BY MRS. MONTOLIEU.
London: Printed by T. Bensley, Bolt-court, Fleet-
street. 1802. 4to. pp. 77.

The Festival of the Rose was instituted under the reigns of Chil-
deric and Clovis, in the fifth century, at the village of Salency in

Picardy, by the Lord of the Manor, and has ever since continued. The village maid who bore the fairest reputation, was rewarded by a crown or garland of roses, and she was certain of being sought in marriage in the course of the year.

FUGITIVE PIECES. BY MRS. DODSWORTH. Canterbury: Printed by Simmons and Kirkby. 1802. 8vo. pp. 107.

CATALOGUE OF THE BOOKS, BOTH MANUSCRIPT AND PRINTED, WHICH ARE PRESERVED IN THE LIBRARY OF CHRIST CHURCH, CANTERBURY.

1802. 8vo.

One hundred and sixty copies of this Catalogue, compiled by the late Rev. H. J. Todd, were printed for the use of public libraries, but it was never intended for sale.

" Of this library, a Catalogue, as it was called, appeared in 1743; but it is merely an alphabetical list of printed books only, without any statements of the place or year in which the books are printed, and without any guide to the shelves on which they had been placed. The present Catalogue, by its two-fold arrangement, is intended to inform the reader of most particulars relating to the books, to point out to him their situation in the library, and at the same time to preserve them in their respective classes.

" The Dean and Chapter, desirous to promote the utility of their library, lately caused it to be carefully examined, as well as considerably enlarged; and, in consequence of the examination, several Manuscripts were found concealed under a heap of rubbish in a private closet. These Manuscripts, having been investigated by some of the members of the Church, are now deposited (as the subjects of them required) partly in the chapter-room, and partly in the library. To the presses in the latter an addition is thus made of twelve volumes, since the publication of a Catalogue of the Manuscripts in this library, by a member of the Church, in 1793. Other manuscripts also, since that period, have been presented to the Dean and Chapter.

"This library, it may be observed, is rich in manuscript materials relating to the civil and ecclesiastical history of the country, and to Saxon literature in general; as the articles under Records, Registers, and Somner, will evince."*—*Extract from the Preface.*

In the answer returned to the Commissioners of Public Records, Nov. 28, 1832, it was said, that no additions had been made, except by bringing together and arranging in chronological order some of the more interesting of a large heap of letters, chiefly upon the business of the Chapter since the Reformation; and it is added, that it is not believed there is anything in the collection likely to be of the least public interest.

The following remarks, upon the use to which Cathedral libraries should be made subservient, together with the anecdote as to the neglect into which one has fallen, justify their insertion here:—

"There are some cases in which cathedral libraries are real libraries and of use. The library of Durham is said to be worthy of the place. But we cannot resist giving publicity to what has reached us as having happened in one of the richest and best cared for of the cathedrals within the past year, a cathedral, too, in which the library is not allowed to be useless. A minor canon is said to have observed that the jackdaws flying over his garden, at times carried in their beaks what seemed like rolls of paper. On one occasion, he was fortunate enough to have one of these rolls dropped at his feet. He took it up, and was surprised, when, on examination, it proved to be an ancient Anglo-Saxon MS. Enquiry was made as to the favourite haunts of the jackdaws; and it was found that they had obtained undisputed possession of a muniment room, in which

---

* Introductory remarks to the catalogue, transcribed from the useful work, " Notes on the Cathedral Libraries of England. By Beriah Botfield." *8vo.* 1849.

sundry old MSS. were preserved, and had got into the expensive habit of using these MSS. to line their nests. The Greek Monks mentioned by Mr. Curzon* were wiser than the canons of this cathedral, for they employed their MSS. for their own convenience, and did not give them to their jackdaws, but used them instead of hassocks to defend their feet and knees from the damp stones."†

BYBLIS; A TRAGEDY.

By WILLIAM DRUMMOND, ESQ.

His Majesty's Envoy Extraordinary and Minister Plenipotentiary at the Court of Naples, and author of a Translation of the Satires of Persius.

London: Printed by W. Bulmer and Co., Clevelandrow, St. James's. 1802. *royal 8vo.* pp. 67.

It is not the intention of the author to publish this Tragedy, or to have it represented, at least for the present. To the reader into whose hands the printed copy may chance to fall, *Hæc ego non multis sed tibi satis magnum, alter alteri theatri sumus.*

The press was corrected by the late Honourable Henry Grey Bennet.

PEDIGREES OF THE FAMILIES OF MILDMAY, OF MOULS-HAM HALL, ESSEX, AND ST. JOHN, OF FARLEY, HAMPSHIRE.

London. 1803. *4to.*

A copy of this book, with two views of Moulsham Hall inserted, was in Mr. Dent's Catalogue, Part II. No. 738.

---

* Tour in the Levant.　　† Edinburgh Review, Jan. 1853, p. 165.

THE PASSAGE OF THE SAINT GOTHARD.
BY GEORGIANA DUCHESS OF DEVONSHIRE,
With an Italian translation, by G. Polidori.
London: Printed by W. Bulmer and Co., Cleveland-
row, St. James's, for Gameau and Co.   1803.   *folio.*
pp. 41.

"Only fifty copies of this brilliant volume were printed; to a few
of which, it is said, Lady Diana Beauclerc lent the aid of her ornamental pencil in some beautiful drawings of the wild and romantic
scenery in the neighbourhood of Mount St. Gothard."*

———

TRIFLES IN VERSE.   (BY HENRY LORD LYTTLETON.)
London: by T. Bensley, Bolt Court.   1803.   *roy. 8vo.*
pp. 52.

A copy in Heber, Pt. I. 6905.

———

AN ACCOUNT OF THE STATUES, BUSTS, BASS-RE-
LIEFS, CINERARY URNS, AND OTHER ANCIENT MAR-
BLES AND PAINTINGS, AT INCE, COLLECTED BY H.
B[LUNDELL].
Liverpool: Printed by J. M'Creery.   1803.   *4to.* pp.
331; with a frontispiece, and six other plates.

---

* Dibdin, Bibliomania, p. 713.

Donations of Peter Blundell, Founder, and other Benefactors to the Free Grammar School at Tiverton,

Originally completed by the late Benjamin Incledon, Esq., and published at his own expense, for the use of the Foundation. Exeter, 1792. Now ordered by the Feoffees to be reprinted, with Notes and Additions, to the present time, 29 June, 1802.

Exeter. 1804. *8vo.*

The school came under the review of the Commissioners for inquiring concerning Charities, and an account of Mr. Blundell's munificent donations will be found in their Report.*

Catalogue Raisonné of the Principal Paintings, Sculptures, Drawings, etc., etc., at Appuldurcombe House, the Seat of the Right Hon. Sir Richard Worsley, Bart. taken June 1, 1804.

London: Printed by William Bulmer and Co., Cleveland-row, St. James's. *folio.* pp. 55; with a view of the House drawn by Davis, and engraved by Fittler.

Twenty-five copies only are said to have been printed. The best pictures have been removed; some to the Earl of Yarborough's house in London, the others to Brocklesby, Lincolnshire. The gems are in London.

---

* Vol. iv.

OPINIONS DELIVERED BY THE EARL OF ESSEX, LORD BURLEIGH, LORD WILLOUGHBY, LORD BURROUGH, LORD NORTH, SIR WILLIAM KNOLLYS, SIR WALTER RALEIGH, AND SIR GEORGE CAREW, ON THE ALARM OF AN INVASION FROM SPAIN, IN THE YEAR 1596, AND THE MEASURES PROPER TO BE TAKEN ON THAT OCCASION.

London: Printed in September 1804, at the Press of the Secretary of State Office. 1804. *8vo.*

Not published nor sold.

———

ACCOUNT OF THE EXTRAORDINARY ESCAPE OF JAMES STUART, ESQ. (COMMONLY CALLED ATHENIAN STUART), FROM BEING PUT TO DEATH BY SOME TURKS, IN WHOSE COMPANY HE HAPPENED TO BE TRAVELLING.

BY ANDREW CALDWELL.

London. 1804. *folio.*

Lowndes states that this was privately printed; it is not so-called in the "Bibliotheca Britannica."

———

POEMS, BY MICHAEL WODHULL, ESQ.
A revised edition.

"Multa dies et multa litura coercuit."—*Horace.*
" Voce tamen noscar, vocem mihi fata relinquunt."—*Ovid.*

London: Printed by Nichols and Son, Red Lion Passage, Fleet-street. 1804. *8vo.* pp. 215.

Portrait of the author drawn by Gardiner, and eight vignettes.

JOURNAL OF A VERY YOUNG LADY'S TOUR FROM CANONBURY TO ALDBOROUGH, THROUGH CHELMSFORD, SUDBURY, AND IPSWICH, AND BACK THROUGH HARWICH, COLCHESTER, ETC., SEPT. 13-21, 1804. WRITTEN HASTILY ON THE ROAD, AS CIRCUMSTANCES AROSE.

Of this little journal not more than 24 copies are printed for use, to save the trouble of transcribing.

London: Printed by Nichols and Son, Red Lion Passage, Fleet Street. 1804. *8vo.* pp. 16.

The Journal is in verse; the author, Anne Susanna Nichols; grand-daughter, it is believed, to John Nichols, whose numerous works on topography, and above all his useful literary anecdotes, are too well known, and esteemed, to require any praise.

MUSCOLOGIÆ HIBERNICÆ SPICILEGIUM.

Auctore Dawson Turner, A.M. Soc. Reg. Art. et Linn.

Yarmouthæ: Typis E. Black, sumptibus auctoris. 1804. *crown 8vo.* pp. 200. With sixteen plates coloured.

Two hundred and fifty copies were printed. Mr. Turner was an ardent cultivator of botany in his younger days, and his fine work on the "Fuci," is a monument of his industry in that branch of natural history. He has published other works on the same subject.

Psyche, or the Legend of Love.

"Castos docet et pios amores."—*Martial.*

London: Printed by C. Whittingham. 1805. 12*mo.* pp. 214.

The first edition of an elegant poem, by the late Mrs. Tighe; afterwards reprinted in 4*to.* and 8*vo.* for sale.

In the "Quarterly Review," May, 1810, is a review of the published edition of Mrs. Tighe's poem; the reviewer closes his strictures with an interesting advertisement from the editor :—"The concluding poem of this collection was the last ever composed by the author, who expired at the place (Woodstock) where it was written, after six years of protracted malady, on the 24th of March, 1810, in the thirty-seventh year of her age. Her fears of death were perfectly removed before she quitted this scene of trial and suffering; and her spirit departed to a better state of existence, confiding with heavenly joy in the acceptance and love of her Redeemer."

———

Notes upon some of the obscure Passages in Shakespeare's Plays;

With Remarks upon the Explanations and Amendments of the Commentators in the Editions of 1785, 1790, 1793.

By the late Right Hon. John Lord Chedworth.

London: Printed by W. Bulmer and Co. 1805. 8*vo.* pp. 375.

Lord Chedworth died in 1804. A service, rendered him professionally by Mr. Penrice, led to a friendship which induced him to leave that gentleman his large property. An attempt was made, on the plea of insanity, to set the will aside : this did not succeed ; Mr·

Penrice printed these notes with the view of affording additional proof of Lord Chedworth's sanity. An account of the noble author, and the proceedings relative to his will, may be found in the Gentleman's Magazine, vols. lxxiv. lxxvi.

A SUPPLEMENT TO NOTES ON THE ANCIENT METHOD OF TREATING THE FEVER OF ANDALUSIA, NOW CALLED THE YELLOW FEVER; ETC. ETC.
(This Treatise is not intended for publication.)
London; Printed by S. Gosnell. 1805. 4*to*. pp. 40; with a folding plate.

ANDALUSIA: OR, NOTES, TENDING TO SHEW THAT THE YELLOW FEVER OF THE WEST INDIES, AND OF ANDALUSIA IN SPAIN, WAS A DISEASE WELL KNOWN TO THE ANCIENTS, ETC. ETC.
BY ROBERT DEVERELL, ESQ. M.P.
January, 1805. (This Treatise is not intended for publication.)
London: Printed by S. Gosnell, Little Queen-street, Holborn. 4*to*. pp. 155; and three plates.

REMINISCENSES,
Written in 1778, for the Amusement of Miss Mary and Miss Agnes B——y.
London: Richard Taylor. 1805.   *folio.*

Twenty-five copies of this entertaining work by Horace Walpole, were printed in this size, at the expense of Lord Frederick Camp-

bell.   Mr. Grenville had a copy copiously illustrated; for which
purpose its size renders it very suitable.

These reminiscences were written for the amusement of the two
ladies whom Horace Walpole was fond of calling his two wives.   The
elder Miss Berry died at her residence in May Fair, in November,
1852, at the great age of ninety, having survived her younger sister
about eighteen months.   Their residence in Curzon Street, was for
many years the reso of the most eminent literary men of the
country, especially in h e higher ranks of society.

" In these Miscellanies (for by that name they should have been
called) are to be found many keen and correct remarks on society,
and on men and manners, with here and there a dash of old reading,
and every now and then a valuable observation or two on the
fashion, and minute details of the age in which Walpole lived."—
Gents. Mag. Jan. 1853, p. 96.

———

JOURNAL OF THREE YEARS' TRAVEL THROUGH DIF-
FERENT PARTS OF GREAT BRITAIN, IN 1795, 1796, 1797.

——— Non ut me miretur turba laboro,
Contentus paucis lectoribus.

London: Printed by J. Brettell, Marshall Street,
Golden Square.   1805.   *roy. 8vo.* pp. 392.   Preface
one leaf.

BY THE DUKE OF RUTLAND.

The Duke also printed for private circulation, a Northern Tour,
in 1810, *roy. 8vo.*   A Southern Tour, in 1810, *roy. 8vo.*

EXTRACTS FROM THE DIARY AND LETTERS OF
MRS. MARY COBB.
London: Printed by C. and R. Baldwin, New Bridge-
street. 1805. 8*vo.*

Engraved coat of arms, with F. E. & M. Cobb, beneath, as a frontispiece. Memoirs xi pages. Extracts from the Diary (which commences August 11, 1791) 324 pages.

Mrs. Cobb was the wife of Francis Cobb, born at St. Peter's, in
the Isle of Thanet, and died at the same place, September 4th, 1802.

Two LETTERS ADDRESSED TO THE LATE RIGHT HON.
WILLIAM PITT, ON THE SUBJECT OF THE ANCIENT
ARIES, OR BATTERING RAM.
BY ROBERT DEVERELL, ESQ., M.P.
(These Letters are not intended for publication.)
London: Printed by S. Gosnell, Little Queen-street,
Holborn. 1805. 4*to.* pp. 40.

CATALOGUE OF THE LIBRARY OF THE WRITERS TO
HIS MAJESTY'S SIGNET.
Edinburgh: Printed at the University Press, for the
Society. 1805. 4*to.* pp. 761; Index, A—CC.

A classed catalogue, with an index of authors and subjects. A
second part was published in 1820; and a third part has since been
published. The first part was compiled by George Sandy, Esq., and
the other portions by Professor Napier.

"One of the best-arranged catalogues, upon De Bure's system,
that has ever been printed. The library of the Writers to the

M

Signet was begun in 1778 ; and now comprises a considerable number of valuable works on history, the belles lettres, and the more
generally cultivated branches of science, beside a very respectable
collection of books of professional utility. The titles of works are
given at length with great correctness, and analyses are inserted of
all the larger series. My copy possesses two supplements, without
which the catalogue is incomplete."—*Horne, Introduction to Bibliography,* vol. ii. p. 636.

Since this was written, there have appeared four alphabetical
catalogues printed in the years 1820, 1826, and 1833, prepared by
Professor Napier, and a separate index of subjects—all in 4*to.*

The present librarian is David Laing, Esq., so well known for his
acquaintance with early Scottish literature, and to whom the editor
of this work is under great obligations for much valuable information.

RHYMES.

"Some rhyme a neebor's name to lash,
Some rhyme (vain thought) for needfu' cash ;
Some rhyme to court the countra clash,
        An' raise a din ;
For me, an aim I never fash ;
        I rhyme for fun."—*Burns.*

London. 1805. 12*mo.* pp. 79.

By the late Octavius Gilchrist, Esq., of Stamford ; and edited,
according to a note in Mr. Haslewood's copy, by Mr. Du Bois. Mr.
Gilchrist died June 30th, 1823. He edited Bishop Corbet's Poems,
and was well read in early English dramatic poetry. Gifford acknowledges his obligations to him, in his valuable edition of the
works of Ben Jonson.

A DISQUISITION UPON ETRUSCAN VASES:
Containing their probable connexion with the Shews
at Eleusis, and the Chinese Feast of the Lanterns; with
Explanations of a few of the principal Allegories de-
picted on them. London: Printed by William Bulmer and Co., for T.
Becket, Pall-Mall. 1806. *Impl. 4to.* pp. 99.

This work, of which the editor believes one hundred copies only
were printed, is well known to be the production of the late James
Christie, Esq., whose learning, combined with the most unassuming
manners, is so generally acknowledged. In some copies, an engraving of the vase in the possession of the late Mr. Edwards, the
bookseller, will occasionally be found. The rarity of the work
induced the author to print, in 1825, a new edition for sale.

HISTORY OF LACOCK ABBEY, OR LOCUS BEATÆ
MARIÆ; FROM DUGDALE, STEVENS, ETC.
With Additions, upon the present state of the Abbey.
Lacock. By the Rev. G. Witham. 1806. *4to.* pp. 53.

This was privately printed by the author, at his own printing
press in the Abbey; he was a Roman Catholic clergyman, and chaplain to Lady Shrewsbury, who then occupied the Abbey; which is
the property, and now the residence of Henry Fox Talbot, Esq., the
ingenious discoverer of the new art of drawing which now bears
his name.

"I saw some time ago, at Mr. Talbot's at Laycock, the original
Magna Charta of Henry the IIId., which I am told is the only perfect one in England; that in the Cotton Library having been very
much damaged by fire."*

---

* Dr. Evetts to Dr. Ducarel; Nichols' Illustrations, vol. iii. p. 587.

A view of the Abbey, which is a very curious building, will be found in Buck's Views: a more modern view will be found in Neale's collection of Gentlemen's Seats.

———

COLLECTANEA;

Or, Collections, consisting of Miscellanies inserted in the European and Monthly Magazines. With an Appendix, containing some Hymns by the same Author.

BY THOMAS TAYLOR.

London.   1806.   8vo.

Fifty copies privately printed at the expense of Mr. Meredith.

———

THE PEDIGREE OF THE RIGHT HONOURABLE THOMAS ANSON, VISCOUNT ANSON OF SHUGBOROUGH AND ORGREAVE, IN THE COUNTY OF STAFFORD, AND BARON SOBERTON OF SOBERTON, IN THE COUNTY OF SOUTHAMPTON, GREAT-NEPHEW OF GEORGE, LATE LORD ANSON AND BARON OF SOBERTON AFORESAID, SOMETIME VICE ADMIRAL OF GREAT BRITAIN, AND COMMANDER IN CHIEF OF HIS MAJESTY'S FLEET, FIRST LORD OF THE ADMIRALTY, AND A PRIVY COUNCILLOR;

Shewing the Descent from Richard de Vernon, Baron of Shipbrooke, and Gilbert Venables, Baron of Kinderton, who both flourished in the reign of William the Conqueror, and were the Progenitors of the several Branches of these Knightly and respectable Families, distinguished in the British Annals for their Loyalty, Bravery, and Virtue; and at length represented by

George Venables Vernon, late Lord Vernon, and Baron of Kinderton, the maternal grandfather of the said Thomas, Viscount Anson; also, through the noble families of Howard, Mowbray, and Segrave, from the Royal House of Plantagenet. And last, from the noble Families of Wentworth, Neville, Ferrers, and many of the most ancient and Illustrious Houses of Great Britain.

Engraved by H. Mutlow, Russell-court, London. 1806. *folio;* three tables, folded.

This pedigree was extracted from the records in the College of Arms. It is not mentioned in Mr. Moule's useful work, Bibliotheca Heraldica.

ON THE ARCHITECTURE OF WALES.
BY SIR RICHARD COLT HOARE, BART.
[London.] 1806. *4to.*

This is a portion of the edition of Giraldus Cambrensis, of which twenty copies were printed, for private distribution.

CATALOGUE OF THE LATE PESARO LIBRARY AT VENICE, NOW FORMING PART OF THE HAFOD LIBRARY. 1806. *8vo.* pp. 155.

Compiled, it is stated, by the late Mr. Johnes, who died in 1816, the purchaser of the collection, which included a fine collection of Aldines. The estate, with the library, was purchased by the fourth Duke of Newcastle; who subsequently parted with it, but the library is now at Clumber, Notts.

Dibdin,* in reference to this collection, says, "These Alduses were purchased of Signor Pesaro of ——; and the room is called the Pesaro Collection. I instigated Mr. Johnes once to part with them: 'As to the *Alduses*' (observed he in reply), 'I must be greatly tempted before I part with them, and you shall see them first.' I did see them; and found them to be, generally speaking, 'no great things.' That collection, however, contains some very desirable copies of early printed books, and among them the *first Lascaris,* 'white as the driven snow.' The beautiful MS. of *Petrarch*, noticed in the first day of this *Decameron* (vol. i. p. cxxxii), is also in this collection."

Mr. Johnes' house was destroyed by fire. Moore, in his Diary,† says, "Johnes of Hafod, delighted when he heard his magnificent house was burnt down, because the sum for which he insured it, 30,000*l.*, would be forthcoming, and he could begin to spend again."

<hr/>

CASSANDRA:

Translated from the original Greek of Lycophron, and illustrated with Notes,

BY VISCOUNT ROYSTON.

Cambridge: Printed by R. Watts. 1806. *Royal 4to.* pp. 106.

"Lord Royston was a very ingenious and learned young nobleman; he was educated, as was his noble and learned father, at Harrow School. He was unfortunately drowned in one of the Northern seas."‡

This translation is reprinted in the Classical Journal, vol. xxv.

<hr/>

* Bibliographical Decameron, vol. iii. p. 359.
† Vol. iv. p. 133.
‡ Bibliotheca Parriana, p. 226.

DESCRIPTION OF NUNEHAM COURTENEY, IN THE COUNTY OF OXFORD [THE SEAT OF THE EARL OF HARCOURT].

12*mo*. 1806. pp. 68.

Originally printed in 1783, and again in 1797.

Now the seat of George Vernon Harcourt, Esq., one of the representatives in Parliament for the county.

CATALOGUE OF [SIR FREDERICK EDEN'S LIBRARY].
1806. 8*vo*. pp. 277.

This is a well-arranged catalogue, compiled by the owner himself; it contains a copious collection of works on political economy. He was the author of a History of the Poor, 3 vols. 4*to*. 1797, and other works.

NEW VIEW OF THE CLASSICS AND ANCIENT ARTS, TENDING TO SHOW THEIR INVARIABLE CONNEXION WITH THE SCIENCES. BY ROBERT DEVERELL, ESQ., M.P. May 19, 1806.

[This Treatise is not intended for publication.]

London: Printed by S. Gosnell, Little Queen-street, Holborn. 4*to*. pp. 160.

THE CHANCELLORS, FROM THE NORMAN CONQUEST TO THE PRESENT YEAR, 1806.

London: Printed by T. Bentley, Bolt-court, Fleet-street. 1806. 4*to*. pp. 22.

LINES, WRITTEN ON SEVERAL OCCASIONS
BY THE LATE HON. CHARLOTTE PENELOPE MONCKTON.

Early, bright, transient, chaste as morning dew,
She sparkled, was exhaled, and went to heaven.—*Young*.

1806.   *oblong* 12*mo*.

This lady was the third daughter of Robert, fourth Viscount
Galway, and died April 26th, 1806.

———

CATALOGUE OF PRINTED BOOKS
IN THE LIBRARY OF THE INNER TEMPLE,
ALPHABETICALLY ARRANGED;
To which is prefixed the Manuscripts therein.

Printed by W. P. Norris, Little Moorgate, London.
1806.   8*vo*.

This was compiled by the brother of the printer; but it was
found to be so imperfect, that the undermentioned Catalogue was
printed in the same year, by order of the Society.

———

CATALOGUE OF THE PRINTED BOOKS AND MANUSCRIPTS
IN THE LIBRARY OF THE INNER TEMPLE;
ALPHABETICALLY ARRANGED.

London: Printed by C. and W. Galabin.   1806.   8*vo*.
pp. 126.

Poems, by Mrs. Cassan, Widow of Stephen Cassan, Esq. Barrister-at-Law, late of Bengal. London: Printed by G. Sidney, Northumberland-street, Strand. 1806. 4*to.* pp. 96.

———

Catalogue of Maps belonging to his Royal Highness the Duke of York, K.G. London: Printed by W. Bulmer and Co., Cleveland-row, St. James's. 1806. 8*vo.* pp. 81.

The Duke of York's library was sold by auction by Sotheby in 1827: but it did not include the maps.

———

Papers relating to the two Baronies of Stafford, claimed by Sir William Jerningham, Baronet, on the death of his Cousin, Lady Anastasia Stafford Howard, 27 April, 1807. [Printed for private use, August, 1807.] 4*to.* pp. 148.

These papers were most probably printed for the use of the House of Lords, at the time when the peerage was claimed; and though it is the usual plan, and they may be in some degree considered *private,* they are too numerous for insertion in this volume; as already stated, they would require a volume to themselves; the claim to the Barony of Stafford was allowed by the House of Lords in 1825.

JOURNEY INTO ENGLAND, BY PAUL HENTZNER,
IN THE YEAR M.D.XCVIII.

Printed at Strawberry Hill, 1757 : Reprinted at the
private press of T. E. Williams, Reading. 1807. *4to.*

"The translation is from the pen of R. Bentley, once the friend
and favourite of Horace Walpole. Mr. Williams reprinted only fifty
copies of Bentley's translation of the part relative to England." *

POEMS, BY FREDERICK, EARL OF CARLISLE,
KNIGHT OF THE GARTER, ETC.

A new Edition, with Addition.

London : Printed by W. Bulmer and Co., Cleveland-
row. 1807. *8vo.* pp. 149.

CATALOGUE OF THE PORTRAITS AND
PICTURES BELONGING TO JAMES, EARL OF FIFE.

1807. *4to.* pp. 94.

THE FILIAL TRIBUTE.

London : Printed by William Bulmer and Co. 1807.
12mo. pp. 43.

By the late Judge Hardinge; printed as *keepsakes* to his friends.

----

* Retrospective Review, vol. i. p. 20.

A Vindication of the Right of the
Universities to a Copy of every New Publication.
By Edward Christian, Esq., Chief Justice
of the Isle of Ely.
Cambridge: Printed at the University Press, by R.
Watts. 1807. 8vo. pp. 36.

A vindication of a right, which it would be to the credit of the
national character speedily to abolish. The tax in support of these
institutions should at least be general, and not imposed on a class,
whose remuneration for their labours is, for the most part, very
precarious. On works of an expensive nature in their production,
such as books on natural history, antiquities, &c., and of which the
number printed is very limited, the tax is most oppressive.

Richardi Bentleii et aliorum Virorum Epis-
tolæ partim mutuæ, accedit Richardi Dawesii ad
Ioannem Taylorum Epistola singularis.
Londini: Typis Bulmerianis. 1807. 4to.

Printed at the expense of the late Dr. Burney: one hundred and
fifty copies on royal 4to., for distribution among his friends, and fifty
on a smaller size, for public libraries.

Dr. Burney died Dec. 28th, 1818; the library of this eminent
scholar was purchased for 13,500l., and deposited in the British
Museum.

Descriptive Catalogue of the Series of Pictures, formed on Subjects selected from the
History of England,

Painted by British Artists for Alexander Davison,
Esq., 1806: in the order in which they are arranged, at
his House in St. James'-square, London.

London: Printed by W. Bulmer and Co., Cleveland-
row, St. James's. 1807. 4to. pp. 49.

In this catalogue are printed the letters from the different artists
who painted the pictures; viz. from West, who selected as his subject, Sir Philip Sidney rejecting the Water — Smirke, Elizabeth
in the Sanctuary receiving the message from the Protector—
Wilkie, Alfred in the Neatherd's Cottage—Northcote, The Earl
of Westmoreland presenting Princess Margaret to James IV.—
W. Devis, Conspiracy of Babington—Tresham, Warren, Earl of
Surrey—Westall, Mary after the battle of Langside—Copley,
Offering of the Crown to Lady Jane Grey.

The pictures were sold by auction by Stanley.

Memoir of the Life of John Sudbury, D.D.,
Dean of Durham.

"Behold I have not laboured for myself only, but for
all that seek wisdom."—*Ecclûs.* xxiv. 34.

[Printed but not published, in *folio.* Wakefield. 1808.]

Reprinted in the works of Dr. Zouch,* edited by the late Rev.
Archdeacon Wrangham. Dr. Zouch assisted in drawing up the Life
and Character of John, Lord Viscount Lonsdale, prefixed to the
Memoir of the Reign of James II. by that nobleman.

---

* Works of Dr. Zouch. 2 vols. 8vo. York, 1820.

Memoir of the Reign of James II. By John, Lord Viscount Lonsdale.

York: Printed by T. Wilson and R. Spence, High Ousegate. 1808. 4*to.* pp. 64.

The author of this work was Sir John Lowther, Bart., first Viscount Lonsdale: the volume was printed from a MS. of that nobleman, by the Earl of Lonsdale. A memoir of his life taken from the history is printed in Sir Egerton Brydges' edition of Collins's peerage. Of the work itself, Sir Egerton says,—"It is very ably and perspicuously written, and throws some curious light on that portentous era." Mr. Heywood,* in quoting this Memoir, says of the author,—"He was united with the Whigs, and deservedly stood high in their confidence." Mr. Macaulay frequently refers to it, in his History of James II.

An Account of the Incidents from which the Title, and part of the Story of Shakespeare's Tempest were derived, and its true State ascertained. By Edmund Malone.

London: Printed by C. and R. Baldwin, New Bridgestreet. 1808. 8*vo.* pp. 36.

In a copy belonging to the late Mr. Planta, was this note:—"Not published; only eighty copies having been printed. It is requested that this pamphlet may not be inadvertently put into the hands of any person who may be likely to publish any part of it."

This essay has been reprinted at the end of the fifteenth volume of Shakespeare, edited by Mr. Boswell, who states that a limited number of copies were printed for distribution among his friends. "One of them, under circumstances which were by no means honourable to its possessor, who has since made himself too well

----

* Vindication of Fox's Historical Work, 4to. p. 236.

known by a posthumous publication full of falsehood and malig-
nity, but whom the grave shall shelter from further reproach, was
sold at an auction, and purchased by Mr. George Chalmers, who lost
no time in putting together the arguments by which he thought
Mr. Malone's theory might be controverted."

> " When modest worth by idle boasting 's shewn,
>   Then, not till then, will I approve Malone :
>   See on the critic, in his pride of place,
>   Laborious Chalmers drops his leaden mace."
>
> *Pursuits of Literature*, pt. 2.

Memoirs of Thomas Brand Hollis, Esq. F.R.S. and S.A.

" Amicitiæ sacrum."

London : Printed by T. Gillet. 1808. 4*to*. pp. 60.
Portrait, and eight plates.

" These Memoirs are not intended to be committed to the ordinary forms of publication. The circle of private friends will accept
with kindness what is presented to them with unmixed good will."

The following extract, though not relating to this work, refers to
the same writer.

" If ever a man of letters lived in a state of energy and excitement which might raise him above the atmosphere of social love, it
was assuredly the enthusiast, Thomas Hollis, who, solely devoted to
literature and to republicanism, was occupied in furnishing Europe
and America with editions of his favourite authors. He would not
marry, lest marriage should interrupt the labours of his Platonic
politics. But his extraordinary Memoirs, while they show an intrepid mind in a robust frame, bear witness to the self-tormentor,
who had trodden down the natural bonds of domestic life." *

---

* D'Israeli, on the Literary Character, p. 256.

CARMINA HOMERICA ILIAS ET ODYSSEI,
A rapsodorum interpolationibus repurgata, et in pristinam formam, quatenus cognosci licuit, tam e veterum monumentorum fide et auctoritate, quam ex antiqui sermonis indole ac ratione, redacta ; cum notis ac prolegomenis, quibus de eorum origine, auctore, et ætate ; itemque de priscæ linguæ progressu, et precoci maturitate, diligenter inquiritur, opera et studio Richardi Payne Knight.
Londini : Ex officina Gul. Bulmer et Soc. 1808. 8*vo.* pp. 201.

"Les *Carmina Homerica Repurgata* de M. Knight n'ont été tirés qu'à cinquante exemplaires ; mais l'ouvrage a reparu avec de nombreuses additions dans les nos. 14, 15, et 16 du *Classical Journal ;* et ensuite à Leipz. 1816, en 1 vol. en 8vo. Dans l'édit. de 1820, qu' accompagne le texte d'Homère, les prolègomènes occupent 108 pp. suivis d'un f pour les *emendanda et corrigenda.* Le texte Grec a 514 pp. et les notes ont 105 pp. M. Knight prétend avoir rétabli, non seulement le véritable texte du poète, mais jusqu'à l'orthographe primitive des mots ; du reste, il rejette absolument le système de M. Wolf. Le sien n'a pas eu l'approbation des savants." *

Mr. Knight published several other learned works, and was one of the principal witnesses examined by the Committee of the House of Commons on the purchase of the Elgin Marbles ; his evidence was severely handled in the "Quarterly Review." He came also under the lash of the author of the "Pursuits of Literature." A notice, said to be "superficial," of the Homer, in the "Quarterly Review," April, 1822, is attributed to Ugo Foscolo. Mr. Knight died in June, 1824.

---

* Brunet, Manuel du Libraire.

SPECIMEN BIBLIOTHECÆ BRITANNICÆ.
Specimen of a digested Catalogue of Rare, Curious,
and Useful Books in the English Language, or apper-
taining to British Literature and Antiquities.
BY THE REV. T. F. DIBDIN, F.S.A. (late of St.
John's College, Oxford).
London: Printed by William Savage, Bedford-bury,
1808. 8*vo*. pp. 77.

On the half title,—"Not published, only *forty* copies printed:"
large paper, of which there are only *eight* copies, with a plate: this
plate only in the large-paper copies. A copy on large paper. Heber
Cat. pt. v. 1360.

A BRIEF ACCOUNT OF THREE FAVOURITE
COUNTRY RESIDENCES.
TO WHICH IS ADDED DEATH, A POETICAL ESSAY,
First printed at Cambridge, in the year 1759.
8*vo*.   pp. 86.

Compiled by Beilby Porteus, Bishop of London.

"Porteus, the *royal* prelate, firm to truth."

In the copy in the Royal Library in the British Museum is the
following note in the handwriting of the Bishop:—"It is my earnest desire that this little volume may never be made public, nor
reprinted. B. LONDON. Aug. 15, 1808."
The following plates are in this work, viz.:—

     Parsonage at Hunton, near Maidstone.
     Gateway to the old Court at Fulham Palace.
     South view of a Cottage at Sundridge.
     View towards the south, from a Cottage at Sundridge.
     View from the east end of Sundridge Church-yard.

"Having spent," says the Bishop, in the preface, "the happiest
period of my life at Hunton, Fulham, and Sundridge, which were

(at different times) my three country mansions, I am desirous to leave behind me a little history of each, as a grateful return for the delight they afforded me for so many years ; and with a view of giving an half-hour's amusement to a few intimate friends and relations, who can alone take any interest in these private details, and for whose use alone, therefore, I shall print a *few* copies of this little volume." The bishop died May, 1809, and was buried in the chapel of Sundridge, Kent.

A NARRATIVE OF THE LAST ILLNESS AND DEATH OF RICHARD PORSON, A.M., PROFESSOR OF GREEK IN THE UNIVERSITY OF CAMBRIDGE, FORMERLY FELLOW OF TRINITY COLLEGE, AND PRINCIPAL LIBRARIAN OF THE LONDON INSTITUTION ; WITH A FAC-SIMILE OF AN ANCIENT GREEK INSCRIPTION, WHICH WAS THE CHIEF SUBJECT OF HIS LAST LITERARY CONVERSATION. London : Printed for the Author, by Richard Edwards. 1808. 8vo. pp. 32; with a large plate of the Greek Inscription.

This Narrative was written by the late Dr. Adam Clarke.

A TOPOGRAPHICAL ACCOUNT OF THE PARISH OF SCAMPTON, IN THE COUNTY OF LINCOLN, AND OF THE ROMAN ANTIQUITIES LATELY DISCOVERED THERE ; TOGETHER WITH ANECDOTES OF THE FAMILY OF BOLLE. BY THE REV. CAYLEY ILLINGWORTH, M.A., F.S.A., ARCHDEACON OF STOW, AND RECTOR OF SCAMPTON AND EPWORTH, IN THE COUNTY OF LINCOLN. 1808. 4to.

" A few impressions only have been printed, to be distributed amongst the author's literary friends: the compiler being actuated

by no other motive than that of forwarding the research of antiquities, and of contributing his mite towards an History of his
County.—*Scampton, 1st March,* 1808."

This work was reprinted in 1810, for the benefit of the widows
and orphans of distressed clergymen in the county of Lincoln. A
collation of the work is given in Upcott's work. In this work will
be found an account of the Knight wooed by the "Spanish Ladye,"
the subject of one of our most interesting ballads.

The Case of Sir John Macpherson, Baronet,
late Governor-General of India; containing a
summary Review of his Administration and Services, prepared by Friends, from authentic Documents. August, 1808.

London: Printed by William Bulmer and Co., Cleveland-row, St. James's.   1808.   4*to.*

A copy of this work was in the sale of Sir James Mackintosh's
library, No. 650. Sir John Macpherson died in 1821, when the
baronetcy became extinct.

Characteristic Sketches of some of the most
distinguished Speakers in the House of Commons,
since the year 1780.

London: Printed by C. and R. Baldwin, New Bridgestreet, Blackfriars.   1809.   8*vo.*   pp. 45.

Written by the late John Courtenay, Esq., formerly member for
Tamworth and Appleby; Surveyor of the Ordnance in 1783; a Commissioner of the Treasury in 1806; died March, 1816.

The Romance of Octavian, Emperor of Rome. Abridged from a Manuscript in the Bodleian Library.

Oxford: Printed by Collingwood and Co. 1809. 8vo.

Edited by the Rev. J. J. Coneybeare. *Fifty* copies only are said to have been printed, from a French MS. in the Bodleian Library.

Catalogue of the Library at Attingham, near Shrewsbury, the seat of Lord Berwick. 1809. 8vo.

This library was sold by auction by Mr. Sotheby in 1843; and produced nearly seven thousand pounds. It was principally distinguished by its collection of Heraldic works.

A Short Statement of the late Trial in the Court of King's Bench, the King *versus* William Dearsley, for an Assault; with the Judgment of the Court pronounced on the Defendant.

Brentford : Printed by P. Norbury. 1809. 8vo. pp. 28.

This trial was distributed by Sir Robert Peat; and contains a report of Lord Ellenborough's decision, that the acceptance of a foreign honour by a British subject, with the King's licence, conferred the honour of knighthood.

CHRONOLOGICAL ABRIDGMENT OF THE HISTORY OF SPAIN.

Printed by E. Harding, Frogmore Lodge, Windsor. 1809.

Fifty copies were printed of this Abridgment, for the use of some of the members of the Royal family: compiled by Miss Knight, author of Dinarbas, a Description of Latium, and other works. A similar Abridgment of the History of Germany was printed in 1810; of France, in 1812; of Rome, in 1817; and of Portugal, in 1817. Twelve copies of a "Hymn" were also printed at the same press, in 1817.

ENGRAVINGS AND ETCHINGS OF THE PRINCIPAL STATUES, BUSTS, BAS-RELIEFS, SEPULCHRAL MONUMENTS, CINERARY URNS, ETC., IN THE COLLECTION OF HENRY BLUNDELL, ESQ. AT INCE.

1809. *2* vols. *folio.*

" Mr. Blundell had nearly attained to his grand climacteric, when having accompanied Mr. Towneley to Rome, he was present when, through the agency of Jenkins, the marbles of the villas Mattei and D'Este were offered to sale: an opportunity so alluring, of becoming possessed of well-known antique statues, and of a collection, without a gradual and tedious acquirement, was a temptation not to be resisted by Mr. Blundell. He purchased, and transferred them to his mansion at Ince-Blundell, near Liverpool: and the multitudinous resort of spectators from that town, soon grew into a serious evil. The present repository, a rotunda of great architectural merit and beauty, was erected in the gardens, in order to obviate this inconvenience, and to display the marbles to greater advantage." *

---

* Nichols, Illustrations, vol. iii. p. 740.

" The most interesting place I have seen in itself, is Mr. Blundell's of Ince, rich in a profusion of antique sculptures and marbles ; we had much entertaining talk about Italy, as he has often been there." *

Ince-Blundell, where this collection of antiquities is deposited, is situated on the left bank of the river Alt, a few miles distant from Liverpool; the mansion has been long in the occupation of the family : it is a spacious and elegant edifice.

The following is the list of the plates, contained in the copy in the British Museum :

Vol. I.

Portrait of Henry Blundell, engraved by Scriven,
from a bust by G. Bullock. 1804.
Frontispiece. View of the Park Pantheon, aquatint.

1 Minerva, from the Lanti Palace.
2 Diana.
3 Theseus.
4 Jupiter.
5 Æsculapius.
6 Roman Consul.
7 Julia Pia.
8 Minerva.
9 Statue representing the Roman Province of Bithynia.
10 Juno.   Thalia.
11 Isis.
12 Apollo.
13 Galatea.   Minerva.
14 Bacchus.   Urania.
15 Venus Victrix.   Bacchante.
16 Anchyrrhoe.
17 Psyche by Canova.
18 Æsculapius.   Ceres.
19 Vertumnus.   An Amorino.
20 Melpomene.   Marcellus.
21 Isis.
22 Spes Etrusca.
23 Mercury.   Apollo.
24 Mercury.
25 Boy and Swan.
26 Silvanus.   Bacchante.   Mercury.
27 Statue on a pillar.
28 Diana.   A Fisherman.
29 Philosopher in contemplation.
30 Pluto.   Cerberus.
31 Cybele.
32 Faun and Goat.
33 Three Egyptian Idols.
34 Bacchus.
35 Marcus Aurelius.
36 Lizard Apollo.
37 Faustina.

---

* Sir J. E. Smith, Life, vol. ii. p. 303.

Vol. II.

140 ⌠One plate, six subjects.
141 ⌡P.-RVBIVS, &c.
142 Three subjects: HYLA, &c.
143 Six subjects, L. APPIAE,
         &c.
144 Vase.
145 Sappho. Torso of a Venus,
         Livia.
146 Large Fragment, and Egyp-
         tian Pots.
147 Osiris. Venus. Hygeia.
148 Two Centaur's heads.
149 Bronze Vase. Julius Cæsar.
150 Bronze Lamps.
151 Gems. [eleven.]
152 This plate is unnumbered,

and undescribed; it con-
tains thirteen engravings
of gems.

153 ⌠Two plates with Greek in-
154 ⌡scriptions; they have
been numbered erro-
neously, 145, 146. The
first plate has three in-
scriptions, numbered I.
II. III., and the second
three, numbered IV.V.VI.
155 S. Hieronymus, from Spag-
noletti, engraved by Piroli.
156 S. Ambrosius, from the same.
157 S. Gregorius, from the same.
158 S. Augustinus, from the same.

The descriptions of the plates are engraved at the bottom, with the exceptions above named. The only letter-press that accompanies the volumes, is a description of plate 78, two title-pages, and a preface to each volume.

Fifty copies were completed of this work. Smith, in his Life of Nollekens, says several of the antiquities were purchased from that artist. Mr. Blundell died in 1812, and his son, C. R. Blundell, Esq., in 1837. He bequeathed this collection and his estates to Thomas Weld Blundell, Esq., a distant relative.

———

Occasional Amusements.

London.   1809.

"The poetical friend, whose nervous lines are an ornament to the 'History of Pleshey,' needs not the additional merit of having written good verses, to enhance that genuine worth by which he has long been distinguished, as one of the most eminent of that honourable and useful body of men of whom Britain justly boasts — whose merchants are princes. Since this note was first written, Mr. Forster (whose name needs no concealment) has printed for the use of his friends a neat little volume (including his 'Pleshey'), under the title," &c.

———

CATALOGUE OF THE MANUSCRIPTS, PRINTED BOOKS, OF THE HISTORY AND ANTIQUITIES, MEDALS, COINS, PORTRAITS, AND TOPOGRAPHICAL ENGRAVINGS AND DRAWINGS, CHARTS, MAPS AND SURVEYS RELATING TO THE COUNTY OF YORK, IN THE COLLECTION OF THE RIGHT HON. JOHN SMYTHE, AT HEATH.

Pontefract : Printed by J. Fox, Market-Place. 1809. pp. 47.

———

POEMATA, QUE DE PRÆMIO OXONIENSIBUS POSITO, ANNIS 1806, 1807, ET 1808, INFELICITER CONTENDE-RUNT; NON IN PUBLICUM EDITA, AMICIS TANTUM PRI-VATIM DEFERENDA.

"Hæc memini, et victum frustra contendere Thyrsin."— *Vir. Ecl.* 7.

Londini : in ædibus Valpianis, pridie idiis Octobres, 1809.

Written by Mr. A. J. Valpy, and the first production from his press, whence issued the Delphin and Variorum classics, and other learned works.

INTRODUCTION TO THE AUTHENTIC COLLECTION
OF THE STATUTES OF THE REALM.
Official Copy, for the use of his Majesty's Commissioners on the Public Records of the Realm. Not published.
[London]; M.DCCC.X. 4to. pp. 180.

Heber's Catalog. pt. v. 2219. "Official copy, not published, only 50 copies printed."

———

CARMINA SELECTA TUM GRÆCA TUM LATINA.
RICHARD PAUL JODRELL, F.R.S.
Londini: 1810.   8vo.

Mr. Jodrell was author of "Illustrations of Euripides," 3 vols. 8vo. London, 1781, highly praised by Adam Clarke; and other works.

———

VIEWS IN ORKNEY, AND ON THE NORTH-EASTERN
COAST OF SCOTLAND, TAKEN IN M.DCCC.V., AND ETCHED
IN M.DCCC.VII.
folio. pp. 27.

This scarce volume is the production of the late Duchess of Sutherland. The plates, says a foreign critic, are executed, "avec un esprit et une correction dont le plus habile imitateur de Rembrandt se ferait honneur." One hundred and twenty copies only were printed.
The following is a list of the plates :—

On the title, Map of Orkneys.	Another view of the same, mark-
Stromna, vignette on p. 1.	ed plate ii.
Orkney Islands seen from the east.	Orkney Islands from the south.

By the permission of her Grace, two or three of the views which illustrated the scenery described by Sir Walter Scott, in the "Pirate," were engraved in the "Landscape Illustrations" of that lamented author's works. A copy is in the Grenville library, with a portrait of the noble Lady.

The Laird of Coul's Ghost, etc.
London : Printed by J. Moyes. [Circa 1810.]

This rigmarole, as it has been styled, was printed some years ago, for private distribution, by Sir James Stuart of Coltness, from a MS.

written by his aunt, Mrs. Betty Stuart. It is supposed to have been a pasquinade against the memory of the Laird of Coul, Mr. Maxwell.

REMARKS ON THE OBSERVATIONS OF THE CHAIRMAN AND DEPUTY-CHAIRMAN OF THE EAST INDIA COMPANY, ON THE EVIDENCE GIVEN BEFORE THE COMMITTEE OF THE HOUSE OF COMMONS APPOINTED FOR THE CONSIDERATION OF INDIA AFFAIRS, ON THE SUBJECT OF THE PRIVATE TRADE WITH INDIA.

London: Printed by Gillet and Son, Crown-court, Fleet-street. 1810. 4to. pp. 92.

These Remarks were written by John Innes, R. C. Bazett, H. Fawcett, and Henry Trail.

MEMOIRS OF NOEL DESENFANS, ESQ.; CONTAINING ALSO, A PLAN FOR PRESERVING THE PORTRAITS OF DISTINGUISHED CHARACTERS; POEMS AND LETTERS.

London: Printed by John Dean, Wardour-street, Soho. 1810. 8vo. pp. 180, and a portrait.

POESIE LIRICHE E PROSE TOSCANE.

Londra: 1810. 4to.

"Edizione non divulgata." By M. Mathias.

Yarico to Inkle; and other Poems.
London: Printed, 1810.   12*mo.*

By Paul Methuen, Esq. (Baron Methuen), of Corsham House, Wilts.

Ode to the Duchess of Newcastle on her Birthday.

4*to.* pp. 30.

Twelve copies only printed by the author, the late Henry Pelham, fourth Duke of Newcastle, K.G.

The Chronology of the History of Modern Europe, from the Extinction of the Western Empire, A.D. 475, to the Death of Louis the Sixteenth, King of France, A.D. 1793, in Ten Epochs.
By Walter Fawkes, Esquire.
York: Printed by Thomas Wilson and Son. 1810. *Royal* 4*to.* A to OO, 4.

"The chronology of the history of modern Europe properly commences with the extinction of the Western Empire; from the ruins of which most of the modern European kingdoms were formed.

"To facilitate the study of history, and to assist the memory, this system of Chronology is divided into Ten Epochs; each distinguished by the name of the most remarkable person or persons who flourished during the different periods under review."

Mr. Fawkes represented the county of York for a short time, before the passing of the Reform Bill. He was a patron of the great artist Turner, R.A., and possessed a considerable number of his drawings in water colour.

190

POEMS, BY THE REV. JEFFEREY EKINS, D.D.,
LATE DEAN OF CARLISLE.

London: Printed by Luke Hansard and Sons, near Lincoln's-inn-fields. 1810. 8vo. pp. 134.

Sixty copies only were printed of this collection of Poems.

———

A CATALOGUE OF BOOKS, POEMS, AND TRACTS, AND SMALL DETACHED PIECES, PRINTED AT THE PRESS AT STRAWBERRY HILL, BELONGING TO THE LATE HORACE WALPOLE, EARL OF ORFORD.

J. Barker, Printer, Great Russell-street, Covent Garden. [1810.]

"As the sale of books, &c., belonging to Mr. Thomas Kirgate, late printer to the Earl of Orford, at Strawberry Hill, has brought before the public a very extensive collection of the productions of that press, and as many of the small pieces are rarely to be met with, I have been induced to attempt making a list of all that has issued from thence, as complete as is in my power.

"Only *twenty* copies are printed, with the intention of distributing them among friends; it is hoped they will kindly make allowance for its imperfections.—G. B."

Compiled by the late Mr. Baker, of St. Paul's Churchyard, whose library was sold in 1810. His collection of Strawberry Hill books was purchased by the late R. P. Cruden, Esq., of Gravesend. In the account of "private presses," &c., which is preparing for publication, will be found, it is believed, a complete catalogue of Horace Walpole's productions at his own press.

SPECIMEN OF AN ENGLISH DE BURE.

London. 1810. *8vo.* Sixteen leaves.

By Dr. Dibdin, who printed *fifty* copies.

FENELON, DEUX DIALOGUES SUR LA PEINTURE.

A Londres. M.DCCC.XI. De l'Imprimerie de Ballantine et Byworth. *12mo.*

THE BRASE NOSE GARLANDE.

M.DCCC.XI. Four leaves. *4to.*

Only twenty copies printed. The author, Thomas Dunbar, Esq., M.A. of Brasenose College, and Keeper of Ashmole's Museum.

It contains only two poems, one entitled "Brase Nose Ale."

The Butler of Brasenose is obliged to furnish an Annual Ode, on Shrove Tuesday, upon the subject of the College Ale. The composition is laid upon the High Table, then removed into the Common Room, and finally transmitted to the Principal's Lodge.

The other is entitled "Brase Nose Chess Club" (recited at the First Anniversary Dinner).

MEMOIRS OF R. F. A.

James Gillett, Printer, Crown-court, Fleet-street. *4to.* pp. 105.

A CATALOGUE OF BOOKS ON ANGLING; WITH
SOME BRIEF NOTICES OF SEVERAL OF THEIR AUTHORS.

London: Printed by T. Bensley, Bolt-court, Fleet-street. 1811. 8vo. pp. 21.

Compiled by Sir Henry Ellis, K.H., principal librarian of the British Museum.

ILLUSTRATIONES THEOPHRASTI IN USUM BOTANICORUM,
PRÆCIPUE PEREGRINANTIUM.
AUCTORE JOHN STACKHOUSE, AM. SOC. LINN. LOND.
HIST. NAT. SOC. (COLLEGII EXON. OXONII OLIM) SOCIO.

Oxonii: E typographeo Clarendoniano. 1811. 8vo. pp. 91.

Privately printed, at the expense of the late Dr. Thackeray, provost of King's College, Cambridge.

LEGACY TO HIS DAUGHTER, ON THE DIVINITY OF
TRUTH IN WRITINGS AND RESOLUTIONS, MATURED IN
THE COURSE OF STUDY, AND EXPERIENCE OF A LONG
LIFE. ENGLISH AND ITALIAN.

1811. 2 vols. 4to.

This work was copied from a bookseller's catalogue. The editor has not succeeded in his attempts to procure an examination of the work itself.

The Little Book (see the Tenth Chapter of Reve-
lation), or, a Close and Brief Elucidation of the
13th, 14th, 15th, 16th, 17th, and 18th Chapters of
Revelations.
By Eben-ezer — "Hitherto hath the Lord helped
us," (Sam. vii. 12)—High Peak, Derbyshire.

"Let him that thinketh he standeth, take heed lest he fall."—
1 Cor. x. 12.

London: Printed by C. Stower, Paternoster-row. 1811.
8vo. pp. 74. Introduction, pp. 61. First Supplement,
pp. 4. Second Supplement, pp. 128. Preface, 4 pp.
The Second Supplement is printed at Sheffield, by J.
Crome, as directed by Ebenezer Al-dred, Printer, Great-
Hucklow, Derbyshire. 1816.

"This extraordinary production is by the Rev. Ebenezer Aldred,
Unitarian minister of Great-Hucklow, Co. Derby. It is of a religious
political nature, and was intended to have been distributed by its
author on the 12th of February, 1811, upon one of the city bridges;
but meeting with a Derbyshire friend, he was by him dissuaded
from his purpose: and by this friend's further intervention, the
whole impression of the book, except a very few copies, was withdrawn effectually, if not destroyed.

"The following paragraph appeared in the London papers of
1812:—'The Rev. Eben. Aldred, a Dissenting minister from the
High Peak in Derbyshire, appeared in a boat upon the Thames, on
Thursday the 28th instant (February), dressed in a white linen robe,
with his long hair flowing over his shoulders, and announced that
the seven vials mentioned in the book of Revelations were about to
be poured out upon the city of London.'

"He printed also (privately I have no doubt), 'Morning and
Evening Prayers for the use of Individuals,' composed by different
Unitarian ministers, and printed at the expense of the Society of
Unitarian Christians. Now reprinted, with a few alterations, by

Eben-ezer Al-dred. 'Pray to thy Father in secret.'—Matt. vi. 6. Printed by J. Crome, Sheffield. 1816. *Small* 8*vo.* or 12*mo.* pp. 50; and one leaf of 'Texts of Scripture.'" *

LETTERS TO ATTICUS.
1811. 12*mo.* pp. 65.

By the late Viscount Fitzwilliam; who presented the fine collection of pictures and engravings to the University of Cambridge, now deposited in the building bearing his name.

GENERAL OBSERVATIONS ON THE WRITINGS OF ST. PAUL.
BY JOHN HEY, D.D.
Printed for the Author, by J. Seeley, Buckingham. 1811. 8*vo.* pp. 143.

JOURNAL OF A TOUR IN ICELAND, IN THE SUMMER OF 1809.
BY WILLIAM JACKSON HOOKER, F.L.S.
Yarmouth: Printed by J. Keymer, King-street. 1811. Not published. 8*vo.* pp. 496. Index, &c., four leaves.

PLATES.
Frontispiece, an Icelandic lady, in her bridal dress.
Plan of an Icelandic house, p. 89.
Eruption of the Geyser, p. 121.
View of the Crater of Geyser, p. 122.

---

* The editor derives this information from William Bateman, Esq., of Middleton Bakewell, to whom he is indebted for several curious additions to his list.

Five hundred copies were privately printed, and *ten* on large paper, given to members of the author's family. A second edition was published in 1813, two vols. 8*vo.*, for sale. Sir William Hooker is now curator of the Botanical Garden at Kew; which is greatly indebted to his exertions to render it worthy the nation.

Account of the Game of Curling.
By a Member of the Duddingston Curling Society.
Edinburgh: Printed at the Correspondent Office. 1811. 8*vo.* pp. 46.

A few copies were printed on thick paper; these are very uncommon.

The Reaper, with Wensley-Dale, enlarged;
and The Tourist [by ——Mander, Esq.].
York: Printed by William Blanshard. *2 vols. 8vo.*

"All but two copies destroyed, at the desire of the representatives.—W. B."
Communicated to the editor by the late Archdeacon Wrangham.

Œdipus Judaicus.
By the Right Honourable William Drummond.

"Œdipo conjectore opus est."—*Plautus.*

London: Printed by A. J. Valpy, Took's-court, Chancery-lane. 1811. 8*vo.* pp. 381. Preface, pp. lxxxii.; and 16 plates.

"I have gotten a book by Sir W. Drummond (printed but not published), entitled 'Œdipus Judaicus,' in which he attempts to prove the greater part of the Old Testament an allegory, particularly Genesis and Joshua. He professes himself a theist, in the preface, and handles the literal interpretation very roughly. I wish you could see it. Mr. W. has lent it me, and I confess to me it is worth fifty Watsons."*

The late Dr. D'Oyly wrote some remarks upon this work in 1812, which were replied to by a writer under the name of Vindex. A review of both works will be found in the ninth volume of the Quarterly Review.

Tre Opera Drammatiche,

Prese nelle Visioni de Dafni, e concatenate istoricamente nell' ordine che segue, cioè, Il Trionfo di Melibeo, La Apria Silene, e La Coronazione di Silene. Scritta da Dafni, ossia timi Dafni, così poeticamente divisato Arcade Pastore essendo nell' estasi del Sonno Magnetico, edora consegnate doverosamente al genio de' Dilettanti della lingua Italiana in ogni parte del mundo.

Londra: della Stamperia de G. Bulmer e Co. 1811. 4to. pp. 238.

Edited by Mr. George Baldwin.

Book Rarities; or, a Descriptive Catalogue of some of the most Curious, Rare, and Valuable Books, of Early Date; chiefly in the Collection of George John, Earl Spencer, K.G. London. 1811.   *8vo.*

By Dr. Dibdin. *Thirty-six* copies only were printed.

---

* Moore, Life of Lord Byron, 4to., vol. i. p. 318.

JUDGMENT OF THE COMMON PLEAS, IN BENYON
AGAINST EVELYN,

BY LORD CHIEF JUSTICE BRIDGMAN, Trin. 14, Cha. II.;
Including a Consideration, how far the Courts of Westminster Hall may adjudicate a Privilege of Parliament, without being concluded by the Votes of either House. Extracted from Lord Chief Justice Bridgman's own Report.

"Non in eos sine observantia, quêis adversari videtur."

London: Printed for W. Clarke and Sons, &c. 1811. 8*vo.* pp. 53.

"Not yet published, nor intended to be so, at present; and when it shall be published, it will be with a preface."—*MS. Note in the title of the copy in the British Museum.*

SKETCH OF THE CHARACTER OF THE LATE
DUKE OF DEVONSHIRE.
BY R. ADAIR, ESQ. M.P.

London: Printed by W. Bulmer and Co. 1811. 4*to.* pp. 28.

This Sketch first appeared in the "Morning Chronicle," within a day or two of the Duke's decease. Fifty copies were afterwards printed in this form, at the expense of the Duchess of Devonshire: a portrait of the Duke usually accompanies the Memoir, engraved from a picture by Sir Joshua Reynolds.

ORATIO DE RIDICULO; HABITA CANTABRIGIÆ IN
SCHOLIS PUBLICIS, ACCEDIT ETIAM AB EODEM SCRIPTUM,
CARMEN COMITIALE. A. COLE.
London. 1811. *4to.*

Reprinted by the late Duke of Marlborough. A copy was in the
White Knights' library, No. 1134.

BIBLIOGRAPHY : A POEM.
[London. 1812.] *8vo.* pp. 24; including Preface.

There is no title-page to this effusion, from the pen of Dr. Dibdin ;
on which is imprinted that only *fifty* copies were struck off.

LETTERS FROM THE REVEREND DR. WARBURTON,
BISHOP OF GLOUCESTER, TO THE HON. CHARLES YORKE,
FROM 1752 TO 1770.
London: Printed by the Philanthropic Society, St.
George's Fields. 1812. *4to.* pp. 105.

About one hundred copies of this edition were printed for private
distribution, at the expense of the Earl of Hardwicke.

CONTES DES FOUS, AND OTHER TRIFLES IN VERSE,
BY THE LATE JOHN BIGGE, ESQ.,
WITH NOTES CRITICAL AND EXPLANATORY.
London: Printed for John Rodwell. 1812.

Not published.

Virgilius.

This Boke treateth of the Lyfe of Virgilius, and of his Deth, and many Marvayles that he did, in hys Lyfe-tyme, by Whychcrafte and Nygromancye, thorough the helpe of the Devyls of Hell.

London. *4to.* pp. *22.*

A reprint by E. V. Utterson, Esq.: who says in the preface, "Mr. Douce's kindness enabled the editor to make the transcript from which this little tract is printed; of it, only *fifty* copies on paper, and *one* on vellum, are taken off, and those solely for private distribution." The vellum copy is in the British Museum; it is a very indifferent specimen of modern vellum printing. There were two copies, it is said, on vellum; the second most probably in the possession of Mr. Utterson.

The publications of Mr. Utterson at his press in the Isle of Wight, are so numerous that it is judged best to print the account of them together; they will be described in the second part of this work, containing the works printed at private presses and by clubs.

Extracts from the Letters of Elizabeth, Lucy, and Judith Ussher,

late of the City of Waterford.

Dublin: Printed by J. Jones, South Great George's-street. 1812.

The Step-mother; a Tragedy.

By Frederick, Earl of Carlisle, Knight of the Garter, etc., etc., etc.

A new edition, with alterations.

London: Printed by William Bulmer and Co., Cleveland-row, St. James's. 1812. *8vo.* pp. 158.

AN HISTORICAL LETTER TO THE REV. CHARLES
O'CONNOR, D.D., HERETOFORE STYLING HIMSELF CO-
LUMBANUS: UPON HIS FIVE ADDRESSES OR LETTERS TO
HIS COUNTRYMEN.
FROM FRANCIS PLOWDEN, ESQ.
London.   1812.   8vo.

Not yet published.   A note in the Grenville copy, calls it "an
impudent libel."

———

THE FATHER'S REVENGE; A TRAGEDY.
BY FREDERICK EARL OF CARLISLE, KNIGHT OF THE
GARTER, ETC., ETC., ETC.
A new edition.
London: Printed by William Bulmer and Co., Cleve-
land-row, St. James's.   1812.   8vo.   pp. 150.

———

TRANSLATIONS FROM THE GERMAN,
IN PROSE AND VERSE.

"Make us eternal truths receive,
And practise all that we believe."—*Dryden.*

Printed by E. Harding, Frogmore Lodge, Windsor.
1812.   12mo.   pp. 112.

Leaf following the title, with this inscription: "The gift of the
Queen, to her beloved daughters, Charlotte-Aug. Matilda, Augusta-
Sophia, Elizabeth-Mary, and Sophia: and, with her Majesty's per-
mission, dedicated to their Royal Highnesses, by the translator,
Ellis Cornelia Knight."

Miss Knight was reader to Queen Charlotte, by whose desire this
volume was composed; thirty copies only were printed.

A Catalogue of Books, relating to the History and Topography of Italy, collected during the years 1786, 1787, 1788, 1789, 1790. By Sir Richard Colt Hoare, Bart. Twelve copies printed. London: Printed by W. Bulmer and Co., Cleveland-row, St. James's. 8vo. pp. 102.

The collection described in this catalogue was most liberally presented to the British Museum, by Sir Richard Colt Hoare, in 1825.

Miscellaneous Poems. Printed by E. Harding, Frogmore Lodge, Windsor. 1812. Small 4to. pp. 90.

This volume contains a selection of poems, by William Robert Spencer, Samuel Rogers, Miss Knight, and others; prefixed is an etching, a view of Frogmore.

Catalogus Librorum qui in Bibliotheca Blandfordiensi Reperiuntur. London: Printed by T. Bensley. 1812. 4to.

Contents.

Fasciculus Primus. Theologia. Critici Sacri. Controversiæ, pp. 35.

Fasciculus Secundus. Technici. Ludorum Graphici. Lexica. Grammatici, pp. 23.

Fasciculus Tertius. De Re Botanicâ et de Re Rusticâ, pp. 13.

Fasciculus Quartus. Poetæ Epici. Drammatici, Lyrici, &c. variis Linguis, pp. 29.

Fasciculus Quintus. Fabulæ et Fabulosa, pp. 29.

Fasciculus Sextus. Facetiæ et Satyræ, pp. 25.

Fasciculus Septimus. Symbola et Emblemata, pp. 11.

Fasciculus Octavus. Chronica. Topographica. Descriptiones Gentium, Hominum, Rituum, &c., pp. 50.

Fasciculus Nonus. Scriptores miscellanei Ingenio, Lepore, Urbanitate insignes, pp. 5.

Catalogus Librorum qui Bibliothecæ Blandfordiensi nuper additi sunt. 1814. pp. 35.

This catalogue was compiled by Mr. Triphook: the library, formerly at White Knights, was sold by auction by Mr. Evans, in 1819: it contained, among other rare works, the celebrated Boccacio of 1481, for which the Marquis of Blandford gave 2260*l.* at the Roxburghe sale; it was purchased by Messrs. Longman and Co. for 918*l.* 15*s.*, and transferred at the same price to the late Earl Spencer, in whose magnificent collection it now remains.

––––––––

Memoirs of Mrs. Jebb.
By George Wilson Meadley, Esq.

London: Printed by Thomas Davison. 1812. 8*vo.* pp. 62.

Mr. Meadley was the author of a Life of Paley, Algernon Sidney, and other works, a list of which will be found in the Gentleman's Magazine, March, 1819.

––––––––

Sketch of the
Life of John Lindsay Crawfurd, Esq.,

Containing a full and impartial Account of his Claim to the Title and Estates of George, Earl of Crawfurd and Lindsay.

Dalry. 1812.   8*vo.*

Descriptive Catalogue
of a Collection of Pictures,
Comprehending Specimens of all the various Schools of Paintings, belonging to Sir Abraham Hume, Bart. London: Printed by G. Smeeton. M.DCCC.XII. 4to. pp. 38.

The late Sir Abraham Hume, a well-known patron of the fine arts; the collection here mentioned was divided between his house in Hill-street, and the country-seat of Wormley-bury, Herts. Since his death, the chief part of the collection was left to the late Viscount Alford and has been removed to Belton.

Studies and Amusements in Pursuit of Knowledge.
Knowledge of Things: Knowledge of the Truth in all Things: Knowledge of the Laws of Nature; or Theseus escaping from the Labyrinth.
By George Baldwin, Londinensis,
born 6–17 May, 1744.
Printed by C. Richards. 1812. 12mo. pp. 32.

The Epistles of Horace,
Translated into English Verse.
Birmingham: Printed by Orton and Hawkes Smith. 1812. 12mo. pp. 88.

This translation is by Mr. Charles Lloyd, of Birmingham. The first, second, third, fourth, seventh, and tenth Epistles, are printed in the Gentleman's Magazine. Mr. Lloyd died at Birmingham, January 16, 1827.

MISCELLANEOUS TRACTS.

I. An Essay on Mystical Theology; or, the Science of sacred Contemplation. II. A Letter on the spiritual Supremacy of the Pope. III. Some Account of Dr. John Taulere. IV. A Discourse pronounced at a Meeting for providing Means for the Education of poor Roman Catholic Children in London. V. A Specimen of an intended Life of Christ: with two Dissertations.—1. On the Genealogy of Christ; 2. On the Prophecy of Isaiah vii. 14.

By CHARLES BUTLER, Esq.

Printed, not published. 1812. 12*mo*. pp. 106.

———

CATALOGUE OF THE ARCHIEPISCOPAL MANUSCRIPTS IN THE LIBRARY OF LAMBETH PALACE; With an Account of the Archiepiscopal Registers, and other Records there preserved.

London: Printed by Law and Gilbert, St. John's square, Clerkenwell. 1812. *folio*. pp. 270.

Compiled by the late Rev. H. J. Todd. Frontispiece, a fac-simile of the first leaf of Adhelmus de Virginitate; at p. 261, a plate, with representations of several curious MSS. in the library.

Five copies were printed on large paper, and one hundred on smaller paper; the latter for distribution among public libraries. One of the five on large paper, formerly Queen Charlotte's, was in Mr. Heber's collection, 4073, pt. 1.

"Not any records here other than those named in the printed catalogue published by the Archbishop, in the year 1812." Answer of the Keeper of the Archives, in the Report of the Commissioners of Public Records. *Folio.* 1837. Appx.

LETTERS ON MISCELLANEOUS AND DOMESTIC SUBJECTS,
Intended for the use of the Writer's Family, and a few select Friends.

Only fifty copies printed.

London: Printed by J. Moyes, Greville-street. M.DCCC.XII. 8vo. pp. 384. Contents and Preface, pp. 12.

Lithographic engravings, twelve portraits. Facing the title, one of the author, Benjamin Oakley, painted by Sir A. W. Callcott, R.A.; and the remaining eleven portraits, busts of the author's children and family connexions.

———

THE HISTORY OF THE COLLEGE OF BONHOMMES, AT ASHRIDGE, IN THE COUNTY OF BUCKS, FOUNDED BY EDMUND, EARL OF CORNWALL.
Compiled from original Records and other authentic Sources.

London: Printed by Law and Gilbert, St. John's-square, Clerkenwell. 1812. 4to.

Compiled by the late Rev. H. J. Todd: it contains six engravings. The collation of this volume will be found in Mr. Upcott's work. One hundred and fifty copies were printed on demy 4to., and fifty on royal 4to., for private distribution, by the Earl of Bridgewater.

———

ACCOUNT OF THE LIFE
OF THE RIGHT HON. WILLIAM WINDHAM.
London: Printed for the Author, not published. 8vo. 1812.

By the late Thomas Amyot, Esq., private Secretary to Mr. Windham, and treasurer of the Society of Antiquaries.

An Account of the Family of Ogle, and of their Estates and Possessions in the County of Northumberland.

Edinburgh: Printed by James Ballantyne and Company. 1812. 8vo. pp. 39.

Sir Walter Scott, in a letter to the late R. Surtees, Esq., says, " I add a flaming sort of pamphlet, published (or printed, I should say, for it is not *published*) by a lady of your country now residing here. It is a genealogical memoir of the family of Ogle; but far too general, and too little supported by dates and references to be interesting. It might be called from the name of the fair, 'Prideaux's Connections.' The editor, Mr. Raine, remarks in a note, that the genealogical lady is believed to have been the late Mrs. Prideaux, who was related by marriage to Sir Chaloner Ogle."

Sir Chaloner is said to have been the Captain Whiffle of Roderick Random.

————

The Bloody Journal, kept by William Davidson, on board a Russian Pirate, in the year 1789.

Mediterranean: Printed on board His Majesty's Ship Caledonia. 1812. 8vo. pp. 34; preface, pp. 4.

"This man served on board H.M.S. Niger, in 1791, then under the command of Admiral Sir Richard Keats. The Journal contains a horrible narration of the enormities committed by the crew of the Pirate, in which Davidson acknowledges that he and the other Englishmen on board took the *most* active lead. He was afterwards accidentally drowned while serving in H.M.S. Royal George.

" At the request of my friend Sir Walter Scott, who had heard of the existence of such a Memoir, and desired to found a poem upon the subject, I obtained for him an authentic copy in 1811, which Sir Richard Keats was so good as to verify to me, with some further particulars of this man's story. But on perusal, Sir Walter Scott pronounced it too horrible for versification, and inserted the substance of it in the Edinburgh Annual Register in 1812.

E. H. LOCKER."

The curiosity of this and the following book has induced the editor to depart from his rule of giving an account of books printed in this country only; he is indebted to the kindness of Mr. Locker for the information connected with them.

A copy of this work is in the library of Corpus Christi College, Oxford; and copies of the two following works will be found in the same library, and also in the Bodleian.

THE SPEECH OF DOCTOR D. ANTONIO JOSEPH RUIZ DE PADRON, DEPUTY TO THE CORTES FROM THE CANARY ISLANDS.

Spoken in the Sitting of January 18, 1813, relative to the Inquisition.

BREAD AND BULLS: AN APOLOGETICAL ORATION ON THE FLOURISHING STATE OF SPAIN IN THE REIGN OF KING CHARLES THE FOURTH,

Delivered in the Plaza de Toros, Madrid,

BY DON GASPAR DE JOVELLANOS.

Mediterranean: Printed on board His Majesty's Ship Caledonia, off Toulon. 1813. 4*to*. pp. 96.

The translation of the two political pamphlets above-mentioned is dedicated to Vice-Admiral Sir Edward Pellew, Bart., afterwards Lord Exmouth, Commander-in-Chief in the Mediterranean, bearing the signatures which follow:—

Lieut. Orlando Felix, Royal Marines, now Major Rifle Brigade.

Lieut. Henry Elton, Royal Navy, now Captain Royal Navy.

Lieut. Alexander Francis Elphinstone, Captain Royal Navy.

Clerk William Pearson Smith, dead.

Lieut. Algernon Percy, Royal Navy, Lord Prudhoe, now Duke of Northumberland.

Rev. John Brickenden Frowd, Chaplain.

Lieut. Robert Turtliff Dyer, Marine Artillery.

The work was revised by Mr. Locker, who wrote the dedication. A notice of both the pamphlets is in the " Quarterly Review," vol. x. p. 203; but Mr. Ticknor says the last pamphlet " is not the work of Jovellanos, though it has always bore his name on the successive editions."*

LIFE OF CHRIST.　C. BUTLER.

1813.

"Printed and circulated among his friends. His design was to frame an harmony of the four Evangelists, by translating them, verse for verse, without any addition or omission,—in such words or phrases, as it might be supposed the Evangelists themselves might have used, if they had written in the English language ; an arduous and an useful undertaking—but which, with great regret, he was obliged to abandon, on account of its extreme difficulty, and the time which a proper execution of it would require."—*Butler's Reminiscences*, page 227.

The first edition of Mr. Butler's Horæ Biblicæ is said to have been printed for private circulation.

ALPHONSO, KING OF CASTILE: A SPANISH TRAGEDY.
Egham: Printed by C. C. Wetton. 1813. 4*to.*　pp. 76.

The author of this tragedy was the late Rev. William Warrington, Vicar of Old Windsor; who printed also, for private circulation—

THE CAMBRIAN HERO; OR, LLEWELLYN THE GREAT:
AN HISTORICAL TRAGEDY.

Wettons, Printers, Egham.　4*to.*　pp. 90.

---

* " History of Spanish Literature," vol. iii. p. 282.

Equanimity in Death, a Poem,
By George Watson, Esq.

London : Printed by J. Moyes, Greville-street, for John Murray, Albemarle-street. 1813. 4*to.* pp. 48.

Written, it is believed, by the late Mr. Watson Taylor, of Earlstoke, before he succeeded to the property of Sir Simon Taylor, and assumed his name.

An Historical and Descriptive Account of
Stoke Park, in Buckinghamshire.

Containing the information relative to that place, supplied by the family now in possession for Mr. Hakewell's History of Windsor, &c., with many additional particulars, and a new arrangement of the matter. In two parts.

London : Printed by W. Bulmer & Co. 1813. pp. 74. Seven plates. 8*vo.*

" The name of Gray the poet is connected with this seat; as the old manor-house furnished the subject of his poem, entitled the *Long Story.* In the year 1789, the ancient mansion appearing to Mr. Penn to demand very extensive repairs, it was thought advisable to take it down. In the same year, the foundation of another noble structure was laid, and the building begun, under the directions of the late Mr. Nasmyth, and completed by Mr. James Wyatt."[*] It has since Mr. Penn's death been purchased by the Right Honourable Henry Labouchere.

---

[*] From the description of the house, in Neale's Seats, by the late Thomas Moule, who furnished the whole of the very careful and interesting accounts in that work.

SERMONS,
WRITTEN BY A LAYMAN.

London. 1813. 8*vo.*

AN ESSAY ON THE CHARACTER OF JONATHAN.

London. 1813. 8*vo.*

"Mr. Hardinge printed a small number of three single 'Sermons, written by a Layman,' and 'An Essay on the Character of Jonathan,' not intended for sale." *

———

RICORDANZA.

MEMOIRS OF ELIZABETH DALTON, WHO DIED ON THE 16TH DECEMBER, 1812, AGED 59 YEARS.

London : Printed by Edward Bridgewater, South Molton-street. 1813. 8*vo.* pp. 225.

Written by James Forbes, Esq., author of "Oriental Memoirs," 4 vols. 4*to.* Mrs. Dalton was his sister.

———

TITI LUCRETII CARI,
DE RERUM NATURA, LIBRI IX.

Londini: in ædibus Ricardi Taylor et Socii. M.DCCC.XIII. 4*to.* pp. 296.

Privately printed by the late Dr. Keate, head master of Eton, for the purpose of presenting to his pupils. Six copies were printed in royal 4*to.* and on tinted paper. Reprinted in 1824, in the same size, with copies on royal 4*to.*; and again in 1832. The copies on large paper of this last edition are a very beautiful specimen of Mr. Taylor's typographical efforts.

———

* Nichols, Illustrations, vol. iii. p. 29,

BOOK OF DREAMS. 1811, 1812, 1813.
London: Printed by C. Richards, 18, Warwick-street,
Golden-square. 4*to.* pp. 150.

The dreams of a young lady, communicated to the late Mr. Baldwin, who printed a few copies of his interpretation of them.

———

CATALOGUE OF BOOKS
IN THE LIBRARY OF THE MILITARY DEPÔT,
QUARTER MASTER GENERAL'S OFFICE.
Printed from *stone* in the year 1813; written with Chemical Ink, by J. Wyld, Draftsman. *folio.* pp. 60.

———

MEMOIR OF MISS ANN BACON, WHO DIED DEC. 24TH,
1809, IN A LETTER FROM HER BROTHER TO MR. B———,
ONE OF HIS INTIMATE FRIENDS.
London: Printed by James Moyes, Greville-street,
Hatton Garden. 1813. 8*vo.* pp. 80.

A sister, it is believed, of Bacon, the sculptor.

———

A FAMILY STORY; A COMEDY, IN FIVE ACTS, OF
WHICH A FEW COPIES ONLY HAVE BEEN PRINTED FOR
THE PRIVATE USE OF THE AUTHOR.

On back of title, "Printed by J. Aston, at the Exchange Herald Office, St. Anne's Street, Manchester, 1814."

Pp. 77. Exclusive of Title and Dedication "to her who so affectionately and assiduously watched the bed of the author, and listened with so much tender sympathy to his tale of symptoms during the continuance of a nervous fever, this comedy, written during the slow convalescence which followed, in common justice ought to be inscribed, a memento of her tenderness and his gratitude."

———

TERENTIUS: THE ANDRIAN, A COMEDY: ATTEMPTED IN ENGLISH METRE.

" Favete, adeste æquo animo."

London: Printed by W. Bulmer and Co., Cleveland-row, St. James's. 1814. Title and preface, pp. x. Prologue, and Persons represented, two leaves. B–M 2, in eights.

This translation was by the late Sir Henry Charles Englefield, Bart. Eight copies were printed on a folio size; of which Lord Spencer possesses one.

———

SUBSTANCE OF A MINUTE RECORDED BY THE HONOURABLE THOMAS STAMFORD RAFFLES, LIEUTENANT-GOVERNOR OF JAVA AND ITS DEPENDENCIES, ON THE 11TH FEBRUARY, 1814; ON THE INTRODUCTION OF AN IMPROVED SYSTEM OF INTERNAL MANAGEMENT, AND THE ESTABLISHMENT OF A LAND RENTAL ON THE ISLAND OF JAVA: TO WHICH ARE ADDED, SEVERAL OF THE MOST INTERESTING DOCUMENTS THEREIN REFERRED TO.

London: Printed (but not published) for Black, Parry, and Co. 1814. 4to. pp. 293.

HEADS OF ANCIENT HISTORY, FROM THE DELUGE
TO THE PARTITION OF ALEXANDER'S EMPIRE.

London: Printed by B. Howlett, 10, Frith-street,
Soho. 1814. 12*mo.* pp. 33.

Written by Hudson Gurney, Esq., F.S.A., of Keswick Hall, Norwich. A copy of this work, bound in *red* leather, was presented by
Mr. Gurney to the late Dr. Sayers, of Norwich, who acknowledged it
in the following lines:—

> " Accept my best thanks for your little red book,
> With delight and amaze on its pages I look,
> And if I can prevent it, it ne'er shall be said
> The *little red* book is a book *little read*."

ANTIQUITIES OF THE HOUSE OF BRUNSWICK,
BY EDWARD GIBBON, ESQ.

London: Printed for John Murray, Albemarle-street.
1814. 4*to.* pp. 206.

When the new edition of Gibbon's Miscellaneous Works was going
through the press, a few copies of this tract were printed separately
in quarto, for Lord Sheffield, to present to different branches of the
Royal family. A copy was in the library of the Duke of York.

THE FIVE WOUNDS OF CHRIST, A POEM, FROM
AN ANCIENT PARCHMENT ROLL, BY WILLIAM BILLYNG.

Manchester: Printed by R. and W. Dean. 1814. 4*to.*
pp. 8; Preface, one leaf.

" Printed from an illuminated parchment roll, about two yards and
three quarters in length, in the possession of Mr. William Yates, of
Manchester. Only *forty* copies printed, for private distribution."

Plates:—I. The Well of Mercy. II. The Well of Pitie. III. The Well of Everlasting Life. IV. The Well of Grace. V. The Well of Comfort. VI. [The Cross, with a wreath]. VII. [Death].

———

The Political Life of William Wildman, Viscount Barrington;
Compiled from Original Papers, by his Brother, Shute, Bishop of Durham.

London: Printed by W. Bulmer and Co. 1814. *Imp.* 4*to.* pp. 207; Index, two pages.

Frontispiece, a portrait, from a picture by Sir Thomas Lawrence, engraved by C. Knight, "by direction of his surviving brothers."

In the preface the Bishop states, that he was assisted in the compilation of the work by Sir Thomas Bernard, Bart.

One hundred copies only were printed; an edition in 8*vo.* was printed in 1815 for public sale. In Sir Henry Ellis's collection of Letters, second series, will be found some letters of this nobleman.

———

An Account of the Visit of His Royal Highness the Prince Regent, with their Imperial and Royal Majesties the Emperor of all the Russias and the King of Prussia, to the Corporation of London, in June, 1814.

London: Printed by order of, and for, the Corporation of the City of London, by Nichols, Son, and Bentley, Red-Lion-passage, Fleet-street. 4*to.* pp. 101.

Frontispiece, View of the interior of Guildhall, as it appeared on the 18th of June, 1814, engraved in outline from a picture painted for the Corporation by W. Daniell, R.A.

An Account of the Entertainment given to Field-Marshal His Grace the Duke of Wellington, by the Corporation of London, in the Guild-hall, on the 9th of July, 1814.

London: Printed by order of, and for, the Corporation of the City of London, by Nichols, Son, and Bentley, Red-Lion-passage, Fleet-street. 4*to.* pp. 59.

A Narrative of the Grand Festival at Yarmouth, on Tuesday, the 19th of April, 1814; With an Appendix, containing Copies of all the Handbills which were published on the Occasion, a List of the Subscribers, and an Account of the Expenditure.

Yarmouth: Printed by T. Keymer, King-street. [Unpublished.] 4*to.* pp. 72.

Fifty copies were printed, for private distribution. Compiled by Robert Cory, jun., Esq., F.S.A.: it contains a few wood-cuts.

Letters and Miscellaneous Papers, by Barré Charles Roberts, Student of Christ Church, Oxford; with a Memoir of his Life.

London: Printed by William Bulmer and Co., Cleveland-row. 1814. 4*to.* pp. 370.

Prefixed is a portrait of the author, engraved by F. C. Lewis; the volume was edited by Mr. Grosvenor Bedford.

" Among the miscellaneous papers, are Notes on Oseney and Boxley Abbeys; in such researches he was indefatigable: the antiquarian collections in this volume are of considerable extent. The

remaining papers are of a lighter description: the first in order
are some remarks on Gibbon's dissertation concerning the Iron
Mask. Among the remaining, is that criticism upon Mr. Pinker-
ton's Essay on Medals, which appeared in the first number of this
Journal." *

His collection of coins is now in the British Museum.

<hr />

RERUM HIBERNICARUM SCRIPTORES VETERES.
TOM. I.

Continens Epistolam nuncupatoriam quæ codicum
vetustissimorum Hibernensium notitiam, et Regum chro-
nologiam complectitur, item Prolegomena ad Annales,
Partibus II. Quarum prima vetustissimorum de Hibernia
Testimonia Historica, secunda Annalium et Carminum
Hibernensium Catalogos comprehendit.

Auctore CAROLO O'CONNOR, S.T.D.

"L'histoire n'est fondée que sur le témoignage des Auteurs qui
nous l'ont transmise. Il importe donc extrêmement, pour la sçavoir,
de bien connoitre quels étoient ces Auteurs. RIEN N'EST A NEG-
LIGER en ce point."—*Hist. de l'Acad. des Inscr.* tom. x.

Buckinghamiæ: Excudebat J. Seeley, veneunt apud T.
Payne, Londini. 1814. 4*to.* Epistola nuncupatoria,
pp. cclxxxvi. Prolegomena, Pars I. pp. clxxxiv; Pars
II. pp. ccvii. After the title, ad Lectorem, one leaf;
Dedication to the Marquis of Buckingham, pp. v.

Tab. I. Ex Missale Hibernico Bobiense Sæculi vii. Epistola, pp. cxxx.
Tab. II. Codex Dublin dictus S. Columbæ, pp. clxxx.

<hr />

* Quarterly Review, vol. xii. p. 509.

Tab. III. Ex Codice dicto S. Ceaddæ, pp. cxcii.

Tab. IV. Ex Psalterio Salabargæ Discipulæ S. Columbani, pp. ccxix.

Tab. V. Ex Codice Rushworthiano, Scripto a Mac Regol, pp. ccxxix.

Tab. VI. Cl. Ptolomæi Geographia Hiberniæ. Prolegomena, Pars I. pp. lviii.

Tab. VII. Codices Hibernici Sæculi, xii. et xiii. Prolegomena, Pars II. pp. clxxiv.

Tom. II.

Complectens Annales Tigernachi, ex Codice Bodleiano, Rawlinson, No. 488, Annales Inisfalenses, ex duobus Codicibus, Dubliniense et Bodleiano, itemque Annales Buellianos, ex Codice Cottoniano Titus A. xxv. nunc primum edidit C. O'Connor, D.D.

> " Ordior audaci, tenebrosa per æquora, velo
> Cimmerium tentare adytum: submersaque lethis
> Sistere de barathro luci. Da, Maxime rerum
> Conditor, ut fugiens syrtes, scopulosque latentes,
> Fœlici inveniam quæsitos littore portus."

Buckinghamiæ: Excudit J. Seeley, prostant Londini apud T. Payne, in Vico dicto Pall Mall. 1825. Dedication to the Duke of Buckingham, one leaf; Samuelis Johnson adhortatio, one leaf. Preface to Tigernachi Annales, pp. xxxii; Tigernachi Annales, pp. 317; Appendix Chronologicus, pp. 4; Errata, one leaf. Annales Inisfalenses, pp. 156; Annales Inisfalenses hactenus inediti, pp. 83. Annales Buelliani, pp. 48. Errata, one leaf.

At the end of this volume the following plates, all engraved by C. J. Smith:—

I. Ornamenta thecæ codicis Stowensis Evangelii S. Johannis. II. A second plate of the same subject, without any inscription above it. III. Two ornamental designs on one plate, without any inscription.

IV. Another representation of the same.   V. Rituale Hibernicum portatile in Bibliotheca Stowense. None of the plates are numbered.

Tom. III.

Complectens Annales IV. Magistrorum, ex ipso O'Clerii autographo in Bibliotheca Stowense. Nunc primum edidit C. O'Connor, D.D.

The motto the same as in Tom. II.

Buckinghamiæ : Excudit J. Seeley.   Prostant Londini apud T. Payne, in Vico dicto Pall Mall.   1826.   Testimonia, et Dissertatio Preliminaris, O'Clerii Epistola nuncupatoria, pp. xxxv. misprinted xxv.   Annales, pp. 840 ; Errata, one leaf.

Tom. IV.

Complectens Annales Ultonienses, ab anno D.CCC.XXXI. ad annum DMCXXXI.   Ex Codice Bodleiano : itemque Indicem Generalem.   Nunc primum edidit C. O'Connor, D.D.

The motto the same as in Tom. III.

Buckinghamiæ : Excudit J. Seeley.   Prostant Londini apud T. Payne, in Vico dicto Pall Mall.   1826.   Annales Ultonienses, pp. 1–398 ; Index Generalis, pp. 1–25.

This laborious and useful work was undertaken at the expense of the first Duke of Buckingham and Chandos : and it is to be regretted that this spirited example has met with so few followers. About two hundred sets were made complete of the four volumes. On its first appearance, it was the intention of the Duke of Buckingham to permit it to be generally sold ; but circumstances induced his Grace to change his determination ; and the work was withdrawn from public sale, when, it is believed, not more than ten copies of the first volume had found their way into the hands of individuals.

Twenty-six copies were printed on large paper : the Grenville library possesses one. Dr. O'Connor had been domestic chaplain to the Marchioness of Buckingham, mother of the Duke ; and after her decease in 1813, remained at Stowe, as librarian. He died 29th July, 1828, æt. about 67.

"The expenses incurred by the Duke of Buckingham for the researches and for the printing of these four volumes, exceeded the sum of 3000*l*. They contain Latin translations from the original Iberno-Celtic MSS. in the library at Stowe.* The most important and interesting works illustrative of the history and antiquities of Ireland were selected, and these volumes embody *no article ever before printed*, or, it might be almost added, ever before known to the literary world, excepting, perhaps, by name. The notes abound in curious and valuable matter, and the learned translator is deservedly deemed more profoundly skilled than any other person of the present day, in the language, figurative expressions, and allusions of the originals. This work must always be deemed essential to any literary collection professing to have the history of Ireland among its objects, as well for the rich mine of curious matter contained in Dr. O'Connor's notes, as for the original texts." MS. note by Sheffield Grace.—Stowe Library Catalogue. No. 3847.

In the same Catalogue, No. 6138, was a set of the cancelled sheets in the four volumes. "Rare, being the only copy preserved, the rest being all destroyed."

JOURNAL OF THE SHRIEVALTY OF
RICHARD HOARE, ESQ., IN THE YEARS 1740–1.
Printed from a Manuscript in his own handwriting.
Bath : Printed by Richard Cruttwell. A.D. 1815.
Royal 4to. pp. 108.

---

* Now in the collection of the Earl of Ashburnham.

DONUM AMICIS. VERSES ON VARIOUS OCCASIONS.
BY FRANCIS NEWBERY, ESQ.
London: Printed for the Author, by Thomas Davison.
1815. 8*vo*. pp. 72.

The author says in his preface, that, " having been frequently soli-
cited to commit his little production to the press, he yields at length
to the wishes of his friends; and, with a grateful sense of their kind
partiality, he requests their acceptance of these pages, as a memorial of his esteem and regard."

———

THE BOOKE OF DEMEANOUR: FROM SMALL POEMS,
ENTITLED, THE SCHOOLE OF VERTVE.
BY RICHARD WESTE.
London: Printed by Edw. Griffin, for Nathanael
Butler, near St. Austin's Gate, by Paul's Church-yard,
Anno Dom. 1619.
London. 1815. 12*mo*. pp. 15.

Thirty-six copies were reprinted by T. Bensley and Son.

———

A CATALOGUE OF BOOKS RELATING TO THE HISTORY
AND TOPOGRAPHY OF ENGLAND, WALES, SCOTLAND,
AND IRELAND.
BY SIR RICHARD COLT HOARE, BART.
London: Printed by William Bulmer and Co., Cleve-
land-row, St. James's. 1815. 8*vo*. pp. 361.

On the back of the title, " This publication is restricted to *twenty-
five* copies. William Bulmer."
Frontispiece, a view of Stourhead, the seat of the Baronet.

Recollections Abroad,
in the Years 1785, 6, 7, 8, 9, 90, 1791.

Bath: Printed by Richard Cruttwell. 1815–1818. 4 *vols*. 8*vo*.

Vol. I. contains the Recollections of the author, the late Sir Richard Colt Hoare, Bart., in France and Italy. Vol. II. Recollections of Germany, Istria, and Italy. Vol. III. Sicily and Malta. Vol. IV. Italy, Abruzzo, &c. Of Vols. I. and II. *twenty-five* copies only were printed. Vols. III. and IV. *fifty* copies.

Abstract of the Evidence taken, or to be produced, in the service of the Right Honourable Sylvester Douglass, Lord Glenbervie, as Heir-Male in General of the Rev. James Douglass, Parson of Glenbervie, next Brother of William IXth Earl of Angus, with Opinion thereon by Thomas Thomson, Esq., Advocate.

Edinburgh: Printed by George Ramsay and Co. 1815. 4*to*. pp. 34; and a Genealogical Table.

Inventory of Worke done for the State, by [Evan Tyler] his Majestie's Printer in Scotland, Dec. 1642–Oct. 1647.

Printed at Edinburgh. M.DCCC.XV. 4*to*. pp. 16.

Printed from the original, in the Lord Registrar's Office, by the late Thomas Thomson, Esq., Depute Clerk Register.

CATALOGUS LIBRORUM QUI IN BIBLIOTHECA CATHE-
DRALIS ELIENSIS ADSERVANTUR.
1815. *Royal 8vo.* pp. 130.

Fifty copies only were printed ; a classed catalogue ; compiled by
Mr. Triphook.

" This collection is chiefly of a Theological character ; it contains
also many valuable Historical works, particularly such as relate to
English history, and a fair proportion of Classics ; though the fasti-
dious Bibliomaniacs will here look in vain for any Editiones Prin-
cipes, or for any other earlier efforts of the Press." *

———

TWO SERMONS, ETC.
[Yarmouth.] 1815. [Not published.] *4to.* pp. 63.

By the Rev. S. Barker, A.M. ; who printed *one hundred* copies, all
for private distribution. The volume contains two Sermons—I. On
the National Jubilee ; II. On the Thanksgiving—and Poems on the
Majesty of the Godhead.

———

AVCTARIVM BIBLIOTHECAE EDINBVRGENÆ, SIVE CA-
TALOGUS LIBRORUM QUOS GIULIELMUS DRUMMONDUS AB
HAWTHORNDEN BIBLIOTHECÆ D.D.Q., ANNO 1627.
Edinburgi : Excudebant Hæredes Andreæ Hart, 1627.
Small 4to., title and 3 leaves " Lectori," &c. pp. 40.
Edinburgh. 1815. *Sm. 4to.* A fac-simile reprint.

A Catalogue of Books presented by Drummond of Hawthornden,
the Poet, to the Library of the University of Edinburgh.
The reprint was limited to about fifty copies.

———

* Mr. Botfield. Notes on Cathedral Libraries, p. 131.

DESCRIPTION OF BROWSHOLME HALL, IN THE WEST
RIDING OF THE COUNTY OF YORK, AND OF THE PARISH
OF WADDINGTON, IN THE SAME COUNTY; ALSO, A COL-
LECTION OF LETTERS, FROM ORIGINAL MANUSCRIPTS,
IN THE REIGNS OF CHARLES I. AND II., AND JAMES
II., IN THE POSSESSION OF THOMAS LISTER PARKER,
OF BROWSHOLME HALL, ESQ.

London: Printed by S. Gosnell, Little Queen-street,
Holborn. Anno Dom. 1815. 4*to.* pp. 130.

Compiled by Mr. Parker; the description of Waddington and the
forest of Bowland from Whitaker's History of Whalley. It was
privately printed by the owner of the estate, for distribution among
his friends; copies have been sold however, I believe, since its first
appearance. It contains twenty plates, a list of which are given in
Mr. Upcott's English Topography. A review of the work will be
found in the *Gentleman's Magazine*, 1815, p. 525.

———

ANOTHER ACCOUNT OF THE INCIDENTS FROM WHICH
THE TITLE AND PART OF THE STORY OF SHAKESPEARE'S
TEMPEST WERE DERIVED, AND THE TRUE ERA OF IT
ASCERTAINED, EVINCING THE ORIGINAL CONNEXION OF
THE ROYAL FAMILY WITH THE POET'S DRAMA.
BY GEORGE CHALMERS, F.R.S., S.A.

London. Only forty copies printed, by R. and A.
Taylor, but not published, nor intended to be. 1815.
8*vo.* pp. 82; preface, &c., pp. viii.

" The Knight of the Leaden Mace," as he was called; see a ballad
on the Shakespeare controversy between Malone and Chalmers in
the "Pursuits of Literature."

BIBLIOGRAPHIANA, BY A SOCIETY OF GENTLEMEN;
Originally published in the " Manchester Exchange
Herald," in the Years 1815 and 1816.
Manchester: Printed by Joseph Aston.

Only twenty-four copies printed.

SOME ACCOUNT OF THE LATE SMITHSON TENNANT,
ESQ., F.R.S., PROFESSOR OF CHEMISTRY IN THE UNI-
VERSITY OF CAMBRIDGE.
London: Printed by C. Baldwin. 1815. 8vo. pp. 46.

Mr. Tennant was killed, owing to the giving way of a drawbridge
he was crossing, near Boulogne. See a notice of him in *Gentleman's
Magazine*, 1815, p. 281.

AN ACCOUNT OF THE VISIT OF HIS ROYAL HIGHNESS
THE PRINCE REGENT, AND THEIR IMPERIAL AND ROYAL
MAJESTIES THE EMPEROR OF RUSSIA AND KING OF
PRUSSIA, TO THE UNIVERSITY OF OXFORD, IN JUNE,
1814.
Oxford: Printed at the Clarendon Press. 1815. 4to.
pp. 98.

Twelve copies of this volume were printed on vellum; the distribution of which will be found in Mr. Moule's Bibliotheca Heraldica. Mr. Upcott possessed the copy which was presented to the
Prince of Orange. The title is engraved: there are also, a ground-
plan of the Radcliffe Library, a view of the interior of the Theatre,
and a sheet, containing specimens of the various types used at the
Clarendon Press. There are copies on large paper; which, with the
ordinary impression, make three different sizes of this work.

Account of the Proceedings at a Meeting held on the 25th January, 1815, in the Church of North Mimms, in the County of Hertford, for the Election of Eight new Trustees of the Charity Estates belonging to and for the Use of the Poor of the Parish of North Mimms:

Together with an Account of the original Foundation of the Charities; of the Exchanges which have taken place in the Lands belonging thereto; of the present State and Condition of the Property; and of the past Management and Expenditure of the Funds. Also, the Plans and Regulations proposed and adopted at the Meeting, for the future Management and Administration of the Charities. With a Supplementary Statement of the Proceedings of the Trustees, up to the 1st of August, 1815.

London: Printed by R. and A. Taylor, Shoe-lane. 1815. 8vo. pp. 64.

Two hundred copies, printed for private distribution. It was drawn up by the late Joseph Sabine, Esq., the distinguished Naturalist.

Fragments of Essays.

" If men intend to observe, they will find much worthy to observe."—*Bacon.*

London: Printed by G. Sidney, Northumberland-street, Strand. 1816. 12mo. pp. 108.

By the late Chandos Leigh, Esq., of Stoneleigh, in Warwickshire, since raised to the peerage by the title of Baron Leigh : there is another volume, called " Verses by Chandos Leigh," 12mo : forming a supplement to a collection of poems, which was printed some time since, and circulated by the Author under the title of " Juvenile Poems." Never published for sale.

REPORT FROM THE COMMITTEE OF ALDERMEN, APPOINTED TO VISIT SEVERAL GAOLS IN ENGLAND. Printed by an Order of the Court of Aldermen, of the 26th September, 1815.

London: Printed by Nichols, Son, and Bentley, Red-Lion-passage, Fleet-street. 1816. *Royal 4to.* pp. 225; including the Title.

"Title, Contents, List of the several Prisons described, and Appendixes. Printed for private distribution only."—*Upcott.*

JOHNSON AND GARRICK.

[Not published.]

London: Printed by Nichols, Son, and Bentley. 1816. *8vo.* pp. 15.

A jeu d'esprit, by the late Sir Joshua Reynolds; of which Mr Croker, in the new edition of Boswell's Life of Johnson,[*] gives the following account:—

" Sir Joshua Reynolds wrote two Dialogues, in illustration of this position; in the first of which, Johnson *attacks* Garrick, in opposition to Sir Joshua, and in the other, *defends* him against Gibbon. They were originally published in a periodical work, but are preserved in Miss Hawkins' Memoirs, vol. ii. p. 110. Lord Farnborough has obligingly communicated to the editor the evidence of the late Sir George Beaumont (who had received copies of them from Sir

---

[*] Vol. iv. p. 169.

Joshua himself) both of their authenticity, and of their correct imitation of Johnson's style of conversation ; and the editor has therefore given them a place in the Appendix."

Two hundred copies were printed, and distributed by Lady Thomond, the niece of Sir Joshua Reynolds.

REFLECTIONS AND RESOLUTIONS PROPER FOR THE GENTLEMEN OF IRELAND, AS TO THEIR CONDUCT FOR THE SERVICE OF THEIR COUNTRY, As Landlords; as Masters of Families; as Protestants; as descended from British Ancestors; as Country Gentlemen and Farmers; as Justices of the Peace; as Merchants ; as Members of Parliament.
Dublin : Printed by R. Reilly, for George Ewing, at the Angel and Bible in Dame-street. 1738. Reprinted, 1816. pp. xxii; 3 leaves ; pp. 1–224. 8vo.

This edition was printed at the expense of Mr. Thomas, Pleasants, Founder of the Stove Tenter-house, Dublin, at a cost of £160. The author was the eminent Dr. Samuel Madden.

The Editor in the preface states that it is reprinted for " wide and gratuitous circulation," and that the first edition was printed in Dublin in 1738 in octavo, without preface, introduction, or table of contents.

A copy is in the library of Earl Talbot, at Ingestrie.

The first edition of the Reflections is rare.

JOURNAL OF A TOUR TO SCOTLAND.
Oxford : Printed by Munday and Slatter. M.DCCC.XVI. 8vo. pp. 131.

By the Rev. Frederick Charles Spenser, a relative of the Duke of Marlborough. He died in 1831.

Q 2

Hortus Gramineus Woburnensis :
Or, an Account of the Results of Experiments on the Produce and Nutritive Qualities of different Grasses, and other Plants, used as the Food of the more valuable Domestic Animals : instituted by John Duke of Bedford. Illustrated with dried Specimens of the Plants upon which these Experiments have been made, and practical observations on their natural Habits, and the soils best adapted to their growth ; pointing out the kinds most profitable for Permanent Pasture, Irrigated Meadows, Dry or Upland Pasture, and the alternate Husbandry ; accompanied with the discriminating Characters of the Species and Varieties.
By George Sinclair,
Gardener to his Grace the Duke of Bedford.
London : Printed by B. M'Millan, Bow-street, Covent-garden. 1816. *folio.* pp. 316 ; Index, two leaves.

This fine illustration of the grasses was prepared and printed at the expense of John sixth Duke of Bedford, one among many instances of the Duke's desire to promote the benefit of agriculture. Mr. Sinclair, the editor, died March, 1834, aged 48.

A second edition of this work, for sale, was published in 1825, in 8vo. with the plates engraved. Its principal merit consists in the experiments.

Description of a Journey to French Flanders, in 1816.
By W. Watts.
London. 1816. 8vo.

From the late Mr. Rodd's Sale Catalogue. Part II. No. 1714.

SELECT PIECES IN VERSE AND PROSE.
BY THE LATE JOHN BOWDLER, ESQ. OF LINCOLN'S INN,
BARRISTER-AT-LAW.
In two volumes.
London: Printed by G. Davidson, Old-Boswell-court,
Carey-street. 1816. 8*vo*.

This work was edited by John Bowdler, Esq., the father of the
author, who died of a decline, in February, 1815. Three editions
have since been printed for sale, the profits arising from which were
given to the Society for the Suppression of Vice.

———

CATALOGUE OF THE LIBRARY OF JOHN BLACKBURN,
ESQ., OF PRESTON HOUSE, HAMPSHIRE.
ARRANGED BY G. J. ROBSON.
Basingstoke. 1816. 4*to*.

———

THREE SERMONS.
BY THE REV. S. BARKER, A.M.
1816. 4*to*.

One hundred copies were printed, for private circulation among
the writer's friends, residing, it is believed, at Yarmouth.

———

LAMENTABLE VISION OF THE DEVOUT HERMIT.
Manchester: Printed in the year 1816. *folio*. pp. 22.

The editor of this work is Mr. W. Yates, who printed *thirty* copies,
for private distribution.

BROMLEY HILL, THE SEAT OF THE RIGHT HON.
CHARLES LONG, M.P.; A SKETCH,
BY GEORGE CUMBERLAND.

London: Printed by T. Bensley and Son, for R. Triphook, 23, Old Bond-street. 1816. 8*vo.* pp. 59.

Bromley Hill was the residence of the late Lord Farnborough; to
whose well-known taste this seat owes much of its beauty.

———

COPY OF A GENEALOGICAL ACCOUNT OF THE BAR-
NARD FAMILY, NOW [1816] IN THE POSSESSION OF MR.
JOHN BARNARD, OF NICOLL's-SQUARE, LONDON, SIL-
VER-FLATTER.

"Printed in 1816, for circulation among the friends and relations
of the family." *

———

CORRESPONDENCE, LEGAL PROCEEDINGS, AND EVI-
DENCES, RESPECTING THE ANCIENT SCHOOL, ATTACHED
TO SAINT PAUL's CATHEDRAL.

A new edition, considerably enlarged.

London. 1816.   4*to.*

By Miss Maria Hackett, of Crosby-square, London. This lady
was subject to the witty remarks of the late facetious Canon of
St. Paul's, Sidney Smith.

———

* Moule, Bibliotheca Heraldica.

Dowland's Musical Banquet.
Chiswick Press: by Charles Whittingham. 1817.

Edited by Mr. Singer. *Twenty-five* copies only were printed. Dowland was the son of an eminent musician of the age of Shakspeare. He printed this Banquet in 1610.

The Long Pack;
A Northumbrian Tale, an Hundred Years Old.
George Angus, Printer, Newcastle. 1817. *8vo.* pp. 24.

Twelve copies only are said to have been printed of this tale, two of which were on vellum.

Catalogue of Books in the Library of Robert Ferguson, of Raith, Esquire.
Edinburgh: Printed at the Caledonian Mercury Press. 1817. *4to.* pp. 102; Index, two leaves.

Essay on the proper Temper of the Mind towards God: addressed by the Earl of Carysfort to his Children. To which is added, a Dissertation on the Example of Christ.
London: Printed by J. M'Creery, Black Horse, Fleet-street. 1817. *12mo.*

"Not published. Only fifty copies printed." Mr. Grenville's copy contains a note from the noble author, John Joshua, K.P. second Lord, who died, April, 1828.

POEMS ON SEVERAL OCCASIONS, IN TWO VOLUMES.
Volume First. Greenock: Printed by Donaldson and
Macfarlane. 1817.
Volume Second. Greenock : Printed by Robert Do-
naldson. 1819. 8vo.
BY JOHN DUNLOP, ESQ.,
Collector of the Customs at Port Glasgow, father of
John C. Dunlop, author of the "History of Fiction,"
3 vols. 1814.

In reference to these occasional poems, the author says in his
preface, " I have not, however, insulted the dignity of the press by
publication, having allowed ten copies only to be thrown off, for particular friends on whose indulgence I can rely."

———

NORTH OF ENGLAND AND SCOTLAND IN M.DCC.IV.
Edinburgh : William Blackwood. M.DCCC.XVII. 12mo.
pp. 71.

Printed from a manuscript in the library of the late Thomas
Johnes, Esq., of Hafod.
At the back of the title page " only 100 copies printed, not for
sale." W. Bell.

———

EXTRACTS FROM THE LIFE OF THE VIRTUOUS CHRISTIAN
AND RENOWNED QUEEN ANNE BOLEIGNE.
BY GEORGE WYATT, ESQ.
Written at the close of the Sixteenth Century. From
the Manuscript Collections of the Rev. John Lewis.
1817. 4to.

" The manuscript from which the present very interesting Memoir
is printed, was purchased at the late Sir Peter Thomson's sale. It

is in the hand-writing of the Rev. John Lewis, of the Isle of Thanet, the celebrated antiquary. It was printed in 1817, for a few noblemen and gentlemen ; but *twenty-seven* copies only having been taken off, it may be considered still to have almost the rarity of a manuscript." *

JOURNAL OF A TOUR THROUGH PART OF FRANCE, FLANDERS, AND HOLLAND; INCLUDING A VISIT TO PARIS, AND A WALK OVER THE FIELD OF WATERLOO; MADE IN THE SUMMER OF 1816.

BY SETH WILLIAM STEVENSON.

Norwich : Printed, not for sale, at the Norfolk Chronicle Press, by Stevenson, Matchett, and Stevenson. 1817. 8*vo*. pp. 349. App. pp. 8. Title, preface, &c., pp. xiv.

The author of this Tour is one of the editors of the Norfolk Chronicle, and in 1833 served the office of mayor of Norwich.

SELECTION OF CURIOUS AND ENTERTAINING GAMES AT CHESS, THAT HAVE BEEN ACTUALLY PLAYED BY JOHN CAZENOVE.

London. 1817. 12*mo*.

"This book has only been circulated among the private friends of the author, who is, or was, the president of the London Chess Club." †

* Cavendish, Life of Wolsey, by Singer, 2nd edit. p. 420.
† Lowndes, Bibliographer's Manual.

The Statutes of the Collegiate Church of Ely, in the original Latin; with Explanatory Notes, and an English Translation.
[By —— Church, of Spital-square.]
London: Printed by Barnard and Farley, Skinner-street. 1817. 8*vo.* Not for sale. pp. 151; including the Title, Dedication to the Gentlemen and Inhabitants of the City of Ely, and Index of the Chapters, in Latin and English.

This collection was not printed from the originals in the posses-sion of the dean and chapter of Ely, and is said to contain many inaccuracies.

———

A Topographical and Historical Description of the Parish of Tixall, in the County of Stafford. By Sir Thomas Clifford, Bart., and Arthur Clifford, Esq.
Paris: Printed by M. Nouzon, 9, Rue de Clery. 1817. 4*to.* pp. 325.

Fifty copies of pp. 153 and 154 were reprinted, on account of mis-nomers.
Sir Thomas Clifford, the principal editor of the second volume, was the eldest son of the late Hon. Thomas Clifford; fourth son of Hugh, Lord Clifford of Chudleigh. He was author of a reli-gious work, entitled, " L'Evangile Medite." At a late period of his life, he imbibed a taste for the study of history, antiquities, topo-graphy, heraldry, and genealogy, in all of which he was conversant. He succeeded, on the death of Francis Constable, Esq., to the great estates of Burton Constable and Wycliff, in the county of York, on which occasion he assumed the name of Constable. He died at Ghent, 25th February, 1823, æt. 60. One copy of this work was in-

laid on elephant folio, for the purpose of illustration ; in the embellishment of which Sir Thomas was employed at the time of his
death. It is very profusely illustrated with portraits and topographical views, and forms two volumes, elegantly bound in russia,
which were in the library at Tixall. The armorial bearings connected with the family, are all emblazoned on the margin of this
copy, under the direction of the late Mr. Moule. Tixall is now the
property of Earl Talbot. The library, it is believed, was removed to
Burton Constable near Hull.

COLLECTANEA CLIFFORDIANA ; IN THREE PARTS:
Containing, I. Anecdotes of Illustrious Personages of
the name of Clifford. II. Historical and Genealogical
Notices respecting the Origin and Antiquity of the Clifford Family. III. Clifford ; a Tragedy.

> Tu facito, mox quum matura adoleverit ætas,
> Sis memor, et te animo repetentem exempla tuorum
> Et pater Æneas, et avunculus excitet Hector.
> *Virgil, Æn.* B. xii. 438-40.

BY ARTHUR CLIFFORD, ESQ.
Paris : Printed by M. Nouzon, 9, Rue de Clery. 1817.
8*vo.*

TWO FABLES IN VERSE.
BY SYDNEY, EARL OF GODOLPHIN.
Never before printed.
[1817]. pp. 15. 4*to.*

Sydney, Earl of Godolphin, was Lord Treasurer in the reign of
Queen Anne. The following note, in the hand-writing of the Editor,

the late Mr. Coxe, the historian, was copied by permission of the late Lord Dover, from the copy in his library :—

" These two Fables in Verse, imitated from La Fontaine, which are printed in these pages from the original manuscripts in the hand-writing of Lord Godolphin, were found among the papers left by Sarah Duchess of Marlborough, and preserved at Blenheim."

A Third Fable in Verse, with a fac-simile of the hand-writing of the author, is attached to the former two.

Twenty copies (ten on demy 4to. and ten on imperial 4to.) were printed of the Two Fables ; and twelve on demy 4to. and ten on imperial 4to., of the Third. A copy is in the Grenville library.

————

TOPOGRAPHICAL ACCOUNT OF THE HUNDRED OF
BOSMERE IN HAMPSHIRE;
Comprising the Parishes of Havant, Warblington, and Hayling.

—— Ego apis Matinæ
More modoque,
Grata carpentis thyma per laborem
Plurimum.　　　　　　　　　HOR.

Havant Press : Printed by Henry Skelton, West-street. 1817. *Small* 4*to.* pp. 112 ; Title, &c., pp. viii.

" The following pages were compiled for the use of an intended History of Hampshire, undertaken by the Rev. William Bingley, under the patronage of the Right Hon. George Rose ; but as that book is laid aside, the Editor was induced to publish a few copies to circulate among his friends."

Only thirty copies printed.

A Genealogical Memoir of the Family of Mont-
morency, styled De Marisco, or Morres, ancient
Lords of Marisco, or De Montemarisco, in the
Peerage of England and Ireland, and respect-
fully addressed to his Majesty Louis XVIII.,
King of France and Navarre.
By Henry de Montmorency-Morres,
Knight of St. Louis, Colonel d'Etat Major in his
Most Christian Majesty's Service.
Printed at Paris. 1817.   4*to*.

This, as well as the Clifford papers, p. 235, illustrative of English
families, and important generally as historical documents, has been
inserted although printed abroad.

———

The Pageant of the Company of Sheremen and
Taylors in Coventry, as performed by them on
the Festival of Corpus Christi;
Together with other Pageants, exhibited on occasion
of several Royal Visits to that City, and two Specimens
of ancient Local Poetry.
Coventry: Printed by W. Reader. 1817. 4*to*. pp.
14; Title and Preface, two leaves.

Edited by Mr. Thomas Sharp, of Coventry, who says in the preface, " The celebrity of the Coventry Pageants gives a particular degree of interest to this portion of our national antiquities ; and he
has been induced to print *twelve* copies, for the purpose of bringing
it more immediately to the knowledge of his antiquarian friends."

BIBLIOTHECA MS. STOWENSIS.
A Descriptive Catalogue of the Manuscripts in the Stowe Library.
Buckingham: Printed by J. Seeley. Vol. I. pp. xvi and 421. 1818. Vol. II. pp. vi and 606. 1819. Appendix to Vol. I. pp. 80. 1819. *3 vols. 4to.*

Compiled by the late learned Dr. O'Conor, librarian to the first Duke of Buckingham and Chandos, who printed *two hundred* copies for private distribution. The MSS. are now in the possession of the Earl of Ashburnham, who purchased them for 8,000*l.* A sale catalogue had been prepared and printed by Messrs. Sotheby and Wilkinson, June 11, 1849, eight days, which the private purchase above mentioned prevented.

———

AN INQUIRY INTO THE SYMBOLICAL LANGUAGE OF ANCIENT ART AND MYTHOLOGY.
BY R. PAYNE KNIGHT.
London. 1818. *8vo.*

" Intended to be prefixed to the second volume of the Select Specimens of Ancient Sculpture, published by the Society of Dilettanti ; but the necessarily slow progress of that work, in the exhausted state of the funds to be applied to it, affording the author little probability of seeing its completion, he has been induced to print this proposed part of it, that any information which he may have been able to collect, on a subject so interesting to all lovers of elegant art, may not be lost to his successors in such pursuits, but receive any additions and corrections which may render it more worthy to appear in the splendid form, and with the beautiful illustrations of the preceding volume."

Richard Payne Knight, of Downton Castle, Herefordshire, Esq., died in 1824 : he bequeathed his medals, drawings, and bronzes, to the British Museum : his library devolved to his brother, Thomas Knight, Esq., who inherited the estates.

This essay is reprinted in the Classical Journal, vol. xxiii.

LETTER TO A NEAPOLITAN FROM AN ENGLISHMAN.
London: Printed by T. Davison. 1818. *8vo.*

Written by the late Lord Holland, to clear up some misconception by Murat, of a conversation which his lordship had held with him. A volume by a foreigner on this subject was in the library of the late Duke of Wellington : the pencil annotations in which by the Illustrious Man were anything but complimentary to the writer's veracity.

INSTITUTIONS; OR, ADVICE TO HIS GRANDSON.
In Three Parts.
BY WILLIAM HIGFORD, ESQ.
London. 1658.
[London : Reprinted by W. Bulmer and Co., Cleveland-row, St. James's. 1818]. pp. 104. *8vo.*

Reprinted at the expense of Lieut.-General Burr. A gentleman of the name of Parsons, obtained a portion of the Scudamore property with General Burr, and assumed the name of Higford. In all probability, this book was written by a connection of the family.

A DREAM.

———— ; Tacitæ quid vult sibi noctis imago ?
*****
*****
Dummodo tale nihil vigilans committere tentem ;
Sæpe licet simili redeat sub imagine somnus.

London: Printed by Bensley and Sons. 1818. *8vo.* pp. 47.

" Not published : very remarkable for the beauty of the dramatic strokes in the dialogue ; a species of excellence which, since

Berkeley, has been rare in English composition. I beg this to be very carefully preserved. I leave the author's name to be guessed." *

By Lord Holland ; who printed a very small number of copies, for private distribution.

———

A DYSSHE OF SOTTLETIES RYGHT RYCHELIE SEA-SONID ; OR, A GOODLIE GARLAND OF DURESME EVER-GREENS PLAITED BY THE INGENIOUS.

> " Her moncks and lordlie priours rise to view,
> And all her faded garlands bloom anew."

Imprynted by Master Francis Humble and his Felowes, for anenst ye Neptune in Foro Dunelmensi. M.DCCC.XVIII. 8vo. pp. 50.

Only *twenty* copies were printed of this collection ; which was edited by the Rev. James Raine, librarian of the Cathedral Library, and the late Richard Surtees, Esq., of Mainsforth, the historian of the county of Durham.

———

RALPH ROYSTER DOYSTER ;
A COMEDY.
London : Reprinted in the year 1818.   8vo.   pp. 88.

This comedy is said to have been written by Nicholas Udal, for-merly Master of Eton College ; where the unique copy, from which this reprint was made, is deposited. This impression, which was limited to twenty-five copies, was printed at the expense of the Rev. Mr. Briggs : it was again printed, in 1821, by Mr. Pulham, of the East India House ; and also in a series of " Old Plays," published in

———

* Note in Sir James Mackintosh's copy.

1830, by T. White, Johnson's-court, Fleet-street. The editor is indebted for this information to Mr. William Holgate, of the General Post Office, who collected a very curious dramatic library, remarkable for its fine condition ; sold by auction, by Sotheby and Son, November, 1831. Mr. Hallam * says, " In spite of its title, it is a play of some merit, though the wit may seem designed for the purpose of natural merriment rather than critical glory. We find in it what is of no slight value, the earliest lively picture of London manners among the gallants and citizens, who furnished so much for the stage down to the civil wars."

CATALOGUE OF THE BOOKS IN THE LIBRARY OF THE COLLEGE OF ADVOCATES, IN DOCTORS' COMMONS.

London : Printed by Charles Baldwin. 1818. 8*vo.* pp. 236.

Compiled by Mr. Henry Butterworth, law bookseller, Fleet-street. A new edition has been published since.

POEMS TO THE MEMORY OF THOMSON, IN THE TEMPLE OF THE MUSES, AT DRYBURGH ABBEY.

Edinburgh. 1818. 8*vo.*

These verses, written by the Rev. John Richmond, of Southdean, were printed at the expense of the late Earl of Buchan, for presents, who printed privately some other trifling effusions. In this abbey are deposited the remains of Sir Walter Scott, Bart.

----

* Literature of Europe, vol. i. p. 612.

R

ACCOUNT OF
LORD BORINGDON'S ACCIDENT AND DEATH.
1818.   4*to.* ; with a portrait.

The subject of this memoir was the eldest son of the Earl of
Morley. He died near Paris, in consequence of accidentally swal-
lowing an ear of rye, in the twelfth year of his age.

MEMOIR OF THE ORIGIN AND INCORPORATION OF THE
TRINITY HOUSE OF DEPTFORD STROND.
London : Printed by J. Darling, Leadenhall-street.
1818.   8*vo.*   pp. 247.

By the late Joseph Cotton, Esq., Deputy-Master of the Trinity
House.

CATALOGUE
OF THE MUSEUM OF JOHN HEAVISIDE, ESQ.,
Comprising Human Anatomy, Natural and Morbid;
Comparative Anatomy ; and Natural History.
London : Printed by G. Woodfall, Angel-court, Skin-
ner-street.   1818.   8*vo.*   pp. 267.   Appendix to Cata-
logue, including Additions to the Morbid Anatomy,
between 1818 and August, 1823.   pp. 4.

This Museum was dispersed by public auction, in 1829. A considerable portion was purchased by John Palmer De la Fons, Esq.,
then residing in the same premises, in George-street, Hanover-
square ; who made some very valuable and curious additions, which
in the season he most liberally threw open for the inspection of his
friends and the scientific world. The Museum was disposed of in
1835.

EAGLE'S-CLIFFE LEGEND.

Stockton. 1818. 4to.

Fifty copies printed as presents.

ORIGINAL LETTERS, FROM THE RIGHT HON. LADY MARY W. MONTAGUE, TO SIR JAMES AND LADY FRANCES STEUART: AND MEMOIRS AND ANECDOTES OF THOSE DISTINGUISHED PERSONS.

Greenock: Printed by Robert Donaldson. 1818. 12mo. pp. 159. Title and preface, pp. vi.

Edited by Mr. Dunlop, Collector of Excise at Greenock.
A copy is in the Marquis of Bute's library.

FAREWELL TO ITALY; AND OCCASIONAL POEMS. BY WILLIAM SOTHEBY, ESQ.

London: Printed by W. Bulmer and Co., Cleveland-row, St. James's. 1818. 4to. pp. 65.

Two hundred and fifty copies were printed. An edition in 8vo. was reprinted subsequently, for sale. Mr. Sotheby died in 1834.

A COLLECTION OF ROYAL GRANTS AND OTHER DOCUMENTS RELATIVE TO THE CONSTITUTION AND PRIVILEGES OF THE ROYAL COLLEGE OF SURGEONS OF EDINBURGH M.DV.—M.DCCC.XIII.

Printed at Edinburgh. 1818. 8vo. pp. 139. Preface and pp. viii.

LETTER TO A HIGHLY RESPECTED FRIEND, ON THE
SUBJECT OF CERTAIN ERRORS OF THE ANTINOMIAN
KIND, WHICH HAVE LATELY SPRUNG UP IN THE WEST
OF ENGLAND, AND ARE NOW MAKING AN ALARMING
PROGRESS THROUGHOUT THE KINGDOM.
BY THE REV. JOHN SIMONS, LL.B.,
Rector of Paul's Cray.
London: Printed by Ellerton and Henderson.   1818.
8*vo*.   pp. 69.

"A Letter never intended for the press, but soon to be published,
with a Preface and Appendix, if it should be thought expedient to
give it a wider circulation."

HINTS ON THE TOPOGRAPHY OF WILTSHIRE.
Queries submitted to the Consideration of the Nobility, &c., of the County of Wilts, with a View to
promote a General History of the County.
Salisbury.   1818.   8*vo*.

Printed for private distribution by Sir Richard Colt Hoare, Bart.

MISCELLANEA.   J. G.
1818.   4*to*.   pp. 83.

This volume, printed at Edinburgh, contains translations of Addison's Machinæ Gesticulantes, Frowde's Cursus Glaciales, &c.   The
author was James Glassford of Dongelston, advocate, who died at
Edinburgh, July, 1845.   He also printed another volume, entitled
" Elegiæ," without place or date; it is a collection of English verse,
pp. 30.   There is another edition of it, pp. 39.

La Prima Musa Clio; translated from the Italian of Cesare Avena de Valdiere. Or, The Divine Traveller; By George Baldwin. Exhibiting a series of Writings obtained in the ecstasy of Magnetic Sleep. Most important for the integrity of the Fact: most interesting to the Curious: most consoling to the Afflicted: and most edifying to the Dubious among Mankind.

[London: Printed by C. Richards, Warwick-street, Golden-square. 1818.]

A thick 8vo. volume, originally intended to form three.

Genealogies of the Hindus, extracted from their Sacred Writings; with an Introduction and Alphabetical Index. By Francis Hamilton, M.D., Fellow of the Royal Societies and of the Societies of Antiquaries of London and Edinburgh, of the Linnæan Society of London, and of the Asiatic Society of Calcutta.

Edinburgh: Printed for the Author. 1819. (Dedicated to James, Duke of Montrose.) 8vo. pp. 126.

Genealogical Tables of the Deities, Princes, Heroes, and Remarkable Personages of the Hindus, extracted from the Sacred Writings of that People. With an Introduction and Index. By Francis Hamilton, M.D., Fellow of the Royal

Society and of the Societies of Antiquaries of London and Edinburgh, and of the Asiatic Society of Calcutta.

Edinburgh: Printed for the Author, by William Aitkin. 1819. *Large folio*. Containing twenty-five engraved general Tables.

Fifty copies of these works were printed for presentations to public libraries and crowned heads.

TOUR IN HOLLAND IN THE YEAR M.DCCC.XIX.

London. 12*mo.*

Privately printed. Title, contents, and errata, vi pages.

Tour (which commences 14th August, 1819) 252 pages. There is no date on the title.

THE ART OF ANGLING.

Not intended for sale.

London: Printed by W. Davy, 41, James-street, Grosvenor-square. [1819.] 12*mo.* pp. 35.

A copy was in Mr. Haslewood's Library, No. 41 of his catalogue; in which is a note stating he had never seen another.

MEMOIR OF THE CLAIM OF MR. JOHN LINDSAY CRAWFURD TO THE TITLE AND ESTATES OF CRAWFURD AND KILBURNY.

Paisley: Printed by John Neilson for Mr. Crawfurd. 1819. 4*to.* pp. 12, and Pedigree.

This tract is very rare.

The Crawfurd estates devolved on the late Earl of Glasgow, as heir of the line of the Crawfurds, and the title has been adjudged to Lord Balcarres, who is now Earl of Crawfurd and Baron Lyndsay. The Earldom of Lyndsay is still in abeyance.

The following anecdote, highly honourable to the late Lord Glasgow, has been communicated by a gentleman to whom the Editor is under very great obligation for different works relating to Scottish history and antiquities.

" John Crawfurd, the forger, having returned to this country, again pursued his claims, but never got the length of the House of Peers. At this time the Crawfurd estates were in the possession of Lady Mary Lyndsay Crawfurd, the sister of the last recognised Earl of Crawfurd and Lyndsay. Her ladyship threw every impediment in the way of investigation ; but dying, Lord Glasgow succeeded to her estates, but not to her mode of opposition. He said, ' If this man be really what he declares, God forbid I should deprive him of his inheritance. Let him have every justice.' Accordingly his lordship furnished ample funds for a fair investigation, the result of which was, that this man, who died in the interim, and was succeeded in his pretensions by a son, was proved to be—what was always the general belief—an impostor. Had the original forgeries not been disclosed by a confederate, there is no doubt that this man would have got both title and estates."

Sermons on the Decalogue ;

To which is added, a Sermon on the Sacrament of the Lord's Supper, preached in the Parish Church of Nuneham Courtenay, Oxon.

By F. Haggitt, D.D.,

Rector of that Parish, and Prebendary of Durham. Not published.

London : Printed for the Author, by J. Brettell, Rupert-street, Haymarket. 1819. 8*vo.* pp. *232.*

Dr. Haggitt was author of several works printed for sale.

CATALOGUE OF THE LIBRARY
OF THE DEAN AND CHAPTER OF NORWICH.
London : Printed by G. Auld, Greville-street. 1819. 8*vo*. pp. 120.

An alphabetical catalogue.

" The books principally relate to Divinity, English History, and Classical Literature ; and are chiefly of recent donation, the greater portion of the existing collection having been presented to the library by Frank Sayers, M.D. It is pleasant also to notice the judicious additions of standard theological and historical works, by purchase from time to time, as the funds admit." Mr. Botfield* speaks in just praise of the preservation of conventual volumes, neither distinguished by excessive rarity, nor remarkable for un-common worth.

———

SURVEY OF TULLAROAN, OR GRACE'S PARISH, IN THE CANTRED OF GRACE'S COUNTRY, COUNTY OF KILKENNY : BEING A GENEALOGICAL HISTORY OF THE FAMILY OF GRACE, FROM THEIR SETTLEMENT IN IRE-LAND, TEMP. HEN. II., TO THE PRESENT PERIOD.
Dublin : Printed at the Faulkner Press. 1819. 8*vo*. pp. 160.

" The impression of this neatly-printed work is restricted to *fifty* copies, for private distribution. The work is accompanied by ' A Descriptive Sketch of the Grace Mausoleum,' containing the monumental inscriptions of the family, with genealogical, biographical, and heraldic details, printed at the same time and place, pp. 106 ; also limited to the same number of copies. The two parts form a handsome and interesting volume, being intended to be bound toge-ther; and contain a variety of graphic illustrations of considerable

———

* Notes on Cathedral Libraries.

local interest, consisting of twenty-nine original family portraits, engraved by R. Grave, London; thirty topographical plates; and eleven heraldic subjects; together with two maps, the one a facsimile of a survey of Grace's Parish, made in 1665, and the other of a survey made in 1818. The above genealogical and topographical descriptions were written by Sheffield Grace, Esq., of Lincoln's Inn, F.S.A.; and the materials, consisting of several volumes in manuscript, evince infinite knowledge of the subject."*

A DESCRIPTIVE AND ARCHITECTURAL SKETCH OF THE GRACE MAUSOLEUM, IN THE QUEEN'S COUNTY; TAKEN FROM THE STATISTICAL ACCOUNT, OR PAROCHIAL SURVEY OF IRELAND,
BY WILLIAM SHAW MASON, ESQ.
Dublin. 1819. *8vo.*

This impression consists of fifty copies: and, as has been stated in the account of Mr. Grace's work, p. 248, usually accompanies that volume.

ANE ADDICIOUN OF SCOTTIS CORNIKLIS AND DEIDIS. 4*to.* pp. 60.

The first part of this volume has this title—" Heir followis ane schort Memoriale of the Scottis Corniklis for addicioun;" and the second part, at p. 29,—" A short Chronicle of the Reign of James the Second, King of Scots." This historical fragment was printed from the Asloan MS. in the Auchinleck Library, at the expense of the late Thomas Thomson, Esq. A fac-simile of the writing is given.

---

* Moule, Bibliotheca Heraldica.

A DISCOURSE DELIVERED IN ST. MARY'S CHURCH, JUNE 11, 1819, BEFORE THE UNIVERSITY OF OXFORD, BEING THE FESTIVAL OF ST. BARNABAS. By J. RADFORD, B.D., Fellow of Lincoln College. Oxford: Printed by J. and T. Bartlett. 1819. *8vo.* pp. 60.

Only thirty copies printed, for private distribution.

KING COAL'S LEVEE; OR, GEOLOGICAL ETIQUETTE; WITH EXPLANATORY NOTES. TO WHICH IS ADDED, THE COUNCIL OF THE METALS. By JOHN SCAFE, ESQ. Alnwick: Printed by J. Graham.   12*mo.*

Twenty-five copies were printed of this work. A second edition was printed in 1819.

A LITERAL TRANSLATION OF THE SAXON CHRONICLE. Norwich: Printed by Stevenson and Co., for J. and A. Arch, Cornhill. 1819. 12*mo.*

Translated by Miss Anna Gurney, of Norwich. Originally intended for sale; but during its progress through the press, the translator hearing of the edition by Dr. Ingram, it was determined to circulate this translation privately.

" The honour of having *printed* the first literal version of the Saxon annals was reserved for a learned lady, the Elstob of her age." *

---

* Ingram, Preface to the Saxon Chronicle. 4to. 1823.

Catalogue of the Pictures, Casts, and Busts, belonging to the Earl of Morley.
Plymouth. 1819.

The seat of the Earl of Morley, Saltram in Devonshire, has been greatly improved by the present noble owner. It contains a fine collection of busts and paintings; among the latter, a very choice collection of the works of Sir Joshua Reynolds, a native of the county.

Poetry of the College Magazine.
Windsor : Printed by Knight and Son. 1819. 8vo. pp. 104.

The College Magazine was circulated in MS. by some Etonians. A selection of the poetry was printed for private distribution. One hundred copies were, it is believed, printed. Mr. Moultrie, one of the writers in the Etonian, a collection of Essays in three volumes octavo, was a contributor.

Memoir of the Life of Lieut.-Col. Spencer Thomas Vassall; with an elegiac Ode upon his Death.
By Miss Holford.
Bristol. 8vo. pp. 59.

Col. Vassall was a gallant officer, Lieut.-Col. of the 38th Foot; which regiment he commanded in the expedition to South America, where he received a mortal wound while bravely leading his men, at the assault of the fortress of Monte Video, in the night between the 2nd and 3rd of February, 1807.

" Every bullet has its billet. The family of the late Colonel Vassall, of the 38th Regiment, have adopted this phrase among their

mottos. In the attack on Monte Video in 1807, where he commanded that regiment, they missed the breach on their approach.
The grape and musketry were so hot, that it drove the men into
confusion, and would have made numbers of them retreat, but for
his exertions. When he observed any of the men stoop or flinch, he
cried out as loud as possible, 'Brave 38th, my brave men, don't
flinch, every bullet has its billet. Push on, follow me, 38th.' He
rallied them repeatedly in this manner, until he got them inside
the breach. He was advancing to the main battery, when a grape
shot broke his leg; and as soon as he fell he cried out— ' Push on,
somebody will take me up, my good soldiers, charge them; never
mind me, it is only the loss of a leg in the service.' He sat up and
helped to tie on a handkerchief to stop the blood, and cried out all
the time of the action, ' I care not for my leg, if my regiment do
their duty, as I hope they will.' As soon as the town surrendered
he heard the men cheer; he joined them with as great spirits as if
nothing had happened, and called them out to be carried at the head
of his regiment. He died in three days after. There is a monument
to his memory in St. Paul's Church, Bristol."—*John Bull*, 15th December, 1833.

PREMONITORY EXTRACTS;

Selected from various Authors of the religious Society
of Friends; with an Appendix, containing similar Extracts from Writers of the Church of England: and
Notes. [Not published.]

Title as above, with " Rose, Printer, Bristol," at the
bottom of the reverse side of the title.

Preface, pp. i to iii, ending with Ninth Month, 1819. Corrigenda
et Addenda, and Index, two leaves, of which the last page is blank;
pp. 252; Appendix, pp. 253 to 338; Notes, pp. 339 to 420.

This work was edited by Dr. Gawen Ball, physician at Bristol.

Some Account of Great Milton, in Oxfordshire.
[By the Rev. Thomas Ellis, late Vicar of the Parish.]
Oxford : Printed by W. Baxter, 1819. 8vo. pp. 48.

The circumstance which gives the greatest interest to the history of this place, is that of its being the residence of the ancestors of our immortal poet of the same name. This manor was once in the possession of Sir Geoffrey Dormer, a wool-stapler in this county, and Lord Mayor of London, 1541; related to the noble family of Dormer, of Wing, Bucks. The Rectory is the corps of a Prebend in the Cathedral Church of Lincoln.

———

Historical and Genealogical Account of the Clan or Family of Macdonald, from Somerlett, King of the Isles, Lord of Argyll and Kintyre, to the present Period, more particularly as relating to the senior Branch of that Family, viz. the Clan Ranald.

In two parts. Part I. From Somerlett to John, Lord of the Isles. Part II. From John to the present Chief.

Edinburgh : Printed by Duncan Stevenson and Co. 1819. Royal 8vo.

———

Guilt ; or, the Anniversary.
A Tragedy, in Four Acts, from the German of Adolphus Mullner.
Edinburgh : Printed by John Ballantyne and Co. 1819. 4to. pp. 104.

Translated by R. P. Gillies, Esq., author of "Childe Alarique;" the impression was limited to *fifty* copies.

THE BOOK OF DEATH.

London: Printed by W. Bulmer and Co., Cleveland-row. 1819. *Crown 8vo.* pp. 408; Index, six leaves; Errata, one page.

The title is inclosed in a wood-cut border, composed of death's heads and shin-bones: in a few copies, this cut is printed in different colours. The work was edited by Samuel Dobree, Esq., of Waltham-stow; sixty copies only were printed, for private circulation. In the title-page is a vignette, a view of the editor's house.

APPENDIX TO A VINDICATION OF THE UNIVERSITY OF CAMBRIDGE FROM THE REFLECTIONS OF SIR JAMES EDWARD SMITH, ETC., ETC.

By JAMES HENRY MONK, B.D., Professor of Greek in that University, now Bishop of Gloucester.

Cambridge: Printed at the University Press, in May, 1819. *8vo.* pp. 55.

Sir James Smith was a candidate for the Botanical chair in the University of Cambridge; but did not succeed, owing to some objections to his peculiar religious principles.

THE FARMER'S VISION.
BY THOMAS, LORD ERSKINE.

London: Printed by C. Roworth, Bell-yard, Temple-bar. 1819. *8vo.* pp. 25.

A satirical poem, by the late Lord Erskine, chiefly intended to show the folly of farmers destroying rooks.

A STATEMENT OF REASONS WHY THE RIGHT REV. BENCH OF BISHOPS OF THE ESTABLISHED CHURCH OF ENGLAND OUGHT NOT TO BE CALLED UPON BY THE FRIENDS OF THAT ESTABLISHMENT TO OPPOSE THE BILL BROUGHT INTO THE HOUSE OF LORDS BY EARL GREY, FOR THE ABOLITION OF THE 25TH AND 30TH OF CHARLES THE SECOND.

By THE HON. MR. CLIFFORD.

London: Printed by Keating, Brown, and Co., 38, Duke-street, Grosvenor-square. 1819. 8*vo.*, pp. 134. Preface, pp. xxviii; Errata, one leaf.

This work was never completed. A very few copies were circulated among the friends of the author, the Hon. Hugh Clifford, since Lord Clifford of Chudleigh.

———

JOURNAL OF THE OPERATIONS OF THE BELVOIR FOXHOUNDS, FROM AUGUST 1ST, 1817, TO APRIL 25TH, 1818.

"Forsan et hæc olim meminisse juvabit."

London: Printed by B. M'Millan, Bow-street, Coventgarden, Printer in ordinary to his Majesty. 1819. 4*to.* pp. 111.

———

LETTERS WRITTEN FROM THE CONTINENT, DURING A SIX WEEKS' TOUR, IN 1818. AFTERWARDS PUBLISHED IN THE YORK CHRONICLE.

York: Printed by Blanshard. 1819. 8*vo.* pp. 119.

By Jonathan Gray, Esq. *Fifty* copies printed.

A Brief Summary of the Contents of a Manuscript, formerly belonging to the Lord William Howard, of Naworth.
Durham. 1819. 8vo. pp. 31.

Fifty copies were printed of this Summary, for private circulation, by Sir Cuthbert Sharp. In the Castle of Naworth, Lord Howard's apartments, containing a bed-room, oratory, and library, are still shown. Many of the books belonging to the original possessor, "belted Will Howard," have his autograph: the valuable collection of MSS. is no longer there: some are deposited in the College of Arms, London.

_____

The Diary of Jacob Bee, from 1682 to 1706.
Durham. 1819. 8vo. pp. 26.

Twenty-five copies were printed for private distribution, by the Editor of the former volume. Jacob Bee was brought up to the sister arts of skinner and glover, and flourished in his native city for three-quarters of a century.

_____

Pedigrees and Memoirs of the Families of Hoare, of Rishford, Com. Devon ; Hoare, of Walton, Com. Bucks ; Hoare, of London, Com. Middlesex ; Hoare, of Mitcham, Com. Surrey ; Hoare, of Stourton, Com. Wilts ; Hoare, of Barn-Elms, Com. Surrey ; Hoare, of Boreham, Com. Essex. Collected and compiled by Sir Richard Colt Hoare, Bart., a.d. 1819.
[Bath.]   4to.   pp. 64.

This account of the several families of Hoare is illustrated by the following plates:—

RICHARD HOARE, Esq., of Barn-Elms; facing title-page.

HENRY HOARE, Esq., of Stourhead; Roth del., Worthington sculpsit, page 9.

RICHARD HOARE, Esq., First Baronet; M. H. del., H. Meyer sculpsit, page 11.

SIR RICHARD COLT HOARE, Bart., of Stourhead; engraved by H. Meyer, from a picture by H. Edridge, A.R.A.

HENRY HOARE, of Mitcham, engraved by Henry Meyer, from a picture by Sir Thomas Lawrence, R.A.

SIR RICHARD HOARE, Knt. }
HENRY HOARE, } four small portraits on one plate
HENRY HOARE, } engraved by Worthington.
SIR RICHARD HOARE, Knt. }

Arms of the Family of Hoare, page 52.

In this volume will also be found a short memoir of the life and works of the highly respected editor, the late Sir Richard Colt Hoare, Bart.; whose various publications on topography are well known and highly esteemed.

The additions made by the learned Baronet to his seat at Stourhead, are two handsome wings; the one appropriated to a picture gallery, and the other to a library.

A CATALOGUE OF THE LIBRARY OF MISS CURRER, AT ESHTON HALL, IN THE DEANERY OF CRAVEN, AND COUNTY OF YORK.

London: Robert Triphook. 1820. 8vo. pp. 308.

This Catalogue was compiled by Mr. Triphook. Fifty copies only are said to have been printed. A new edition has since appeared, compiled by Mr. Stewart; an account of which will be found in a subsequent page.

" Frances Mary Richardson Currer, only daughter and heiress of the Rev. Henry Richardson Currer, was born at Eshton Hall, the 3rd of March, 1785. She is in possession of both the Richardson and Currer estates; and inherits all the taste of the former family;

having collected a very large and valuable library, and also possesses a fine collection of prints, shells, and fossils, in addition to what were collected by her great grandfather and great uncle." *

MEMORIALS OF THE HALIBURTONS.
Edinburgh: Printed by James Ballantyne and Company, at the Border Press.   1820.   4to.

Engraved frontispiece of the burial aisle of the Haliburtons (and of Sir Walter himself), in the chancel of the Abbey Church of Dryburgh ; no name, but etched from a drawing by Mr. Skene, of Rubislaw.   Preliminary Notice, 1 leaf, or pages iii and iv, in which it is stated that "Walter Scott, of Abbotsford," was served heir to his grand-uncle, Robert Haliburton, of Newmains.   This Notice is dated Abbotsford, March, 1820.

The "History of the Haliburtons in Dryburgh" ends at p. 63.

The Notice by the Editor (Sir Walter Scott), begins, — "Thirty copies have been thrown off of these Genealogical Memorials, intended only to gratify the wish of some respectable friends of the present possessor of the Manuscript, whose families are mentioned in it." Sir Walter was the representative of the family, as grand-nephew of Sir Robert Haliburton, of Newmains.

In 1824, Sir Walter Scott reprinted some copies of the volume on rather larger paper than the edition of 1820, printed by James Ballantyne and Company at the Border Press.   4to. front. pp. iv and 63.   Two leaves, numbered i—iv, are added, entitled, "Declaration of the Persons within named, anent Muirhouselaw's Death" (extracted from the Sheriff Court Record of Roxburghshire, May, 1716).   In other respects this is a literal reprint of the edition in 1820.   The Notice also begins,—"Thirty copies," &c., but now the Editor is styled "Sir Walter Scott" of Abbotsford, and the date is changed to November, 1824.   The above Declaration is added to illustrate a passage, "On the 50th page of the foregoing Memorials," &c.

---

* Nichols, Illustrations, vol. i. p. 252.

BIBLIOTHECÆ REGIÆ CATALOGUS.

Londini: Excudebant Gul. Bulmer and Gul. Nicol.
M.DCCC.XX—M.DCCC.XXIX. *5 vols. folio.*

CATALOGUE OF MAPS, PRINTS, DRAWINGS, ETC.,
Forming the Geographical and Topographical Col-
lection attached to the Library of his late Majesty King
George the Third; and presented by his Majesty King
George the Fourth, to the British Museum.*

London: Printed by order of the Trustees of the
British Museum, by G. Woodfall, Angel-court, Skinner-
street. M.DCCC.XXIX. *Folio.* pp. 373; Index, pp. liii.

Prefixed to the first volume is a portrait of the royal and illustrious founder, George III., engraved by S. W. Reynolds, from a bust
by John Bacon, R.A. On the first leaf of the Introduction is a representation of the library at the Queen's House; and at the end of
the Introduction, a view of the octagonal room, in which a portion
of the library was kept: they are engraved on wood by J. Byfield,
from drawings by Frederick Nash; in the alterations of the Palace,
these rooms have disappeared.

The Catalogue of the Books was compiled by the late Sir Frederick Barnard, assisted by the late Nicholas Carlisle, Esq., and John
Hulbert Glover, Esq., librarian to the Queen.

The Geographical Catalogue was compiled by Alexander Macpherson, who assisted Mr. Arrowsmith in drawing some of the maps
for Rees' Cyclopædia.

This noble collection, which has been well styled, " a gift greater
than has been bestowed by any sovereign upon any nation, since the
library of the Ptolemies was founded at Alexandria," † was presented to the Nation by his late Majesty George IV. The letter of

---

* This portion of the Royal Catalogue is also printed in 2 vols. 8vo. for
general sale.

† Sir Henry Ellis, Dedication to " Original Letters," First Series.

the Royal donor, together with a few extracts from the Report of the Committee appointed by the House of Commons, are here introduced, as necessary to the history of the library.

"DEAR LORD LIVERPOOL,

"THE KING, my late revered and excellent father, having formed, during a long series of years, a most valuable and extensive Library, consisting of about one hundred and twenty thousand volumes, I have resolved to present this collection to the British Nation.

"Whilst I have the satisfaction, by this means, of advancing the literature of my country, I also feel that I am paying a just tribute to the memory of a parent, whose life was adorned with every public and private virtue.

"I desire to add, that I have great pleasure, my Lord, in making this communication through you.

"Believe me, with great regard,

"Your sincere friend,

"*Pavilion, Brighton, January* 15, 1823. "G. R."

The Committee appointed to report upon the Library proceed to state, that "the general plan of its formation appears to have been determined upon by his late Majesty King George the Third, soon after his accession to the throne; and the first extensive purchase which he made, was that of the library of Mr. Joseph Smith, the British consul at Venice, in 1762.

"In 1768, Mr. Barnard, the librarian, was sent to the Continent by his Majesty; and in France, Italy, and Germany, he bought numerous books of great rarity and value. Previous to his departure, he received a letter from Dr. Johnson,* who frequently visited the

---

* The admirable letter of this eminent man, forming part of the history of the Royal collection, is not, it is trusted, inappropriately introduced.

"SIR,

"It is natural for a scholar to interest himself in an expedition undertaken like yours, for the importation of literature; and therefore, not having travelled myself, I am very little qualified to give advice to a traveller; yet, that I may not seem inattentive to a design so worthy of regard, I

Library, pointing out the best means of completing it. The rules laid down in that letter have been followed with unremitting attention. The Library has been considered as very complete, for its extent, in all branches of science and literature : it is very rich in classics, in English history, in Italian, French, and Spanish literature, and in the scarce, early printed books of the fifteenth century.

---

will try whether the present state of my health will suffer me to lay before you what observation or report have suggested to me, that may direct your inquiries, or facilitate your success. Things, of which the mere rarity makes the value, and which are prized at a high rate, by a wantonness rather than by use, are always passing from poorer to richer countries ; and therefore, though Germany and Italy were principally productive of typographical curiosities, I do not much imagine that they are now to be found there in great abundance. An eagerness for scarce books, and early editions, which prevailed among the English about half a century ago, filled our shops with all the splendour and nicety of literature ; and when the Harleian Catalogue was published, many of the books were bought for the library of the King of France.

" I believe, however, that by the diligence with which you have enlarged the library under your care, the present stock is so nearly exhausted, that, till new purchases supply the booksellers with new stores, you will not be able to do much more than glean up single books, as accident shall produce them ; this, therefore, is the time for visiting the Continent.

" What addition you can hope to make by ransacking other countries, we will now consider. English literature you will not seek in any place but in England. Classical learning is diffused everywhere, and is not, except by accident, more copious in one part of the polite world than in another ; but every country has literature of its own, which may be but gathered in its native soil. The studies of the learned are influenced by forms of government, and modes of religion; and therefore, those books are necessary and common in some places, which, where different opinions or different manners prevail, are of little use, and for that reason, rarely to be found.

" Thus, in Italy you may expect to meet with canonists and scholastic divines; in Germany with writers on the feudal law ; and in Holland with civilians. The schoolmen and canonists must not be neglected, for they are useful to many purposes ; nor too anxiously sought, for their influence among us is much lessened by the Reformation. Of the canonists, at least, a few eminent writers may be sufficient. The schoolmen are of more general value. But the feudal and civil law I cannot but wish to see complete. The feudal constitution is the origin of the law of property, over all the civilized part of Europe ; and

The sum expended in the purchase of Mr. Smith's library was about 10,000*l.*, and the sum applied for the purchase of books, for a period of sixty years, has been about 2,000*l.* annually. It is also to be observed, that additions have been made to the collection by persons anxious to shew their respect to his late Majesty, and to promote his views. Among these, the late Jacob Bryant deserves particularly to

the civil law, as it is generally understood to include the law of nations, may be called, with great propriety, a regal study. Of these books, which have been often published, and diversified by various modes of impression, our Royal Library should have at least the most curious edition, the most splendid, and the most useful. The most curious edition is commonly the first, and the most useful may be expected among the last. Thus, of Tully's Offices, the edition of Fust is the most curious, and that of Grævius the most useful. The most splendid, the eye will discern. With the old printers you are now become well acquainted : if you can find any collection of their productions to be sold, you will undoubtedly buy it ; but this can scarcely be hoped, and you must catch up single volumes where you can find them. In every place things often occur where they are least expected. I was shewn a Welsh Grammar, written in Welsh, and printed at Milan, I believe, before any Grammar of that language had been printed here. Of purchasing entire libraries, I know not whether the inconvenience may not overbalance the advantage. Of libraries collected with general views, one will have many books in common with another. When you have bought two collections, you will find that you have bought many books twice over, and many in each which you have left at home, and therefore did not want ; and when you have selected a small number, you will have the rest to sell at a great loss, or to transport hither, at perhaps a greater. It will generally be more commodious to buy the few that you want, at a price somewhat advanced, than to incumber yourself with useless books. But libraries collected for particular studies, will be very valuable acquisitions. The collection of an eminent civilian, feudist, or mathematician, will perhaps have very few superfluities. Topography, or local history, prevails much, in many parts of the Continent. I have been told, that scarcely a village of Italy wants its historian. These books may be generally neglected, but some will deserve attention, by the celebrity of the place, the eminence of the authors, or the beauty of the sculptures. Sculpture has always been more cultivated among other nations than among us. The old art of cutting on wood, which decorated the books of ancient impression, was never carried here to any excellence ; and the practice of engraving on copper which succeeded, has never been much employed among us in adorning books. The old books with wooden cuts are to be diligently sought ;

be mentioned, as having enriched the Library with some of the rarest specimens of the art of printing, at its commencement in this country.

"The examination of the contents of the Royal Library, furnishes the strongest reason for placing it in the same building as the Museum Library; the former being very rich in many of those classes in which the latter is very deficient; particularly in works illustrative of the history of printing, in geography, in heraldry and antiquity, in theology, in various branches of belles lettres, in grammars and dictionaries, in Italian and Spanish literature, and in general history."

---

the designs were very often made by great masters, and the prints are such as cannot be made by any artist now living. It will be of great use to collect in every place maps of the adjacent country, and plans of towns, buildings, and gardens. By this care you will form a more valuable body of geography than can otherwise be had. Many countries have been very exactly surveyed; but it must not be expected that the exactness of actual mensuration will be preserved, when the maps are reduced by a contracted scale, and incorporated into a general system.

"The King of Sardinia's Italian dominions are not large; yet the maps made of them in the reign of Victor, fill two atlantic folios. This part of your design will deserve particular regard, because, in this, your success will always be proportionate to your diligence.

"You are too well acquainted with literary history, not to know that many books derive their value from the reputation of the printers. Of the celebrated printers you do not need to be informed; and if you did, might consult Baillet 'Jugemens des Scavans.' The productions of Aldus are enumerated in the Bibliotheca Græca, so that you may know when you have them all, which is always of use, as it prevents needless search. The great ornaments of a library furnished for magnificence as well as use, are the first editions, of which, therefore, I would not willingly neglect the mention. You know, Sir, that the annals of typography begin with the Codex, 1457; but there is just reason to believe, that there are latent in obscure corners, books printed before it. The secular feast in memory of the invention of printing, is celebrated in the fortieth year of the century; if this tradition, therefore, is right, the art had in 1457 been already exercised nineteen years.

"There prevails among typographical antiquaries a vague opinion, that the Bible had been printed three times before the edition of 1462, which Calmet

The Library thus presented to the Nation is now deposited in the particular portion of the British Museum expressly built for its reception. An endeavour * has been made to convey an idea of the noble repository in which it is placed. At each end of the room is an inscription, recording the gift, in English and Latin : the following is a copy of the latter :—

REX . GEORGIVS . IIII .

LECTISSIMAM . HANC . LIBRORVM . COPIAM .

A . PATRE . GEORGIO . III . COMPARATAM .

IN . MUSEO . BRITANNICO . COLLOCARI . JVSSIT.

ET . PVBLICAM . ESSE . VOLVIT .

ANNO . REGNI . SVI . III .

---

calls ' la première edition bien averée.' One of these editions has been lately discovered in a convent, and transplanted into the French King's Library. Another copy has likewise been found, but I know not whether the same impression, or another. These discoveries are sufficient to raise hope, and instigate inquiry. In the purchase of old books, let me recommend you to inquire with great caution, whether they are perfect. In the first edition, the loss of a leaf is not easily observed. You remember how near we both were to purchasing a mutilated missal at a high price.

" All this, perhaps, you know already, and therefore my letter may be of no use. I am, however, desirous to shew you, that I wish prosperity to your undertaking. One advice more I will give, of more importance than all the rest ; of which I, therefore, hope you will have still less need. You are going into a part of the world, divided, as it is said, between bigotry and atheism : such representations are always hyperbolical ; but there is certainly enough of both to alarm any mind solicitous for piety and truth ; let not the contempt of superstition precipitate into infidelity, or the horror of infidelity ensnare you into superstition. I sincerely wish you successful and happy, for,

" I am, Sir,

" Your affectionate humble servant,

" *May* 28, 1768. " SAM. JOHNSON."

" To F. A. BARNARD, ESQ."

* Vide title-page of this work : drawn by Mackenzie ; engraved by John Le Keux.

The collection of books here deposited is considered to consist of about 80,000 volumes ; exclusive of the valuable collection of maps, plans, and topographical views, the catalogue of which is contained in the volume before mentioned. About * thirty-five works, consisting, for the most part, of books printed in the fifteenth century, and which had been presented to his Majesty George III. by the celebrated Jacob Bryant, were retained ; and a MS. volume of Memoranda by Dr. Johnson, presented to the King by Bennet Langton, Esq.†

Two hundred copies of the Catalogue were printed, the expense of which was defrayed by a parliamentary vote. A very liberal distribution was made of them ; viz. to the members of the Royal Family, the Cabinet Ministers, the Universities, and other literary establishments of the United Kingdom ; to most of the foreign Potentates, Academies, and literary Societies of the Continent.

In addition to the library, maps, and topographical drawings, a very valuable cabinet of ancient and modern coins and medals was also presented to the British Museum. It contains nearly 16,000 pieces, and is particularly rich in German coins, early Italian, English, and Dutch medals.

Brunet in his notice of the catalogue, says, "Nous n'avons rien à en dire sous le rapport bibliographique, car ce n'est guère qu'une simple table, où les titres, fort peu devéloppés, sont rangés par ordre alphabétique des noms des auteurs, ou du mot principal du titre, lorsque le livre est sans nom d'auteur."

The Report previously quoted gave an account of the sums granted by Parliament for the purchase of works of art, science, and literature, since the foundation of the British Museum, in 1755 : the following is the list :—

		£
1753	For the Sloanian Collection . . .	20,000
1758	„ the Harleian Collection . . .	10,000
1772	„ the Hamilton Collection of Vases .	8,410

---

* An excellent Bibliographical Notice of the Royal Library is in the "Gentleman's Magazine," 1834, p. 235.

† See Mr. Croker's edition of "Boswell's Johnson," vol. v. p. 299.

		£
1805	For the Townley Collection of Statues .	20,000
1807	„ the Lansdown Manuscripts . .	4,925
1810	„ the Greville Minerals . . .	13,727
1813	„ the Hargrave Library . . .	8,000
1814	„ the remainder of the Townley Collection	8,200
1815	„ the Phigalian Marbles . . .	15,000
1816	„ the Elgin Marbles	35,000
1818	„ the Burney Library . . .	13,500

Since that Report, the following Special Parliamentary Grants have been voted :—

		£	s.	d.
1820	Mrs. Dorville—Collection of Zoology	1,127	10	0
1824	Mr. Salt's Egyptian Antiquities .	2,000	0	0
1825	Mr. Rich's MSS. and Coins . .	7,500	0	0
1831	Arundel MSS. by purchase and exchange—estimated value . .	3,559	3	0
1834	Mr. Sam's collection of Egyptian Antiquities	2,500	0	0
„	Mr. T. Hawkins' collection of Fossil Saurian remains	1,310	5	0
1835	Egyptian Antiquities . . .	6,000	0	0
1836	Egyptian Antiquities . . .	918	4	0
„	Antique Vases	3,473	18	7
„	Etchings by the Dutch Masters .	5,000	0	0
„	Charlemagne Bible	750	0	0
1837	Mr. Broderip's Collection of Shells .	1,575	0	0
„	Antique Vases	1,136	3	6
1838	Egyptian Antiquities . . .	650	13	3
„	Signor Campanari's Etruscan Antiquities	600	0	0
1839	Signor Anastasy, for Egyptian Antiquities	1,600	0	0
„	Mr. Mantell's Geological Collection .	4,212	0	0
1840	Mr. Hawkin's Collection of Fossils .	1,800	0	0
1841	Mr. Stewart—Collection of Coins .	880	0	0

		£	s.	d.
1841	Mr. Burgon—Collection of Coins .	4,000	0	0
„	Mr. Butler—Collection of Manuscripts	2,200	0	0
1842	Messrs. Smith — Collection of En-			
	gravings	2,390	0	0
„	Mr. Gould—Collection of Zoology .	350	0	0
„	Mr. Cuming—Collection of Zoology	650	0	0
„	Mr. Tattam — Collection of Syriac			
	Manuscripts	730	0	0
„	Mr. Burgon—Collection of Antiquities	600	0	0
1843	Strawberry Hill — Collection of			
	books, &c.	1,018	0	0
„	Prince of Canino's Antique Vases .	1,300	0	0
„	Mr. Lambert's Botanical Specimens .	384	0	0
„	Mr. Tattam—Syriac Manuscripts .	1,000	0	0
„	Engravings, the works of Raphael			
	Morghen	1,575	0	0
1844	Mr. Koch's Collection of Fossils .	1,000	0	0
„	Mr. Tattam—Syriac Manuscripts .	45	0	0
„	Sculptures from Xanthus . .	1,000	0	0
„	Coins from the Collection of the Duke			
	of Devonshire	1,200	0	0
„	Books, &c., from the Libraries of the			
	Duke of Sussex, &c. . .	3,304	6	9
„	Coins from the Collection of the late			
	Mr. Thomas	2,500	0	0
1845	Duke of Sussex, &c., Collection of			
	Books, &c.	1,095	13	3
„	Xanthian Antiquities . . .	1,387	0	0
„	M. de Falconnet, Collection of Fossils	1,000	0	0
„	Messrs. Smith, Collection of Prints, &c.	7,705	0	0
1846	Fossils from the Sub-Himalayan Moun-			
	tains (classifying) . . .	541	12	3
1847	Fossils from the Sub-Himalayan			
	Mountains	127	8	11
„	Marbles from Bodroon . . .	351	2	6

		£	s.	d.
1847	Marbles from Kurdistan . . .	2,382	8	5
1848	Marbles from Assyria . . .	561	10	6
„	Messrs. Smith—Collection of Prints, &c.	4,200	0	0
„	Verstolk's Prints, &c. . . .	566	16	0
1849	Marbles from Assyria . . .	837	9	4
1850	Marbles from Assyria . . .	2,649	8	0
„	Ibrahim Pacha's Gold Coins . .	1,050	0	0

HISTORICAL ACCOUNT OF THE
ORIGINE AND SUCCESSION OF THE FAMILY OF INNES,
Collected from Authentick Writs in the Chartor-Chist
of the Samen. From an original Manuscript in the
Possession of His Grace the Duke of Roxburghe.
Edinburgh: Printed by George Ramsay and Co., for
Waugh and Innes, Hunter Square. 1820.

Large 4to. pp. 74, with a folding engraved plate, Insignia D. Henrici Innes ab eodem Junioris, &c.
"Two hundred copies printed at the Duke's expense." Lowndes,
p. 998.

SOME ACCOUNT OF ST. JOHN'S HOSPITAL, AND THE
FREE SCHOOL, COVENTRY.
1820. 4to.

This forms part of a volume of collections for the History of
Coventry, privately printed by Thomas Sharp, Esq., an eminent
antiquary of that city ; who printed *six copies only*, for private distribution. The following is a list of the collection :—

I. Illustrations of the History and Antiquities of St. Michael

Church, Coventry ; from original, and mostly unpublished documents. By Thomas Sharp. Coventry : Printed by W. Reader. 1818. 4to. pp. 55.

II. Illustrations of the History and Antiquities of the Church of the Holy Trinity. Coventry. 1818. 4to. pp. 45.

III. St. Nicholas' Church, Coventry. No title. 4to. pp. 3.

IV. Bablake Church, or Chapel, Coventry. No title. 4to. pp. 21.

V. Account of St. John's Hospital.

VI. Grey Friars, Coventry. No. title. 4to. pp. 12.

VII. St. Mary Hall, Coventry. 4to. pp. 5.

Enumeration of the Inhabitants of the City of Glasgow, and its connected Suburbs ; Together with Population and Statistical Tables, relative to Scotland and England.

Compiled and arranged by James Cleland, Member of the Chamber of Commerce and Manufactures ; late one of the Magistrates, and Convener of the Trades' House, Glasgow.

" An increase of population, when it follows its natural order, is not only a positive good in itself, but absolutely necessary, in the farther increase of the annual produce of the land, and labour of the country."—*Malthus.*

" An active and industrious population is the stay and support of every well-governed community."—*Colquhoun.*

Glasgow : Printed by James Hedderwick, for the Hon. the Magistrates and Council, the Governors of the Town Hospital, and the Commissioners of Police. 1820. *Folio.* pp. 40 ; Postscript, one leaf.

Mr. Cleland was the author of a History of Glasgow, noticed in the Edinburgh Review.

MISCELLANIES :
BY FREDERICK, EARL OF CARLISLE, K.G.

Meditans nugarum, et totus in illis.

London: Printed by J. F. Dove, St. John's-square.
8*vo.* pp. 114.

The noble author died 4th September, 1825.

————

THE PROFLIGATE ;
A COMEDY, BY GEORGE WATSON TAYLOR, ESQ.
[London.] Bulmer and Nicol. 1820. 4*to.* pp. 17.

Two hundred copies were printed of this comedy. At the sale of
the library at Earlstoke, several copies, which had not been distributed, were sold by auction.

————

MEMOIRS HISTORICAL AND ILLUSTRATIVE OF THE
BOTANICAL GARDEN AT CHELSEA, BELONGING TO THE
SOCIETY OF APOTHECARIES OF LONDON.

London: Printed by R. Gilbert, St. John's-square,
Clerkenwell. 1820. 8*vo.* pp. 111.

Compiled by Henry Field, Esq., treasurer of the company, for the
use of the members of the society only.

————

LA DANCE MACABRE.

Uiuans qui voyez cesti dance
Se souvent la regardez
Vous scaires se bien la gardez
Q' hòneur mòdain nest pas cheunce.

The above is the title of a reprint, in small 4*to*. (consisting of five leaves), of part of " La Dance Macabre," printed at Paris, by Nicole de la Barre, the 23d July, 1500 ; preserved in the British Museum. The reverse of the title-page is blank. The other four leaves are printed on both sides, have a wood-cut on the top of each page, and two stanzas of eight lines each, underneath.

The wood-cut on the title, and above the colophon on the last page, are the same ; all the other wood-cuts are different, suiting the subjects.

" Bibliographical Analysis of La Dance Macabre, preserved in the British Museum," on the two pages of leaf 6, with the colophon, " London : Printed by Samuel and Richard Bentley, Dorset-street, Fleet-street ;" with their certification, that only twenty-five copies on paper, and only six copies on vellum, were printed.

Then follow, on the recto of leaf 7, some observations on the poem ; and an extract from Warton's History of Poetry.

CYLLENIUS ; A POEM.

Pochi compagni avrai per l' altra via
Dice la turba, al vil guadagno intesa.—*Petrarca.*

Farley-Hill : Printed by J. Magennis. 1820. *8vo.*

In Dr. Valpy's copy, at the sale of his library in 1832, it was stated that only *twelve* copies were printed, by the author himself, at his private press. Farley-Hill is distant seven miles from Reading. A second edition has since appeared, in two volumes. Mr. Dickinson, the author, died February 5, 1827.

The following additional particulars have been forwarded to the Editor by a friend of Mr. Dickinson's :

" I was acquainted for many years with Charles Dickinson, Esq., of Somersetshire, a gentleman of large fortune and of great accomplishments in literature ; he, during a portion of his life, dedicated his leisure hours to auto-printing ; he kept presses and types in his apartments, and composed in a leaden style—I mean to say, that the patriotic, ultra-liberal principles which he professed he embodied in excellent poetry, and as Apollo gave him the verse, he printed; but he wrote not his poem. Mr. Dickinson read his poems to me, portions indeed, for they formed some volumes quarto, of perhaps 800 pages each, in large type, and with margins to receive his corrections. One volume was, I think, a poem with this title, 'India;' the date of printing prior to 1812."

HISTORICAL VIEW OF THE FORMS AND POWERS OF THE COURT OF EXCHEQUER, IN SCOTLAND; To which is added, an Appendix, containing the Rules of Procedure, and certain Minutes of Court, relating thereto.
BY BARON SIR JOHN CLERK, BARONET, and
MR. BARON SCROOPE.
Edinburgh: Printed by J. Hays and Co. 1820. *Large* 4*to.* pp. 343.

Printed from a MS. written before the year 1724, at the expense of the Court of Exchequer of Scotland, but not for sale.

CATALOGUE OF THE PRIVATE LIBRARY OF THE RIGHT REVEREND THE LORD BISHOP OF LONDON.
London: Printed by Luke Hansard and Sons. [Circa 1820.] 4*to.*

Twelve copies only were printed of this Catalogue, compiled for the private convenience of his Grace the late Archbishop of Canterbury (Dr. Howley), when Bishop of London. Since it was printed, his Grace had made very large additions to his collection.

An Attempt at a Glossary of some Words used in Cheshire ; communicated to the Society of Antiquaries, by Roger Wilbraham, Esq., etc.

From the Archæologia, Vol. xix., with considerable Additions.

London : Printed by W. Bulmer and Co. 1820. 12*mo.* pp. 91.

This volume was reprinted for general sale in 1826. Mr. Wilbraham was a member of the Roxburghe Club, and died in 1829. A portion of his library, containing rare Italian literature, was sold by auction by Mr. Evans, in June, 1829.

———

A Trewe and Feythfull Hystorie of the redoubtable Prynce Radapanthus.

London : Reprinted by R. and A. Taylor, Shoe-lane. 1820. *Square* 18*mo.* 20 leaves, black letter.

Edited by John Adey Repton, Esq., who states that there was not a copy of the original in the British Museum, or Bodleian Library. Seventy-five copies were printed on plain paper, three on coloured paper, and two on vellum. Mr. Repton is the author of several papers on architecture, which have appeared in the Archæologia.

———

Queen Mab, by Percy Bysshe Shelley.

pp. 240. 8*vo.*

Original edition, privately printed without a title-page ; a copy was in Mr. Hanrott's library, pt. 3, 2407, bound up with which was a handbill, folio, entitled "a Declaration of Rights," a seditious paper, printed for circulation in Ireland.

T

274 M.DCCC.XXI.

CATALOGUE OF THE LIBRARY OF THE ATHENÆUM, LIVERPOOL.
BY GEORGE BURRELL, Principal Librarian.

"Sine libris, Deus jam silet, justitia quiescit, torpet medicina, Philosophia manca est, Literæ mutæ, omnia tenebris involuta cimmeriis."—*Bartholinus.*

Liverpool: Printed by Harris and Co. M.DCCC.XX. *8vo.* pp. 404.

A classed catalogue. The building in which this library is placed, was opened in 1799, it is situated in Church-street, said to be the first of the kind established in the kingdom. It contains the MSS., &c., of the late William Roscoe, collected for his Lives of Lorenzo de Medici and Leo X. A new edition of the catalogue is said to be in preparation.

REMORSE, AND OTHER POEMS.
BY BARRY ST. LEGER.
London. 1821. *12mo.*

Fifty copies only were printed of this volume. Mr. St. Leger was the editor of the "Album," a short-lived periodical, "Gilbert Earle," and other works. A memoir of him is in the "Gentleman's Magazine," 1829, p. 642.

THOUGHTS, CHIEFLY ON SERIOUS SUBJECTS.
BY WILLIAM DANBY, ESQ., of Swinton Park, Yorkshire.

Exeter: Printed for the Author by E. Woolmer, Gazette Office. 1821. *8vo.*

This work has been reprinted, with considerable alterations, and the addition of another volume.

The residence of the author is at Swinton, near Masham. He was sheriff of the county of York in 1784: he died Dec. 4th, 1833, æt. 82.

" It is a book in which his neighbours could find nothing to amuse them, or which they thought it behoved them to admire ; but I have seldom seen a more amiable or a happier disposition portrayed than is there delineated."*

SELECT POEMS OF EDWARD HOVEL THURLOW, LORD THURLOW.
Chiswick: Printed by C. Whittingham. 1821. 8vo. pp. 91.

Lord Thurlow, the second of that title, assumed the name of Hovel, as lineal descendant of Richard Hovel, an esquire of the body to Henry V. Besides this volume, he published several others, for sale. He died in 1829. Lord Thurlow's works were the subject of a severe article in the "Edinburgh Review," vol. xxxi., by T. Moore.

TALES OF THE CORDELIER METAMORPHOSED, AS NARRATED IN A MANUSCRIPT FROM THE BORROMEO COLLECTION, AND IN THE CORDELIER CHEVAL OF M. PIRON; WITH TRANSLATIONS.
London: Printed at the Shakspeare Press, by William Bulmer and W. Nicol. 1821. 8vo. pp. 54.

Printed at the expense of George Hibbert, Esq., for private circulation, from a manuscript in the collection of the late Count Borromeo, of Padua ; at the sale of whose library, in 1817, it came

---

* Southey, Life, vol. vi. p. 78.

into Mr. Hibbert's possession; it contains eleven etchings by Robert Cruickshank; sixty-four copies only were printed.

The frontispiece originally represented a female on her knees before a crucifix; the editor, with propriety, made the alteration as it now appears in the volume; few copies possess both prints.

POESIAS LYRICAS DE FRANCISCO DE VOYA GANCAO STOCKLER, do Conselho de sua Magistade, Tenente general dos suos Exercitos, Commendador da Ordem de Christo; Socio da Academia Real das Sciencias de Lisboa, da Sociedade Real de Londres, e da Sociedade Philosophica da Philadelphia.

Londres: Impresso por T. C. Hansard, Peterborough-court, Fleet-street. 1821. 8*vo.* pp. 250.

DRAMAS, TRANSLATIONS, AND OCCASIONAL POEMS, BY BARBARINA, LADY DACRE.

In two volumes.

"Per desio di Lode
Non canto io, no; ben per chi m'ama e m'ode."

Vittoria Colonna.

London: John Murray. M.DCCC.XXI. 2 vols. 8*vo.*

"For you, then, my friends, I print a few copies of my Plays, Translations, and other trifling compositions; that if ever you should be disposed to look at them again, the second perusal may at least be less troublesome than the first."—*Preface.*

Lady Dacre, "whose Dramas," says the "Quarterly Review,"*

---

* No. XCVII.

"both tragic and comic, have been much and justly admired," is the second daughter of the late Admiral Sir Chaloner Ogle, Bart., and widow of Valentine Wilmot, Esq., married to Lord Dacre, November, 1819, who died March, 1851.

A CATALOGUE OF THE PRINTED BOOKS IN THE LI-BRARY OF THE INNER TEMPLE; ARRANGED IN CLASSES. London: Printed by George Woodfall, Angel-court, Skinner-street. 1821. 8vo. pp. 139.

Compiled by the Rev. W. H. Rowlatt; who informed the editor, that *twenty-eight* copies only were printed.

FORTIGUERRI:
Translation from the Italian of Fortiguerri, of the First Canto of Ricciardetto; with an Introduction, concerning the principal Romantic, Burlesque, and other Mock-heroic Poems. [Not published.] London: Printed by T. Davison, Whitefriars. 1821. 12mo.

Translated by the late Lord Glenbervie: it was reprinted for sale, in 8vo., in 1822.

MEMOIR ON THE ANTIQUITY OF THE ZODIACS OF ESNEH AND DENDERA. London: Printed by A. J. Valpy. 1821. 8vo. pp. 111; with two plates.

Written by the late Sir William Drummond, who died March 29, 1827, at Rome.

278 M.DCCC.XXI.

Memoir of the late Captain Joseph Huddart, F.R.S.

London: Printed by W. Phillips, George-yard. 1821. 4*to.* pp. 102.

Prefixed is a portrait of the Captain, from a picture by J. Hoppner, R.A.: he was an elder brother of the Trinity House, and died in 1816. The Memoir was written by his son, Sir Joseph Huddart, of Brynkir, Caernarvonshire.

A Writing, or Declaration, from the Law Book, to obliterate the House of the Revolver, or Solar System. Second Edition.

By C. Houseman.

London: Printed by A. J. Valpy, Red-Lion-court, Fleet-street. 1821. 8*vo.* pp. 354.

Twenty-five copies only are said to have been printed of this strange compilation, which is an attack on the Newtonian system. The following illustrations will be found in it:

Page		Page	
8	The form of the Tabernacle.	172	Sacrifice of Apis.
10	Abram's Sacrifice.	177	Tomb of Psammuthis.
13	The Altar of Earth.	211	Flying Roll.
33	The Molten Calf.	216	Isis.
44	Device, shewing the Planetary System.	243	Daniel and the Priests of Beli.
47	Sennacherib's Death.	285	Chamminim.
87	The Tabernacle.	289	The Wedding Feast.
107	Portable Orrery.	307	Nebuchadnezzar.
116*Osiris.		327	Molten Sea.
117	Solar System.	340	From the Tomb at Thebes.
146	Brahma, Veshnoo, Siva.	350	Interior of the tomb at Psammis.
165	Osiris, from the tomb at Thebes.		

SKETCH OF THE LIFE OF SIR HUGH INGLIS, BART.
London. 8*vo.* 1821.

With a portrait. Privately printed.

POEMS BY ALEXANDER SCOTT,
From a Manuscript written in the year M.D.LXVIII.
[Edinburgh: Printed by Balfour and Clarke.
M.DCCC.XXI.] 8*vo.* pp. xvi and 104.

One hundred copies of this volume were printed for private distribution, by Mr. David Laing. The Poems were printed from Bannatyne's MS. collection, and this is the only collected edition of the works of an author who has been styled the "Scottish Anacreon."

REPORT TO THE RIGHT HONOURABLE THE LORD CHIEF BARON, AND THE HON. THE BARONS OF HIS MAJESTY'S COURT OF EXCHEQUER IN SCOTLAND, BY THE KING'S REMEMBRANCER, RELATIVE TO THE TOMB OF KING ROBERT THE BRUCE, AND THE CATHEDRAL CHURCH OF DUNFERMLINE.
Edinburgh: Printed by Hay, Gall, and Co., Niddry-street. 1821. 4*to.* pp. 67.

This Report was drawn up by Sir Henry Jardine, King's Remembrancer; and contains the following plates :—

1. Sketch of the new Church of Dunfermline.
2. Plan of the old and new Churches.
3. Fac-simile of the Inscription on the plate of copper on Bruce's coffin.
4. Measurement of the skeleton.

Memoir of the Life of Lieut.-Gen. Daniel Burr ; With a Supplement, containing Letters, Documents relative to the Succession to the Estates of the Duchess of Norfolk, Inscriptions, &c. London : Printed by W. Bulmer and W. Nicol, Cleveland-row, St. James's. 1821. 8vo. pp. 180.

At the death of the Duchess of Norfolk, many claimants to the Scudamore estate appeared. E. F. Stanhope, Esq., who has taken the name of Scudamore, obtained half ; the remainder has been divided between Lieut.-Gen. Burr and Mr. Parsons, who has taken the name of Higford.

———

Journal of the Operations of the Belvoir Fox-hounds from August 7, 1820, to April 18, 1821.

"Forsan et hæc olim meminisse juvabit."

London: Printed by M'Millan, Bow-street, Covent-garden. 1821. 4to. pp. 92.

The Belvoir Fox-hounds are an old and celebrated pack ; the Journals of their operations are very numerous ; the editor has met however, with those only which he has enumerated : the management has been transferred by his Grace the Duke of Rutland to Lord Forester.

———

Diciere di Annibal Caro, e di altri. A' Re Della Virtu. Calveley Hall. 1821. 8vo. pp. 117.

Privately printed by W. Davenport, Esq. Calveley Hall is near Barbridge, Cheshire.

Thomæ Craigi Epithalamium, quo, Henrici Darnleii et Mariæ Scotorum Reginæ nuptias celebravit.

Impressum Edinburgi anno M.D.LXV. Denuo editum anno M.DCCC.XXI.

12mo.

Edited by Mr. David Laing: who says in the preface, "Amicis nonnullis gratificaturi, et simul qualecunque Carmen, haud sua laude carens, ab oblivione vindicaturi, perpauca tantum exemplaria iterum typis mandari jussimus."

———

Bibliotheca Herefordiensis:

Or, a Descriptive Catalogue of Books, Pamphlets, Maps, Prints, &c., &c., relating to the County of Hereford: compiled by John Allen, Jun.

Hereford: Printed by J. Allen, High Town. 1821. 8vo. pp. 120.

The compiler of this Catalogue was a bookseller at Hereford; twenty-five copies were printed for private distribution. One copy was said to be printed on vellum. Mr. Allen died in 1831.

See an account of the contents of the library, "Gentleman's Magazine," July, 1825.

———

Repertorium Wiltonense.

[Privately] printed with a view to facilitate inquiry into the Topography and Biography of Wiltshire, collected by Sir R. C. Hoare, Bart. [consisting of Members of Parliament, High Sheriffs, Gentry, &c.]. Fol.

Bath. 1821.

Only fifty copies privately printed for presents.

Selection from the Papers of John St. Mawe, A.B., late of Trinity College, Cambridge.

ἱερὸν ὕπνον
Κοιμᾶται· θνήσκειν μὴ λέγε τοὺς ἀγαθούς.
Call. Epig.

"The wintry blast of death
Kills not the buds of virtue ; no, they spread,
Beneath the heavenly beams of brighter suns,
Through endless ages, into higher powers."
Thomson's Summer.

London: Printed by W. M'Dowall, Pemberton-row, Gough-square. 1821. 8*vo.* pp. 198.

The author of this volume, a young man of considerable talents, died July 10, 1820. He was educated at St. Paul's School, and was a member of Trinity College, Cambridge.

Essays on Petrarch.
By Ugo Foscolo.

Irrequietus homo perque omnes anxius annos
Ad mortem festinat iter. Mors optima rerum.
Petrar. Africa, lib. vi.

London: Printed for the Author, by Samuel and Richard Bentley, Dorset-street, Fleet-street. M.DCCC.XXI. *Imperial* 8*vo.* pp. 121.

In a note in Mr. Hanrott's copy, it is said that only sixteen copies were printed of this edition. It was published for sale by Mr. Murray in 1823.

MONASTICON WILTONENSE:
Containing a List of the Religious Houses in North and South Wiltshire; compiled chiefly from Bishop Tanner's Notitia Monastica.
Shaftesbury: Printed by J. Rutter. 1821. *folio.* pp. 46; Introduction, pp. vii.

This work was edited by the late Sir Richard Colt Hoare, Bart., whose object was to gain information respecting these establishments by the circulation of a few copies, as well as to facilitate the labours of his coadjutors in the topography of the County of Wilts.

ETCHINGS OF
VIEWS IN THE VICARAGE OF LETHERHEAD, SURREY,
BY HARRIET DALLAWAY.
London: G. Woodfall, Printer, Skinner-street. *8vo.* M.DCCC.XXI. pp. 46.

There are thirteen etchings, of which the following is a list:—
1. Letherhead, on the north-west, from Norbury Park.
2. Letherhead Church, from the south-west.
3. The Vicarage.
4. The Vicarage, with additions made in 1820.
5. The Vicarage, from the Vicarage-lane.
6. In the Garden; the Nut-tree Walk.
7. The Water-walk, looking down the River.
8. The Colonnade.
9. The Grotto.
10. The Engine-house.
11. The Vicar's Willow, *Salix Babylonica.*
12. River Mole, from the Vicarage-lane.
13. The Ale-house of Elinour Rummyng.

Prefixed is a short account of the village, by the Rev. James Dallaway, (who died June 6, 1834,) in two letters to Richard Duppa, Esq., of Lincoln's Inn.

Memoir of William Wilson, of Nether-Worton, Co. Oxon., Esq. Anno 1821.

Mr. Wilson died August, 1821.

A Collection of Fugitive Pieces in Verse, with some Originals.

Never published.

Edinburgh : Printed by J. H. m.dccc.xxi.   8*vo*.

The following is a list of the contents :—

1. The Thimble. A Poem, by [Allen] Ramsay. pp. 4.

2. The Election. A New Song, by Burns. pp. 4.

This related to the contest for Kirkcudbright, between Murray of Broughton and Sirdon of Balmaghie. pp. 4.

3. Antiquum carmen Scoticum cui nomen Maggy Lauder, Latine nec non metrice redditum et exinde facile cantandum. 12mo. 1 leaf.

4. Scraps. By the late Sir Alexander Boswell. pp. 4.

5. The Pledge ; or, the Real State of the Matter. By Sir M. S. Stewart, Bart. 1 leaf.

6. Multum in Parvo. pp. 4.

7. Cockembendie. Part II.* pp. 4.

Journal of the Operations of the Belvoir Fox-hounds, from August 7, 1821, to April 6, 1822.

" Forsan et hæc olim meminisse juvabit."

London : Printed by B. M'Millan, Bow-street, Covent-garden. 1822. 4*to*. pp. 97.

---

* This was a supplement to the preceding article.

Select Sonnets of Petrarch, with Translations and illustrative Notes.

By James, late Earl of Charlemont.
Dublin: Printed by William Folds and Son. 1822.
pp. 113.

" The object of these Translations may be best ascertained from
the Introduction. They form a small portion of a work found in a
state nearly ready for publication among the author's papers, and
intended to illustrate, in a similar manner, the writings of the great
Italian poets, from Dante to Metastasio. A limited number of
copies has been printed, for the perusal of his friends and admirers,
at the desire of his nearest relative, to shew that the leisure mo-
ments of a life devoted to the cause of his country, were devoted
with equal ardour to that of literature ; and to teach those who
come after, to what a height of elevation rank and talents can raise
their possessor, by being unremittingly applied to the purposes for
which they are vouchsafed by our Creator."

" Lord Charlemont appears to have had a particular partiality for
the people, as well as for the climate and literature, of Italy; and
his voluminous MS. history of the poetry of that country, commencing with Dante, and ending with Metastasio, furnishes most
pleasing, accurate, and critical accounts of their best poets. From
this MS. the Rev. Edward Groves has edited a privately printed and
highly interesting volume." *

Russell's Natural History of the Bee.
1822. 8vo.

From the catalogue of the late Sir F. Freeling's library, No. 1205,
where it is stated only two copies were privately printed by the
Author from types cut by himself.

----

* Memoirs of the Family of Grace, p. 81.

ANE DECLARATIOUN OF THE IUST AND NECESSAR
CAUSES, MOVING VS OF THE NOBILLITIE OF SCOTLAND,
AND VTHERS, YE KING'S MAIESTEIS FAITHFUL SVB-
IECTIS, TO REPAIR TO HIS HIENES' PRESENCE, AND TO
REMANE WITH HIM, FOR RESISTING OF THE PRESENT
DAINGERIS APPEARING TO GODDIS TREW RELIGION,
AND PROFESSOURS THAIROF, ETC., ETC.
Derectit from Stirling, with speciall command and li-
cence to be prentit.   Anno M.D.LXXXII.
[Edinburgh.   1822.]   12*mo.*

" The tract here presented to the public, is reprinted from a copy,
supposed to be unique, preserved in the library of the Faculty of
Advocates."
Forty-five copies only were reprinted by the editor, Mr. Maidment.

THE POET'S PILGRIMAGE : IN FOUR CANTOS.
" But how shall I, apprentice of the skill,
   That whilom in divinest wits did reign,
Presume so high to stretch my humble quill ?"—
           Spenser's Faery Queen, Introduction to Book iii.

London: Printed by L. Harrison, 373, Strand.
M.DCCC.XXII.

Of this work, 100 copies were privately struck off on foolscap
quarto, intended only for presents to the author's friends ; and
there was nowhere any mark of authorship.   Afterwards it was
found to be so much liked by a few people who read it, that Mr.
Collier was persuaded to publish and put his name to it.   A new
title-page was printed in 1825, the only difference being that he
described it as " An Allegorical Poem," and that the author's name,
I. Payne Collier, was inserted.   There is also some change in the
introduction, particularly by the insertion of a translation of one

of *Ariosto's Capitoli Amorosi.* It was advertised in a few news-papers, but the advertisement was recalled instantly, as the author repented of what he had done, and not a copy was sold. Of the one hundred copies originally printed, eighty-five were destroyed.

———

CONCISE VIEW OF THE ORIGIN, CONSTITUTION, AND PROCEEDINGS OF THE HONOURABLE SOCIETY OF THE GOVERNOR AND ASSISTANTS OF LONDON, OF THE NEW PLANTATION IN ULSTER, WITHIN THE REALM OF IRE-LAND, COMMONLY CALLED THE IRISH SOCIETY.
Compiled, principally, from their Records. 1822.
Printed by order of the Court, by Gye and Balne, No. 38, Gracechurch-street, London. *8vo.*

In the Appendix is an account of the siege of Londonderry, from Leland's History of Ireland; a translation of the Charter granted by Charles II. to the Irish Society, and of James I. to the town of Coleraine; Inquisitions; Fishery cause, between the Society and the Marquis of Donegal, by David Babington, Law Agent; Narrative of a Journey to the north of Ireland, in the year 1802, by Robert Slade, Secretary; the General Agent's Report on that Journey, on the Timber, and on Coleraine School.

———

TWELVE ETCHINGS AFTER DRAWINGS AND ENGRAVINGS BY PARMIGIANO AND ANDREA MELDOLLA, IN THE COLLECTION OF RICHARD FORD.
London. 1822. *4to.*

The plates are etched by Richard Ford, Esq., who possesses a very valuable collection of engravings from the works of the old masters. There were never more than *twenty* printed. Mr. Ford is well known by his admirable works on Spain.

DOCUMENTS RELATIVE TO THE RECEPTION AT EDIN-
BURGH OF THE KINGS AND QUEENS OF SCOTLAND,
A.D. M.D.LXI.
Printed at Edinburgh. A.D. M.DCCC.XXII. 4*to.* pp.
124.

By Sir Patrick Walker, Heritable Usher of the White Rod.

———

NUGÆ DERELICTÆ QUAS COLLEGERUNT J. M. ET R. P.
Edinburgi. 1822. 8*vo.*

This title is prefixed to a volume containing eighteen or twenty
tracts, printed in a separate form, at different periods; afterwards
collected, and a title, with list of contents added : a prefatory note
states that it is probable not more than six complete sets are in
existence. The initials on the title-page designate James Maidment, Esq., Advocate ; and Robert Pitcairn, Writer to the Signet.

———

TWO COPIES OF VERSES ON THE MEETING OF KING
CHARLES THE FIRST AND HIS QUEEN HENRIETTA
MARIA, IN THE VALLEY OF KINETON, BELOW EDGE-
HILL, IN WARWICKSHIRE, JULY 13, 1643.
Birmingham. 1822. 4*to.*

By the late William Hamper, Esq., of Birmingham.

In the title-page is an engraving of the unique medal by Rawlins,
struck upon this occasion, from the collection of William Staunton,
Esq., of Langbridge. A short introduction, by Mr. Hamper, dated
Deritend House, Birmingham, February 9th, 1822, states, that "the
verses, more interesting from their locality than any poetical merit,
have been preserved in manuscript, among the private papers of
that distinguished antiquary, Sir William Dugdale ; and from his

interleaved almanacks the Queen's route, from Newark to Kineton, is now, for the first time given."

The number printed was very limited, for private circulation alone; twenty-five copies are on large paper. William Hamper, Esq., was a very eminent antiquary, and author of many valuable communications to the Archæologia. His principal work is the "Life and Diary of Sir William Dugdale;" 1827. 4to. The latter period of his life was employed in preparing an appendix, consisting of several additional letters of that celebrated antiquary. Mr. Hamper died at Highgate, near Birmingham, May 3, 1831, æt. 54.

REPORTS FROM THE BOARDS OF CURATORS OF THE MUSEUM OF THE COLLEGE, TO THE COURT OF ASSISTANTS OF THE ROYAL COLLEGE OF SURGEONS OF LONDON.

London : Printed by B. Carpenter and Son, 16, High-street, Aldgate. 1822. 8vo. pp. 221.

Ten triennial reports; after which the mode was altered, both as to time and publication.

COLLECTIONS FOR A HISTORY OF THE ANCIENT FAMILY OF CARLISLE.

Humilitate.

London. 1822. 4to. pp. 414; Contents and Introduction, xvi.

A wood-cut on the title-page, engraved by Bewick, with the inscription, "Fuimus."

The author says in the conclusion, "In this compilation, no solicitude of an author need be entertained, as it is written solely for private amusement; no hopes of emolument can be indulged, as the work is not printed for sale; and no thoughts of resentment can be intended—for of the long-forgotten dead, who would speak with unkindness? I knew the name to be honourable—I wished it might have an historian." It was edited by the late Nicholas Carlisle,* F.R.S., M.R.I.A., Assistant Librarian to his Majesty, and Fellow and Secretary of the Society of Antiquaries of London. One hundred copies were printed, for distribution among the author's friends, one of whom † says, "It is worthy the author's taste and various erudition."

MISCELLANEOUS NOTICES RELATING TO CHINA, AND OUR COMMERCIAL INTERCOURSE WITH THAT COUNTRY, INCLUDING A FEW TRANSLATIONS FROM THAT LANGUAGE.

London. 1822. 8vo.

"Privately printed."—*Grenville Catalogue*, p. 687.

---

* N. Carlisle, for more than forty years Secretary to the Royal Society of Antiquaries, died at Margate on Friday, the 27th August, 1847, in the seventy-seventh year of his age. He added to his name the distinctions of K.H., D.C.L., F.R.S., F.A.S., &c., &c., and was the author of several works on archæological subjects. His publications began about forty years ago, the first we can refer to being his "Topographical Dictionary of England," 2 vols. 4to. in 1808; the "Topographical Dictionary of Ireland" followed, in a 4to. volume, 1810; that of Wales, another 4to., in 1811; and that of Scotland and the Islands of the British Seas, 2 vols. 4to., in 1813. In the arduous office which he held, Mr. Carlisle was a straightforward and upright functionary, setting his face against the intrigues and party movements which have so frequently distracted and injured the Society.

† Dr. Parr.

Records of the Origin and Proceedings
of the Outinian Society,
Founded for securing the advantages of Benevolence
and Justice; with aid of Monitory Suggestions in Critical and Ethical Lectures, where no other provision can
easily be made for that purpose; or, particularly, pro-
posing to lessen those Evils incident to the pursuit of
Happiness by Marriage, or otherwise, from which the
Complaint has sprung, that " the business of Every-body
is that of Nobody."
London: Printed by W. Nicol. 1822. 4to.; with
plates.

This society held their meetings at the house of the late John
Penn, Esq., in New-street, Spring-gardens. The record of its proceedings was intended for sale; but as the editor believes no purchaser was ever obtained for a single copy, and those which have
found their way from the warehouse of the printer were distributed
gratis, he has thought it entitled to insertion here.

Outline Engravings and Descriptions of the
Woburn Abbey Marbles.
[London]. M.DCCC.XXII. *folio.*

This splendid representation of the valuable collection of marbles,
in the possession of John, sixth Duke of Bedford, was printed at the
expense of his Grace, and has been very liberally distributed among
the friends and patrons of art.

The gallery in which this collection is deposited " was built in
the year 1789, from designs by Henry Holland, Esq. Its dimensions
are, 138 feet in length; 25 feet in breadth; and 22 feet, 7 inches, in
height. In the centre of the building are eight magnificent columns,
supporting a dome; each column consists of one entire stone: they

are all ancient, and were discovered in excavations made at Rome, by the late Mr. Brand, of the Hoo. Two of them of Breccia Africana, and two of Rigio. Their white marble capitals are also antique, and were discovered in the same excavations : they are of a very rich composite order, containing ornaments added to the combined decorations of the Ionic and Corinthian styles. At the eastern end of the Sculpture Gallery is the Temple of Liberty. At the western end is the Temple of the Graces. The visitor is conducted into the Gallery, through a small ante-room, on the walls of which are engravings of some of Canova's most beautiful statues and groups of sculpture. Opposite to the entrance is a marble bust, by Garrard, of Mr. Holland, who built the Sculpture Gallery ; and another bust, by Chantrey, of Nollekens, whose works adorn the interior of the Temple of Liberty."

The following is a list of the plates contained in this volume :—

I. South elevation of the Sculpture Gallery and Temples ; engraved by H. Moses.

II. Ground-plan of the Sculpture Gallery and Temples.

III. Section of the Sculpture Gallery and Temples ; engraved by E. Turrill.

IV. Antique Bacchic Vase ; engraved by H. Moses.

V. Apollo Musagetes, Minerva, and the Muses ; engraved by Charles Heath.

VI. Triumphal Procession of Bacchus and Hercules ; engraved by H. Moses.

VII. Achilles at Scyros ; engraved by H. Moses.

VIII. The Death of the Boar at Calydon ; engraved by E. Finden.

IX. Luna and Endymion ; engraved by E. Goodall.

X. Meleager and Atalanta ; engraved by H. Moses.

XI. Symbolical Animal, destroying a Deer ; engraved by George Corbould.

XII. Bacchanalian Procession ; engraved by H. Moses.

XIII. Phædra and Hippolytus ; engraved by H. Moses.

XIV. Ancient Mythological Basso-relievo.

XV. The Lanti Vase ; Plate I. ; engraved by H. Moses.

XVI. The Lanti Vase ; Plate II. ; engraved by H. Moses.

XVII. Bacchus ; Plate I. ; engraved by H. Moses.

XVIII. Bacchus ; Plate II. ; engraved by H. Moses.

XIX. Minerva ; engraved by H. Moses.

XX. Ceres ; engraved by H. Moses.

XXI. Antique Bronze Faun ; engraved by H. Moses.

XXII. Torso of Venus ; engraved by G. Corbould

XXIII. Torso of Apollo ; engraved by H. Moses.

XXIV. Antoninus Pius. Septimius Severus ; engraved by G. Corbould.

XXV. Ælius Verus. Marcus Aurelius ; engraved by H. Moses.

XXVI. Trajan. Diadumenianus ; etched by Henry Corbould.

XXVII. Hercules. Antique Larva, or Sepulchral Mask, Persius ; etched by Henry Corbould.

XXVIII. Fragment of the statue of a Boy. Matidia. Ancient marble disk ; engraved by H. Moses.

XXIX. Hector recommending his Son to the protection of the Gods ; an alto-relievo, by F. Chantrey, R.A. ; engraved by Henry Moses.

XXX. Penelope's reluctance to produce the Bow of Ulysses : an alto-relievo, by F. Chantrey, R.A. ; engraved by Henry Moses.

XXXI. The Wrath of Achilles : a basso-relievo, executed by Thorvaldsen, in 1815 ; etched by Henry Corbould.

XXXII. Priam supplicating Achilles ; by the same artist as the former plate ; etched by Henry Corbould.

XXXIII. Hector reproaching Paris ; basso-relievo, by Sir Richard Westmacott, R.A., executed in 1821 ; engraved by Henry Moses.

XXXIV. Hero and Leander; by Sir R. Westmacott, R.A. ; engraved by H. Moses.

XXXV. Psyche, Plate I., ⎫ by Sir Richard Westmacott, R.A., ex-
XXXVI. Psyche, Plate II., ⎬ ecuted in 1822; both engraved by H.
　　　　　　　　　　　　　　⎭ Moses.

XXXVII. Western elevation of the Temple of Liberty ; engraved by H. Moses.*

---

* The foundation of this Temple of Liberty was laid by Francis, Duke of

XXXVIII. Group in the pediment of the Temple of Liberty ; by J. Flaxman, R.A. ; engraved by Charles Heath.

XXXIX. Group in the south front of the Temple of Liberty ; by Sir R. Westmacott, R.A. ; engraved by H. Moses.

XL. Eastern elevation of the Temple of the Graces ; erected from designs by Sir Jeffry Wyattville, R.A. ; engraved by H. Moses.

XLI. The Graces, plate I. ; Canova, sculptor ;* engraved by G. Corbould.

XLII. The Graces, plate II. ; engraved by G. Corbould.

XLIII. Lady Georgiana Elizabeth Russell (Romilly), eldest daugh-

---

Bedford, a short time before his death ; and it was completed by his brother, John, sixth Duke. On the architrave is a Latin inscription, from the classical pen of the Rev. Dr. Parr :—

HANC . ÆDEM . LIBERTATI . SACRAM .

ET . A . VIRO . PATRIÆ . BONORUM . QVE . CIVIVM . AMANTISSIMO .

FRANCISCO . RVSSELL . BEDFORDIÆ . DVCE . INCHOATVM .

IOANNES . RVSSELL . HÆRES . EIVS .

EX . VOLVNTATE . FRATRIS . MORIENTIS . PERFICIENDAM . CVRAVIT .

ANNO . . CHRISTI . CIƆ IƆCCC III .

In this temple is the bust of Charles James Fox, by Nollekens, with some verses on the pedestal, by Georgiana, Duchess of Devonshire : also the following busts of some of the most intimate friends of that statesman, by Nollekens, viz. Earl Grey, Lord John Townshend, Lord Robert Spencer, Lord Holland, General Fitzpatrick, and Mr. Hare.

* The following elegant tribute to the memory of this eminent man is taken from the list of his works, in this volume.—" Whilst the foregoing testimony to the wonderful talents which Canova has displayed in this group of the Graces, was passing through the press, the afflicting intelligence of his death reached England. It may therefore be permitted to the possessor of this Collection to add to the page, the tribute which he feels to be due to the memory of that great sculptor; as it was his good fortune, whilst visiting Italy, to enjoy the happiness of his society, and the benefit of his refined taste; and to possess him, afterwards, as a guest at Woburn Abbey. During this intercourse, he had the means of observing, that the estimable qualities and amiable disposition of Antonio Canova, joined to his engaging simplicity of manners, endeared him to private friends, as much as his transcendant abilities had done, to the admirers of whatever is sublime, or graceful, or attractive, in the highest departments of art."

ter of the sixth Duke of Bedford; Thorvaldsen, sculptor; engraved by W. Finden.

XLIV. Lady Louisa Jane Russell; now Marchioness of Abercorn; by F. Chantrey, R.A., engraved by W. Finden.

XLV. Group in the south front of the Temple of the Graces; by Sir R. Westmacott, R.A.; engraved by H. Moses.

XLVI. Cupid. Ancient Roman Sarcophagus. Cupid, engraved by H. Moses.

In the title-page is a vignette of a Bull, by Garrard; on the leaf of description of the vignettes, is the Bird of Jove, grasping a thunderbolt; also by Garrard: the drawings were made by the late Henry Corbould. The text is beautifully printed by Mr. Nicol, at the Shakspeare Press; it is not paged. The following is a collation:—title, one leaf—list of plates, one leaf—Sculpture Gallery, half title, one leaf—description of the Sculpture Gallery, two leaves—Marbles in the Sculpture Gallery one leaf—Descriptions of Plates V. VI. VII., two leaves each—VIII. IX. X. XI. XII. XIII., one leaf each—XIV. XV. XVI., two leaves—XVII. XVIII., one leaf—XIX. to XXXIV., each one leaf of description—XXXXV. XXXVI., one leaf—XXXVII. two leaves—XXXVIII. to XL. each one leaf—XLI. XLII., the Graces, six leaves—XLIII. XLIV. XLV., each one leaf — XLVI., three leaves — vignettes' description, one leaf—a single leaf, giving a description of the copies in marble of some of the most admired statues and busts of antiquity—Appendix, one leaf—Dissertation on the Lanti Vase, by the late James Christie, Esq., two leaves—Dissertation on an ancient Hymn to the Graces, by Ugo Foscolo, 23 pp.

The descriptions which illustrate the marbles were, for the most part, written by the late Duke of Bedford; who printed one hundred and eighty copies, for private distribution. Copies are in the British Museum, and in the library of the Society of Antiquaries. The copper plates were destroyed, by desire of the Duke.

STATUTA COLLEGII REGINALIS APUD CANTABRIGI-
ENSES ANNO M.D.LIX. A REGIIS COMMISSARIIS RE-
FORMATA : QUIBUS ACCEDUNT INTERPRETATIONES STA-
TUTORUM A PRÆSIDE ET SOCIIS SANCITÆ.

"Volumus quod Statuta hujus Collegii sint tripartita ;
quorum hæcce vera copia semper remaneat in Turri, cum
sigillis et Jocalibus Collegii ; secunda remaneat in Camera
Præsidentis ; tertia vero remaneat catenata in vestibulo
Capellæ Collegii."—*Stat.* cap. 28.

Cantabrigiæ : Typis academicis, sumptibus Collegii
Reginalis, excudit Joannes Smith. 1822. 4*to.* pp. 76 ;
Introduction, pp. vii.

A FORM FOR THE COMMEMORATION OF BENEFACTORS,
TO BE USED IN THE CHAPEL OF ST. MARGARET AND ST.
BERNARD, COMMONLY CALLED QUEEN'S COLLEGE, CAM-
BRIDGE.

Cambridge : At the University Press, by J. Smith,
1823. pp. 18.

A copy of the " Statutes," with the " Form," formerly belonging
to the Rev. G. C. Gorham, of Queen's College, was sold at Mr. Hibbert's sale, and contained the following memorandum :—

" Only fifty copies of this work were printed, under my care, from
the autograph, now in the Muniment Tower of Queen's College, besides three copies on vellum. (See Note *a*, p. 1, Preface.)* The
three vellum copies are appropriated according to the directions

---

* (*a*) Vide Librum MS., in camera Præsidis, cui titulus, " *Order Book.*"—
" 8. Jan. 1822, agreed ; That a correct transcript be made of the original
Statute Book ; that from such transcript, fifty copies be printed, which shall be
deposited in the custody of the master, for the use of the fellows ; and that three
be printed on vellum, to be deposited according to the directions of the 28th
chapter of the Statutes."

in the 28th chap. of the Statutes. (See the title-page, motto.) The fifty copies were deposited with the President, for the sole use of the Society. The College *granted* one copy to the British Museum; none being *sold* by the Society, the Museum had no claim.

" This copy belonged to myself, as one of the five senior fellows of Queen's College : and was transferred by me to George Hibbert, Esq., of Portland-place.

" *The Initial Letters* were drawn by myself on wood, and engraved over my drawings by Hughes. For the *subjects* of these illustrations see the published Catalogue of Queen's Coll. Library, Pref.

" *The Prolegomena* were drawn up by me, not without a laborious search among the College records and muniments.

" *The Seals* (which form a complete series) were drawn by B. Howlatt, under my eye, from casts made by myself, by permission of the Society, from the actual impressions attached to College deeds. Of the seal, 1447, only *one* original exists ; the seal, 1460, exists only at Corpus Christi College ; and some of the others are recovered from fragments of several impressions, so that they may be said to be lost to the Society.

" *Clapham*, 6 *Sept.* 1827. " G. C. Gorham."

Poetical Sketches
of a Tour in the West of England.
Printed for the Author, by J. Montgomery, Sheffield, for private distribution only. 1822. 8*vo.* pp. 79.

Written by Marmaduke Middleton, Esq., of Leam, in Co. Derby.

" Robert Middleton, the last heir-male of this family, died in 1736. His daughter and heiress married Mr. Jonathan Oxley, of Sheffield ; pursuant to whose will, Marmaduke Carver (son of the Rev. Mr. Carver, of Morstham, in Yorkshire) took the name of Middleton, in 1795, and is the present proprietor of Leam." *

---

* Lysons, Magna Britannia. Derbyshire.

POETICAL TRANSLATIONS,
BY HENRY GOSSE.

London: Printed by A. J. Valpy, Red-Lion Court, Fleet Street. 1822. 8vo. pp. 146.

Printed for private gifts among the friends of the author, Henry Gosse, Esq., a magistrate for Surrey, residing at Epsom.

THE ΠΕΡΙ ΜΟΥΣΙΚΗΣ OF PLUTARCH, translated. Chiswick: From the Press of C. Whittingham, College House. 1822. 12mo. pp. 115.

This translation is by J. H. Bromdy, of Hull; the original text accompanies it. Prefixed is a frontispiece, representing Clio, from a drawing by Harriet Cheney. A copy in Mr. Eyton's Catalogue, No. 1175.

"HERE BEGYNETH A LITTEL TOME, AND HATHE TO NAME, 𝕿𝖍𝖊 𝕷𝖎𝖓𝖈𝖔𝖑𝖓𝖊 𝕹𝖔𝖘𝖊𝖌𝖆𝖕: BEYNGE A BREFE TABLE OF CERTAINE BOKES IN THE POSSESSION OF MAISTER THOMAS FROGNALL DIBDIN CLERK; WHICH BOOKES BE TO BE SOLD TO HIM WHO SHALL GYUE THE MOSTE FOR Yᵒ SAME." London. Printed by W. Bulmer and Co. 1822. 8vo. pp. 16.

Only thirty-six copies were printed. Lowndes says, "this tract has been surreptitiously reprinted."

A full account of the books obtained by the "practised hand of Rosicrusius" will be found in Mr. Botfield's interesting volume, "Notes on the Cathedral Libraries of England," who well remarks, in printing Mr. Garvey's letter, the librarian, "that those who are anxious for the integrity of those great collections which the wise and the good of former ages have handed down to us, may learn from hence the necessity of devising means, whereby such treasures may be preserved unimpaired and intact for posterity, more effectual than those which the venerable consort of Michael Honeywood, happily in no wise prescient of the future fate of these literary treasures, devised." In a copy in Thorpe's catalogue, 1835, is a note, part of which is here inserted:—"Only thirty-six copies were printed. Common copies have sold as high as four guineas. The books, nineteen in number, were purchased for five hundred guineas."

Mr. Botfield further remarks, "the loss thus sustained by the ancient library of Lincoln Cathedral by the sale of the volumes thus inconsiderately, and, in my opinion, unjustifiably, detached, was compensated, in some degree, by the purchase of other books with the proceeds, and the addition to the original collection of the books thus purchased."

In this opinion of the loss, we think most of our readers will coincide ; and we hope it is not the forerunner of the destruction of the ancient Cathedral libraries, whose books, and their grave and curiously-bound volumes, harmonise gracefully with the noble structures they adorn, in exchange for the poor utilitarian cheap *railroad* editions, hastily got up and carelessly edited, which swarm on the publisher's counter and railroad station. It is due, however, to the curators of the library of Lincoln, to add, that the books obtained by the exchange are not of the character alluded to ; "many would do honour to any library."

A Tour in the Isle of Wight, in the Autumn
of 1820. Currente calamo.

" Let us become acquainted with the beauties of our own country before we explore those of a foreign land."— *Hints to Travellers.*

London : Printed by A. and R. Spottiswoode, New-street Square. 1822. 12*mo.* pp. 84.

In Mr. Eyton's catalogue, celebrated for a very large collection of privately printed books, it is said to be by the late Countess of Blesinton.

A CATALOGUE OF THE SUBSCRIPTION LIBRARY AT
KINGSTON ON HULL, ESTABLISHED IN DECEMBER, 1775.
Liverpool: Printed by G. F. Harris's Widow and Bro-
thers. M.DCCC.XXII. 8*vo.* pp. 672.

A classed Catalogue, for the most part on the plan of that of the
Royal Institution, London. Compiled chiefly by Mr. Joseph Clarke,
brother of the late Vicar of Holy Trinity Church, Hull. Nine
copies were on large paper.

AN ESSAY ON SCULPTURE.
No Title-page. 8*vo.* pp. 59, including false title
and preface.

The author is Philip B. Duncan, Esq. It was printed at Oxford,
about 1822.

ON INSTINCT. (BY THE SAME AUTHOR.)
No title. 8*vo.* pp. 32.

About the same period.

ON MIGRATION. (BY THE SAME.)
No title. 8*vo.* pp. 38.

Same period.

CASTLES OF ALNWICK AND WARKWORTH, ETC., FROM
SKETCHES BY C. F., DUCHESS OF NORTHUMBERLAND.
[London.] 1823. 4*to.* pp. 39.

These representations of the splendid residences of the House of

Percy, are all from the original designs of the accomplished lady of the late noble owner. They are drawn on stone by J. D. Harding; the impression was limited to two hundred and fifty copies.

The following is a list of the views:—

Frontispiece—Saxon Gateway of the Inner Court.

Distant view of Alnwick.

Alnwick Castle, from the north demesne.

Alnwick Castle, from the north-west.

East view of Alnwick Castle.

Alnwick Castle, from an old picture.

The Barbican.

Avener's Tower,
Caterer's Tower,
Guard-house,
Hotspur's Seat, } on one plate.

Constable's Tower,
Postern Tower, on
Armourer's Tower, one
West garret, Abbot's plate.
Tower, }

The Dungeon.

The Second Gateway.

Quarterings.

General Plan.

Plan of ground floor.

Plan of principal floor.

Malcolm's Cross,
Monument of Wil- } vignettes on text,
liam the Lion, p. 15.

Recess in Saloon, vignette, p. 16.

Entrance Gateway.

Ancient Well, vignette, p. 18.

Hulne Abbey, vignette, p. 19.

Interior of Hulne Abbey.

Plan of Hulne Abbey.

Gateway of Hulne Abbey, vignette, p. 22.

———

Warkworth Castle, from an old picture.

North view of Warkworth Castle.

Entrance Gate and Keep of Warkworth Castle.

Keep of Warkworth Castle.

Lion Tower, Warkworth.

Gate-house of Warkworth Castle.

Warkworth Castle, plan.

Warkworth Castle, plan of ground floor.

Warkworth Castle, plan of second floor.

Hermitage, vignette, p. 32.

South view of Hermitage.

Vignette, p, 34.

Coquet Island.

Percy's Cross.

Hotspur's Tower, vignette, p. 39.

The volume is also embellished with illuminated capitals, having historical allusion.

Leisure Hours;
By Richard Whitfield Ashworth.

Sed tamen et parvæ nonnulla est gratia musæ.—*Martial.*

Bishop's Stortford: Printed by William Thorogood, North-street. 1823. 8*vo.* pp. 73.

———

Journal of the Operations of the Belvoir Fox-Hounds, from August 7, 1822, to April 12, 1823.

"Forsan et hæc olim meminisse juvabit."

London: Printed by B. M'Millan, Bow-street, Covent-garden. 1823. 4*to.* pp. 80.

———

De Capta a Mehemethe II., Constantinopoli.

Leonardi Chiensis et Godefredi Lange Narrationes, sibi invicem collatæ : accessere Isidori Cardinalis, e duplici monumento, Epistola et Ducæ super Urbe capta deletoque Christianorum in Oriente imperio Monodia : recensebat et notis illustrabat Joann. Bapt. L'Ecuy Doctor Sorbonicus, Abbas Præmonstrati.

Lutetiæ Parisiorum: Sumptibus illustrissimi Domini D. Caroli Stuart, equitis aurati, Magnæ Britanniæ Legati apud Regem Christianissimum. M.DCCC.XXIII. 4*to.* pp. 131 ; Præfatio Editoris, pp. xii.

Printed for private circulation, from a fac-simile of the manuscript in the Royal library at Paris, which is inserted in the volume, at the expense of the late Lord Stuart de Rothsay; sixty copies only are said to have been printed. His Lordship printed also, for private circulation—

1. Catalogue des Livres de la Bibliothèque du Chevalier Stuart. Paris: Imprimé a l'hotel de sa Majesté Brittanique. 1821.

2. Fragmentos de Cancioneiro Portuguez inedito do Seculo XIII. Paris: Teico de S. M. Brittanico. 1822.

Of the first work, copies are in the library of the Duke of Bedford and Earl Spencer. The "Fragmentos de Cancioneiro Portuguez" is the subject of a long note in Mr. Hallam's "Literature of Europe;"[*] he mentions that "an account of this book by M. Raynouard will be found in the 'Journal des Savans' for August, 1825." The late Lord Holland possessed the catalogue of Lord Stuart de Rothsay's library, which is particularly rich in Spanish and Portuguese literature.

DESCRIPTION OF THE SHIELDS OF ARMS RECENTLY PUT UP IN THE HALL OF WOTTON HOUSE, IN THE COUNTY OF BUCKS.
London: Printed by William Nicol, Cleveland Row, St. James's. 1823. 4*to.* pp. 1–22; and *Impl. 8vo.*

Printed at the expense of the late Sir Scrope Morland, Bart., who left it incomplete. It comprises one plate, drawn on stone, containing the arms of Brydges and Bruce, 1728; and Grenville and Brydges, 1796. The shields were put up on the rebuilding of Wotton House; the old pile having been destroyed by fire, October, 1820: it has since been rebuilt, under the direction of the late Sir John Soane, R.A.

---

[*] Vol. i. p. 55: Lond. 1837.

INSTRUMENT OF FALSING OF DOOMS. M.CCC.XL.
Printed J. H. Edinburgh. 1823. pp. 3 and Title.

Ten copies printed.

INDENTOUR BETWYX ROBERT LORD FLEMYNG AND
GILBERT LORD KENNEDY AND SIR ALEXANDER BOID
OF DUCHOL KNYCHT.
Maid at Strivelyn the tend day of februar, the Year
of God M.CCC.LXV.

Stirling. M.DCCC.XXIII. J. H. 8*vo*. pp. 3. Title
and prefatory note, by James Maidment, Esq. pp. 4.

Ten copies only were printed.

INSTRUCTIONS FOR THE LORD FLEMYNG LIEUTENENT
AND WARDOUN OF THE WEST BORDOUR.
[1823.] pp. 4. 8*vo*.

The preceding three articles were privately printed at the expense of the late James Hill, Esq., Writer to the Signet, afterwards Deputy Keeper of the Register of Sasines at Glasgow, for Lanarkshire. This gentleman was the eldest son of Robert Hill, Esq., of Firth, also a Writer to the Signet; and he married a lady of the name of Kelly. He died in the prime of life, leaving no issue. The manuscripts, from which these brochures were printed, are, or were, in the Charter chest of the Representatives of the Earl of Wigton, a title now believed to be extinct. The Indentour was thought so valuable as illustrating a dark period of Scottish History, that the late lamented P. F. Tytler obtained permission for its being reprinted in the Appendix to one of his Volumes of the History of Scotland.

THE HISTORY OF THE COLLEGE OF BONHOMMES, AT
ASHRIDGE, IN THE COUNTY OF BUCKINGHAM, FOUNDED
IN THE YEAR 1276, BY EDMUND, EARL OF CORNWALL.
Compiled from original Records, and other authentic
sources : to which is added, a Description of the present
Mansion, erected on the site of the ancient College.

> " A pleasanter place than Ashridge is, hard were to find,
>   As Skelton rehearseth with words few and plain,
>   In his distichen, made in verses twain ;
>   *Fraxinus in clivo frondetque viret sine rivo,*
>   *Non est sub divo similis sine flumine vivo.*"

London: Printed by R. Gilbert, St. John's-square.
1823. *folio.* pp. 91 ; Table of Descents, folded, marked
p. 93 ; a single leaf, B 6, unpaged, containing an account
of John, Earl of Bridgewater.

This volume was edited by the late Rev. H. J. Todd ; who says in
the preface, " From records belonging to the demesnes of Ashridge,
with which he became acquainted, through the Earl of Bridgewater's friendly means, long before the death of the late possessor,
the illustrious Duke of Bridgewater, and from other documents,
which passed, according to the Duke's bequest of his books and
manuscripts, to the present Marquess of Stafford, now Duke of
Sutherland, have been extracted many curious particulars of Ashridge while a convent, and after it became the residence of Lord
Chancellor Egerton and his descendants. Thus, from the retired-
ness of monastic manners, the reader will be led to many notices
of courtly splendour, and finally, from the demolition of this ancient
edifice, to the mansion erected on nearly the conventual site, per-
petuating the venerable name of Ashridge."
The foundation of the splendid pile described in this work was
laid on the 25th October, 1808, in the presence of the late noble
owner, John William, Earl of Bridgewater ; and the building was

inhabited on the 11th of October, 1814. The founder of the mansion died on the 21st of October, 1823 ; and bequeathed this estate
to his great nephew, fettered with singular conditions, which the
annexed extract from the Will itself will shew."*

---

* Extracted from the Registry of the Prerogative Court of Canterbury :—

" In the Will of John William, Earl of Bridgewater, dated 31st March, 1823,
is the following clause :—

"Provided, that if John Hume, Lord Viscount Alford, shall die without
having acquired the title of Duke or Marquis of Bridgewater, then the estate
directed to be limited to the heirs male of his body shall be void ; and that if
the Earldom of Brownlow shall descend to him, and he shall not have acquired
the title of Duke or Marquis of Bridgewater, before the end of five years after
he become Earl of Brownlow, then the several estates directed to be limited to
Viscount Alford shall cease ; and that my estates before devised, shall be
enjoyed as if Viscount Alford were actually dead, without issue male. Provided also, that if it shall happen that Viscount Alford shall not acquire the
title of Duke or Marquis of Bridgewater, with the immediate limitation over of
such title to Charles Henry Cust; and that if the Earldom of Brownlow shall
descend to the said Charles Henry Cust, and he shall not have acquired the
title of Duke or Marquis of Bridgewater before the end of five years next after
he shall become Earl of Brownlow, then the several estates directed to be
limited to Charles Henry Cust shall be void. Provided also, that if my
brother, Francis Henry Egerton, shall be created Duke or Marquis of Bridgewater, with such limitations over of the title, that the same may immediately
after the failure of issue male of my brother, come to John, Viscount Alford,
and his heirs male, and after them to Charles Henry Cust, and his heirs male,
then my estates shall be enjoyed as if the several provisos had not been contained in this my Will. Provided, that if John, Earl Brownlow, shall, in case
of the failure of issue male of my brother in his lifetime, be created Duke or
Marquis of Bridgewater, the title being limited to him and his heirs by Sophia,
Lady Brownlow, his late wife, only, and not being inheritable by any other
issue of John, Earl Brownlow, the same shall be equivalent to the acquisition
of such title by Viscount Alford; and my estates shall be settled so as to be
enjoyed for the future as if the several provisos had not been contained in this
my Will. Provided, that if John, Earl Brownlow, shall hereafter take any
other title than Duke or Marquis of Bridgewater, so as to be inheritable by his
issue male by Sophia, Lady Brownlow, his late wife ; then the estates directed
to be limited to Viscount Alford, and Charles Henry Cust, and to their heirs

The following is the list of the plates which illustrate this volume :—

North front of Ashridge, as it was in 1768. Mackenzie, del., Charles Pye, sculp. ; to face the title.

General plan of Ashridge. James Wyatt, R.A., Jeffry Wyatville, R.A., delin^{t.} ; E. Turrell, sculp. ; page 1.

Seals : Ex originali carta penes Comitem de Bridgewater. J. Basire, del. et sculp. ; page 10.

Monument of Thomas Waterhous. Copied from Morgan's Sphere of Gentry. No engraver's name ; page 24.

King Edward VI. R. Westmacott, R.A., sculp. ; drawn on stone by Richard Lane, from the original drawing by Henry Corbould ; page 31.

Queen Elizabeth ; by the same artists ; page 32.

Thomas Egerton, Baron of Ellesmere, Lord Keeper to Queen Elizabeth ; engraved by Edward Scriven ; page 34.

The Hon. Thomas Egerton, fourth son of John, first Earl of Bridgewater ; engraved by W. Evans ; page 43.

---

respectively, shall cease ; and that my estate shall be enjoyed according to this my Will, as if the said Viscount Alford and Charles Henry Cust were actually dead, without issue.

"Proved by the Right Hon. John, Earl Brownlow, Lord Viscount Clive, and the Right Hon. Sir Charles Long, now Lord Farnborough, 18th December, 1823."

On Lord Alford's death, 2nd January, 1851, leaving two sons, and without having obtained the Dukedom or Marquisate of Bridgewater, a suit was instituted in the Court of Chancery to try the validity of the condition in Lord Bridgewater's Will as to obtaining one of those titles. If the condition was valid, the Hon. Charles Henry Cust, Lord Alford's brother, was entitled to the estates, but subject to the same condition ; if the condition was not valid, Lord Alford's eldest son was entitled to the estates as tenant in tail male. Vice-Chancellor Lord Cranworth gave a judgment in favour of the validity of the condition. (See 1 Simons's Reports, New Series, 464.) From this decision there was an appeal to the House of Lords. The appeal has been heard, and questions were referred to the judges ; the decree of the Lord Chancellor has been reversed, and the estates now pass to Lord Alford, a minor, grandson of Earl Brownlow.

The Lady Alice Egerton, daughter of John, first Earl of Bridgewater; engraved by W. Evans; page 43.

John, Lord Viscount Brackley, eldest son of John, first Earl of Bridgewater; engraved by W. Evans; page 44.

Francis, Duke of Bridgewater (oval); engraved by James Heath; page 56.

Elevations (two) in outline; F. Mackenzie, del.; E. Turrell, sculp.; page 68.

North front of Ashridge; drawn by F. Mackenzie; engraved by H. Le Keux; page 70.

Hall, Ashridge; drawn by F. Mackenzie; engraved by J. Le Keux; page 71.

Stair-case, Ashridge; drawn by F. Mackenzie; engraved by J. Roffe; page 71.

Senchia, wife of Richard, Earl of Cornwall; R. Westmacott, R.A., sculp.; drawn on stone by Richard Lane, from the original drawing by Henry Corbould; page 72.

Richard, Earl of Cornwall, King of the Romans; by the same artists; page 72.

Edward the Black Prince; by the same artists; page 72.

Edmund, son of Richard, Earl of Cornwall; by the same artists; page 72.

Richard de Walford; by the same artists; page 72.

Thomas de Cantelupe, Bishop of Hereford; by the same artists; page 72.

St. Benedict; by the same artists; page 72.

A Monk; by the same artists; page 72.

East Front, Ashridge; drawn by F. Mackenzie; engraved by W. R. Smith; page 73.

North-west view of the Chapel Tower; drawn by F. Mackenzie; engraved by William Woolnoth; page 74.

South-west end of the Chapel; by the same artists; page 74.

Interior of the Chapel, looking towards the Altar; F. Mackenzie, del.; J. Heath and A. Freebairn, sculp.; page 74.

View of the Altar in the Chapel, Ashridge; F. Mackenzie, del.; A. Freebairn, sculp.; page 74.

Crypt, Ashridge; drawn by F. Mackenzie; engraved by Henry Le Keux; page 75.

South Front of Ashridge; drawn by F. Mackenzie; engraved by H. Le Keux; page 76.

Seal appended to the acknowledgment of the King's supremacy, in 1534, vignette, on page 81, is, of course, the insignia of the priory, and bears in the base, the lion rampant, the arms of the founder, the Earl of Cornwall.

John William, seventh Earl of Bridgewater; painted by W. Owen, R.A.; engraved in mezzotint by S. W. Reynolds; before the table, page 93.

On the title-page; vignette, the holy lamb.

Two hundred copies were printed of this work, for private distribution.

STONEHENGE.

" Thou noblest monument of Albion's Isle !
　　Whether by Merlin's aid, from Lythia's shore,
　　To Amberes' fatal plain Pendragon bore,
　Huge frame of giant hands, thou mighty pile,
　T' entomb his Britons, slain by Hengist's guile ;
　Or Druid priests, sprinkled with human gore,
　Taught 'mid thy many maze their mystic lore ;
　　Or Danish chiefs, enriched with savage spoil,
　To Victory's idol vast, an unhewn shrine,
　　Raised the rude heap ; or, in thy hallowed round,
　Repose the kings of Brutus' genuine line ;
　　Or here those kings in solemn state were crowned ;
　　We muse on many an ancient tale renowned."
　　　　　　　　　　　　　　　　　　　　Warton.

Printed by A. Stark, Market-place, Gainsborough. [1823.] pp. 30.

This tract was written by Mr. Adam Stark, author of the History of Gainsborough, and of an account of Stowe, the *Sidnanster* of the Romans. The object was to prove that Stonehenge was erected by the Saxons.

MEMOIR OF THE LATE REV. HUGH MOISES, M.A.,
Head Master of the Royal Grammar School,
Newcastle-upon-Tyne.
Newcastle: Printed by Edward Walker, Pilgrim-street.
1823. 8*vo.* pp. 59.

Written by the Rev. J. Brewster; who says in the preface, " The impression is private; and I have distributed copies of it only to my friends, or such as were yet alive of Mr. Moises' scholars. Amongst these, to two valuable men who were my townsmen at Newcastle-upon-Tyne, and whom I had known from early youth, Lords Stowell and Eldon."

MEMOIRS OF THE FAMILY OF GRACE;
BY SHEFFIELD GRACE, ESQ., F.S.A.

Τὸ γὰρ γέρας ἐστὶ θανόντων.—*Hom.*

These on tradition's tongue still live, these shall
On history's honest page be pictured bright
To latest times.—*Grahame.*

London. M.DCCC.XXIII. 8*vo.* pp. 104.

Some copies of this work have another title; with a wood-cut, the armorial badge, with the mottos of the family,—" Concordant nomine facta," and " En grace affie ;"—with the letters S. G. A list of plates which are in this work will be found at the end of the volume ; they consist of topographical views, armorial bearings, and portraits ; the principal part are from old copper-plates, which Mr.

Grace obtained, and with impressions from which he has illustrated his volume.

At the end, the following additions will generally be found,— Lines to Sheffield Grace, Esq., by Charles Symmons, D.D., one leaf: Lines written at Jerpoint Abbey. 1820. pp. 16: Verses in Irish, entitled, "Grace's Country;" two leaves: Descent of the Family of Grace; two leaves: a Table, Descent of the Graces of Gracefield: Monumental and other Inscriptions; pp. 34.

The volume is dedicated to the Duchess of Buckingham and Chandos, with whose noble family the author is distantly connected.

———

An Account of Greek Manuscripts, chiefly Biblical, which had been in the possession of the late Professor Carlyle, the greater part of which are now deposited in the Archiepiscopal Library, at Lambeth Palace.

London: Printed by Richard Gilbert, St. John's-square, Clerkenwell. 1823. *8vo.*

Two hundred copies were printed of this Catalogue, compiled by the Rev. Henry John Todd. In it will be found an account of those MSS., which, being claimed by the Patriarch of Jerusalem, were returned to him.

———

Sketch of the Life and Writings of Ferdoosee.

Manchester: Printed for the Author. 1823. *12mo.* Dedication, Advertisement, &c., 3 leaves, and pp. 56.

"A small number of copies is printed separately, not for publication, but for the use of a few friends."

BIBLIOTHECA HIBERNICA:
Or a Descriptive Catalogue of a Select Irish Library, collected for the Right Hon. Robert Peel, &c., &c.

"Attamen audendum est et veritas investiganda," &c. — *Shaw Mason's Parochial Survey of Ireland.*

"For not to be able to find what we know to be in our possession, is a more vexatious circumstance than the mere want of what we have neglected to procure. This catalogue will not only assist the forgetful, but direct the inquisitive."—*Dr. Johnson.*

Dublin : Printed by W. Folds and Son, Great Strand-street. 1823.   8*vo.*

This impression consists of fifty copies only. 8*vo.* pp. 57 ; Introduction, pp. v ; and a fac-simile of Sir John Davies's tract on Ireland. It was compiled by W. Shaw Mason.

" A BALLAD BOOK."
[Edinburgh. 1823.] 12*mo.* pp. 123.

This volume, which is dedicated to the late Sir Walter Scott, was printed at the expense of Charles Kirkpatrick Sharpe, Esq. ; who thus commences his address to the "Courteous Reader :"—" As this book, of which only *thirty* copies were printed, shall cost thee nothing, saving a little time thrown away on its perusal, which most antiquaries can very well spare, I will make no apology to thee for compiling it." It contains fragments of forty-three ballads, chiefly from tradition.

Sir Walter Scott styles it, "a curious collection, under the modest title of a 'Ballad Book,' which indicates, by a few notes only, the capacity which the editor possesses for supplying the most extensive and ingenious illustrations upon antiquarian subjects." *

---

* Poetical Works, by Lockhart, vol. i. pp. 25, 84.

Travels in Egypt and Nubia, Syria and Asia Minor, during the Years 1817 and 1818. By the Hon. Charles Leonard Irby and James Mangles, Commanders in the Royal Navy.

London : T. White and Co. 1823. 8*vo*. pp. 560.

Printed for private distribution.

" They are very valuable compositions, characterised throughout by a degree of modesty which sheds around them a peculiar grace." —*Translator of Laborde's Journey through Arabia Petræa*, p. xix.

" Well written, and full of accurate information." — *Robinson, Biblical Researches*, vol. iii. Appx. p. 24.

———

The Odes of Anacreon of Teos : translated into English Measure, By Edward Hovel Thurlow, Lord Thurlow.

London. J. Warwick, Brooke-street, Holborn. 8*vo.* pp. 81. 1823.

———

The Flower and the Leaf, after Geoffrey Chaucer. By Edward Hovel Thurlow, Lord Thurlow.

London. J. Warwick, Brooke-street, Holborn. 1823. 8*vo*. pp. 30.

A note in the copies of these works, in Mr. Hanrott's sale, No. 541, pt. iv, states, that no copies of these poems had been distributed among the friends of the author.

Lord Thurlow died at Brighton, June 4, 1829, aged 47.

REMARKS UPON CERTAIN OBJECTIONS PUBLISHED IN
THE DUBLIN NEWSPAPER CALLED "THE WARDER,"
AGAINST THE TITHE-COMPOSITION BILL, NOW PENDING
IN PARLIAMENT.
[BY RICHARD LAURENCE, Archbishop of Cashel.]
London: Printed by A. and R. Spottiswoode. 1823.
8vo. pp. 15.

Not published: very few copies printed.

———

MEMOIR OF THE LIFE AND FAMILY OF THE LATE
SIR GEORGE LEONARD STAUNTON, BART.;
With an Appendix, consisting of Illustrations and
Authorities; and a copious selection from his private
Correspondence.

> "His various learning and elegant accomplishments at-
> tracted my attention and reverence; his long political
> career, ever marked by honour, integrity, talent and bene-
> ficence, was beheld by his numerous friends with delight
> and respect; and in these feelings no one participated
> more than myself."—*Charles Butler's Reminiscences.*

Havant Press: Printed by Henry Skelton, West-street
[for private circulation only]. 1823. 8vo. pp. 400; Dedication and Contents, pp. xiii.

Prefixed is a private plate of Sir George Leonard Staunton, Bart.;
Engleheart pinxit, 1792, engraved by C. Picart; at p. 369, a vignette
from Sir George Staunton's account of Lord Macartney's embassy to
China. He died January 14, 1801, and was buried in Westminster
Abbey. He was succeeded by his son, the editor of this volume,
formerly member of parliament for Hampshire.

NOTES OF PROCEEDINGS AND OCCURRENCES
DURING THE BRITISH EMBASSY TO PEKIN, IN 1816.
Havant Press: Printed by Henry Skelton, West-street
[for private circulation only]. 1824. 8*vo*. pp. 480.

Written by Sir George Staunton, Bart., of Leigh House, Hampshire, formerly member of parliament for the southern division of
that county.

A DESCRIPTIVE CATALOGUE OF A COLLECTION OF
PICTURES, COMPREHENDING SPECIMENS OF ALL THE
VARIOUS SCHOOLS OF PAINTING; BELONGING TO ———
[London.] M.DCCC.XXIV. 4*to*. pp. 77.

This Catalogue is descriptive of the collection belonging to
Sir Abraham Hume, Bart. The pictures, on the death of Sir A.
Hume, were bequeathed to the late Lord Alford, eldest son of
Earl Brownlow.

EGYPT; A DESCRIPTIVE POEM, WITH NOTES.
BY A TRAVELLER.
Alexandria: Printed for the Author, by Alexander
Draghi, at the European Press. 1824. 8*vo*. pp. 55.

"This poem was printed with a view to divert the author's attention, whilst suffering under severe affliction, as well as to give
encouragement to a very worthy man, the printer. It is the first
English work carried through in Alexandria; and as the compositor
was entirely ignorant of the language in which it is written, the difficulties that existed in correcting the proof-sheets may be easily
imagined."
By Henry Salt, Esq. Fifty copies were printed.
This work, from being printed out of the country, did not come
within the editor's list; but as it was the first English work printed

in Alexandria, and from its being, in all probability, very little known, he has departed from his usual rule, by inserting it here.

Mr. Salt was the companion of Lord Valentia, during his travels in India; subsequently, consul-general in Egypt; where he died, leaving behind him a well-earned reputation for his proficiency in Oriental literature. "I have not printed it with my name, but as a 'Traveller,' nor will a single copy be sold." It is reprinted in Mr. Hall's Life of Salt, vol. ii.

An Inquiry, on the grounds of Scripture and Reason, into the Rise and Import of the Eucharistic Symbols.
Dublin: Printed by Richard Beere and Co., 28, Little Strand-street. 1824. 8vo. pp. 93.

By Alexander Knox, private Secretary to Lord Castlereagh, before the union with Ireland. Fifty copies only are said to have been printed. It will be found in Mr. Knox's Remains, third edition. 4 vols. 8vo. London. 1844.

Statement
of the Services of Sir Stamford Raffles.
London: Printed by Cox and Baylis, Great Queen-street, Lincoln's Inn Fields. Nov. 1824. 4to. pp. 72.

A memoir of this eminent public servant was printed by his widow. London. 1830.

"His heart was full of enjoyment; and, in the retirement for which he had so long sighed, and surrounded by all the ties which it had pleased God to spare to him, he indulged his happy spirit. In the midst of all these best of worldly treasures, in the bosom of his family, that spirit which had won its way through a greatly chequered course, was suddenly summoned to the throne of God, on the day previous to the completion of his forty-fifth year, the 5th of July, 1826." In the same suburban school, where Sir Stamford Raffles received his education, the editor of these pages was also brought up. The reviewer, in the "Quarterly," of his widow's "Memoir" affects to sneer at suburban schools; but that could not be a very bad one, where Sir Stamford laid the foundation of an education, which in after life raised him to such well-deserved eminence—and it should be recollected that these "Academies" were the only places accessible for the instruction of the sons of the middle class, now happily supplanted by such institutions as King's College, the City of London, and other schools.

To-Day and Yesterday; a Satire.
Chiswick: Printed by C. Whittingham. 1824. 8vo. pp. 29.

Written by Sir Henry Lytton Bulwer, Minister to the Court of Tuscany; author of another little tract published in the same year, called "The Life of Thomas Shovewell."

Southendiana: or, Bagatelles produced in the Season of 1823, at Southend.
Prittlewell: At the private Press of the Rev. F. Nolan. 1824. 8vo.

This little tract is introduced here, principally with the view of stating that the Rev. Frederic Nolan, vicar of Prittlewell, with the curacy of Southend attached to it, has a *private press* at the former place, where he printed this pamphlet for private circulation; and also several other works at the same press, which are for sale.

INDEX AD SPECIMEN GEOGRAPHICUM. AUCTOR
D'ANVILLE, Regiæ Humaniorum Litterarum Academiæ
et Scintiarum Petropolitanæ Socius.   M.DCC.LXII.
London.   1824.   4*to*.   pp. 26.

Drawn up by the late Matthew Raper, Esq., of Wendover Dean,
Bucks, and printed for private circulation.   Its object was to facilitate the reference to the map of ancient Greece, by D'Anville.

———

THE CONDUCT OF THE BISHOP OF PETERBOROUGH
EXPLAINED, WITH RESPECT TO THE RECTOR AND CU-
RATE OF BYFIELD.
London: Printed by R. Gilbert, St. John's-square.
1824.   8*vo*.   pp. 131.

On reverse of the title page is this note :—
" The following pages are printed for the purpose of vindicating
my conduct to those who are willing to read what is necessary for
that purpose.   But as the subject has too little interest for general
readers, they are not intended for publication and sale.
" 30*th Nov.* 1824.   HERBERT PETERBOROUGH."
The Rector was the Rev. Charles Wetherell.
The Curate was the Rev. Samuel Stanley Paris.

———

MENU DE LA MAISON DE LA ROYNE, FAICT PAR
MONS. DE PINGUILLON.   M.D.LXII.
Edinburgh.   [1824.]   4*to*.   pp. 45.

This curious household book of Mary Queen of Scots was printed
at the expense of the late Thomas Thomson, Esq., Deputy Clerk
Register, and President of the Bannatyne Club.   At the end is a fac-
simile of Queen Mary's signature, dated at Stirling, 16th July, 1562.

Τεκμηρια Μετρικα.

Symptoms of Rhyme, original and translated.

"Fulgebat
Inter minora sidera."

London: Printed by Thomas Davison, October 15, 1824. 4to. pp. 69.

By the late Rev. Peter Hall, of Brazen-nose College, Oxford; editor of Picturesque Memorials of Salisbury, and various other works. Twenty-five copies only were printed.

Abstract from the Public Records, of Charters, Acts of Parliament, Treaties, etc.,

Concerning — 1. The Stewartry and Principality of Scotland; II. The Duchy of Cornwall; III. The Principality of Wales, and Earldom of Chester; IV. The Duchy of Normandy; V. The Dauphiné of France.

Edinburgh: Printed by P. Neill. 1824. 4to. pp. vii. and 86.

Printed at the expense of the Court of Exchequer in Scotland, for private circulation.

Nugæ Metricæ.

"Nos hæc novimus esse nihil."

(Oxford: Printed by J. Collingwood). M.DCCC.XXIV. 4to. pp. 89.

By Lord Grenville; who says in the preface, "Of the following trifles, written at very different periods of the author's life, some were attempted as translations, others as paraphrases only, or still more distant imitations of the poetry to which they refer: the very few original pieces are entirely occasional. He prints this small collection for private distribution among those who may perhaps attach to it, as a slight memorial of him, a value to which it has no other claim: and he requests of each of them, in the words of his favourite Flaminius, but with far more reason for the wish—

> 'At tu quicquid id est ineptiarum
> Ne prodire sinas in ora vulgi.' "

Two hundred and fifty copies were printed by the noble writer, for distribution among his friends and relatives.

"One or two by Lord Wellesley, written long ago, and a piece of very good Greek humour by Lord Holland." *

"Whatever," says a writer in the Quarterly Review,† "may be the proper intrinsic merit of the verses, much of their charm consists in their having afforded amusement to the declining years of Lord Grenville; they are a grave and a grateful testimony to the value of such studies from the highest authority." A few of the poems are printed in the Review.

Lord Grenville died in 1834.

Monastic Remains of the Religious Houses at Witham, Burton, and Stavordale; Collected by Sir Richard Colt Hoare, Bart. Anno 1824.

Crockers, Printers, Frome.   *4to.*

Fifty copies printed for private circulation, at the expense of Sir Richard Colt Hoare, Bart. These priories are in Somersetshire.

---

* Lord Tenterden to Sir E. Brydges. Memoirs, vol. i. p. 118.
† Vol. lix. p. 465.

Memorials of the Bagot Family :
Compiled in 1823.

"As every man's house is his castle, so is his family a private
commonwealth."

Printed at Blithfield, by William Hodgetts. 1824. 4*to*.
pp. 172 ; Appendix, pp. xxxi.

These Memorials were drawn up by William, the second (and present) Lord Bagot.   The book contains the following plates :—

> Lord Bagot (the compiler), in his robes ; lithograph.
> Seals of the family; A.D. 1210, &c.; page 8.
> Seals of the family; A.D. 1295, &c.; page 9.
> Seals of the family; temp. Edward I. &c.; page 10.
> Seals of the family; temp. Henry II. &c.; page 12.
> Sir William Bagot, and Margaret his wife, in Baginton
>   church, Warwickshire ; page 20.
> And four printed tables of the Bagot pedigree.

The honour of the peerage was conferred on this family, October
17th, 1780.

———

Diary of a Traveller (James Forbes), over Alps and Appennines.
1824.   8*vo*.

———

North Countrie Garland.
Edinburgh.   1824.   pp. 57.   Title, Preface, and Contents, pp. vi.   12*mo*.

"Many of the pieces in it had never before been published.
Small as is the volume, it makes considerable additions to our catalogue of ancient ballads."—*Motherwell's Minstrelsy*.

Edited by James Maidment, Esq., who printed *thirty* copies.

Y

LA BELLE MARIANNE: A TALE OF TRUTH AND WOE.
London: Printed by J. Nichols and Son, 25, Parliament-street. 1824. 8vo. pp. 54.

This tale was written by Dr. Dibdin, in the year 1802. In a note
in the copy in Mr. Haslewood's library, it is said, "that the narrative grew out of facts."*

MEMOIRS OF THE LIFE OF MASTER JOHN SHAWE,
sometime Vicar of Rotherham: afterwards Minister of
Saint Mary's Church, Lecturer of the Holy Trinity
Church, and Master of God's-House Hospital, at Kings-
ton-upon-Hull: written by Himself. With Notes explanatory and biographical, by JOHN BROADLEY, F.S.A.,
F.L.S., Fellow of the Royal Society of Literature, &c.
Hull: Printed by J. Ferraby, Market-place. 1824.
8vo. pp. 121; Errata, one leaf.

"This biographical sketch is now for the first time printed; it is
taken from a manuscript preserved in the British Museum, made by
Dr. Thomas Birch from the original manuscript, corrected and interlined in several places by Mr. Shawe himself."

One hundred copies were printed, and four on large paper, at the
expense of the editor, the late Mr. Broadley, for private circulation
among his friends.

A CATALOGUE OF PROCESSES IN THE REGISTRY OF
THE HIGH COURT OF DELEGATES, FROM 1609 TO 1823.
Printed by A. and R. Spottiswoode, New-street-square.
8vo. pp. 84.

This catalogue was printed privately for the College of Advocates.
It was prepared by Dr. Addams, and contains nearly 1500 cases.

---

* See Dibdin's "Reminiscences," p. 194.

Catalogue of the

Library of Samuel Butler, Bishop of Lichfield, Manuscripts and Autographs.

1824. 4to.

This catalogue was in Mr. Eyton's collection, No. 327; but it appears to be very rare, as it is unknown to the learned prelate's son. A note in Mr. Eyton's copy says, "Never completed." It contains the whole of the printed books, and one page of manuscripts.

Narrative of a

Journey from Santiago de Chili to Buenos Ayres, in July and August, 1821.

Published by John Murray. London. 1824. 8vo.

Fifty copies of this Journal have been printed for the gratification of the writer's (Lieutenant Edward Hibbert) family, who, from their regard to his memory, will attach to it a value which it might otherwise not possess.

Of this amiable and gallant young officer a memoir will be found in the "Gentleman's Magazine," vol. xciv. part. i. p. 185.

The author states "that his Journal is only the catalogue of vexations that assailed him. With his mind sufficiently occupied in surmounting the difficulties that obstructed his journey, he had little leisure to profit by those few opportunities of remark which might have presented themselves during his rapid progress. Fatigued to death, hardly awake, memory failing, he hastily wrote what first occurred, and frequently fell asleep whilst noting down the events of the day."

The Journal will well repay the reader. The descriptions of scenery are striking, and his portraits of his travelling companions and others, are alike spirited and clever.

JOURNAL OF A TRIP TO PARIS,
BY THE DUKE AND DUCHESS OF RUTLAND, JULY, 1824.
London. 1824.   4*to.*

JOURNAL OF A SHORT TRIP TO PARIS, DURING
THE SUMMER OF 1825.
London. 1825.   4*to.*

These volumes are the production of his Grace the Duke of Rutland; and are embellished with plates, from the pencil of the late accomplished Duchess; who died November 28, 1825. These two were only printed for private distribution; but the "Journal of a Tour in Belgium and Holland" (printed in 1823. 4*to.*) was sold.

———

OUTLINES

SELECTED FROM THE BLOTTING BOOK OF AN INVALID.

"Vix ea nostra voco."—*Ovid.*

London. 1825.   8*vo.*

Only fifty copies were printed of this miscellany, consisting of Essays in prose and poetry, by the Hon. Robert Fulke Greville, son of Louisa, Countess of Mansfield, by her second marriage with the late Hon. Robert Fulke Greville, brother of the late Earl of Warwick.

———

POEMS. BY WILLIAM SOTHEBY.
London: Printed by William Nicol, Cleveland-row, St. James's. 1825. 8*vo.* pp. 281.

Two hundred and fifty copies were printed by Mr. Sotheby, of this edition of his poems, for private circulation among his friends.

CATALOGUE OF THE LIBRARY OF JOHN DENT, ESQ.

Printed by W. Nicol, Shakspeare Press. 1825. 4*to.*

This Catalogue, of which twenty copies only were printed, was made by Messrs. Payne and Foss. " Quoique rangé par ordre alphabétique, il est en quelque sorte systématique ; par exemple, les ouvrages de typographie y sont placés sous le nom de comté, et plusieurs articles sous le nom du sujet, comme: *Scotland, Ireland, Coin, Entertainments,* &c.; les ouvrages de chaque auteur sont dans l'ordre chronologique, les titres donnés tout au long et accompagnés de notes."—*Brunet.*

The Library was sold by Mr. Evans, in the year 1827. Copies of this catalogue have produced 12*l.* Among other rarities in this Library was the celebrated vellum "Livy," printed at Rome, 1469; purchased by Messrs. Payne and Foss for 250 guineas, and afterwards transferred to the choice collection of the late Right Hon. Thomas Grenville.

A TOUR TO THE RHINE ;

WITH ANTIQUARIAN AND OTHER NOTICES.

London: Printed by S. and R. Bentley. 1825. 8*vo.* pp. 106.

By W. G. Meredith, Esq., who died at Cairo in 1831, aged 27. He was the only son of the late George Meredith, Esq., of Nottingham Place, London, and Berrington Court, Worcestershire.

OUTLINES FOR THE CLASSIFICATION OF A LIBRARY ;

Respectfully submitted to the consideration of the Trustees of the British Museum.

London: Printed by G. Woodfall. 1825. 4*to.*

By the Rev. Thomas Hartwell Horne : one hundred copies were

printed for private circulation at the expense of the trustees of the British Museum. Mr. Panizzi, a good authority, states it to be the best he has ever seen, and in his evidence, printed in the report on the British Museum, 1835, says,—" I thought it an extremely good, as well as an elaborate outline of classification ; but I believe Mr. Horne has changed his mind on various portions of it, and that his own copy, which is interleaved and interlined, would now give you a very different, as well as enlarged, classification, to what he then proposed."

The Reverend author says, in a communication to the editor, that having seen many schemes put forth since his own was published, for the arrangement of Libraries, when reduced to plain matters of fact, they do not really deviate from his own method. Though the writer looks upon a classed catalogue as an useless and expensive matter for a library like that in the British Museum, he believes Mr. Horne's arrangement, as Mr. Panizzi observes, to be " extremely good." Mr. Horne states that, in the sixth class, he should in future substitute " Linguistics," or " Linguistical Science," for Grammar, as it comprehends all languages. Brunet is said to be the first who adopted this term, in his last edition of the " Manual," vol. 5.

Mr. Horne is the author of a valuable work, entitled " An Introduction to the Study of the Scriptures," which has gone through several editions.

EPITAPHS.

Some of which have appeared in the " Literary Gazette " of March and April, 1823.

London : Printed by W. Nicol. 1825. 8*vo.* pp. 24.

By William Beckford, Esq. Printed for private circulation : a few of them appeared in the " Literary Gazette," and were accompanied by the following note from the author, addressed to the editor :—

" SIR,—In my rambles about this neighbourhood, I collected the following verses from the tombstones of different churchyards.

Some of the most whimsical, though nearly effaced, are still to be found in the cemetery of a rather considerable town on the high road from London to Bristol, and are, probably, the production of the same goose quill; but whether wielded by the Sexton, Clerk, or even Parson of the Parish, I could not learn : all I discovered upon the subject was, that some of them have been inscribed a good many years ago, apparently enough before the dawn of our present most wonderful poetical era.

" I remain, Mr. Editor,

" Viator."

Excerpta Scotica.

Edinburgi.   1825.   *8vo.*

By James Maidment, Esq.

The volume contains twenty-nine articles, printed on separate sheets. A note at the commencement says, " The preceding tracts were privately printed, and not more than six complete sets can be made up, in consequence of the limited impression of some of them."

A Catalogue of Miniature Portraits in Enamel, By Henry Bone, Esq., R.A., in the Collection of his Grace the Duke of Bedford, at Woburn Abbey.

" ——— Et te, repetentem exempla tuorum,
    Et pater Æneas, et avunculus excitet Hector."

Virg. Æn. lib. xii.

London : Printed by William Nicol, Shakespeare Press. 1825.   *8vo.*   pp. 63 ; Introduction, Title, &c. pp. viii.

The historical notices in this Catalogue were written by his Grace John, the sixth Duke of Bedford, who states in the Introduction, that " the idea of transferring these portraits from the perishable materials of oil paintings on panel or canvass, to the more durable and brilliant representations in enamel, was first suggested by a view of Mr. Bone's interesting Gallery of Portraits of the most distinguished characters that flourished in the reign of Queen Elizabeth ; a collection worthy of decorating the walls of that splendid residence of our kings, Windsor Castle."

The following are the portraits which have been executed by Mr. Bone :—

1. Philip, Archduke of Austria, afterwards King of Castile ; ob. 1506.

2. Joanna, his consort, second daughter of Ferdinand and Isabella, King and Queen of Castile and Arragon.

These two portraits are copied from original pictures, painted probably by Mabuse, in 1506.

3. John Russell, first Earl of Bedford, and patriarch of the family.

4. Francis, second Earl of Bedford, only son of the first Earl.

" It is probable that the originals of both these portraits are from Holbein."

5. Sir Francis Russell, third son of Francis, second Earl of Bedford.

" There are no portraits," says the Duke, " of the first Countesses of Bedford, nor of the wife of this Lord Russell, in the collection at Woburn Abbey, or in any other with which I am acquainted."

6. William, Lord Russell of Thornhaugh, fourth son of Francis, second Earl of Bedford ; ob. 1613.

7. Elizabeth, Lady Russell of Thornhaugh, wife of the preceding ; ob. 1611.

It is related of this lady, that she accompanied her husband in wolf-hunting, when she was in Ireland.

8. Edward, third Earl of Bedford, only son of Francis, Lord Russell.

9. Lucy, Countess of Bedford ; ob. 1628 ; from a portrait said to be by Gerard Honthorst.

10. Francis, fourth Earl of Bedford ; ob. 1641 ; " the principal pro-

moter of that truly stupendous work, known by the name of the Bedford Level." Taken from a very fine whole length, by Vandyck.

11. Katherine, Countess of Bedford, wife of the preceding Earl; from an original whole length, by Cornelius Jansen.

12. William, first Duke, and fifth Earl of Bedford; ob. 1700.

"This enamel is taken from a picture of two whole-length portraits, of William, Earl of Bedford, and his brother-in-law, George Digby, Earl of Bristol, a copy (or perhaps a duplicate, by Vandyck himself) from the fine picture in Earl Spencer's collection at Althorp."

13. Anne, Countess of Bedford, wife of the preceding; ob. 1684.

14. William, Lord Russell, "the well-known martyr to the cause of his country."

15. Rachel, wife of William, Lord Russell, the author of the Letters.

16. Wriothesley, the second Duke, and sixth Earl of Bedford; ob. 1711; from an original enamel, by Boit.

17. Elizabeth, wife of the preceding Duke; ob. 1724.

Taken from the same enamel as the preceding.

18. Wriothesley, third Duke; ob. 1732; from a picture by Isaac Whood.

19. Anne, Duchess of Bedford, wife of the preceding; ob. 1762.

20. John, fourth Duke; from a portrait by Sir Joshua Reynolds.

21. Diana, first wife of John, Duke of Bedford; ob. 1735.

22. Gertrude, second wife of John, Duke of Bedford; ob. 1794; from a portrait by Sir Joshua Reynolds.

23. Francis, Marquis of Tavistock; ob. 1767; from Sir Joshua Reynolds.

24. Elizabeth, Marchioness of Tavistock, wife of the preceding; ob. 1768; from Sir Joshua Reynolds.

25. Francis, fifth Duke of Bedford; ob. 1802.

There are five outline plates, representing the frames in which the miniatures are hung.

There have been added the following:—

26. John, sixth Duke of Bedford, from a picture by Sir Thomas Lawrence.

27. Georgiana Elizabeth, first wife of John, sixth Duke of Bedford.

28. Georgiana, Duchess of Bedford, second wife of John, sixth Duke of Bedford, from a picture by Hayter.

29. Francis, seventh Duke of Bedford, from a picture by Casterton Smith, enamel by John Harlam.

30. Anna Maria, Duchess of Bedford, from a picture by Casterton Smith, enamel by John Harlam.

31. William, Marquis of Tavistock, from a picture by Frank Stone, enamel by John Harlam.

HORTUS ERICÆUS WOBURNENSIS:
Or, a Catalogue of Heaths, in the Collection of the Duke of Bedford, at Woburn Abbey. Alphabetically and systematically arranged.

M.DCCC.XXV. 4to. Engraved Title; Introduction and Preface, pp. xiv; Explanation of the plates, one leaf; Alphabetical arrangement, pp. 29; Systematic arrangement, four leaves, paged 31 to 37; Letter from George Hayter, two leaves, paged 39, 40, 41.

The Introduction was drawn up by John, sixth Duke of Bedford, K.G., at whose expense the work was printed, for private circulation. It contains the following plates :—

1. East view of the Heath-house.
2. West view of the same.
3. Plan, elevation, and section of the Heath-house.
4. Plan of the Parterre, for hardy Heaths.

Habit of the leaves of Heaths, coloured figures, Plate I.
Anthers, Flowers, and Inflorescence, coloured, Plate II.
Flowers, coloured, Plate III.
Flowers, coloured, Plate IV.
Diagram of colours ; George Hayter invent. et J. Scott fecit.
Gradations from black to white ; and from brown to white.

LETTER FROM THE HON. ALEXANDER MACONOCHIE
(LORD MEADOWBANK), TO THE EARL OF ELDON.
Edinburgh.   1825.   4to.   pp. 30.   Appendix, pp. 9.

Relative to an attack on his Lordship by the late Chief Commissioner Adam in relation to certain jury proceedings.
Very few copies printed and circulated.

OBSERVATIONS ON THE ELECTION LAW OF SCOTLAND.
Edinburgh.   1825.   Not published.   4to.   pp. 34.
Appendix pp. 10.   Title, &c., pp. 4.

By Lord Auchinleck, father of James Boswell, and grandfather of
Sir Alexander Boswell, Bart.
Sixty copies were printed, by James Allan Maconochie, Sheriff of
Orkney.

CATALOGUE OF THE LIBRARY OF THE ROYAL SOCIETY.
London: Printed by William Nicol, Cleveland-row,
St. James's.   M.DCCCXXV.   4to.   pp. 604.

An alphabetical Catalogue, made by Messrs. Payne and Foss.   A
new Catalogue of the scientific portion of the Library, by M. Panizzi,
is described subsequently.

ELIDURE, AND EDWARD;
TWO HISTORICAL DRAMATIC SKETCHES.
London: Printed by Thomas Davison, Whitefriars.
1825.   8vo.

By Mrs. Fletcher, of Edinburgh. Mrs. Fletcher was an English lady, and the wife of Archibald Fletcher, Esq., Advocate, whom she survived. Mr. Fletcher was termed the Father of Scottish Reform, from his early advocacy of what are termed liberal principles. By his lady he had two sons (1), the late Myles Angus Fletcher, Esq., Advocate, who married Miss Clavering, niece of the last two Dukes of Argyle, and by this lady he had issue. After her husband's demise, Mrs. Myles Fletcher married John Christison, Esq., Advocate, brother of Professor Christison, of Edinburgh. (2) Angus, who was bred to the law, but who is now celebrated as a sculptor.

Journal of a Week in Holland, in the Summer of 1824.

Hull: Printed by Isaac Wilson, Lowgate. 1825. 8vo. pp. 16.

By Jonathan Gray, Esq.

Genealogical Memoirs of the Royal House of France;

Forming a Commentary upon the Genealogical Table of that illustrious and ancient House. M.DCCC.XVIII.

By the late Richard Barré, Lord Ashburton.

London: Printed by William Nicol, Shakspeare Press, Cleveland-row, St. James's. 1825. *folio.* pp. 199; with a large Table of the Royal Family of France.

At the back of the title is the following quotation from Gibbon, on the House of Courtenay: "Of all the families now extant, the most ancient doubtless, and the most illustrious, is the House of France, which has occupied the same throne above eight hundred years, and descends in a clear and lineal series of males, from the middle of the ninth century."

This work was left ready for the press, at the death of Lord Ashburton, in 1823, when the title became extinct; it was printed for private circulation, in compliance with the noble author's wish, by his executors. His lordship was the son of the celebrated lawyer, John Dunning, on whom the honour of the peerage was conferred.

The Charter and Grant of the Company of Stationers [1741].
Reprinted for private distribution by William Tyler. London. 1825. 8vo. pp. 64.

The original Charter bears date 1556. It was printed in 1741, by some dissatisfied freemen, with their own partial, and, as the editor is informed, erroneous statements.

The Private Theatre of Kilkenny;
With introductory Observations on other private Theatres in Ireland, before it was opened. 1825. 4to. pp. 134.

This volume contains portraits of Richard Power, Esq., Right Hon. H. Grattan, John Lyster, Esq., George Rothe, Esq., Humphrey Butler, Esq., Thomas Moore, Esq., James Corry, Esq., Miss Smith (now Mrs. Bartley), and Miss Walstein—all performers at that theatre. The portraits were all privately engraved for this work.* In the "Edinburgh Review" (vol. xlvi. p. 368) is an interesting paper on private theatricals. "With the Theatricals of Kilkenny expired the last

---

* Note in Mr. Hanrott's copy.

faint remains of what may be called the Social Era in Ireland. In the list of the actors at Shane's Castle, in 1785, there occurs one name, which, in the hearts of all true Irishmen, awakens feelings which they can hardly trust their lips to utter — Lord Edward Fitzgerald."

Hints on Rural Residences.

> Its roof with weeds and mosses covered o'er,
> And honey-suckles climbing round the door ;
> While mantling vines along its walls are spread,
> And clustering ivy decks the landscape head.
>
> *Knight's Landscape.*

London. 1825. 4*to.* pp. 107.

By the late Nicholas Carlisle, Esq., F.S.A.; who printed only seventy-five copies of this work, for private circulation. It is dedicated to Lord Grenville. The author once contemplated erecting a cottage ; and these " Hints " arose out of his intended design.

A Gyfte for the Newe Yeare ;
Or, a Playne, Plesaunt, and Profytable Pathe Waie to the Black-Letter Paradyse.

Emprynted over the grete Gate-waie offe Saincte Jhonnes Colledge, Cambridge, by Wyntonne Hattfelde. Anno 1825. 12*mo.* pp. 20.

Only twenty copies were printed of this little work, by the Rev. C. H. Hartshorne, author of the " Book Rarities of Cambridge." 8*vo.*

GENEALOGICAL HISTORY OF THE FAMILY OF BRABAZON;
From its Origin, down to Sir William Brabazon, Lord
Treasurer, and Lord Chief Justice of Ireland, temp.
Henry VIII., who died in 1552, the common ancestor of
the Earls of Meath, and of the Brabazons of Brabazon
Park, by Elizabeth Clifford, of the illustrious House of
Clifford; and thence from his only younger Son, Sir
Anthony Brabazon, of Balinasloe Castle, Governor of
Connaught, down to his present Representative, and Heir
Male of this Branch, Sir William John Brabazon, of
Brabazon Park, in the county of Mayo, Bart., now sur-
viving.
Paris: Printed by J. Smith, Rue Montmorency [for
private distribution only]. 1825. 4*to.* pp. 21; Ap-
pendix, pp. lvi; Fragment, par le Chevalier Courcelles,
pp. 4.

This work was edited by Hercules Sharp, Esq., of Domons,
Northiam, Sussex; and from its being closely connected with
English history, the editor has introduced it here, although printed
abroad. *Fifty* copies only are said to have been printed: this, however, there is reason to think is an error. The author married the
sister of Sir William John Brabazon, Bart., which circumstance
induced him to undertake this history of the family. The arms are
in lithography, indifferently executed.

TRIFLES IN VERSE; BY MARIANNE BAILLIE.
London. 1825. [Not published.] 12*mo.* pp. 48.

Mrs. Baillie died in 1831. She was author of a "Tour on the Continent," in one volume 8*vo.*, and "Sketches of the Manners and Customs of Portugal," in two volumes.

MEMORANDA OF CONVERSATIONS WITH LORD ED-
WARD O'BRYEN, DURING THE LAST FEW WEEKS OF
THE ILLNESS WHICH TERMINATED IN HIS DECEASE.
London : Printed by Ellerton and Henderson, Gough-
square. 1825. 8*vo*. pp. 83.

Lord Edward O'Bryen, brother of the Marquis of Thomond,
married Lady Elizabeth Susan Somerset, second daughter of the
Duke of Beaufort, the editor of this volume. He died March 9,
1824. His widow married, secondly, November 11, 1829, Major-
General James Orde.

A MEMOIR OF THOMAS GREEN, ESQ., OF IPSWICH ;
With a Critique on his Writings, and an Account of
his Family and Connexions.

"Non omnis moriar."

Ipswich : Printed by John Raw. 1825. 4*to*. pp. 82.

At p. 72 is a portrait of Mr. Green, engraved by Worthington.
The volume was edited by the Reverend Dr. Ford ; who says in
the preface, " It may be necessary to state, that the impression of
this Memoir has been limited to *one hundred* copies ; which will be
presented to the more immediate and intimate friends of the deceased." A list of Mr. Green's different works is given ; the most
important of which was, " Extracts from the Diary of a Lover of
Literature." 1810. 4*to*.

THE EARLS OF DERBY, AND THE VERSE WRITERS
AND POETS OF THE SIXTEENTH AND SEVENTEENTH
CENTURY. BY THOMAS HEYWOOD, F.A.S.
Manchester: Printed by Robinson and Bent.
M.DCCC.XXV. 4*to*. pp. 44.

Sixty-four copies were printed of this work, for private circulation.

A NARRATIVE OF AN EXCURSION TO IRELAND, BY THE
DEPUTY GOVERNOR, TWO MEMBERS OF THE COURT,
AND THE ASSISTANT SECRETARY, OF THE HONORABLE
IRISH SOCIETY OF LONDON. 1825.

" ———hæc olim meminisse juvabit."—*Virg.*

BY THE DEPUTY GOVERNOR.

London: Printed by Charles Skipper, St. Dunstan's-
hill. [1826.] 4*to.* pp. 103.

Prefixed is a view of the Salmon-leap. The narrative was compiled by Gilpin Gorst, Esq.

———

CATALOGUS LIBRORUM IN BIBLIOTHECA UNIVERSI-
TATIS ANDREANÆ, SECUNDUM LITERARUM ORDINEM DIS-
POSITUS.

Impensis Academiæ Andreanæ. Typis Roberti Foulis.
Academiæ Typographi. 1826. *folio.*

Engraved in the title-page, the seal of the University.

———

LIBRORUM IMPRESSORUM, QUI IN BIBLIOTHECA SCHOLÆ
MERCATORUM SCISSORUM ADSERVANTUR, CATALOGUS.

Londini: Impensis Mercatorum Scissorum Societatis,
excudebat Gulielmus Barry, in vico dicto *Bishopsgate.*
M.DCCC.XXVI. pp. 42.

An alphabetical Catalogue. In the introduction will be found
various minutes of the Court of the Merchant Tailors' Company,
and a list of some of the donors. The library contains a fair collection of Hebrew and other Oriental books of reference; some
good copies of the Fathers; nearly all the standard classical and
other Lexicons, and the best writers in English Theology.

The Merchant Tailors' Company devote twenty guineas per annum to the increase and keeping up of the Library ; and frequent presents have been made to it by Members of the Court.

TRANSLATIONS FROM THE SERVIAN MINSTRELSY : To which are added some specimens of Anglo-Norman Romances.

London. 1826.   4*to.*

" Of this volume a very small edition only has been printed for private circulation." * The reviewer adds a hope, that the use he has made of the " Minstrelsy " may lead to its publication.

Some of the minor songs of the Servians have been translated in the " Westminster Review."

PRECIS OF THE WARS IN CANADA, FROM 1755 TO THE TREATY OF GHENT IN 1814. WITH MILITARY AND POLITICAL REFLECTIONS.

BY MAJ. GEN. SIR JAMES CARMICHAEL SMYTH, BART.

" The study of history, and the knowledge of past events, afford the best instructions for the regulation and conduct of human affairs."—*Polybius.*

London. 1826. 8*vo.* pp. 185. Preface, &c., pp. xxii.

On the half-title :—" N.B. This volume is printed by desire of His Grace the Master-General, for the use and convenience of official people only. It is requested it may be considered as confidential by those persons to whom copies may be sent."

----

* Quarterly Review, vol. xxxv. p. 66.

Nugæ Canoræ, quas in Amicorum Gratiam
imprimi fecit Etonensis, G. Booth.
Typis J. Ham, Oxoniæ. m.dccc.xxvi. 4*to.* pp. 146.

From Mr. Eyton's Catalogue, No. 376 ; the presentation copy to
Archdeacon Wrangham, with two autograph letters.

An Account of the Corporation of Beech's Fen,
in the County of Suffolk ;
With a translation of their Charter, and copies of
various other Documents relating to the said Corpora-
tion. Drawn up in the year 1807, for the use of the
Corporation.
Reprinted, with various Notes and Additions, in 1826.
Jarman, Printer, Bucks. 8*vo.*

Weeds and Wild Flowers. By E. G. L. B.
Paris. 1826. Not published.

A juvenile production of Sir Edward Bulwer Lytton, Bart. ; although printed abroad, it is recorded here as a guide when the *opera
omnia* of this distinguished writer shall be collected.

Catalogue of the principal Pictures in
Flanders and Holland. 1822.
London: Printed by W. Nicol. 1826. 8*vo.* pp. 88.

Only fifty copies were printed by the author, the late Lord Dover.
It is dedicated to the present Duke of Sutherland ; the preface occu-

pies two pages; at the end is an alphabetical list of painters, place and date of their birth, date of death, whom they studied under, and the style they principally painted in.

Some Account of the Personal Religion of Margaret Gray.
By her Father, Jonathan Gray, Esq., of York.

"I thought upon my ways, and turned my feet to thy testimonies, in all haste, and delayed not to keep thy commandments."

Printed by J. Wolstenholme, York. 1826. pp. 112.

A Catalogue of the English Portion of the Library of the Venerable Francis Wrangham, M.A., F.R.S.

"How many square feet of reading," cried I, "are here collected!"

Malton. 1826. 8vo. pp. 642.

This Catalogue was compiled by its learned owner; it includes an account of most of the books contained in it, their author, their subject, or their edition. Only seventy copies were printed; which have never been distributed. In this Catalogue will be found the most numerous collection in the kingdom of that class of works which it is the endeavour of the editor of this work to describe; and he was under the greatest obligations to Archdeacon Wrangham, for much valuable assistance, as well as information of several interesting works which, but for his kindness, would in all probability have escaped his notice. The library, since his death, was sold by auction by Messrs. Sotheby.

A Part of the Life of Lady Margaret Cunningham, Daughter of the Earl of Glencairn. Edinburgh. 1826. *4to.*

Edited by Charles Kirkpatrick Sharpe, Esq. A limited number of copies were printed for private distribution.

———

Catalogue of some Books in the possession of H. Jadis, Esq., in Bryanstone-square. London : Printed at the Temple printing office, by J. Moyes, Bouverie-street. M.DCCC.XXVI. *8vo.* pp. 48.

Compiled by Mr. Rodd. Mr. Jadis' library was sold by auction, by Mr. Evans, in 1828.

A portion of this Catalogue is sometimes found with this title : —Shaksperiana : a complete collection of the books and pamphlets which have been published, relative to the life, or illustrative of the writings of Shakspeare, in the possession of H. Jadis, Esq.

———

Collections for
A History of the Ancient Family of Bland.

"Dispute it like a man.———
I shall do so ;
But I must also feel it as a man;
I cannot but remember such things were,
That were most precious to me."

London. 1826. *4to.* pp. 305 ; Introduction, pp. xxx.

This work was printed and privately distributed by Nicholas Carlisle, Esq., F.S.A.

It consists of collections relating to families of Bland, resident in the several counties of York, Westmoreland, Middlesex, and the city of London, Wilts, Hertford, Nottingham, Berks, Oxford, North-ampton, Derby, Bucks, Cambridge, Worcester, Essex, Norfolk, Lan-caster, Lincoln, Kent, and Durham; Brecknock, and Montgomery; and in the counties of Kerry, and Queen's County, in Ireland; and in the State of Virginia, in North America. One hundred copies only were printed.

CATALOGUE OF THE LIBRARY OF THE DEVON AND EXETER INSTITUTION; WITH AN ABSTRACT OF THE RULES.

Exeter: Printed by Mary Flindell, at the Western Luminary Office, Gandy-street. 1826. 8vo. pp. 159.

A classed Catalogue. "This institution was established at Exeter in 1813, by some gentlemen of the city and its neighbourhood. A handsome building has been fitted up for the purpose, with two spacious libraries, galleries for a museum, and reading-rooms. The collection of books is already extensive and valuable."* Another edition was published in 1836.

THE HISTORY OF GORHAMBURY;
BY CHARLOTTE GRIMSTON.
[Circa 1826.] 4to. pp. 90.

This volume was edited by the Hon. Charlotte Grimston, who died January, 1831.

Gorhambury derives great interest from being the patrimonial inheritance of the great Sir Francis Bacon. It obtained its name

---

* Lysons, History of Devonshire.

from Gorham, eighteenth Abbot of St. Albans.   The present edifice was built by the late Viscount Grimston, and completed in 1785, from the designs of Sir Robert Taylor, and is generally esteemed a good specimen of that architect's talents.   A valuable collection of portraits is in the gallery at Gorhambury.   The plates in illustration of this work are executed in lithography, and are as follows :—

Plan of the Grounds.

South View of Gorhambury, built by Sir Nicholas Bacon.

North View of the same.

Ground plan of the same.

Portrait of Sir Nicholas Bacon, from the original at Gorhambury.

Painted Glass in the Gallery.

Gorhambury: view of the present House.

Ground Plan of the same.

Remains of the Interior Court at Gorhambury.

Report of the Committee of Magistrates, appointed to make inquiry respecting the Public Bridges in the County of Middlesex.   London: Printed by J. Rider, Little Britain.   1826.   4to.   pp. 460.

This report was presented on the first day of the General Quarter Sessions, in October, 1825.   Signed, George Saunders, Samuel Purkis.

Memoir of the Origin and Incorporation of the Trinity House, of Deptford Strond.   London : Printed by J. Darling, 31, Leadenhall-street.   8vo.   pp. 247.

Compiled by the late Joseph Cotton, Esq., one of the masters. The Trinity House was incorporated by Henry VIII.

The Life of Addison. By Nathaniel Ogle. London: Printed by Thomas Davison, Whitefriars. 1826. *Crown 8vo.* pp. lxxxvi.

On the back of the title,—" Fifty copies of the following preface have been printed separate from the edition of the ' Spectator ' to which it is to be prefixed, for private distribution among the author's friends."

———

Strange Newes from Warwick;

Which happened on Thursday last, being the 17th day of November, 1642. Manifesting how one Jeremiah Shore, a Corporal of Dragooners under his Excellence, being wounded at the Battel at Keynton, came to the Anchor at Warwick, a little Inne, and gave the Hostesse of the House a Bagge of Money to keepe for him untill such time as hee had recovered his Health. Also, how the said Hostesse conspired with her Husband to couzen the said Souldier of his Money, causing him to be imprisoned for offering to demand it. With the manner how they forswore themselves before the Bench ; and how God's just Judgment immediately fell before them, to the terror and amazement of all that great Assembly. Whereunto is annexed, another fearfull Example which happened at Coventry.

[Nov. 23.]   Printed by T. F. for R. C.   1642.

Stratford on Avon. Reprinted by James Ward. 1826.

" The editor, in presenting to a few of his friends this reprint of a curious Warwickshire tract in his possession, does not venture to assert, whatever his opinion may be, that this little volume is unique. But he may confidently say that it is extremely scarce because during an eager search of many years for rarities of this kind, no other copy has come to his knowledge, either in any cata-logue of public or private libraries, or by the information of friends well versed in the knowledge of books. If this tract be considered of little or no interest in the present day, yet its rare occurrence will perhaps make a republication of it acceptable to those for whom it is intended; and therefore a very limited impression, of twenty copies only, is taken for private distribution.—W. S.

"*Longbridge, near Warwick, November* 24, 1826."

In a letter to Thomas Sharp, Esq., of Coventry, to whom the editor is indebted for this communication, Mr. Staunton, at whose expense this tract was reprinted, says, "I have burnt the blocks, which were cut for the purpose of making the copies, as nearly as possible, fac-similes of the original."

A List of the Knights and Burgesses who have represented the County and City of Durham in Parliament.

Durham: Printed by Francis Humble. 1826. 4*to.* pp. 41.

Fifty copies of this list, edited by Sir Cuthbert Sharp, were printed for private distribution. A second edition was printed in 1831, at Durham, 4*to.*, pp. 55, consisting of one hundred copies.

The Mill;

A Moravian Tale, founded on Fact.

London: Printed by Samuel and Richard Bentley, Dorset-street. 1826. 12*mo.*

Written by Lord Francis Leveson Gower, now Earl of Ellesmere: fifty copies were printed for private distribution. It originally ap-peared in a magazine, without the consent of the noble author.

The following is a list of the other privately printed publications of Lord Ellesmere, who kindly took the trouble to furnish it to the Editor ; it was thought it would be more convenient to place them all together, though they can scarcely be called books.

1. Boyle Farm.　A Poem.

1827.

This was published first in the "Literary Gazette," without the author's permission, and subsequently published for sale, and went through eight editions.

2. The Paria.　A Tragedy in one Act.
Translated from the German of Michael Beer.

1836.

3. Town and Country.　A Poem in one Canto.

1836.

4. Blue Beard, or dangerous Curiosity.
A Justifiable Homicide.　A Tragedy, in two Acts.

1841.

5. The Pilgrimage.　A Poem.

1841.

This was subsequently published with additions, in a volume called "Mediterranean Sketches."

6. Donna Charitea.　Queen of Castille.
A Drama, in three Acts.

1843.

7. Alfred.　A Drama, in one Act.

1844.

THE CONNECTION OF BATH
WITH THE LITERATURE AND SCIENCE OF ENGLAND.
Read before the Literary and Philosophical Association,
November 6th, 1826.
BY THE REV. JOSEPH HUNTER, F.A.S.

Et nos aliquod nomenque decusque Gessimus.—Virg.

Printed by Richard Cruttwell, St. James's-street, Bath.
1827. 12*mo.* pp. 22.

Of this Address only fifty copies were printed.

Those who are acquainted with the distinguished Historian of
South Yorkshire, and know how deeply he is imbued with the love
of literature, will regret that this Tract is so limited in its impression. It eminently deserves a more important form and a more
extensive circulation.

CONSIDERATIONS, ADDRESSED TO THE ARCHBISHOP
OF DUBLIN AND THE CLERGY WHO SIGNED THE PETI-
TION TO THE HOUSE OF COMMONS FOR PROTECTION.
Dublin. 1827. ("Not published.") 8*vo.* pp. 33.

A LETTER FROM THE COUNTESS OF NITHSDALE,
ETC.; WITH REMARKS BY SHEFFIELD GRACE, ESQ.,
D.C.L. AND F.S.A.

Splendide mendax.—Hor.

London. M.DCCC.XXVII. 8*vo.* pp. 37; with a Table
of Descent.

Mr. Grace says, he " met with the original among a highly interesting collection of MSS. at Wardour Castle, while on a visit to my noble and accomplished friend, Lord Arundel." The letter is from Winifred Herbert, Countess of Nithsdale, to her sister, the Lady Lucy Herbert, abbess of the English Augustine nuns at Bruges, containing a circumstantial account of the escape of her husband, William Maxwell, fifth Earl of Nithsdale, from the Tower of London, on Friday, the 23rd of February, 1716. A beautiful ballad on the capture of Lord Nithsdale at the battle of Preston, originally printed in Cromek's Nithsdale and Galloway Songs, entitled "Lament for the Lord Maxwell," is by the late Allan Cunningham, and will be found in his "Poems." 12*mo.* London. 1847.

RAMBLES IN WALTHAM FOREST, A POEM,
Illustrated with Lithographed Engravings. Privately printed.

1827. *Small 4to.*

By the late Countess of Blessinton. Twenty-five copies only printed.

THE FORM OF MORNING AND EVENING PRAYER, TO THE USE OF THE UNITED CHURCH OF ENGLAND AND IRELAND;
Together with the Psalms of David, and the Second Lessons, as they are appointed to be said every Morning in the Year: to which are added, the First Lessons to be read on Sundays: with Notes.

London: Printed for J. Hatchard and Son. 1827. 2 *vols.* 12*mo.*

Five hundred copies were printed of this work : compiled by the late Hon. Charlotte Grimston, sister of the late Earl of Verulam, for the purpose of being sold; but on application for permission, it was refused; they were therefore circulated privately. A new edition has since been printed, which, by an arrangement with the King's printer, is for sale.

STOWE;

A Description of the House and Gardens of the Most Noble Richard Grenville Nugent Chandos Temple, Duke of Buckingham and Chandos; Knight of the Most Noble Order of the Garter.

Printed by J. Seeley, Buckingham. 1827. *Imp.* 4*to.* pp. 92.

Twenty-five copies were printed on large paper of the description of Stowe, for private circulation; containing the following plates, which are not to be found in the editions printed for sale :—

1. View of the Arch at Stowe, inscribed "Ex Bibliotheca Stowense."

2. Portrait of the Duke of Buckingham; engraved by Cooper, after a miniature by Saunders; opposite the title-page.

3. Plan of the Gardens: drawn and etched by William James Smith.

4. The Buckingham Lodges; vignette wood-cut.

5. The Hermitage; vignette wood-cut.

6. The Temple of Bacchus; vignette; engraved by Charles John Smith.

7. Gothic Cross; vignette wood-cut.

8. Urn, in memory of the Marquis of Buckingham; vignette wood-cut.

9. Fac-simile of an autograph document, with the signatures of the French court, attesting the planting of some elm trees by Louis XVIII. and his family, in grateful remembrance of the liberal hospitality shown to them by the Marquis of Buckingham.

10. The Fountain ; vignette wood-cut.
11. The Grotto ; engraved by C. J. Smith.
12. Temple of Concord and Victory ; engraved by C. J. Smith.
13. Fane of Pastoral Poetry ; vignette wood-cut.
14. Lord Cobham's Pillar ; engraved by C. J. Smith.
15. The Gothic Temple ; by the same artist.
16. The Palladian Bridge ; by the same artist.
17. Stowe, in 1660 ; by the same artist.
18. Stowe, in 1827 ; by the same artist.
19. Interior of Wotton Church ; by the same artist.
20. Wotton House, east front ; by the same artist.
21. Wotton Church ; engraved by C. J. Smith.
22. Wotton House, west front ; by the same artist.
23. Chapel and Chantry in Wotton Church ; by the same artist.
24. Wotton Church, south view ; by the same artist.

This book contains, besides, all the engraved plates by Medland, which have appeared in various editions of the description of Stowe.

CLIFFORDIANA.

Exeter: Printed by T. How, High-street. 12*mo.* pp. 99.

Edited by the Rev. George Oliver, a Roman Catholic clergyman resident at Exeter : it contains an account of the Cliffords of Chudleigh, and a list of the pictures at their family seat, Ugbrooke, Devonshire. Mr. Oliver is the author of a volume, entitled " Historic Collections relating to the Monasteries in Devon." 8*vo.* 1820.

THE DUKE OF WELLINGTON'S VISIT TO SUNDERLAND.
Sunderland. 1827. 8*vo.* pp. 33.

Edited by Sir Cuthbert Sharp ; who printed thirty copies.

SUBSTANCE OF THE SPEECH OF HIS GRACE THE DUKE OF WELLINGTON, IN THE HOUSE OF LORDS, ON WEDNESDAY, MAY 2, 1827.

London : J. Hatchard and Son, 187, Piccadilly. 1827.

8vo.

Of the speech of this illustrious nobleman, one hundred copies were privately printed. In it will be found the passage so often mentioned, containing the reasons why his Grace declined taking office, when Mr. Canning formed his administration.

––––––

WYL BUCKE, HIS TESTAMENT; THE LEGACIES PALATABLY PREPARED FOR THE LEGATEES.

Reprinted (not for publication) at the Chiswick Press. 1827. *Small 4to.* pp. 36.

Edited by the late Joseph Haslewood, one of the members of the Roxburghe Club; who printed forty copies for private circulation. In the copy sold in his library, it appeared that he charged some of his friends five shillings per copy.

––––––

CHRONICON MIRABILE, SEU EXCERPTA MEMORABILIA E REGISTRIS PROVINCIALIBUS COM. PAL. DUNELM.

"Pondere non numero."

Bishop Wearmouth : George Garbett, typographer. 1827. *8vo.* pp. 27.

This work consists of three parts : the first was printed in 1819, 8vo. pp. 26; the second, in 1825, 8vo., pp. 23; and the third, in 1827. It is edited by Sir Cuthbert Sharp; who printe d thirty copies for private circulation.

CERTAINE OBSERVATIONS TOUCHING Y^e ESTATE OF THE COMMON WEALTH, COMPOSED PRINCIPALLY FOR THE BENEFIT OF THE GENTRY OF THE COUNTY OF DURHAM.

"Ortus nostri partem patria vindicat partem amici."—*Cicero.*

Durham : F. Humble and Co., Printers. M.DCCC.XXVII. 4*to.* pp. 22.

On the back of the title-page, M. S. Eccles. Cath. Dunelm. c. iii. 20, No. 3, p. 93.—R. S. J. R.

Privately printed at the expense of the late Richard Surtees, Esq., and the Rev. James Raine.

———

OBSERVATIONS OR NOTES UPON THE WRITINGS OF THE ANCIENTS, UPON THE MATERIALS WHICH THEY USED, AND UPON THE INTRODUCTION OF THE ART OF PRINTING;

Being from Papers read before the Philosophical and Literary Society, annexed to the Bristol Institution, at their evening meetings, in 1827.

BY JOHN MATTHEW GUTCH.

Bristol: Printed by J. M. Gutch, at the office of " Felix Farley's Bristol Journal." 1827.

Only twenty-five copies printed, for private distribution. *Imp.* 8*vo.* pp. 170.

———

DESCRIPTIVE CATALOGUE OF SOME OF THE CU-RIOSITIES, AND OF THE MINERALS AND FOSSILS, IN THE LEDSTONE MUSEUM, OF THE REV. GEORGE DODD. Rochdale. 4*to.* 1827.

REMARKS UPON AN ESSAY ON GOVERNMENT BY JAMES MILL, PUBLISHED IN THE SUPPLEMENT TO THE ENCYCLOPÆDIA BRITANNICA.

London: Ridgway.   1827.   4*to.*

(By Leweson Smith, son of the Right Hon. Vernon Smith ;) published for private circulation by his father.

———

CATALOGUE OF THE LIBRARY AT BELVOIR CASTLE, THE SEAT OF THE DUKE OF RUTLAND.

London.   1827.   4*to.*   41 leaves.

Fifty copies were printed.

———

ILLUSTRATIONS OF STONE CIRCLES, CROMLECHS, AND OTHER REMAINS OF THE ABORIGINAL BRITONS, IN THE WEST OF CORNWALL.

From Drawings made on the spot in 1826.

BY WILLIAM COTTON, ESQ., M.A.

London: Printed by James Moyes.   4*to.*   pp. 46.

Back of the title, "Donum Amicis — only twenty-five copies printed."

" Mr. Cotton's little volume is indeed replete with details most attractive for the studious in our aboriginal monuments. It cannot, therefore, but be a matter of regret that the private impression has been limited to such a small number as twenty-five copies, which, by giving it the rarity of a MS., deprives a stranger of the hope of ever adding it to the shelves of his library."*

———

* A. J. Kempe, F.S.A.   Gent.'s Magazine, Feb. 1833.

A A

A CATALOGUE OF THE BOOKS BELONGING TO THE
LIBRARY OF THE ROYAL OBSERVATORY, GREENWICH.
London: Printed by William Nicol, Cleveland-row,
St. James's. 1827. 8*vo.* pp. 66.

An alphabetical Catalogue, made by Mr. Foss. The library is said
to be very incomplete in that class of books which it would be
expected to contain.

ANCIENT SCOTTISH BALLADS, RECOVERED FROM
TRADITION, AND NEVER BEFORE PUBLISHED;
With Notes, Historical and Explanatory, and an Ap-
pendix, containing the Airs of several Ballads.
Edinburgh. 1827. 8*vo.*

Collected by G. R. Kinloch; noticed by Sir W. Scott in his introductory remarks on popular poetry, prefixed to the Minstrelsy of
the Scottish Border.

AN ESSAY ON THE MODERN PRONUNCIATION OF THE
GREEK AND LATIN LANGUAGES.
BY UVEDALE PRICE, ESQ.
Oxford: Printed by W. Baxter. 1827. 8*vo.* pp. 249.

"This small volume is a part only, but a considerable part, of
what I have written on the subject; it contains, however, the leading positions and principles upon which my notions are founded.
I thought it best to print, but not to publish it. Mine is a direct,
undisguised, unqualified attack on the whole, and every part of our
system."—*Extract from the Preface.*
The writer of this Essay was the author of a highly-esteemed
work, entitled "An Essay on the Picturesque," and was subsequently
created a Baronet.

A CATALOGUE OF THE ILAM GALLERY. 1827.
Ashbourn: Printed by W. Hoon. 1828. *Imp.* 4*to.*
pp. 21.

Twenty-five copies were printed of this Catalogue for presents, at the expense of the owner, Jesse Watts Russell, of Ilam, co. Stafford, Esq.

MEMORIAL OF THE
CONVERSION OF JEAN LIVINGSTON, LADY WARISTOUN;
With an Account of her Carriage at her Execution, July, 1600.

Edinburgh. 1827.   4*to.* pp. 37.

Only a very few copies privately printed by C. K. Sharpe, Esq., for presents. It is a most striking account of the repentance of a beautiful woman, who murdered her husband, and was executed for the horrid fact at Edinburgh, the 4th or 5th of July, 1600. It is printed from the original MS. in the handwriting of an eye-witness, preserved in the Advocates' Library.

CATALOGUE OF WORKS ON THE PEERAGE AND BARONETAGE OF ENGLAND, SCOTLAND, AND IRELAND, IN THE LIBRARY OF SIR CHARLES GEORGE YOUNG, GARTER.

London. 1827.   8*vo.* pp. 87.

The preface states,—"The following pages present a catalogue of such printed works as can be designated Peerages, and occur in the library of the collector; they will be found to contain nearly all that have issued from the press, to the year 1827."

Fifty copies were printed, and ten on large paper.

REGISTRUM WILTUNENSE, SAXONICUM ET LATINUM, IN MUSEO BRITANNICO ASSERVATUM, AB ANNO REGIS ALFREDI 892, AD ANNUM REGIS EADWARDI 1045. Nunc demum Notis illustraverunt, J. Ingram, S.A.S.; Sharon Turner, .A.S.S; T. D. Fosbroke, S.A.S.; Thomas Phillipps, Bart., S.A.S.; Richard Colt Hoare, Bart., S.A.S.
Sumptibus R. C. HOARE.
Londini : Typis Nicolsianis. 100 exemplaria impressa. Anno 1827. *folio.* pp. 56; Preface, pp. xi.

An engraving of the seal of the Abbey of Wilton, engraved by Basire.

This volume was printed at the expense of Sir Richard Colt Hoare, Bart. The editorial part was entrusted principally to the care of the late Sharon Turner, historian of the Anglo-Saxons.

———

A BRIEF ACCOUNT OF MICROSCOPICAL OBSERVATIONS, MADE IN THE MONTHS OF JUNE, JULY, AND AUGUST, 1827, ON THE PARTICLES CONTAINED IN THE POLLEN OF PLANTS; AND ON THE GENERAL EXISTENCE OF ACTIVE MOLECULES IN ORGANIC AND INORGANIC BODIES.
BY ROBERT BROWN, F.R.S.,
President of the Linnean Society.
[Not published.]
London. 8vo. 1827.

"This little unpublished pamphlet, consisting of sixteen pages, has excited more curiosity at home and abroad, than anything we recollect for many years. It is the production of a gentleman who is acknowledged by every one to stand at the head of botanical science, *princeps botanicorum*, and who deserves confidence for the correctness of his observations, and for the faithfulness with which he records them. His discovery is no less than this, that the ultimate particles he can obtain from all bodies, organic and inorganic, have inherent motion, like unto vital action."*

BIBLIOTHECA MARSDENIANA, PHILOLOGICA
ET ORIENTALIS:
A Catalogue of Books and Manuscripts, collected with a view to a general comparison of Languages, and to the study of Oriental Literature.
BY WILLIAM MARSDEN, F.R.S., ETC.
London: Printed by J. L. Cox, Great Queen-street, Lincoln's-Inn-Fields. 1827. 4*to.* pp. 309.

This catalogue contains—I. An Alphabetical Catalogue of Authors. —II. A Chronological Arrangement, in each Class of Literature.— III. Manuscripts.

A LETTER, STATING THE TRUE SITE OF THE
ANCIENT COLONY OF CAMULODUNUM.
Printed by John Rutter, Shaftesbury. A.D. 1827.

This tract was written by Sir Richard Colt Hoare, Bart. It is noticed in the "Gentleman's Magazine;" where the reviewer states that Sir Richard has completely settled the point, as to Colchester being the undoubted Camulodunum. It was a reply to a tract by the Rev. John Skinner, read at the Philosophical and Literary Society of Bristol, Feb. 8, 1827, who contended for Camerton, near Bath, as the Roman colony. Twenty-five copies printed.

---

* Loudon, Magazine of Natural History, vol. ii. p. 46.

ODYSSEY, BOOK V.

London: James Ridgway, Piccadilly. 1827. 8*vo.*
pp. 24.

A translation, by Lord John Russell; who printed only twenty-five copies, for private distribution.

VERSES WRITTEN ON
THE ALAMEDA AT AMPTHILL PARK.
BY J. H. WIFFEN.

"Here, then, is the true Parnassus, Castalia, and the Muses: in the walks and shades of trees, the noblest raptures have been conceived. Here Poets have made their verses, Orators their panegyrics, Historians grave relations, and the profound Philosophers have passed their lives, in repose and contemplation. Paradise itself was but a kind of nemorous temple."—*Evelyn.*

London: Printed by James Moyes. 1827. 4*to.*
pp. 28.

"Thirty copies only have been printed, for private distribution."
Mr. Wiffen is well known as the translator of Tasso, and the historian of the House of Russell.

CATALOGUE OF THE LIBRARY OF THE CORPORATION OF THE CITY OF LONDON: INSTITUTED IN THE YEAR 1824.

Printed for the use of the Corporation of the City of London. 1828. 8*vo.* pp. 189.

This Library was established in the year 1824, by a grant from the Corporation of 500*l.* as an outfit, and 200*l.* per annum, for the purchase of books: it is placed under the management of thirteen members of the court of Common Council. It is to be hoped that, ere long, more suitable apartments will be found for the Library, than the dark rooms it now occupies at Guildhall. It is open from ten till four, each day; Mr. Herbert, author of the "History and Antiquities of the Inns of Court," is librarian. The collection of newspapers is the completest known, with the exception of that in the British Museum.

The Nightingale
warbling forth her owne Disaster;
Or, the Rape of Philomela, new written in English Verse.
By Martin Parker.

London: Printed by G. P. for William Cooke, and are to be sold at his shop neere Furneval's Inne gate, in Holbourne. 1632. [Reprinted by J. Moyes, Greville-street, Holborn.] 12mo. pp. 25.

Reprinted for private circulation, by the late Amos Strettell, Esq.

Ritson styles the author "A Grub-street scribbler, and great ballad-monger of Charles the First's time."

On the Landscape Architecture of the
great Painters of Italy.
By G. L. M., Esq.
1828. 4to. With 55 plates on stone.

The author is Mr. Laing Meason. One hundred and fifty copies only are said to have been printed. It is believed, however, that several copies were subsequently sent to the publisher (Mr. Carpenter) for sale.

PRACTICAL DISCOURSES :
A Selection from the unpublished Manuscripts of the late Venerable Thomas Townson, D.D., Archdeacon of Richmond; one of the Rectors of Malpas, Cheshire; and some time Fellow of St. Mary Magdalen College, Oxford.

ἀποθανὼν ἔτι λαλεῖται.

Not published.
London : Printed by A. and R. Spottiswoode, New-street-square. 1828. 8*vo*. pp. 400.

Five hundred copies of these Discourses were printed, for private distribution; they were edited by the late John Jebb, D.D., Lord Bishop of Limerick.

———

SUMMARY OF A MORE COMPREHENSIVE AND CIRCUM-STANTIAL NARRATIVE; RELATING TO THE CONDUCT OF CERTAIN ENGLISH PERSONS AT VERSAILLES IN FRANCE.
To be published hereafter, if deemed expedient.
Dublin : Printed in 1828.   8*vo*.   pp. 60.

———

A NARRATIVE OF AN ASCENT TO THE SUMMIT OF MONT BLANC, MADE DURING THE SUMMER OF 1827, BY MR. WILLIAM HAWES AND MR. CHARLES FELLOWES.
Printed, for Benjamin Hawes, Junior, by Arthur Tay-lor. M.DCCC.XXVIII. 4*to*. pp. 35.

This Narrative is drawn up by Benjamin Hawes, Esq., Under Se-cretary at War, from materials furnished by his brother at his request. "It is printed in order to gratify the inquiries of numerous friends, and to prevent the wearisome repetition and verbal detail of the same story; and it is hoped it will be acceptable to those for whom alone it is intended." The party reached the summit on the 25th of July, 1827. "The view and the scenery around them were objects of intense curiosity; and here they found themselves more than compensated for all their labours." The Narrative, which was obligingly lent to the editor, was illustrated with several views of the scenery in this wild spot; autographs of the travellers and their guides, written when on the summit; and an attestation of the Syndic at Chamouny, of the completion of the enterprise by Mr. Hawes and his companion.

RENTALS OF THE EARLDOM AND BISHOPRIC OF ORKNEY;

With some other explanatory and relative Documents. Collected by Alexander Peterkin, Esq., Sheriff Substitute of Orkney.

Edinburgh. 1828. 8vo.

Printed by order of the Barons of the Court of Exchequer in Scotland; and, it is believed, for private circulation.

TEMPLARIA.

Papers relative to the History, Privileges, and Possessions of the Scotish Knights Templars, and their successors the Knights of St. John of Jerusalem.

[Edinburgh.] M.DCCC.XXVIII.

Four parts. Four copies on large paper, and twenty *small 4to*.
Privately printed by James Maidment, Esq., and now of extreme

rarity.   It contains a variety of documents from original MSS. and scarce printed papers relative to these two Orders.

———

POETRY, ORIGINAL AND SELECT;
Written by several distinguished Characters.

Printed for private distribution.   pp. 30.   No copy has come into the editor's hands.

———

JOURNAL OF A TOUR MADE BY A PARTY OF FRIENDS, IN THE AUTUMN OF 1825, THROUGH BELGIUM, UP THE RHINE TO FRANCKFORT AND HEIDELBERG, AND ACROSS THE EASTERN SIDE OF FRANCE, AND PARIS.
BY T. B.
Norwich: Printed by S. Wilkin, Upper Haymarket. 1828.   8vo.   pp. 88.

With a view of Huy Castle, lithographed by Johnson, from a sketch by the author, Thomas Brightwell, Esq., a solicitor at Norwich, and a great promoter of the study of natural history. His entomological collection is now deposited in the Museum of Natural History recently established in that city.

———

LETTRES SUR LA COUR DE LA CHANCELLERIE, ET QUELQUES POINTS DE LA JURISPRUDENCE ANGLOISE.
PAR M. C. P. COOPER, Avocat Anglois.
Nouvelle édition, revue et corrigée.
A Londres.   1828.   8vo.

The first edition of this book was published anonymously in the month of October, 1827; but the sale was immediately suspended,

—for what reason is not very apparent, as the author distributed all the remaining copies among his professional friends. The above edition was privately printed; and it is said that only one copy has ever occurred in a sale catalogue. The work, being much sought after as containing the original sketch of the legal reforms that have lately taken place, or that are now in progress, as well as numerous curious details respecting the English judges and bar, foreign codes, &c., has been twice reprinted on the Continent, at Paris and Bruxelles. Mr. Cooper, of the Chancery bar, and the Secretary to the Record Board, is the author both of the Letters and the Notes; although the Continental editions, following the first edition, represent the Letters to have been actually written by a Frenchman.

FIDELITY; OR, LOVE AT FIRST SIGHT.
A TALE, WITH OTHER POEMS.
London: Printed (not for sale) by Savage and Easingwood, James-street, Buckingham Gate. 1828. 4*to.* pp. 92.

The name of the author was cut out in the only copy seen of this volume.

A LETTER TO THE RIGHT HONOURABLE THE EARL OF ABERDEEN, K.T., PRESIDENT OF THE SOCIETY OF ANTIQUARIES, ON THE EXPEDIENCY OF ATTACHING A MUSEUM OF ANTIQUITIES TO THAT INSTITUTION.
BY JAMES HEYWOOD MARKLAND, ESQ., F.R.S.
London. 1828. 8*vo.* pp. 19.

This, although only a pamphlet, is inserted as a memorandum of an attempt to draw the attention of the Society of Antiquaries to an object which, it is hoped, will be eventually accomplished. "A museum of Antiquities, properly organised, would not only tend to the preservation of the objects, but ultimately show the real use to which they are to be applied. By an assemblage of details, the observer may be led to generalize."*

ESSAYS ON GOVERNMENT, JURISPRUDENCE, THE LI-
BERTY OF THE PRESS, PRISONS, AND PRISON DISCI-
PLINE, COLONIES, THE LAW OF NATIONS, AND EDU-
CATION.
BY JAMES MILL, ESQ., Author of the "History of
British India."
Reprinted by permission from the Supplement to the
" Encyclopædia Britannica." (Not for sale.)
London. 1828.

It is reviewed by Lord Jeffrey, in the "Edinburgh Review," vol. xlix. p. 159. A reply from Bentham, in the "Westminster," was again the subject of a severe castigation by Jeffrey, in a critique, from which it has been said utilitarianism received a blow from which it never recovered.

CARTA CONSTITUCIONAL DA MONARCHIA PORTU-
GUEZA DECRETADA, E DADA REI DE PORTUGAL E AL-
GARVAS D. PEDRO, IMPERADOR DO BRAZIL, AOS 29
DE AVRIL, DE 1826.
London. 4to. 1828.

Printed, as the editor is informed, for private circulation among those who took an interest in the dispute for the throne of Portugal.

---

* Quarterly Review of this Letter, vol. xxxvii.

Beware lest any Man spoil you through Philosophy and vain Deceit, after the Tradition of Men, after the Rudiments of the World, and not after Christ.—Col. ii. 8.

London: Printed by W. Marchant, Ingram-court, Fenchurch-street. 1828. 8vo. pp. 500.

Printed solely for private distribution : the question being, whether the Sacred History alludes only to our earth ? Admitting that it speaks of another, what is that unknown earth?

———

The Promissory Note Question, considered as a Case between the great Capitalist and the daily Labourer, or the Monied Interest and the Nation at large.

"Thou shalt not muzzle the ox that treadeth out the corn."

London : Printed by J. B. Nichols and Son, Parliament-street. 1828. 8vo.

———

Psychæ; or, Songs of Butterflies, By T. H. Bayly, Esq., Attempted in Latin Rhymes (to the same Airs); with a few additional Trifles.

"They flutter through life's little day."—Gray.

Malton. 1828. 8vo. pp. 40.

By the late Archdeacon Wrangham; who says, "I feel assured that, without any intercession on my part, the kind and candid reader, for whom alone these trifles are intended, will treat them kindly and candidly; and admit, that the editor of Bishop Walton's Prolegomena to the Polyglott Bible, may venially indulge in a little innocent recreation."

Only a few copies printed for private distribution.

––––––

THE STATUTES OF THE ORDER OF THE GUELPHS. William Pickering, Chancery-lane, London. 1828. 4*to.* pp. 17.

One hundred copies of this volume, edited by the late Sir Nicholas Harris Nicolas, were printed for the use of the members of the order.

––––––

THE STATUTES OF THE ORDER OF THE THISTLE. William Pickering, Chancery-lane, London. 1828. 4*to.* pp. 39.

Fifty copies of these Statutes, edited by Sir Harris Nicolas, were printed for private circulation.

––––––

A CATALOGUE RAISONNE OF THE SELECT COLLECTION OF ENGRAVINGS OF AN AMATEUR. London. M.DCCC.XXVIII. 4*to.* pp. 279. Memorandum of the Collections to which various Specimens described in the foregoing Collection have belonged; List of Plates; and Index of Engravers, pp. viii.

This Catalogue describes the collection of Thomas Wilson, Esq., one of the most eminent collectors of choice engravings, and generally admitted a most excellent judge.

Twenty copies were printed on large paper, which were distributed among the most distinguished collectors of the day. This collection, considering its extent, is esteemed one of the most select ever formed by a single individual. In the Introduction, the author says, "An admirer of the art of engraving wishes to leave some testimony of the pleasure he has derived from his pursuit as the collector and possessor of these specimens ; and he could not, therefore, deny himself the additional amusement of describing them ; of prefixing a short biography of each master, where it was practicable ; and of adding such anecdotes of the prints collected, as seemed to him to be interesting."

In the volume are forty-three plates, consisting of initial letters, vignettes, tail-pieces, &c., designed by Frank Howard, George Cruikshank, and other artists : and in the index are a few monograms, used by different engravers.

The collection has since been disposed of by auction.

***

Seaham Harbour.

Durham. 1828.   8vo. pp. 23.

Thirty copies printed by the editor, Sir Cuthbert Sharp. The harbour has been recently made, at the expense of the Marquis of Londonderry, who has a seat in the neighbourhood, and whose eldest son, by his second marriage, bears the title of Lord Seaham.

***

Reliquiæ Scoticæ. Scotish Remains in Prose and Verse, from original MSS. and scarce Tracts.

Edinburgh. 1828.   8vo.

This collection contains eighteen different articles, separately paged ; with title, preface, and contents, pp. 6. It was privately printed by James Maidment, Esq., and Alexander Pitcairn, Esq., and very few copies were thrown off. Two copies on thick paper were taken for the two editors.

A DESCRIPTIVE CATALOGUE OF BOOKS IN THE LIBRARY OF JOHN HOLMES, F.S.A.; With Notices of Authors and Printers.

> "———— cum transierint mei
> Nullo cum strepitu dies,
> Obscurus moriar senex."

Norwich: Printed by Matchett, Stevenson, and Matchett, Market Place. 1828. 8vo. pp. 340; Errata, one leaf.

A DESCRIPTIVE CATALOGUE OF BOOKS IN THE LIBRARY OF JOHN HOLMES, F.S.A.; With Notices of Authors and Printers. Vol. II. Containing also additional Notes to the First Volume.

> "Multi mei similes hoc morbo laborant, ut cum scribere nesciant, tamen a scribendo temperare non possunt."— *Erasmus, in Pref. in tertiam seriem quarti tomi Hieronymi,* p. 408.

> "Nullus amicus magis libet, quam liber."

Norwich: Printed by Matchett, Stevenson, and Matchett. 1830. 8vo. pp. 286; Errata, one leaf; Title, Preface, &c. pp. vii. Frontispiece, a view of the Library in Mr. Holmes' grounds.

A Descriptive Catalogue of Books in the Library of John Holmes, F.S.A.; With Notices of Authors and Printers. Vol. III. Containing also a second Series of additional Notes to the First Volume, and some additional Notes to the Second Volume.

> " Incipit et dubitat, scribit, damnatque tabellas ;
> Et notat et delet, mutat, culpatque, probatque."

> " From grave to gay, from lively to severe."

Norwich : Printed by Matchett, Stevenson, and Matchett, Market Place. 1832. *8vo.* pp. 295 ; Title, Preface, &c., pp. viii.

"The owner of the Library described in this Catalogue was one of the younger sons of a worthy and highly respected clergyman of the Church of England, and in early life had neither the thought nor the means of indulging his fancy for the acquisition of a library. "The whole is compiled," says the reviewer in the "Gentleman's Magazine,"* "with taste and judgment ; and the notices of the authors, and the list of the plates in their works, may be referred to as useful sources of information."

Canzone, per la morte dello Cavaliero Guglielmo Drummond, morte in Roma, 29 de Marzo, 1828.

Londra. 1828. *8vo.*

"Stampata privamente."

---

* December, 1832.

LIFE OF HENRY SMITH.

Appendix. Evidences relating to the Estates of Henry Smith, Esquire, some time Alderman of the City of London. Collected by JOSEPH GWILT, ESQ., F.S.A., one of his Kindred. London: Printed by George Woodfall. M.DCCC.XXVIII. (only twenty-five copies printed.) 8vo. pp. clxxx.

This volume is intended to form the Appendix to a Life of Alderman Henry Smith, which Mr. Gwilt purposed to print. The celebrated Henry Smith, who was a liberal benefactor to every parish in the county of Surrey, and to numerous places in other counties, died 3rd January, 1627, and lies buried in the chancel of the church at Wandsworth, his native village. Mr. Gwilt is a lineal descendant of the alderman's sister. An account of him will be found in Nichols's Anecdotes, vol. ii. p. 382.

A DESCRIPTION OF A SERIES OF ILLUSTRATIONS TO G. P. HARDING'S MANUSCRIPT HISTORY OF THE PRINCES OF WALES, FROM THE TIME OF EDWARD OF CAERNARVON, TO THE PRESENT SOVEREIGN OF ENGLAND; Containing a List of all the Portraits, Armorial Bearings, Royal Badges, Monuments, Seals, Illuminated Views, and other Decorations. London: Printed for G. P. Harding, Hercules-buildings, Lambeth; by W. Davy, Gilbert-street, Grosvenor-square. 1828. 8vo. pp. 31.

Mr. G. P. Harding, an artist eminent in his profession, who excelled in copying ancient portraits, devoted a period of ten years to illuminating a very beautiful manuscript History of the Princes of Wales; which many of the nobility and gentry had an opportunity of seeing. This little tract is descriptive of its illustrative decorations, derived from authorities not very commonly resorted to, particularly the heraldic badges and cognizances of the several princes, distinguishing the different royal families. In this part of his work, consisting of not less than one hundred and seventy drawings, Mr. Harding was assisted by Sir Charles Young, Mr. Willement, and the late Mr. Moule; by the last of whom this account of the heraldic devices was written.

The "Illustrations" have been purchased by the Prince of Wales, for two hundred pounds.

***

THE LIFE OF THE CELEBRATED SIR FRANCIS DRAKE, THE FIRST ENGLISH CIRCUMNAVIGATOR; REPRINTED FROM THE BIOGRAPHIA BRITANNICA.

Together with the Historical and Genealogical Account of Sir Francis Drake's Family, from Betham's Baronetage: and Extracts from Nicholson's History of Cumberland, containing an Account of the Richmond Family of Highead Castle. Not published.

London: Printed by J. Moyes. 1828. 8vo. pp. 83.

With a portrait of Sir Francis Drake, drawn on stone; and a representation of the chair made out of Drake's ship, which was sent to the University of Oxford, and is placed in the picture gallery.

***

REMARKS UPON THE LAWS AFFECTING ECCLESIASTICAL PLURALITIES IN IRELAND.

Dublin: Printed by Bentham and Hardy. 1829. 8vo. pp. 39.

The tract is by the late Dr. Richard Laurence, Archbishop of Cashel. It was not for sale.

HOUSEHOLD EXPENSES, FOR ONE YEAR,
OF PHILIP, THIRD LORD WHARTON.
Newcastle-on-Tyne.   1829.   4*to*.

Privately printed for presents, by W. C. Trevelyan, Esq.

———

EPITOME OF THE CASE ON THE CLAIM OF THE DILLON
FAMILY OF PROUDSTON, TO THE GREAT CHAMBERLAIN-
SHIP OF ALL ENGLAND.
BY SIR JOHN JOSEPH DILLON, KNT. AND BARON S.R.E.
London.   1829.   4*to*.   pp. 20.

Notwithstanding the London impress on the title, these pages
were printed in Paris, at the press of Didot, sen. Sir John Dillon
was also the author of a Memoir upon the same subject; printed
for private use, in 1820 (fol. pp. 10), upon the occasion of the claim
of Charles Baron Dillon, of the Roman Empire, to the office of Lord
Great Chamberlain, presented to the Court of Claims previously to
the coronation of King George IV.

In this argument, it is contended that the judgment of the House
of Lords in 1626, which gave that high and distinguished office to
the Earl of Lindsay (the ancestor of the Marchioness of Cholmon-
deley, and the Lady Burrell, afterwards Lady Willoughby d'Eresby,
to whom the House awarded it upon their claim in 1781, on the
death of Robert Duke of Ancaster) was wrong, and proceeded upon
erroneous principles ;—that, in fact, the office was then vested in
the co-heirs of John, *fourteenth* Earl of Oxford, and Baron Dillon is
now one of the co-heirs.

That decision has frequently, it appears, been considered a singular one ; and the Memoir as well as the Case contains a statement,
not only curious, but interesting to those who devote their time to
genealogical and juridical antiquities. The noble houses of Percy
and Murray maintain the same arguments as the Baron Dillon ; the
Duchess of Northumberland and the Duchess Dowager of Atholl,

were claimants in 1781, as co-heirs of the fourteenth Earl of Oxford; so that the House had knowledge of their pretensions before it decided the question.

The Baron subsequently to the printing of this argument petitioned the Crown, and the consideration of his petition was referred to the Attorney-General.

THE MUSIC OF THE SOUL; OR, THE EFFUSIONS OF A RENEWED HEART, EXPRESSED IN FAMILIAR VERSE.

By J. W., deceased, in usum amicorum.

London: Printed by J. Haddon, Castle-street, Finsbury. 1829. 12mo. pp. 144.

By John Wilson, Esq., of Islington; who died in January, 1826, aged seventy-five.

FIFTY SELECT POEMS OF MARC-ANTONIO FLAMINIO;

Imitated by the late Rev. EDWARD WILLIAM BARNARD, M.A., of Trinity College, Cambridge; with a short Memoir of the Author. Edited by the Ven. Archdeacon Wrangham, M.A., F.R.S. Θανὼν λάμπεις.

Chester. 1829. 8vo. pp. 69. Preface pp. xxii.

PRIVATE LETTERS NOW FIRST PRINTED FROM THE ORIGINAL MSS. 1694–1732.

Edinburgh. 1829. 8vo.

The prefatory memorandum by the editor, James Maidment, Esq., explains the reasons why the publication was private:—

"Although the ensuing Letters are both curious and interesting, their peculiar and local nature renders them best suited for PRIVATE CIRCULATION among those persons who think there is no very great harm in being diverted with such (antiquated) scandal as afforded amusement to a person so truly respectable and virtuous as Mr. RO-BERT WODROW, Minister of the Gospel at Eastwood, to whom (with the exception of a very few) they are all addressed."

Wodrow was the historian of the persecution of the Presby-terians. A review of this very scarce little work will be found in "Frazer's Magazine."

PORTRAITS OF THE SPRUGGINS FAMILY, ARRANGED BY RICHARD SUCKLETHUMKIN SPRUGGINS, ESQ. With descriptive letter-press.
1829. 4*to*. 44 plates.

The authorship of this clever volume has been erroneously attri-buted to the Dowager Countess of Morley. Her Ladyship's share consisted in lithographing the drawings, but the text was by a writer unknown to the editor.

NUGÆ SCOTICÆ. MISCELLANEOUS PAPERS, ILLUS-TRATIVE OF SCOTISH AFFAIRS FROM 1535 TO 1781. Edinburgh. M.DCCC.XXIX. 8*vo*.

On the title an etching of a blue-gown, with these lines,—

> "Behold, courageous Collonel Munro,
> A Higland Hero, turn'd a blue-goun Beau."

Privately printed by James Maidment and G. R. Kinloch, Esqs.; contains twenty-two articles separately paged. Title, preface, and contents, pp. 8. Complete sets of the different articles are of great rarity.

THE HISTORY OF LITHOGRAPHY,
Reprinted with considerable additions from the "Foreign Review," No. vii. for July, 1829.
By T. CROFTON CROKER, ESQ., Superintendent of the Admiralty Lithographic Press.
For private circulation.
London. 4*to.* pp. 87. (With Illustrations.)

The illustrations in the History of Lithography varied in all the copies, and they were very few. Among them were transfers from the hands of Sir Walter Scott, the Rev. W. Lewes, D'Israeli (the elder), Dr. Maginn, Theodore Hook (a sketch of Buonaparte, from his recollections of him at St. Helena), sketch by Sir William Beechey (two impressions only taken in an altered state), sketch by Wilkie (one impression, and he is known only to have made another sketch upon stone, from which Hullmandel took one impression, Dr. Young's first attempts at reading the Rosetta stone, &c., &c.

The review led to the following :—

A REPLY TO SOME STATEMENTS IN AN ARTICLE ENTITLED THE HISTORY OF LITHOGRAPHY, PUBLISHED IN THE "FOREIGN REVIEW," No. VII., FOR JULY, 1829.
BY C. HULLMANDEL.
London: Printed by J. Davy. 1829. 8*vo.* pp. 11.

———

TUMULI WILTUNENSES: A GUIDE TO THE BARROWS ON THE PLAINS OF STONEHENGE.
BY SIR RICHARD COLT HOARE.
Printed by J. Rutter, Shaftesbury. 8*vo.* pp. 50. With 6 plates of Barrows, Urns, &c.

Memoranda relating to Coleopterous Insects, found in the Neighbourhood of Swansea.

Not published.

Printed by W. C. Murray and D. Rees, Cambrian Office, Swansea. [1829.] 8vo. pp. 75.

These Memoranda were compiled by Lewis Weston Dillwyn, Esq., of Penllergare, North Wales; who says in the preface, " Our district has probably already afforded more interesting additions to the British Fauna than any other."

Poems, by W. T. Moncrief.

"Lasso, a tal che non m'ascolta, narro."—*Petrarch.*

Printed (for private distribution only) at the Author's private Press, Saville House, Lambeth. M.DCCC.XXIX. 12mo. pp. 176.

The author, a well known dramatic writer, in the preface, says, " I commenced printing this volume to please one who, alas! has not lived to witness its completion; the praise or censure of others is now, therefore, of little import to me."

Sermons, at St. John's College, Oxford. By the Rev. Doctor Bell.

York. 1829. 8vo. pp. 278.

Dr. Bell also printed the following Sermons and Lectures, for private distribution:—

I. Lectures on the Catechism. York. 1805. 12mo. pp. 92. Fifty copies were printed.

II. A second edition of the same work. York. 1816.

III. Six Sermons on the Liturgy. York. 1819. 12*mo.* pp. 111. One hundred copies.

SPEECHES OF THE RIGHT HON. CHARLES ABBOT, IN COMMUNICATING THANKS IN THE HOUSE OF COMMONS, TO MILITARY COMMANDERS, 1807–1816: WITH A BIOGRAPHICAL MEMOIR, AND APPENDIX.

[Not published.]

London : Printed by James and Luke G. Hansard and Sons. 12*mo.* pp. 295.

This volume is edited by John Rickmann, Esq., Clerk Assistant to the House of Commons. The Right Hon. Charles Abbot, created Lord Colchester, June 3, 1817, died May 8, 1829, æt. 72.

THE MOST PLEASANT SONG OF LADY BESSY, THE ELDEST DAUGHTER OF KING EDWARD THE FOURTH; AND HOW SHE MARRIED KING HENRY THE SEVENTH, OF THE HOUSE OF LANCASTER.

With Notes, by THOMAS HEYWOOD, F.A.S.

> "——— Sermones ego mallem
> Repentes per humum."

London : Printed by Richard Taylor, Red-Lion-court, Fleet-street. M.DCCC.XXIX. 12*mo.* pp. 82; Introduction, &c., pp. xvi.

This Song is copied from a manuscript in the possession of William Bateman, Esq., F.A.S. ; the hand-writing is of the age of Charles the Second. Lady Bessy was the eldest daughter of Edward the

Fourth, by the ill-omened marriage of that monarch with the daughter of Earl Rivers. The British Museum possesses a copy of this MS., of the time of Queen Elizabeth.

The ballad itself presents some curious historical notices, which, whether real or fictitious, deserve the attention of writers upon the historical events of the period to which it refers. The Introduction and Notes, from the pen of Mr. Heywood, will be found to afford information both valuable and interesting.

INDEX TO THE PUBLIC GENERAL STATUTES OF THE UNITED KINGDOM, FROM JANUARY, 1801, TO JULY, 1828. BY B. SPILLER, LIBRARIAN, House of Commons. London : Printed by James and Luke G. Hansard and Sons. 1829. 4to. pp. 306.

INDEX TO THE ROLL OF ARMS, OF THE SOVEREIGN, AND OF THE SPIRITUAL AND TEMPORAL PEERS, WHO SAT IN THE PARLIAMENT HELD AT WESTMINSTER ON THE 5TH OF FEBRUARY, IN THE SIXTH YEAR OF THE REIGN OF KING HENRY THE EIGHTH, ANNO DOMINI 1515:

In the possession of Thomas Willement. London. 1829. Not printed for sale. Royal 4to., and one copy on atlas 4to. pp. 17.

Mr. Willement, who has done more than any other artist of his day toward a restoration of the true character of heraldic design, published a lithographed fac-simile of this contemporary roll in his possession, in which the arms were emblazoned in strict imitation of the original vellum ; and dedicated it to the Earl of Abergavenny,

K.T. Such rolls, or lists of the peers of parliament, it was the custom, at least as early as the reign of Henry VIII., for Garter King of Arms to prepare ; they were similar, excepting with respect to the arms, to those lists which, since the Restoration, Garter has regularly presented to the House at the commencement of each session. This publication, as a fac-simile, is valuable in an heraldic point of view, as affording contemporary evidence of armorial bearings, and as specimens of the style of emblazoning heraldry at the commencement of the sixteenth century.

Mr. Willement, in this publication, which was confined to fifty copies, adapted it to the provisions of the Acts of Queen Anne and George III. for the *encouragement* of learning, to avoid the obligation of delivering eleven emblazoned copies out of the fifty ; he afterward gratuitously distributed this tract, replete with information relative to the Roll, to prevent the obnoxious claim on the part of the Libraries. Beside a preface, at the end of which is the author's mark, T.W., with the motto, 𝔞𝔲𝔰𝔰𝔶 𝔟𝔦𝔢𝔫 𝔠𝔬𝔪𝔢 𝔧𝔢 𝔭𝔬𝔲𝔯𝔬𝔶, there is an explanatory index of the coats of arms, fifty in number, consisting of nine pages.

FUGITIVE PIECES. BY DR. BELL.
Second edition.
York.   1829.   *8vo.*   pp. 89.

A previous edition, without date, pp. 82, consisted of fifty copies.

FIFTY LYRICAL BALLADS.
BY THOMAS HAYNES BAYLY.
Bath.   1829.   *12mo.*

" We must say we like the comic songs the least : we doubt not they have had considerable success in society—but they want good singing, good humour, bright lamps, and bright eyes, supper, and champagne ; they are not for quiet criticism. This volume is intended for private circulation ; and we cannot but say that Mr. Bayly's friends are greatly indebted to him."

———

THE GENEALOGIE OF THE MACKENZIES, PRECEEDING
YE YEAR M.DC.LXI. WREATTIN IN YE YEAR M.DC.LIX.
By a Persone of Qualitie (MACKENZIE OF
APPLEGARTH).
Edinburgh. 1829.   *4to.*

Printed from a MS. written by Sir George Mackenzie, of Rosehaugh, afterward Earl of Cromarty, Viscount Tarbet, and Lord Clerk Register of Scotland. The editor was J. W. Mackenzie, Esq., Writer to the Signet. Fifty copies were printed.

———

SUGGESTIONS SENT TO THE COMMISSIONERS APPOINTED
TO INQUIRE INTO THE LAWS OF REAL PROPERTY ;
WITH MINUTES OF THE EVIDENCE GIVEN BEFORE THEM.
BY JOHN TYRELL, ESQ., of Lincoln's Inn, Barrister.
London: Printed for the Author. 1829. [Not published.] *8vo.* pp. 388 ; Appendix, pp. cx. ; Index, thirty leaves.

The author in the Introduction says, "I have been induced to print these remarks, by the request of several of my professional friends, who have expressed a desire to see them, and the hope that, by distributing a few copies in a convenient form, principally among the members of the Bar, I might contribute to promote that consideration and discussion, without which no important alteration in the laws can prudently be made." Mr. Tyrell died Aug. 20, 1840.

" Many of his suggestions were adopted by the Real Property Commissioners, and he was shortly afterwards made one of the Commissioners, a step that may have increased his rank at the Bar, but which considerably diminished his income from his profession, and impaired his health by the laborious nature of his duties. His incessant application to his office sowed the seeds of the complaint which carried him off in the prime of life, and the full vigour of his mental faculties."*

SALICTUM WOBURNENSE:
Or, a Catalogue of Willows, Indigenous and Foreign, in the Collection of the Duke of Bedford, at Woburn Abbey : systematically arranged.

> " ———— Genus haud unum, nec fortibus ulmis,
> Nec Salici."— *Virg. Georg.* ii. 83.

London. M.DCCC.XXIX. *Imp.* 8vo. pp. 294.

Privately printed at the expense of John, sixth Duke of Bedford ; who says in the Introduction, " My late gardener, Mr. George Sinclair, to whose practical knowledge I was so much indebted in arranging my Catalogue of the Genus Erica, first called my attention to the plan of forming a collection of the numerous species and varieties of the genus Salix. The genus Salix is a tribe, of which it may perhaps be said, that they claim no peculiar interest, except to the botanical inquirer. Yet Sir James Smith, in his able Dissertation, has called it a vast, important, and most natural genus. Of the whole family of Willows, the *Salix Babylonica* (weeping-willow) seems to be the only one that has hitherto found its way into our dressed gardens, or pleasure grounds : this, from the graceful nature of its growth, must ever be a pleasing object in our home scenery :

---

* Hardy. Memoirs of Lord Langdale, vol. i. p. 384.

and an interesting one, from the record of the Psalmist, which gives a sanctity to its name :—

"'By the rivers of Babylon there we sat down, yea, we wept when we remembered Zion. We hanged our harps upon the *willows* in the midst thereof.'—Ps. cxxxvii."

Only fifty copies were printed. The frontispiece represents Johnson's Willow, which was destroyed by a storm, April, 1829 ; it was the *Salix Russelliana,* measured thirteen feet in girth, and not sixty feet in height. The volume contains coloured representations of the different species of willows ; for the arrangement of which, his Grace states he is entirely indebted to the botanical skill of his gardener, Mr. James Forbes.

————

Some Account of the Worshipful Company of Grocers, of the City of London. By John Benjamin Heath, Esq.

"Mercibus hic Italis mutat sub sole recenti
Rugosum piper et pallentis grana cymini."

Persius, Sat. v.

London. 1829. Not published. 8*vo.* pp. 358 ; Dedication, Preface, and Contents, pp. viii.

Prefixed is a portrait of St. Anthony, tutelar saint of the Company of Grocers, from an ancient carved figure, preserved at Grocers' Hall. The arms of the Company, which previously existed under the title of Pepperers, are on the title-page : the south view of Grocers' Hall, as it was restored after the fire of London, 1666, will be found at p. 42.

The author of this volume is nephew of Dr. Heath, whose valuable library was disposed of by public auction in 1810, by the late Mr. Jeffrey.

"The Grocers' Company," says the author, in his preface, "is the most ancient of the twelve great companies in London ; and as it was, undoubtedly, the first commercial corporation ever known in England, and one from which sprung, in after-times, some of our great mercantile establishments, it has frequently been a source of surprise and regret that there should exist no account of the origin and proceedings of this venerable body."

A reviewer, in the "Gentleman's Magazine,"* says,—"We cannot pass over Mr. Heath's masterly vindication of Sir John Cutler, whose memory has been 'damned to everlasting fame,' by Pope. Our author shows that he was a liberal benefactor to the Company in his life-time, by erecting buildings at the hall after the fire of London, and the founder of a lecture at Gresham College, for the benefit of Stock the mathematician ; beside which, he repaired St. Margaret's church at Westminster, and built a gallery for the sole use of the poor. Upon these facts, Mr. Heath adds, 'Surely these are not the acts of a man who,

> " ——————— saw tenants break, and houses fall ;
> For very want, he could not build a wall :' "

one part of the charge of meanness, so forcibly put by the satirist—

> " His only daughter in a stranger's power,
> For very want, he could not pay a dower ;' "

sinks into groundless slander : for Mr. Heath shows that he had two daughters ; to one of whom he gave a marriage-portion of 20,000*l.*, and settled on the other, on her marriage with the Earl of Radnor, the magnificent mansion and estate of Wimpole Hall, in Cambridge-shire, which he had purchased for that purpose."

It is hardly to be expected, that Mr. Heath's spirited example will find many followers among the other City Companies : but it is hoped that it may induce those, who manage their affairs, to devote some portion of their revenues to the investigation of their early history ; and we think it would well become a Company like that of the Stationers, so intimately connected with the early literary his-

---

* December, 1832.

tory of the country, not to be the last in following so liberal an example.*

Mr. Heath's own copy of this History of the Grocers, is illustrated, to a very great extent, by drawings and prints of every member of the Company, as well as the arms of every distinguished person connected with it: among them is a very fine copy of the portrait of Sir John Cutler, now in their hall. The drawings were made by G. P. Harding: the illustrations added form four volumes in folio size.

CATALOGUE OF THE ARUNDEL MANUSCRIPTS, IN THE LIBRARY OF THE COLLEGE OF ARMS.

Not published.

M.DCCC.XXIX.   *Royal 8vo.*   pp. 136.

This volume was printed, for private distribution, at the expense of Sir Charles George Young, Garter, F.S.A. It was compiled under his direction by Mr. W. H. Black; and contains an account of that portion of the Arundel Library which was given by Henry, Duke of Norfolk, to the College of Arms, in 1678.

The rest of the Arundel MSS. were given to the Royal Society; and have, in pursuance of a bargain between the Council of that learned body and the Trustees of the British Museum, made in 1829, become the property of the latter. They appear to have been valued at 3559*l.* 3*s.*; which sum was to be paid to the Royal Society in books computed of that value; the Trustees of the Museum undertaking to sell certain of their duplicates, and to apply the funds arising therefrom to the purchase of such scientific works as the Council and Fellows of the Royal Society should choose; eventually, however, books to the amount of 455*l.* only, were taken, and

---

* Mr. Collier has done something with this view, in his curious volumes, " Extracts from the Registers of the Stationers Company, 1557 to 1587." 2 vols. 8vo. Printed for the Shakespeare Society. 1849.

the remainder was paid in money. It is not very probable that learned body will ever again have the opportunity of bartering so valuable a gift ; for few persons will hereafter be disposed to leave anything to a Society, whose Council could recommend, and whose Fellows sanctioned, that disposal of them.

One hundred copies of this Catalogue were printed, for private circulation.

THE HEART'S EASE;
OR, A REMEDY AGAINST ALL TROUBLE.
BY SYMON PATRICK, D.D.

London : Printed. 1682. Reprinted by R. Gilbert, 1829. 12*mo*. pp. 94.

Reprinted, at the expense of the Venerable Archdeacon Thorp, for private distribution.

THE BOOK OF COMMON PRAYER, AND ADMINISTRA-
TION OF THE SACRAMENTS,

According to the use of the United Church of England and Ireland : together with the Psalms of David, and explanatory Annotations, chiefly selected from the edition of the Common Prayer, published by the Right Rev. Richard Mant, Bishop of Killaloe.

1829.   12*mo*.   pp. 463.

Fifty copies of this edition, which is beautifully executed by Mr. Nicol, were printed by the editor, the Hon. Elizabeth Cust ; with the following dedication :—

" To my godson, I dedicate this edition of the Book of Common Prayer. May our established religion be loved by him ' with all his

C C

heart, with all his soul, and with all his strength :' and walking in the steps of his Father, following the example of his Mother (whose virtues live in blessed remembrance), may he 'fear God and the king, and meddle not with them who are given to change.'—E. C."

The godson, to whom this is dedicated, was the late Lord Alford, eldest son of Earl Brownlow by his first wife, daughter of Sir Abraham Hume, Bart. An edition of this work has been printed for sale, in 1832 ; but it does not contain the dedication.

———

Reports of Deputations

Who, in pursuance of Resolutions of the Court of Assistants of the Drapers' Company, of the 23rd January, 1817 ; 3rd August, 1818 ; 2nd August, 1819 ; 7th August, 1820 ; and 7th April, 1827 ; visited the Estates of the Company, in the County of Londonderry, in Ireland, in those years ; and which were ordered by the Court to be printed, for the use of its Members.

London : Printed by J. L. Cox, Great Queen-street, Lincoln's-inn-Fields. 1829. 4*to.* pp. 211.

Plates on stone, from drawings by W. J. Booth :—

I. Plan of the town of Moneymore.
II. Church, Drapers' Town.
III. Drapers' Town.
IV. Mill, Moneymore.
V. Moneymore.
VI. Moneymore, from a window of the Inn.
VII. Moneymore, from the road.
VIII. The Church, Moneymore ; vignette on text, p. 149.
IX. Drapers' Town.
X. Ballinascreen ; Plan.
XI. Crany Free School.

BIBLIOTHECA COLEIANA;

A Catalogue of the Collection of Books, the private
Property of John Cole, of Scarborough; comprising
illustrated Copies of all those Works, of which he is the
Author: beside numerous Elucidations, both by Prints
and MSS., of the Productions of several other Writers.
Scarborough: Printed by John Cole, for the perusal of
his Friends, and not for sale. 1829. 8*vo*. pp. 33.

Mr. Cole printed fourteen copies of this Catalogue on drawing
paper, four on pink paper, and fifty on crimped paper.

Mr. Cole has, also, edited the undermentioned works; and as the
number printed of each is very limited, the editor thought a list of
them would not be unacceptable:—

1. Descriptive Catalogue of a Portion of the Collection of Books
of John Cole. With plates, wood-cuts, &c. 1825. 8*vo*. It contains the following plates: I. House in which George Villiers, second Duke of Buckingham, died. II. Folding wood-cut fac-simile
of a figure on a glazed tile. III. Rudston Church and Obelisk; and
numerous wood-cuts. Twenty-five copies only were printed, and
two on drawing paper.

2. Scarborough Worthies; collected by John Cole. Scarborough.
1826. 8*vo*. Only eighteen copies printed.

3. A Tour round Scarborough, historically and bibliographically
unfolded. By John Cole, author of the History and Antiquities of
Ecton, &c. Scarborough. 1826. Only twenty-five copies printed.

4. Le Petit Visiteur; containing a Sketch of the History of Scarborough; a Series of Cabinet Views, and Scarborough Lyrics; by
a Lady. Scarborough. 1826. *Foolscap* 8*vo*. Only twelve copies
printed.

5. Bookselling Spiritualized. Books and Articles of Stationery
rendered Monitors of Religion. By John Cole, editor of Herveiana,
&c. Scarborough. 1826. Only sixty copies were printed.

6. An Unique Bibliomaniac displayed, in a Biographical Account
of the late Mr. William Abbott, of Scarborough. By John Cole

c c 2

Scarborough. 1827. 8*vo*. With a catalogue of his books. Only six copies were printed, with the Catalogue, complete.

7. A pleasant and profitable Journey to London ; performed and described by John Cole, author of the "History and Antiquities of Weston Favell." Scarborough : Printed for private distribution, by John Cole, Newborough. 1828. Only fifty copies were printed.

8. An Account of the Proceedings at the Commemoration in honour of Hervey, at Weston Favell, June 18, 1833. Under the direction of John Cole, the projector of the Jubilee. Northampton : Printed for John Cole, Market Square, for private distribution. 1833. *Foolscap 8vo.* Only fifty copies printed ; it contains views of Weston church, and the rectory house.

THE PRESENT LAND TAX IN INDIA,

Considered as a measure of Finance, in order to show its effects on the Government and the People of that Country, and on the Commerce of Great Britain. In Three Parts.

By JOHN BRIGGS, Lieutenant-Colonel in the Madras Army.

London : Printed for Longman, Rees, Orme, Brown, and Green, Paternoster-row. 1830. 8*vo*. pp. 476.

BIBLIOTHECA RODESIANA.

A Catalogue of the Library at Barlborough Hall, taken September, 1830.

Printed by Thomas Combe, Junior, Leicester. 8*vo*. pp. 43.

An alphabetical Catalogue.

Barlborough Hall is ten miles from Mansfield.

A Vindication of the Theory of Mahometanism
Unveiled,
Against the Strictures of a Writer in No. XIII. of the
British Critic, and Quarterly Theological Review. In a
Letter to the Rev. Hugh James Rose, B.D., Christian
Advocate in the University of Cambridge. [Not pub-
lished.]
    [London.]   m.dccc.xxx.   8*vo.*

"Mahometanism Unveiled," 2 vols. 8*vo.*, is the work of the Rev.
Charles Forster, examining chaplain to the Bishop of Limerick;
who wrote this vindication of his own work.

Caius Gracchus; a Tragedy:
From the Italian of Monti.
London: Printed by J. Moyes. 1830. 8*vo.* pp. 120.

Fifty copies were printed of this translation, by the late Lord
George William Russell, second son of John, sixth Duke of Bedford.

The Genealogy of the House and Surname of
Setoun, by Sir Richard Maitland, of Ledington,
Knight; with the Chronicle of the House of
Setoun, compiled in Metre, by John Kamington,
alias Peter Manye, etc., etc.
Printed at Edinburgh.   m.dccc.xxx.   4*to.* pp. 64;
Preface, pp. xiii.

Prefixed, engraved in outline on the same plate, are portraits of
Robert, first Earl of Winton; Lady Margaret Montgomerie, Coun-

tess of Perth ; and Lady Isabella Seton, Countess of Perth. Fac-
simile of the MS. ; H. Gavin, sculp. ; prefixed to the Preface. Quarterings of the Countess of Winton ; p. xiii. Seton Chapel, an
etching ; prefixed to the Genealogy.

The editor, in the preface, states, that " The text of this volume
is printed from a manuscript in the possession of Mr. Hay, of
Drummelzier, great grandson of the Hon. Elizabeth Seton, daughter
of Alexander, first Viscount of Kingston. From an expression in
one of the notes, it seems to have been written by George, third
Earl of Wintoun ; and is remarkable for the extreme laboriousness
and precision of the character."

The Life and Miracles of St. Edith, the
Daughter of King Edgar,

An Ancient (about 1420) English Poem, now first
printed from a MS. in the British Museum, with Glos-
sarial Notes, by W. H. Black.

1830. *Folio.*

To the English philologist, as a genuine specimen of the ancient
Wiltshire Dialect, it will be found exceedingly valuable. It also
may with propriety be called the legendary history of Wilton Abbey
in metre.

One hundred copies printed for private circulation, by Sir R. C.
Hoare, Bart.

A Catalogue of Books in the Library of the
Company of Clock-makers, of the City of London.

London : Printed by M'Millan, Bow-street, Covent-
garden. 1830. 8*vo.* pp. 27.

An alphabetical catalogue of books, almost entirely relating to
horology. The preface states, that " A collection of specimens of

watches, principally of those made in the early state of the art, to illustrate the progress of watch-making from its first commencement, has been begun ; and a considerable number of specimens, some of no small value and rarity, collected together. But this collection is in too infant a state to be further noticed at present."

JOURNAL OF A TOUR THROUGH THE HIGHLANDS OF SCOTLAND, DURING THE SUMMER OF 1829. Edinburgh : Printed by James Johnstone. 1830. 8vo. pp. 376 ; Preface, pp. xvi.

Five hundred copies of this Tour were printed, for private circulation, by the author, Beriah Botfield, Esq., of Norton-House, Northamptonshire.

Two copies only possess the portrait of the author ; the drawing of which was on stone, and destroyed by the frost.

CHRONICON VILODUNENSE ; Sive de Vita et Miraculis Sanctæ Edithæ Regis Edgari filiæ carmen vetus Anglicum. E Codice unico Cottoniano in Museo Britannico adservato, nunc demum in lucem editum ; cura Gulielmi Henrici Black ; sumptibus RICARDI COLT HOARE. Londini : Typis Nicholsianis ; Centum exemplaria impressa. 1830. Folio. pp. 141.

The archæologist is greatly indebted to the munificence of Sir Richard Colt Hoare, Bart., for various valuable favours, and for this volume among the rest ; and every praise is due to Mr. Black, as the editor, a gentleman well known for his knowledge of ancient manuscripts. This volume generally accompanies the Registrum Wiltunense; copies of it having been presented by Sir Richard Colt Hoare to the same friends to whom the other work was given.

OBSERVATIONS ON THE DIMENSIONS OF THE SHIPS OF THE LINE AND FRIGATES IN THE FRENCH NAVY. By M. TUPINIER, Director of Naval Constructions, Knight of St. Louis, Officer of the Legion of Honour. Translated from the French, by a British Officer. (CAPT. WILLIAM JONES, R.N.) London : Printed for private distribution. 1830. 8*vo.* pp. 119.

NOTES OF THREE TOURS IN IRELAND, IN 1824 AND 1826. By J. B. [J. Chilcot, Printer, Wine-street, Bristol.] 12*mo.* pp. 337.

In the preface (dated Clifton, 1st Dec. 1830) it is stated, that " The following Notes were written during the course of several journeys, undertaken for the purpose of examining the state of education in Ireland."

LETTERS WRITTEN BY MRS. BIRCH, OF BARTON LODGE, IN THE 99TH AND 100TH YEARS OF HER AGE. With several fac-simile plates, and portrait of the venerable lady (about 1830). 4*to.*

This work was in the late Earl of Mornington's library.

Magni Rotuli Scaccarii Normaniæ de Anno ab Incarnatione Domini m.c.lxxxiiii.

Willielmo filio Radulfi, Senescallo quæ extant.

1830. 4*to.* pp. 12; Title and Preface, pp. iv.

This is the fragment of a great Roll for Normandy, of the thirtieth year of Henry II., exhibiting accounts similar to those contained in the Pipe Rolls of the Exchequer. The first part of this fragment contains part of the annual account of William, Earl of Arundel.

Printed at the expense of the late Henry Petrie, Esq., Keeper of the Records in the Tower of London, for private circulation.

———

Remains of William Ralph Churton.

" ——— non sotto l'ombra in piaggia molle
    Tra fonti e fior, tra Ninfe e tra Sirene,
        Ma in cima all' esto e faticoso colle
    Della virtù riposto è il nostro Bene."

Tasso, Ger. I. xvii.

Private impression. 1830. 8*vo.* pp. 179.

This volume was edited by Dr. Churton, formerly one of the under masters of the Charter-house, and head master of the grammar school at Hackney; brother to W. R. Churton, who died in September, 1828; of whom this volume contains a memorial.

———

The Worme of Lambton.

Durham. 1830. 4*to.* pp. 15.

Thirty copies were printed, for private circulation, by Sir Cuthbert Sharp. The story of the Worme of Lambton being a very in-

teresting one, the editor has introduced the account, from Surtees'
valuable History of Durham :—

"The heir of Lambton,* fishing, as was his profane custom, in
the Wear on a Sunday, hooked a small worm or eft, which he carelessly threw into a well, and thought no more of the adventure.
The worm (at first neglected) grew till it was too large for its first
habitation ; and issuing forth from the *Worm Well*, betook itself to
the Wear, where it usually lay a part of the day, coiled round a crag
in the middle of the water ; it also frequented a green mound near
the well (*the Worm Hill*), where it lapped itself nine times round,
leaving vermicular traces, of which grave living witnesses depose
that they have seen the vestiges. It now became the terror of the
country; and amongst other enormities, levied a daily contribution
of nine cows' milk, which was always placed for it at the green hill,
and in default of which it devoured man and beast. Young Lambton had, it seems, meanwhile, totally repented him of his former
life and conversation ; had bathed himself in a bath of holy water,
taken the sign of the cross, and joined the Crusaders. On his
return home he was extremely shocked at witnessing the effects of
his youthful imprudences, and immediately undertook the adventure. After several fierce combats, in which the Crusader was foiled
by his enemy's *power of self-union*, he found it expedient to add
policy to courage, and not perhaps possessing much of the former
quality, he went to consult a witch, or wise woman. By her judicious advice, he armed himself in a coat of mail studded with razor
blades ; and thus prepared, placed himself on the crag in the river,
and awaited the monster's arrival. At the usual time the Worm
came to the rock, and wound himself with great fury round the
armed knight, who had the satisfaction to see his enemy cut in
pieces by his own efforts, whilst the stream washing away the se-
vered parts, prevented the possibility of re-union. There is still a

---

* " The tradition, however, is not constant as to young Lambton, the hero of
the tale, being the original fisherman. The transgression is sometimes attributed to a wicked *quidam*, with many vulgar additions.

sequel to the story: the witch had promised Lambton success only on one condition, that he should slay the first living thing which met his sight after the victory. To avoid the possibility of human slaughter, Lambton had directed his father, that as soon as he heard him sound three blasts on his bugle, in token of the achievement performed, he should release his favourite greyhound, which would immediately fly to the sound of the horn, and was destined to be the sacrifice. On hearing his son's bugle, however, the old chief was so overjoyed that he forgot the injunctions, and ran himself with open arms to meet his son. Instead of committing a parricide, the conqueror again repaired to his adviser, who pronounced, as the alternative of disobeying the original instructions, that no chief of the Lambtons should die in his bed for seven, or (as some accounts say) for nine generations—a commutation which to a martial spirit had nothing probably very terrible, and which was willingly complied with.

" The story, such as it is, full of plot and incident, certainly ranks amongst the most popular traditions of this country, and has been transmitted, with very little variation, for centuries from father to son ; and various facts have been pressed into the service, to establish the commination of sudden death that has been supposed to hang over the family. The date of the story is of course uncertain ; but nine ascending generations from the late General Lambton (in whom popular tradition affirmed the curse to expire) would exactly reach to Sir John Lambton, knight of Rhodes, of whom this curious entry stands in an old MS. pedigree, lately in the possession of the family of Middleton, of Offerton :—

" ' Johan Lambeton that slewe yᵉ Worme was knight of Rhoodes and Lord of Lambeton and Wod Apilton efter the dethe of fower brothers sans esshewe masle. His son Robert Lampton was drowned at Newebrigg.' That the knight ever succeeded to the family estates, however, contradicts the proven pedigree.

" The Worm Hill stands not within the domain of Lambton, but on the north bank of the Wear, in the estate of North Biddick, a mile and a half, it may be, from *old* Lambton Hall. The Hill is a small artificial cone, formed of common earth and river gravel. The

Worm Well lies betwixt the Hill and the Wear.* Half a century ago, the Worm Well was in repute as a *Wishing Well*, and was one of the scenes dedicated to the usual festivities and superstitions of Midsummer eve ; a *crooked pin* may sometimes be still discovered, sparkling amongst the clear gravel at the bottom of its basin.†

"The Lambton Worm belongs to a class of household tales, the genuine appendages of ancient families long occupying the same ground and station ; and perhaps no other certain deduction can be drawn from such legends, excepting that the families to which they relate are of ancient popular reputation, against whose gentle condition ' the memory of man runneth not to the contrary.' Sometimes, indeed, the tale relates to the founder of the family, the true story of whose establishment being long forgotten, tradition has thrown a misty halo round his brows. Like the preux chevalier of romance, the *homo propositus* of the name goes forth to slay wolf, bear, or wivern ; and if on his return he does not marry the king's daughter, he at least receives broad lands and livings as his guerdon. To this class belong the Worm of Sockburn, the Brawn of Pollard's Dene (both which have faulchion evidence), the Boar of Kentmere, and that other Brawn of Brancepath, whom Roger de Fery slew treacherously in a pit-fall at Cleves Cross.‡ But the Lambtons

---

* " The Worm Well had formerly a cover, and an iron dish or ladle."

† " Distance from the Hill to the Well, 26 yards ; from the Well to the River, 48 yards."—C.S.

‡ "And exactly in point is that Worm of Linton, in Roxburghshire, whom the wily Scotch knight (said to be one of the Somervilles), watching when the wind was in the right quarter, slew, with a sod of blazing peat on the point of his spear, which answered the double purpose of stifling the monster, and preserving the assailant from the effects of its pestilent breath ; the achievement is still visible in stone, over the south door of Linton Church, ' a rude sculpture, representing a knight with a falcon on his arm, encountering with his lance, in full career, a sort of monster, which the people call *a Worm*.'—*Border Minstrelsy ; notes to Kempion*.

> ' The wode Laird of Lariestoun
> Slew the wode worme of Wormistoune,
> And wan all Linton paroschine.'   " The

were a family of good and valorous repute long before the date of their family legend (which only ascends to the fourteenth century); and it does not appear that the hero of the tale reaped anything from his adventure, except the honour of the achievement, and a very singular curse on his descendants to the ninth generation."

DESCRIPTION OF THE RESIDENCE OF JOHN SOANE, ARCHITECT;

With some general Remarks on the State of Architecture in England in the Nineteenth Century, and on the Qualifications and Duties of an Architect; &c., &c., &c. — Description of the House and Museum on the north side of Lincoln's-inn Fields, the Residence of John Soane, Professor of Architecture in the Royal Academy, &c., &c.

London: Printed by James Moyes, Took's-court, Chancery-lane. M.DCCC.XXX. 4*to.* pp. 56.

The residence of Sir John Soane, R.A., in Lincoln's Inn Fields, is well known to contain the most important collection of sculpture and specimens of architecture ever collected by one individual; which the owner, under certain restrictions, bequeathed to the British nation.

" The title *Worm* was certainly used with great latitude; Dante calls that venerable quadruped Cerberus, *Il gran Verme inferno.*

" One would suppose, that sometimes the sculpture said to commemorate the legend has, vice versâ, given rise to the fable. At Kirkby-Stephen, the first Lord Wharton (who won his title by hard blows with the Scotch) sleeps in effigy on an altar tomb, and presses with his feet the family crest, a bull's head; and this bull's head is in popular opinion thought to represent the Devil, and to allude to some very ghastly encounter sustained by the gallant Warden of the Borders, against the common Enemy of Man."

The following plates accompany this volume :—

Recollections of the Character of
Henry Hoyle Oddie, Esq.

> Strongest minds
> Are often those of whom the noisy world
> Hears least ; else surely this man had not left
> His graces unrevealed and unproclaimed.
> But as the mind was filled with inward light,
> So not without distinction had he lived,
> Beloved and honoured far as he was known.
> And something that may serve to set in view
> The doings, observations, which his mind
> Had dealt with—I will here record.—*Wordsworth.*

Private impression.   M.DCCC.XXX.   *8vo.*   pp. *23.*

Prefixed is a portrait of Mr. Oddie, who was auditor, during forty-five years, to the noble family of Montagu ; and died at Barnwell Castle, a seat of that family, July 27, 1830, in the 87th year of his age.

An Historical and Genealogical Account of the Noble Family of Neville, particularly the House of Abergavenny ; And also a History of the old Barony of Abergavenny ; with some Account of the illustrious Family of the Beauchamps, and others, through whom it descended to the present Earl of Abergavenny ; accompanied with Notices of the Castles, Seats, and Estates, belonging to the Family, and their Heraldic honours.

By Daniel Rowland, Esq.

London: Printed by S. Bentley. 1830. *folio.* pp. 227. Appendix, pp. xxi. At the end of the work, four large Genealogical Tables, marked i–iv.

This volume is compiled by Daniel Rowland, Esq. To all readers of English history, the name of Neville is familiar ; and until the close of the reign of the Tudors, few events of historical importance occurred, without the association of the names of some of this aspiring and powerful family. The distinguished and able historian of Durham, speaking of this noble race, remarks : "The Earls of Westmoreland, though extremely powerful, possessed only the natural influence of their high rank and extended property, and remained uniformly loyal to the reigning line ; whilst the issue of their father's second bed, the Nevills of Salisbury and Warwick, soared to the highest offices of the state, and were the chief agents in the destruction of their kindred blood of Lancaster. Salisbury, Warwick, and Montagu, perished in the storm which they had raised ; and their blood, mingled with that of Plantagenet, flowed on the scaffold, under the Tudors.   The succeeding age saw the House of Westmoreland plunged in irretrievable ruin : and now, of all this stately-branching cedar, whose boughs once shadowed the land, the line of Abergavenny, not distinguished in the modern Peerage either by superior titles or splendid fortunes, alone remains."—I. lvii.

It is to be regretted that the plates are not executed in a manner more worthy the character of the noble House, and the design of the valuable work which they are intended to illustrate.   The following is a list of them :—

Right Hon. Henry Neville, second and present Earl, and forty-fourth Baron, of Abergavenny, K.T. ; anno 1830 ; facing the title-page.

Charles Nevill, the sixth and last Earl of Westmoreland ; page 44.

Seals of the Nevill Family ; Plate I.—marked 1, 3, 4, 7 ; page 70.

Seals of the Nevill Family ; Plate II.—marked 2, 5, 6, 8 ; page 70.

Richard Nevill, Earl of Warwick ; page 78.

George Nevill, Lord Bergavenny, K.G., ob. 1535; page 143.

Henry Nevill, Lord Bergavenny, ob. 1586; page 147.

Lady Bergavenny; page 147.

Raby Castle, Durham ; page 189.

Branspeth Castle, Durham ; page 197.

Abergavenny Castle, Monmouthshire ; page 208.

Eridge Castle, Kent ; the residence of the present Earl.

Of Eridge Castle, Mr. Rowland says,—"The castle, as a dwelling, may be said to be possessed of much elasticity in its construction. It is calculated to hold a very large establishment ; and it is a place, at the same time, in the arrangement of its apartments, well adapted to afford great domestic comfort to a more limited family.   It is situated in a well wooded and watered park, containing above three thousand acres of land.   It is surrounded by an ample demesne of ten thousand acres.   It is laid out in rides and drives, which measure fifty-four miles.   In one direction, from Tonbridge Wells to Rotherfield, the demesne is seven miles, and from east to west five miles long."

PIECES OF POETRY; WITH TWO DRAMAS.

Privately printed.

Chiswick : Printed by C. Whittingham, College House. M.DCCC.XXX. *2 vols.* 12*mo.*

After the title is a leaf, containing the following note :—

" No one can entertain a less favourable opinion of these trifles than their author, who has had them privately printed, merely for the satisfaction of his family, and of a few partial friends.— G. W. T."

Prefixed is a portrait of the author, Mr. Watson Taylor. Painted by George Sanders ; engraved by Edward Scriven. The " PROFLI- GATE," mentioned in page 270, is here reprinted.

ABSTRACT OF THE CHARTERS AND OTHER PAPERS RECORDED IN THE CHARTULARY OF TORPHICHEN, FROM 1581 TO 1596.

Edinburgh : M.DCCC.XXX. *small* 4*to.* pp. 35. Preface, pp. x.

Thirty-five copies were printed for John B. Gracie, Esq., Writer to the Signet ; with an introductory notice by James Maidment, Esq., advocate.

A similar tract is entitled—

NOTES OF CHARTERS, ETC., BY THE RIGHT HON. THOMAS, EARL OF MELROSE, AFTERWARDS EARL OF HADDINGTON, TO THE VASSALS OF THE BARONY OF DREIM, FROM 1615 TO 1627.

Edinburgh. M.DCCC.XXX. 4*to.* pp. 12. Preface, pp. iv.

Thirty-five copies were printed by Mr. Gracie.

D D

REGISTRUM CARTARUM PRIORATUS TUTTEBURIENSIS.
MS. No. LIX. INTER CODICES ARUNDELIANOS IN
BIBLIOTHECA FECIALIUM LONDINI ASSERVATUM. — RE-
GISTRUM CARTARUM PRIORATUS DE NOVO LOCO. MS.
No. LX. INTER CODICES ARUNDELIANOS IN BIBLIO-
THECA COLLEGII FECIALIUM LONDINI ASSERVATUM.
Royal 8vo. pp. 26.

These two tracts are in fact embodied in the Arundel Catalogue,
mentioned at page 384: they give the titles of the instruments
contained in the respective chartularies; the rubrics of the MSS.
themselves having only been used where they were sufficiently
comprehensive.

The Chartularies of Tutbury Priory and Newstead Abbey, being
exceedingly curious and valuable, a few copies of these tracts were
printed in this separate form, and distributed by Sir Charles Young
among friends, to whom the contents were more immediately interesting.

———

A LETTER ON THE BELGIC REVOLUTION.
JUNE, 1831.
(BY SLVAIN VAN DE WEYER.)
1831. *8vo.*

Privately printed. The author is Ambassador at the Court of St.
James's; an ardent encourager of literary pursuits.

———

BIBLIOGRAPHICAL NOTICES OF SOME EARLY
EDITIONS OF THE ORLANDO INNAMORATO AND FURIOSO.
London: William Pickering. 1831. *12mo.*

Twenty-four copies only of these Notices have been taken off, for
private distribution, from the "Orlando Innamorato" and "Furioso," published by Mr. Pickering.—A. PANIZZI.

One copy on vellum is in Mr. Grenville's library. See Brunet's notice of the plagiarism of which he thought himself accused in the Grenville catalogue.

––––––––

First Part:

On the Advantages of substituting an Income Tax for the present Taxes.

Second Part:

On the Objections to the plan of the late Property Tax, and on Modifications of it; and on the different Plans of an Income or Property Tax.

Third Part:

On the superior Means afforded by an Income or Property Tax, of reducing the National Debt.

Appendix, Estimates of Income, Scales of Charge, &c., &c.

Printed by F. Thorogood, Grocers'-hall-court, Poultry, London. 1831. *8vo.* pp. 317; Appendix, pp. 63.

"Although the writer of the following pages communicates them through the press, yet as he is desirous to confine the distribution of them within a particular limit, so it is his earnest wish that his production may not be considered as a publication seeking general notice."

––––––––

A History, Antiquarian and Statistical, of the Parish of Great Totham, in the County of Essex. By George W. Johnson, F.L.S., etc.

Great Totham: Printed for private circulation only, by Charles Clark. 1831. *8vo.* pp. 62.

Frontispiece: a view of Great Totham Church, engraved on wood; from a drawing by Miss Hayler.

The Genealogy of the most Noble and Ancient House of Drummond. By the Honourable William Drummond, afterwards Viscount of Strathallan. m.dc.lxxxi. Edinburgh. m.dccc.xxxi. Printed by A. Balfour and Co. 4to. pp. 331.

" The Genealogie of the most Noble and Ancient House of Drummond ;

" Containing a true Accompt of the original Extractione, the Offspring, and Allayes of that Family; deduced from the first of that Name, ane Hungarian gentleman, and continowed to the present Age.

" By a Friend to Vertue and the Family.

" The memory of the just is blessed : but the name of the wicked shall rot."—*Prov.* x. 7.

" Stemmata quid faciunt ? quid prodest, Pontice, longo Sanguine censeri."—*Juven.*

" Satius est me meis rebus gestis florere, quam majorum opinione niti, et ita vivere ut sim posteris nobilitatis et virtutis exemplum."—*Cicero.*

" Collected in the year 1681.

" Nobility is that which cannot be bought ; for it consists in a high descent, and undegenerat race of Ancient Worthies, more adorned with eminent vertues than riches or outward pomp."—*Hathornden, in Epist. ad Com. Perth.*

In the preface it is stated, " The present genealogical history, which is now printed for the first time, was compiled in the year 1681, and has always been esteemed a work of authority. The Hon. William Drummond, youngest son of John, second Lord Maderty, was raised to the dignity of the peerage, on the 6th of September,

1686, by the title of Viscount of Strathallan. In the Appendix is inserted an account of the family, written by William Drummond of Hawthornden, the celebrated poet, which was thought worthy of preservation, as a literary relique. The impression of this volume, which is intended for private circulation, is limited to one hundred copies." It was edited by Mr. David Laing, Librarian to the writers to the Signet.

THE SHERIFFS OF SHROPSHIRE, WITH THEIR AR-
MORIAL BEARINGS; AND NOTICES, GENEALOGICAL AND
BIOGRAPHICAL, OF THEIR FAMILIES.
By the late REV. JOHN BRICKDALE BLAKEWAY, M.A.,
F.A.S., Minister of St. Mary's, Shrewsbury.
Shrewsbury: Printed by William and John Eddowes,
Corn-market. 1831. *folio.* Title, Preface, &c., 4 leaves;
Sheriffs, pp. 1-245; alphabetical Index of the Sheriffs,
on page 246; Index of Persons and principal matters,
7 leaves.

On the title a view of the old Town Hall, Shrewsbury, which was taken down in 1784. There are large and small paper copies of this volume.

Mr. J. B. Blakeway, in conjunction with Mr. H. Owen, was author of a "History of Shrewsbury," 2 vols. 4*to.* London, 1825.

PAPERS ELUCIDATING THE CLAIM OF
SIR AUGUSTUS D'ESTE, K.C.H.
London. 1831. 8*vo.* pp. 38.

The peculiar interest of the question discussed in this volume, as relating perhaps remotely to the succession of the Hanoverian crown, has procured for it some considerable attention. It was privately printed and circulated, with a view to put the friends of Sir Augustus d'Este in possession of the opinions of Dr. Lushington and Mr. Richards, respecting the marriage of his Royal Highness the Duke of Sussex to Lady Augusta Murray, at Rome, in 1793. That marriage was dissolved by the Court of Arches in 1794. Some additional evidence respecting it having been obtained by Sir Augustus d'Este (not formerly before the Court of Arches), which induced him to consider that a marriage beyond sea, and out of the jurisdiction either of the British Crown or British Parliament, was not affected by the Royal Marriage Act of 12 Geo. III., he submitted a case to those learned counsel ; who, after " great consideration," have pronounced their opinion, that the Act in question does not extend to marriages of the descendants of George II., solemnized *bonâ fide* out of Great Britain, and beyond the limits of British jurisdiction ; and that the marriage at Rome was *not* impeachable under that statute.

The subject having attracted public attention, this volume was reprinted for sale in 1832, and published with another, entitled, " The Case of the Children of His Royal Highness the Duke of Sussex, elucidated : a Juridical Exercitation, by Sir John Dillon, Knt. and Bn. S.R.E. London. 1832." 4*to.* pp. 53. A copy of the original edition, with an autograph letter, was in the Stowe Library, No. 1634.

A Narrative
of the French Expedition to Dantzig, in 1734.
Edinburgh. M.DCCC.XXXI. 4*to.* pp. 84 ; Dedication, and Prefatory Notes, pp. xl.

Printed at the expense of the late Alexander Henderson, Esq., of Edinburgh : it is inscribed to the late M. Pancoucke, the celebrated publisher at Paris, and is lavish in ardent praise of the French Revolution of that time.

A printed leaf, prefixed to the work, states as follows :—

"Of this edition, fifty-eight copies have been printed on paper, and four on vellum.

"One copy on vellum, for M. Pancoucke; one for the Royal Library, Paris ; and two copies with the Editor.

"Thirty copies on paper to M. Pancoucke ; twenty-seven with the Editor ; and one with the Printer."

LETTER TO LORD PALMERSTON BY A FORMER DE-PUTY OF THE BELGIAN CONGRESS SENT TO LONDON IN 1831, TO TREAT WITH PRINCE LEOPOLD OF SAXE-COBOURG.

By COUNT FELIX DE MERODE.

1831.   8vo.

GLANCES AT VARIOUS OBJECTS,

During a Nine Weeks' Ramble through Parts of France, Switzerland, Piedmont, Austrian Lombardy, Venice, Carinthia, the Tyrol, Schaffhausen, the Banks of the Rhine, and Holland.

By RICHARD HOLLIER.

"Let him also keep a diary. Let him not stay long in one city or town, more or less as the place deserveth: but not long."—*Bacon's Essay on Travel.*

For private distribution only.

London : Printed by James Moyes, Took's-court, Chancery-lane. M.DCCC.XXXI. 4to. pp. 244.

One hundred copies were printed.

EXAMINATION OF THE CLAIM OF JOHN LINDSAY CRAU-
FURD TO THE TITLE AND ESTATES OF CRAUFURD AND
LINDSAY, WITH REFUTATION OF "THE CRAUFURD
PEERAGE," ETC.
1831.   4to.

By James Dobie, Esq. A very clever *exposé* of the claim of John
Lindsay Craufurd to the Craufurd and Lindsay titles, who, after
having been tried and convicted of forging documents to support
his pretensions, after his return from Botany Bay again resumed
operations.

———

REPORT ON THE MILITARY EXPENDITURE OF THE
HONOURABLE EAST INDIA COMPANY, ADDRESSED TO
MAJOR-GENERAL THE HONOURABLE SIR JOHN MAL-
COLM, G.C.B.
By LIEUT.-COLONEL EDWARD FREDERICK.
London: Printed by Richard Taylor, Red-Lion-court,
Fleet-street. 1831. [Not for sale.] *folio.* pp. 137.

The document is intended only for private distribution among a
select few.

———

OF THE VOCATION OF OUR AGE FOR LEGISLATION
AND JURISPRUDENCE.
Translated from the German of Frederick Charles von
Savigny, by ABRAHAM HAYWARD.
London: Printed by Littlewood and Co., Old Bailey.
Not for sale. [1831.] *8vo.* pp. 192.

This translation is by Abraham Hayward, of the Inner Temple,
Esq., Barrister-at-Law : translator of the "Faust" of Goethe in prose.

Thoughts on Orkney and Zetland, their Antiquities, and capabilities of Improvement; With Hints towards the formation of a Local Society for the investigation and promotion of these Objects; to to which are annexed, Extracts from curious Manuscripts, together with useful Lists.

Not printed for sale.

Edinburgh: Printed by Neill and Co. M.DCCC.XXXI. 8vo. pp. 47.

Sketch-book of Inigo Jones.

1831. 8vo.

A fac-simile of the original, in the possession of his Grace the Duke of Devonshire; executed in lithography at the expense of his Grace. One hundred copies only were printed; which have been liberally distributed among the friends of the noble owner of the original manuscript.

The editor feels that the best account he can give of this very curious volume, will be found in the subjoined letter from Mr. Collier, addressed to the late Thomas Amyot, Esq., Treasurer of the Society of Antiquaries.

"23, *Hunter-street, Brunswick-square,*
"*Dec.* 22, 1831.

"My dear Sir,

"I am directed by the Duke of Devonshire to present to the Society of Antiquaries a Fac-simile of the Sketch-book of Inigo Jones; and I may with peculiar propriety make you the medium of this communication, inasmuch as his Grace in the first instance, and as a personal testimony, gave you a copy of it. The original is a relic of extraordinary value and curiosity, consisting of drawings in pen and ink, with accompanying illustrative remarks and general observations, entirely by the hand of the architect of the Banquet-

ing House at Whitehall ; and it affords evidence of the great diligence, as well as of the skill and taste of the author. It was made
while he was in Italy, in the year 1614.

" The Sketches are not only from statues and reliefs, but from
pictures by the most celebrated masters of the Italian schools ; and
the motto chosen by this distinguished man, and prefixed to his
Sketch-book, supplies an interesting characteristic, shewing that at
the age of forty-two, Inigo Jones thought himself happy only while
he was improving his taste, enlarging his mind, and laying in fresh
stores of science—

' *Altro diletto che imparar non trovo.*'

" Another circumstance connected with this production deserves
notice. It is known that Inigo Jones evinced his earliest fondness
for the arts in Landscape Painting, and in the Duke of Devonshire's
collection at Chiswick is a rare specimen of his skill in this department. Although Inigo Jones had been appointed Architect to the
King of Denmark before the year 1606, the Sketch-book does not
contain a single design, hint, or note, of or for any building, public
or private ; while it is obvious from every page, that the author was
studying the human figure with great care, and delineating the features of the human face in minute detail. Hence it would seem,
that in 1614 he was devoting his attention very much to painting
and sculpture ; as if anxious to supply deficiencies of which he was
aware, and as if this, his second visit to the Continent, had been
undertaken chiefly with that purpose. It will be seen that nothing
was too great for his ambition, nothing too insignificant for his observation—from the Last Judgment of Michael Angelo to the sim-
plest folds of drapery.

" The Sketch-book of Inigo Jones also serves to clear up a point
in his biography ; of the more importance, because it has relation
to his quarrel with Ben Jonson. On the first page it bears the date
of ' Rome, 1614,' which at once settles the question disputed by Mr.
Gifford and Mr. A. Chalmers, whether the disagreement between
Inigo Jones and Ben Jonson ' commenced in 1614.' Of course, it
could not ' commence ' while Inigo Jones was in Italy ; and the

hostility certainly did not break out until a much later period, viz. Christmas, 1631-2. Inigo Jones at that date took offence that Ben Jonson had omitted his name on the title-page of the Masque of ' Chloridia,' on the preparations and scenery for which Inigo Jones had been engaged. This circumstance establishes that Ben Jonson had no reference to Inigo Jones, in his ' Bartholomew Fair,' acted in 1614, the very year when Inigo Jones was in Italy, while it tends to fix upon him the ridicule contained in ' The Tale of a Tub,' which was performed in 1633.

" The precise date when Inigo Jones returned to England has not been ascertained, but his departure has been erroneously stated to have taken place in 1612. It appears by a Privy Seal, published by me in ' The Annals of the Stage, and History of Dramatic Poetry,' that Inigo Jones was engaged in January, 1612-13, in making arrangements for a Masque at Court. He probably left this country soon afterwards.

" The Sketch-book is only a very small part of the valuable remains connected with the life and reputation of Inigo Jones, transmitted to the Duke of Devonshire by the celebrated Earl of Burlington. Inigo Jones, with some interruptions in consequence of absence from England, superintended most of the court entertainments, from the accession of James the First to the commencement of the Civil Wars ; and at Devonshire House are preserved the original designs, not only of the scenes but of the characters, for the Masques at the different royal residences. The details of all the fantastic habiliments are given with the utmost minuteness, both as to form and colour ; and the sketches for large views of rocks, waterfalls, woods, palaces, or temples, illustrate most remarkably the contrivances for the representation of those splendid shows which were the peculiar delight of our first Stuart, and of his unfortunate successor.

" With regard to the execution of the Fac-simile which accompanies this letter, as I carefully watched its progress through the hands of the lithographer, I may be allowed to say that it is both faithful and spirited, and that it gives an exact notion, externally and internally, of the original. Having gone over the pages of the manuscript while it was in my custody, you also can bear testimony to the accuracy of the imitation.

" The impressions were limited very far below the demands upon the liberality of the Duke of Devonshire; but his Grace felt that antiquaries must take a peculiar interest in the subject; and, although not himself a member, his known attachment to the objects of this Society, and his strong desire to promote them, have induced his Grace to send a copy for its acceptance.

" I am, dear Sir, your sincere and obliged,

"J. PAYNE COLLIER."

BIBLIOTHECÆ COLFANÆ CATALOGUS.

Catalogue of the Library of the Free Grammar School at Lewisham, founded by the Reverend Abraham Colfe, M.A.

BY WILLIAM HENRY BLACK.

Printed by order of the Worshipful Company of Leather-sellers of the City of London, Governors of the Grammar School. M.DCCC.XXXI. 8vo. pp. 176; Preface and Memorials, pp. lvi.

A view of the School at Lewisham, C. Hill delineavit, faces the title-page; the arms of the Company, those of the Rev. A. Colfe, prefixed to a pedigree; a fac-simile specimen of his handwriting; a vignette view of his Almshouses, with an impression of the book-plate of the Library; and two pages of fac-similes of autographs, illustrating the Memorials, will be found in the work. The introductory pages contain Memorials of the family of Colfe, and of the life and character of the founder of the Library, as also a list of benefactors to the Library. " The books consist chiefly of old Bibles and commentaries, the works of the Fathers and other theologians, historians, classics, grammarians, and critics." * In the examination

---

* Gentleman's Magazine, October, 1832.

before the Commissioners of Charities, it was stated that some of the books were valuable, but the only one mentioned is Walton's Polyglott. Seven years ago the Company put the collection into good bindings. No books had been added since the witness who was examined by the Commissioners, was master. Twenty shillings a year is left by the founder's will for increasing the library.

The Pitney Pavement,

Discovered by Samuel Hasell, Esq., of Littleton, A.D. 1828; and illustrated with his Notes,

By Sir Richard Colt Hoare, Bart.

Crocker, Printer, Frome. 1831.   8*vo.*   pp. 20.

At the back of the title, "fifty copies, not printed for sale."

Plate I. Roman Villa at Littleton; S. Hassell, del.; J. Basire, sculp.

Plate II. Mosaic Pavements at Pitney.

Plate III. Roman Villa at Pitney; marked Plan II.

Plate IV. Baths at Pitney; marked Plan III.

Nine plates engraved in outline, marked Figures I—IX.

Two Heads, inscribed, "in the four angles," on one plate.

Two plates, with four figures, marked Figures A—D.

A second edition, for sale, has been published by Messrs. Nichols and Son.

Travels in Russia, Persia, Turkey, and Greece, in 1828–9,

By Thomas Alcock, Esq.

[Not published.] London: Printed by E. Clarke and Son, Well-street. 1831. 8*vo.* pp. 227.

Plate, Cavern of Makoo; drawn and engraved by W. Daniell, R.A.: and a map of the country, by Arrowsmith.

The author says, in his preface, that he " shall neither fatigue the reader with remarks on places and antiquities which have already been described at full length by former travellers, nor shall I lead him stage by stage through the provinces of the Rhine and Austria, but rather at once conduct him to the less frequented parts of my tour."

———

ESSAYS,

By the late ROBERT HAMILTON, LL.D., F.R.S.E., Professor of Mathematics in the Marischal College, and University of Aberdeen.

Aberdeen: Printed by D. Chalmers and Co. M.DCCC.XXXI. 8vo. pp. 217.

" The following three Essays by the late Dr. Hamilton, are printed for distribution among the friends of the author. The Essay on *Peace and War* was published anonymously, in the year 1790 ; and has long been very rare. *On the Management of the Poor* was published in 1822, when an idea was entertained of establishing poor rates in the city of Aberdeen. The *Essay on Government* was written during the progress of the French Revolution."

———

STATUTES AND ORDINANCES
OF THE MOST ILLUSTRIOUS ORDER OF ST. PATRICK.

Dublin: Printed by G. A. and J. F. Grierson, Printers to the King's Most Excellent Majesty. 1831. 12mo. pp. 151.

These Statutes were first printed in 1809 ; again in 1814, with the additional Statutes ; making pp. 112; and to this edition, printed in 1831, with two additional warrants issued since, is added a list of the grand masters and knights from the foundation of the order.

MEMOIR OF THE LIFE OF THOMAS YOUNG,

M.D., F.R.S.,

Foreign Associate of the Royal Institute of France,

&c., &c.

With a Catalogue of his Works and Essays.

London :   John   and   Arthur   Arch,   Cornhill.

M.DCCC.XXXI. *Royal 8vo.* pp. 62.

This Memoir was drawn up by Hudson Gurney, Esq., V.P.S.A. ; it is prefixed to the late Dr. Young's Egyptian Dictionary. A few copies of the Life were printed separately, on royal octavo size, for private distribution.

Record Commission.

On the accession of William IV., a new commission was issued under the great seal, appointing Commissioners to inquire into the state of Public Records, and to take measures for their more convenient use and better preservation. The proceedings of the old Commission had long been subjected, through the press, to strong animadversions. Considerable abuses had no doubt prevailed under the old system ; and a most extravagant expenditure had taken place. The appointment of a new Commission, with a new Secretary, naturally induced some inquiry as to the proceedings of the former one, and into the conduct and remuneration of the parties employed under it. Such inquiry, as might be expected, led to charges and explanations, which appeared in the form of letters and pamphlets, addressed chiefly to the Commissioners in general, or to individual Members of the Board. As some of them contain valuable information connected with the Public Records, and the subject being, in every way, interesting and important to the public in general, the Editor has obtained an account of such as were privately printed, either by order of the Board, by the Secretary, or by the authors of the different pamphlets. The impressions, in most cases, were very limited in number, and confined to private circulation. Upon the merits or demerits of the several questions agitated, it is neither necessary nor within the scope of the Editor's work to enter.*

1. RECORD COMMISSION.

On the back of the title :—

" Printed for the use of the Commissioners.

" *May*, 1832.   " C. P. COOPER, *Sec.*"

8*vo.*   pp. 14.

This is merely a copy of the commission, dated 12th March, 1831, printed for the members, whose names are prefixed, viz :—

William, Lord Archbishop of Canterbury.

Henry, Lord Brougham and Vaux, Lord Chancellor.

William, Viscount Melbourne, Secretary of State for the Home Department (or Secretary of State for the time being).

Rt. Hon. Charles Manners Sutton, Speaker (or Speaker of the House of Commons for the time being).

Rt. Hon. John Charles Spencer, commonly called Viscount Althorp, Chancellor of the Exchequer (or Chancellor and Under Treasurer of the Exchequer for the time being).

Rt. Hon. Sir John Leach, Master of the Rolls (or Master for the time being).

William Dundas, Lord Clerk Register of Scotland (or Lord Clerk Register for the time being).

George John, Earl Spencer, K.G.

George, Earl of Aberdeen.

Edward, Bishop of Llandaff.

Rt. Hon. Thomas Grenville.

Rt. Hon. Charles Watkin Williams Wynne.

Rt. Hon. Sir James Mackintosh.

Rt. Hon. Henry Hobhouse.

Rt. Hon. George Agar Ellis (afterward created Lord Dover).

Sir James Parke, Justice of the King's Bench.

Sir John Bernard Bosanquet, Justice of Common Pleas.

---

* In the Gentleman's Magazine, April, 1804, there will be found some information relative to the proceedings of the old and new Commissions.

Sir Robert Harry Inglis, Bart.
Louis Hayes Petit, Esq.
Henry Bellenden Ker, Esq.
Henry Hallam, Esq.
John Allen, Esq.
Edward Protheroe, Esq.
Edward Vernon Utterson, Esq.
William Brougham, Esq.

2. OBSERVATIONS ON THE PUBLIC RECORDS OF THE FOUR COURTS AT WESTMINSTER, AND ON THE MEASURES RECOMMENDED BY THE COMMITTEE OF THE HOUSE OF COMMONS IN 1800, FOR RENDERING THEM MORE ACCESSIBLE TO THE PUBLIC.

Drawn up by the desire of his Majesty's Commissioners on the Public Records.

BY WILLIAM ILLINGWORTH, of the Hon. Society of Gray's Inn, F.S.A., and late Deputy Keeper of his Majesty's Records in the Tower.

8vo.　pp. 67.

Fifty copies ordered by the Commissioners to be printed for their use, 20th May, 1831.

3. REPORT OF THE COMMITTEE, ON THE " REPORT," " ADDITIONAL STATEMENT," AND " LETTER," OF MR. PALGRAVE.

May, 1831.　　　　　　　　　　　　8<i>vo.</i>　pp. 31.

Fifty copies printed for the use of the Commissioners, June, 1832.

4. REPORT OF THE COMMITTEE, ON THE MODE OF REMUNERATING THE SUB-COMMISSIONERS.

May 13, 1831.　　　　　　　　　　　8<i>vo.</i>　pp. 15.

Fifty copies printed for the use of the Commissioners, June, 1832.

5. Observations on the Calendar of the Proceedings in Chancery, edited by John Bayley, Esq., F.R.S., and F.S.A.; and on the Parliamentary Writs, edited by Francis Palgrave, Esq., F.R.S., and F.S.A., under the Authority of the Record Commission.

To which is added, an Appendix of Illustrative Documents.

London. 1832.   8*vo.*   pp. 36.   Appendix, pp. lxx.

This statement is by the Secretary to the Commission, Charles Purton Cooper, Esq.

6. Papers relative to a Complaint made by the Editor of "The New Edition of the Rolls of Parliament."

London.   May 9th, 1832.   8*vo.*   pp. 24.

7. A Reply to those Portions of the Statement drawn up by C. P. Cooper, Esq., which relate to the Editor of the New Edition of the Rolls of Parliament; etc.

London.   9th May, 18th May, 1832.   8*vo.*

This is by Francis Palgrave, Esq.; and very few copies were said to have been circulated. From a Letter addressed to the Lord Chancellor by Sir Nicholas H. Nicolas (8*vo.* 1832), upon the subject of the Record Commission, it would appear that some copies extended to pp. 69, others to pp. 80.

8. AMPLIFICATION, BY HENRY COLE, OF MR. PAL-GRAVE'S EXPLANATORY NOTE, IN PAGES 66 AND 67 OF HIS REPLY.

9. OFFICE OF SECRETARY. — LETTER FROM MR. COOPER TO H. B. KER, ESQ., ONE OF THE COMMISSIONERS, ETC., ETC., ETC.
London. 13th June, 1832.   8*vo.* pp. 7.

This relates to the mode merely in which the duties of Secretary had been executed.

10. LETTER FROM FREDERICK DEVON, ONE OF THE CLERKS OF THE. CHAPTER HOUSE, WESTMINSTER, TO THE RIGHT HONOURABLE THE LORD CHANCELLOR, RESPECTING A FALSE AND CALUMNIOUS STATEMENT, PRINTED AND PRIVATELY CIRCULATED BY F. PAL-GRAVE, ESQ., F.R.S., F.S.A., AND BARRISTER-AT-LAW, AMONGST HIS MAJESTY'S COMMISSIONERS OF THE PUBLIC RECORDS.
9th June, 1832.   8*vo.* pp. 8.

11. A LETTER TO HIS MAJESTY'S COMMISSIONERS FOR PUBLIC RECORDS, IN ANSWER TO CERTAIN PASSAGES IN MR. PALGRAVE'S "REPLY TO THE STATEMENT OF THE SECRETARY TO THE COMMISSION, IN RESPECT TO THE PARLIAMENTARY WRITS."
BY THOMAS DUFFUS HARDY, F.S.A., Member of the Inner Temple, and one of the Clerks in the Record Office at the Tower.
12th June, 1832.   8*vo.* pp. 56.

12. REMARKS UPON THE " REPLY OF FRANCIS PAL-
GRAVE, ESQ., TO THOSE PORTIONS OF THE STATEMENTS
DRAWN UP BY MR. C. P. COOPER, WHICH RELATE TO
THE EDITOR OF THE NEW EDITION OF THE ROLLS OF
PARLIAMENT ; " ETC.

 London. June, 1832.   8vo. pp. 31.

 These remarks are by Mr. Cooper.

13. LETTER FROM THE RIGHT REV. THE BISHOP OF
LLANDAFF,* TO THE RIGHT HON. THE SPEAKER,
CHAIRMAN OF THE COMMITTEE UPON THE PARLIAMEN-
TARY WRITS.

 London. July, 1832.   8vo. pp. 13.

14. LETTER FROM EDWARD PROTHEROE, JUN., ESQ.,
M.P., TO THE SECRETARY, UPON THE CONTINUATION
OF SIR FRANCIS PALGRAVE'S EDITION OF THE PAR-
LIAMENTARY WRITS.

 London. September, 1832.   8vo. pp. 43.

 Mr. Protheroe is one of the Commissioners.

15. REPORT OF THE COMMITTEE APPOINTED BY THE
ORDER OF THE BOARD, DATED 30TH JUNE, 1832, TO
INQUIRE INTO THE CIRCUMSTANCES CONNECTED WITH
MR. BAYLEY'S PUBLICATION OF THE CALENDARS OF
THE PROCEEDINGS IN CHANCERY, AND HIS CHARGES
FOR THE SAME.

 London.   8vo. February, 1833.

 From the peculiar nature of the contents, twenty-five copies only

---

* Edward Copleston, D.D., one of the Commissioners.

have been printed, for the private use of the Right Honourable Members of the Board. The names of the Commissioners are pre-fixed; and in the copy which belongs to each, the name is there printed in red ink, as well as on the title-page. Why a Report of gentlemen named to inquire into the conduct of a public servant, and the expenditure of public money, should be *printed*, yet con-fined in its circulation to the Commissioners only, does not appear.

Proceedings of His Majesty's Commissioners on the Public Records of the Kingdom.
folio.   1832–1833.

Only twenty-five copies are printed, for the use of the Board. This work is said to be full of curious historical and archæological information; but as it is printed (like the House of Commons' papers) simply to facilitate the transaction of the public business of the Commissioners at their different meetings, if the number of copies printed corresponds with the number of the Commissioners, it seems not improbable that a perfect copy will be of very rare occurrence; a circumstance very much to be regretted.*

The Manner of Proceeding on Bills in the House of Lords.
Not intended for sale.
London: James and Luke G. Hansard and Sons, near Lincoln's-inn-Fields.   1831.   4*to*.   pp. 88.

By George Bramwell, Esq., of the Inner Temple, who has printed for sale a similar work with respect to proceedings in the House of Commons.

---

* The Editor had hoped that the list of the publications of the Record Com-mission would have had the benefit of the revision of Mr. Cooper, who supplied

DISSERTATION ON THE MANNER AND PERIOD OF THE
DEATH OF RICHARD II., KING OF ENGLAND;
Delivered from the Chair of the Royal Society of Li-
terature, at the Anniversary Meeting, on Friday, 4th
May, 1832.
BY THE RIGHT HON. LORD DOVER, President.
London: Printed by T. Brettell, Rupert-street, Hay-
market. M.DCCC.XXXII. 4to. pp. 20.

Fifty copies were printed on this size, for the noble author of the
Dissertation, for private distribution: to this nobleman, whose pre-
mature death has been generally lamented, the editor owed many
acts of personal kindness, and several important communications
to this volume. Lord Dover died 10th July, 1833.

———

THE SCROPE AND GROSVENOR ROLL.
De Controversia in Curia Militari, inter Ricardum Le
Scrope et Robertum Grosvenor, Milites: Rege Ricardo
Secundo, M.CCC.LXXXV.–M.CCC.XC.
1832. Imp. 8vo.

These beautiful volumes emanate from the press of Mr. SAMUEL
BENTLEY, and reflect high credit upon the typographical art.
The impression is strictly limited, and no copies are printed for
sale. The publication originated with a few individuals, who associated themselves together, and obtained a subscription for the pur-

———

him with the information which appeared in the first edition. That gentleman's
engagements have prevented his doing so.
In the Life of Lord Langdale by Mr. Hardy, vol. ii., will be found much information on the subject of the proper keeping of these valuable documents. Mr.
Hardy states it to be his intention to publish a History of the Public Records of
the Realm.

pose of presenting to the public, under the editorship of the late Sir Nicholas Harris Nicolas, this curious roll, accompanied by historical and biographical illustrations. Its subject is the celebrated dispute between Sir Richard Scrope and Sir Robert Grosvenor, in the reign of King Richard the Second, and which was carried on in the Court of Chivalry during a period of five years, with considerable spirit and perseverance by both parties, who enlisted on their respective sides as witnesses, some of the most distinguished knights and warriors who flourished in that age of chivalry.

Two volumes only are at present printed. The *first* contains a literal copy of the Roll, from the original in the Tower, with some relative documents, to which a title-page and Historical Introduction are promised, on the completion of the work. The *second*, which is complete (with the exception of a title-page), consists of a History of the House of Scrope, down to the reign of King Henry the Fourth, accompanied by pedigrees of the two leading Houses of Bolton and Masham, followed by biographical notices of the deponents in favour of Scrope, and a translation of the material parts of their depositions. The notices of Scrope's witnesses are not concluded in this volume; and the whole of those of Grosvenor remain to be produced.

The *third* volume, therefore (not yet, however, in the press), is intended to contain the conclusion of the notices of Scrope's deponents, as well as similar notices of those of Grosvenor; the latter to be preceded by an account of the ancient family of Grosvenor, and accompanied by other historical and illustrative notes.

The work, from its limited impression, must be always rare.*

The Vision.

London: James Fraser, 215, Regent-street. 1832. 12*mo.* pp. 283.

The editor is informed that this work was originally intended for

---

* A review of this work is in the Quarterly, vol. lvi. p. 1.

publication, but not more than four copies ever passed out of the publisher's hands. He has been unable to obtain a sight of a copy, or to ascertain the reasons for its being withdrawn.

HAMLET, AND AS YOU LIKE IT.
A specimen of an Edition of Shakespeare.
BY THOMAS CALDECOTT, ESQ.

Φασι δε και Αρατον πυθεσθαι αυτου, [Τιμωνος] πως την Ομηρου ποιησιν ασφαλως κτησαιτο· τον δε ειπειν, Ει τοις αρχαιοις αντιγραφοις εντυγχανοι, και μη τοις ηδη διωρθωμενοις.—*Diog. Laertii Timon.* Amst. 4to. 1698, p. 600.

"And surely, if men, by the help of that blessed art of correcting old copies, proceed to amend, and upon private fancie doe presumne thus to alter publike records, shortly wee shall have just cause generally to esteeme those copies most correct, which least have been corrected."—*Explication of a place in Polybius,* at the end of *Sir H. Savile's Tacitus,* Fo. 1622, p. 224, *John Bill.*

"Quæ in veteribus libris reperta mutare imperiti solent, dum Librariorum insectari inscitiam volunt, suam confitentur."—*Quint.* l. ix. c. iv.

London: Printed for the Editor, by William Nicol, Cleveland-row, St. James's. 1832. 8vo.

Title and Preface, pp. xvi. Hamlet, pp. 1–178; Notes, pp. 1–150. As you Like it, pp. 1–115; Notes, pp. 1–43.

Two hundred and fifty copies of this edition were printed, for private distribution. It contains considerable additions to that which was published for sale in 1820.

Mr. Caldecott's library, rich in early English poetry, was sold by auction, by Messrs. Sotheby, in 1833.

OUTLINES OF THE GEOGRAPHICAL DISTRIBUTION OF BRITISH PLANTS, BELONGING TO THE DIVISION OF VASCULARES, OR COTYLEDONES.

BY HENRY COTTRELL WATSON.

" With such a liberal hand, has nature flung their seeds abroad."

Edinburgh : Printed for private distribution.   [1832.] 12*mo.*   pp. 335.

" As this work is not to be purchased, it may to some readers seem unjust to occupy space in pointing it out to them. But not so ; for, to our botanical readers, no book more interesting, on British plants, has ever been published ; and it is, to the best of our knowledge, the most interesting book, in relation to them, which has been published these twenty years." *

———

NOTES OF THREE TOURS IN IRELAND IN 1824 AND 1826.

BY JAMES GLASSFORD, ESQ., Advocate, one of the late Commissioners of Inquiry into the State of Education in Ireland.

Bristol: Published by W. Strong, and J. Chilcott; and sold by Hamilton, Adams, and Co. London. 1832. 12*mo.* pp. viii. and 373.

In the advertisement it is stated, *The following sheets were printed about a year ago for private distribution.* . . . The volume is now offered to the public as at first printed in January, 1831, without

———

* Loudon, Magazine of Natural History, May, 1833.

any alteration, except a new title-page, and the addition of this advertisement.—J. G., Clifton, February, 1832.

Mr. Glassford, of Dugalston, in Dunbartonshire, admitted a member of the Faculty of Advocates, 1793, succeeded to Dugalston on the death of his elder brother ; and died at Edinburgh in July, 1845.

An Historical Account of his Majesty's First, or the Royal Regiment of Foot: General George Duke of Gordon, G.C.B., Colonel.
Compiled by Major Joseph Wetherall.
London: Printed by W. Clowes, 14, Charing Cross. M.DCCC.XXXII. *8vo.* pp. 225.

"*London, 26th June,* 1832.
" Gentlemen,

" A manuscript copy of the following historical account of the 'Royals,' having been presented to me by Major Wetherall, I have, as a mark of my approval of this valuable Memoir, been induced to order a few copies of it to be printed for your use ; and from the perusal of which I hope you will derive as much gratification as I feel pleasure in presenting it to you.

" I remain, Gentlemen,
" &c., &c.,

" The Officers of the First   " Gordon,
  (or the Royal) Regt."   " Colonel, the 'Royals.' "

The Spirit of the Age.
By Chandos Leigh, since Baron Leigh, of Stoneleigh.
1832.   *12mo.* pp. 45.

Lord Leigh published, also for private distribution, " Vasa," *8vo.* pp. 70 ; and " A Fragment," *8vo.* pp. 17.

Memorials of the Malignant Cholera in Oxford, 1832.

" ʼΕγὼ δὲ οἷόν τε ἐγίγνετο λέξω, καὶ ἀφ' ὧν ἄν τις σκο-
πῶν, εἴ ποτε καὶ αὖθις ἐπιπέσοι, μάλιστ' ἂν ἔχοι τι προειδὼς
μὴ ἀγνοεῖν.—*Thucyd.* lib. ii. cap. 48.

Oxford: Printed by W. Baxter. 1835. *oblong 4to.*
pp. xii., and 48.

By the Rev. Vaughan Thomas, B.D., with three engravings.

A Letter to Lord Viscount Goderich, on the
Patronage of the Arts by the English Government.

By William Wilkins, A.M., formerly Fellow of
Caius College, Cambridge, R.A. and F.R.S.

" Learning and science repay the State with usury
the assistance which the State affords to those who
profess and cultivate them."—*Necker, Comptes Ren-
dus,* i. 157.

London: Printed for J. Rodwell, New Bond-street.
1832. [Not published.] *8vo.* pp. 80.

This letter to the present Earl of Ripon has been reprinted, by
permission of the writer, in the "Annals of the Fine Arts," vol. iii.
It is very justly severe on the miserable economy displayed by this
country in the encouragement of the fine arts. Some remarks
having been made in the "Literary Gazette" upon Mr. Wilkins' proposed design for the National Gallery, that gentleman was induced
to make a very singular defence of his building, in the "Athenæum" of March 2, 1833: it called forth, naturally, many severe

remarks from his professional brethren ; among others, the following, which was printed by the author for private circulation :—

"Observations on the Communication of Mr. Wilkins to the
Editor of the ' Athenæum,' relative to the National Gallery. By
Joseph Gwilt, F.S.A., F.R.A.S., author of a Translation of Vitruvius,
&c., &c., &c.

"London : Printed for the Author, by George Woodfall, Angel-
court, Skinner-street. 1833." *8vo.* pp. 16.

A Biographical Memoir of the Right Hon. Wil-
liam Huskisson ; derived from authentic sources.
London : Printed by J. L. Cox, Great Queen-street,
Lincoln's-inn-Fields. 1831. *8vo.* pp. 275.

A portrait of this eminent statesman is prefixed, engraved by W.
Finden, from a picture by Sir Thomas Lawrence. The memoir is by
the late Mr. John Wright, many years Editor of " Hansard's Debates in Parliament."

Statement of the Issues used in the Court of
Session for the Trial of Civil Causes by Jury,
By Lord Chief Commissioner Adam.
With a prefatory Letter addressed to the Lord Chancellor.
1832. *8vo.* Statement, pp. 56 ; Appx. pp. 94 ; a duplicate page *15, 16. Title and preface, pp. 10.

A very valuable work. The following notice by the Commissioner,
of Mr. Justice Gould, coming from one who knew him, is valuable :—

" Gould was a very conscientious Judge. He never fancied that
because a jury differed from him they were therefore wrong. He
might think them wrong, but not because they differed from him."

CHRISTIANISM; OR, BELIEF AND UNBELIEF RECONCILED:
BEING EXERCISES AND MEDITATIONS.

" Mercy and truth have met together,
Righteousness and peace have kissed each other."

Not for sale; only seventy copies printed. (1832.)
8*vo.* pp. 59.

Said to be written by Mr. Leigh Hunt, when in Italy.

––––––––

OBSERVATIONS IN SUPPORT OF THE TITLE OF THE
KING, JURE DUCATUS, TO ALL ESCHEATS AND FOR-
FEITURES, ARISING WITHIN THE FEES OR LIBERTIES
OF THE DUCHY, OUT OF THE COUNTY PALATINE; 28TH
SEPTEMBER, 1831: AND STATEMENT OF THE CASE
OF THE BULMER ESCHEAT, WITHIN THE LIBERTY OF
THE SAVOY, PARCEL OF THE DUCHY OF LANCASTER;
5TH APRIL, 1832.

London: Printed by William Clowes, 14, Charing-
cross. 1832. *folio.* Part I., pp. 51; Part II., pp. 104.

Of this work, only thirty copies were printed, at the expense of
Sir George Harrison, K.C.H., one of the King's Council, and Auditor
of the accounts of his Majesty's Duchy of Lancaster.

The volume, which is dedicated to his late Majesty, William IV.,
contains the result of an investigation, into which Sir George Harrison entered, in the discharge of his duty as one of the Council,
and in support of the King's rights, arising within the fees and
liberties of the Duchy, OUT of the County Palatine.

The first part of the work, entitled OBSERVATIONS, was written in
consequence of the opinion of the Attorney and Solicitor General
(Sir James Scarlett and Sir Edward B. Sugden), that a certain property within the liberty of the Savoy, had, by the death of H. M.

Bulmer, Esq., escheated to the King *jure Coronæ*, and not *jure Ducatus*. The dissent of the Chancellor and Council of the Duchy from that opinion led to the submission of the case to the successors in office of Sir J. Scarlett and Sir E. Sugden—Sir Thomas Denman and Sir William Horne—who concurred with their predecessors, and thought "the property belonged to the Crown, by virtue of its prerogative, not in right of the Duchy of Lancaster."

The Auditor, notwithstanding those eminent legal opinions to the contrary, contended that the property escheated to the Crown, JURE DUCATUS; and some of his positions having, in the course of the discussions occasioned by the second reference, been questioned by the law authorities, he was induced to enter into a more extended investigation; the result of which was, the Statement of the CASE, which follows the Observations, and forms the second part. The inquiry was evidently one of laborious research; and Sir George Harrison has in this volume presented a curious and interesting detail respecting the King's rights, as lord of the Duchy of Lancaster.

———

THE ROYAL INTELLECTUAL BAZAAR:
A Prospectus of a Plan for the Improvement of the Fashionable Circles.

THE FLYING BURGOMASTER.
A Legend of the Black Forest.
1832.

These two productions of the Dowager Countess of Morley are inserted to prevent their escaping the notice of some future Horace Walpole, in a new edition of Noble Authors. Though, as pamphlets, they do not come within the scope of this work, the wit and talents of this distinguished Lady, so universally known, entitle them to be recorded with the view mentioned. Two other small productions from the same ready pen are, "Nina," a tale in verse, and a little squib, entitled the "Lady's last Strike."

CORRESPONDENCE AND EVIDENCES RESPECTING THE ANCIENT COLLEGIATE SCHOOL ATTACHED TO ST. PAUL'S CATHEDRAL.

1832. 4to. pp. 80. Appendix of Documents and Authorities respecting the ancient Collegiate Foundation attached to St. Paul's Cathedral, pp. xiv.

By Miss Hackett, of Crosby-square. A new edition, with some additions, of the work mentioned at page 230. Since that account was printed, the editor has been favoured with a copy of the work; as well as of the following, by the same indefatigable lady.

REGISTRUM ELEEMOSYNARIÆ D. PAULI LONDINENSIS.

Now first printed from a Manuscript in the Harleian Collection, by permission of the Trustees of the British Museum; with corroborative and explanatory Notes.

London: Printed by J. B. Nichols, 25, Parliament-street. 1827. 4to.

A collection of documents, including the greater part of the benefactions to St. Paul's Cathedral, for the purpose of eleemosynary distribution, prior to the reign of Richard II.

THE MANIFESTO OF HIS MOST FAITHFUL MAJESTY, THE KING OUR LORD, DOM MIGUEL THE FIRST.

London: Printed by Redford and Robins, 95 and 96, London-road, Southwark. 1832. 4to. pp. 40.

In Portuguese and English; with the arms of Portugal in the centre of the title-page. Printed in double columns.

COPIES OF THE POLLS TAKEN AT THE SEVERAL
ELECTIONS FOR MEMBERS TO REPRESENT THE COUNTY
OF NORTHAMPTON IN PARLIAMENT, IN THE YEARS
1702, 1705, 1730, 1745, AND 1806, AT NORTHAMPTON.
Reprinted from Poll Books in the possession of Mr.
George Baker.

Northampton: Printed by T. E. Dicey, Mercury
Office. 1832. 4*to*. pp. 399.

To which is added :—

A COPY OF THE POLL FOR TWO KNIGHTS OF THE
SHIRE FOR THE COUNTY OF NORTHAMPTON, WHICH
COMMENCED AT NORTHAMPTON ON THE 7TH, WAS CON-
TINUED DURING THE 9TH, 10TH, 11TH, 12TH, 13TH,
14TH, 16TH, 17TH, 18TH, 19TH, 20TH, 21ST, AND
CLOSED ON THE 23RD OF MAY, 1831.

Printed from the official Documents at Northampton.
1831. pp. 168.

Printed for private distribution only, at the expense of Beriah
Botfield, Esq., of Norton Hall, high sheriff for the county, during
the year in which the election took place.

————

THE LYRICS OF HORACE;
Translated by
the VENERABLE ARCHDEACON WRANGHAM.

"In magnis voluisse sat est."

Second edition. Chester. 1832.

Of this translation, one hundred copies were printed in quarto, and ten in octavo, all for private distribution. Archdeacon Wrangham printed several other small pamphlets privately, but it is impossible, with regard to the plan of this work, to include them. The following forms an exception—" Homerics," Chester, Feb. 1834. *8vo.* pp. 16.

THE BENEDICTIONAL OF ST. ÆTHELWOLD, BISHOP OF WINCHESTER.

An illuminated Anglo-Saxon MS. of the Tenth Century, in the library of his Grace the Duke of Devonshire, with a Prefatory Dissertation, and a Description of the Benedictional of Archbishop Robert, an illuminated Anglo-Saxon MS. of the same Century, in the Public Library at Rouen.

Communicated to the Society of Antiquaries.

BY JOHN GAGE, ESQ., F.R.S., Director.

London: Printed by J. B. Nichols and Son, 25, Parliament-street. 1832. *royal 4to.* pp. 136.

Twenty-five copies of this very curious manuscript have been printed by the learned editor, on this size, separate from the " Archæologia," vol. xxiv., where it first appeared.

The importance of the work has induced the editor to deviate in this instance from his rule of excluding the separate tracts of contributors to different literary and scientific transactions—it being usual to allow them a certain number of copies of their communications separate from the transactions themselves.

Mr. Gage says, in the preface, " St. Æthelwold's Benedictional is perhaps the most precious of all the MSS. in the Cavendish collection ; and deep are our obligations to the Duke of Devonshire, who, with a full sense of its value, and in order to promote the

F F

knowledge of Anglo-Saxon art, has had the munificence to allow us the free use of the volume." It contains thirty-two plates, engraved by G. F. Storm, an artist of great industry and fidelity in this department of art. Mr. Gage's copy has some of the plates illuminated, in imitation of the original, by the same artist.

———

OBSERVATIONS ON THE PRINCIPLES TO BE ADOPTED IN THE ESTABLISHMENT OF NEW MUNICIPAL CORPORATIONS;
Together with the heads of a Bill for their future Regulation and Government.
BY FRANCIS PALGRAVE, of the Honourable Society of the Inner Temple, Barrister-at-Law.
Not published.
London. 1832. 8vo. pp. 71. Heads of proposed Bill, pp. xlvi.

The tract was subsequently printed for sale.

———

JOURNAL OF MR. JAMES HART, ONE OF THE MINISTERS OF EDINBURGH, AND ONE OF THE COMMISSIONERS DEPUTED BY THE CHURCH OF SCOTLAND TO CONGRATULATE GEORGE I. ON HIS ACCESSION TO THE THRONE, IN THE YEAR 1714.
Edinburgh. 4to. 1832.

Edited by Principal Lee, and printed privately, it is understood, at the expense of Mr. Duncan Stewart.

The Pindar of Wakefield's Legend ;
With two lithographic Engravings.

London : Printed by J. Moyes, Castle-street, Leicester-square. 1832. 8*vo.*

The work was printed at the request of an Archery club, who hold their meetings alternately at Benham Park, and Sparsholt Place, in the county of Berks. Two hundred and fifty printed : it contains two views of the place of meeting, in lithography.

Lansdowne MSS. 78. No. 67. Burghley Papers.

The Names of all such Gentlemen of Accompte, as were residing within yᵉ Citie of London, Liberties and Suburbes thereof, 28 Novembris, 1595, Anno 38 Elizabethæ Reginæ, &c.; endorsed, " Strangers beying not Citizēs, lodgȳg in London."

pp. 8.

Fifty copies only were printed, by Sir C. G. Young, Garter, in 1832. The original was written evidently to inform Lord Burghley what country gentlemen were then residing in London.

Memorials of a Departed Friend.
" She being dead, yet speaketh."—Heb. xi. 4.

London : Printed by James and Luke G. Hansard and Sons, near Lincoln's-Inn-fields. 1833. 12*mo.* pp. 333.

The preface is signed by the editor, C. D. [Mr. Charles Dyson], by whose wife the papers contained in the volume were written.

F F 2

POETRY;
By the late HENRY F. R. SOAME, ESQ., H.E.B.
London. 1833. 12mo. pp. 41.

Edited by Sir Henry Edward Bunbury, Bart., cousin to the deceased author.

FUGITIVE PIECES.
By the late ADAM PATERSON, ESQ., of Edinburgh,
Advocate.
Presented as a memorial of him, to his Friends and Companions.

" The Lord gave, and the Lord hath taken away; blessed
be the name of the Lord."

London. 1833. 8vo. pp. 43.

Prefixed is a memorial of the writer, a very excellent and talented young man, who died of a consumptive malady, in the thirty-first year of his age.

AN ENQUIRY INTO THE EARLY HISTORY
OF GREEK SCULPTURE.
By the late JAMES CHRISTIE, a Member of the
Society of Dilettanti.
London: Printed by William Clowes, Charing Cross,
M.DCCC.XXXIII. 4to. pp. 54.

Prefixed is a portrait of the late Mr. Christie, from a bust by Henry Behnes, drawn by Henry Corbould, engraved by Robert Graves.

" The following pages were drawn up with the intention of offering them as an introduction to the second volume of select specimens of Ancient Sculpture, published by the society of Dilettanti. The design was not completed ; and they are now printed as a fragment of the History of Sculpture, originally intended."

Fifty copies only were printed, under the direction of Mr. Stirling Christie.

ESSAY ON THE MINES OF ENGLAND, THEIR IMPORTANCE AS A SOURCE OF NATIONAL WEALTH, AND AS A CHANNEL FOR THE ADVANTAGEOUS EMPLOYMENT OF PRIVATE CAPITAL.

BY G. ABBOTT.

1833. *8vo.*

CALEB KNIVETON, THE INCENDIARY. A TALE.

(Not published.)

Oxford : Printed by W. Baxter. 1833. 12*mo*. pp. 43.

Dated Blithfield, Feb. 11, 1833, by F. E. P., *i. e.* the Rev. Francis Edward Paget, student of Christ Church, Oxford.

A CATALOGUE OF THE BOOKS OF THE RIGHT HON. CHARLES VISCOUNT BRUCE OF AMPTHILL (SON AND HEIR-APPARENT OF THOMAS EARL OF AILESBURY), AND BARON BRUCE OF WHORLETON, IN HIS LIBRARY AT TOTENHAM, IN THE COUNTY OF WILTES.

Oxford: at the Theater. M.DCCC.XXXIII. pp. 316. 4*to.*

FANCIES OF A RHYMER.

Not published.

Printed by Davison, Simmons, and Co., Whitefriars, London. 1833. 12*mo.* pp. 118.

A juvenile production of the Rev. Alfred Gatty, Author of an interesting little volume called " The Bell."

BIBLIOGRAPHICAL NOTES ON THE BOOK OF JASHER.
BY THOMAS HARTWELL HORNE, B.D.

London : Printed by A. Spottiswoode, New-street Square. M.DCCC.XXXIII. 8*vo.* pp. 11.

Mr. Horne printed only fifty copies of these Notes, for private circulation ; and, though they have been since inserted in the sixth and following editions of his " Introduction to the Study and Knowledge of the Holy Scriptures," the history of this " literary forgery " is sufficiently curious to justify its insertion in this catalogue. The following account of it is given by Rowe Mores, in his Dissertation upon English Typographical Founders and Foundries, published in 1778 :—" In the year 1751, Mr. Ilive published a pretended translation of the Book of Jasher, said to have been made by one Alcuin, of Britain. The account given of the translation is full of glaring absurdities : but of the publication, this we can say, from the information of the only one who is capable of informing us, because the business was a secret between the two.—Mr. Ilive, in the nighttime, had constantly a Hebrew Bible before him, and cases in his closet. He produced the copy for Jasher, and it was composed in private, and the forms worked off in the night time, in a private press room, by these two, after the men of the printing house had left their work." Jacob Ilive, the person here mentioned, was a type-founder and printer, who carried on business in London between the years 1730 and 1763, in which last year he died. Being not perfectly sound in his mind, he produced some strange works. In 1733, he published an Oration, intended to prove the plurality of worlds—and asserting that this earth is hell; that the souls of men are apostate angels; and that the fire to punish those confined to this world at the day of judgment, will be immaterial. In November, 1751, he published the Book of Jasher, an account of which was given in the "Monthly Review" for December in the same year, which is printed in Mr. Horne's tract; who says, "With this quotation from the 'Monthly Review,' the author would have dismissed the pretended Book of Jasher, had it not come to his knowledge that very many individuals have been induced to purchase the reprint of this forgery, of which the following is the title:—

"'The Book of Jasher: with testimonies and notes, critical and historical, explanatory of the text: to which is prefixed, various readings, and a preliminary dissertation, proving the authenticity of the work. Translated into English from the Hebrew, by Flaccus Albinus Alcuinus, of Britain, abbot of Canterbury, who went a pilgrimage into the Holy Land and Persia, where he discovered this volume in the city of Gazna.

"'Is not this written in the book of Jasher?—Joshua x. 13.

"'Behold, it is written in the book of Jasher.—2 Sam. i. 18.

"'Bristol: printed for the Editor, by Philip Rose, 20, Broadmead. Sold by Longman, London. M.DCCC.XXIX.'" 4to.

Outlines of Ancient History, from the Deluge to the Division of the Roman Empire. Compiled from the Writings of the most approved Authors.

London: Printed for the Author, by A. J. Valpy. 1833.

The work, though advertised as sold by Valpy, was never published. A few copies were given by the author, W. R. Gray Bates, to his friends.

A Chronological Table of the principal Greek Philosophers mentioned by Cicero, in his Books, "De Natura Deorum."
By W. R. Gray Bates.
Printed by R. Todd, Oundle, 1833.

———

Portraits by an Amateur.
1. Earl and Countess of Winton.
2. Lady Marie Stewart.
3. The Duke and Duchess of Lauderdale.
4. The Duke of Lauderdale.
5. Viscount and Viscountess Dundee.
6. Madame de Staël.
Not published for sale.
M.DCCC.XXXIII. 4to.

The amateur was the late Charles K. Sharpe, Esq. Twenty copies, and four on India paper, were thrown off. The etching of Madame de Staël is the best likeness extant.

———

Maitland's Narrative of the Principal Acts of the Regency, during the Minority; and other papers relating to the History of Mary, Queen of Scotland.
(Ipswich): R. Root. 4to. 1833. Twenty-five leaves, including Title and Preface.

"Fifty copies printed by W. S. Fitch, for private circulation."— *Grenville library.*

MEMOIR OF THE REV. CORNELIUS NEALE, M.A., FORMERLY FELLOW OF ST. JOHN'S COLLEGE, CAMBRIDGE.

To which are added his Remains, being Sermons, Notes, and various other compositions in prose and verse. Collected and edited by the REV. WILLIAM JOWETT, M.A., late Fellow of St. John's College, Cambridge. London. M.DCCC.XXXIII. (Not published.) *8vo.* pp. 368. Preface and Contents, pp. xiv.

Three editions have subsequently been published, in *fcap. 8vo.*

SONNETS. BY EDWARD MOXON.

" In truth, the prison, into which we doom
Ourselves, no prison is ; and hence to me,
In sundry moods, 't was pastime to be bound
Within the Sonnet's scanty plot of ground."—*Wordsworth.*

London. M.DCCC.XXXIII. *8vo.* pp. 46.

Mr. Moxon is a publisher of celebrity : these Sonnets were for private circulation.

BUBBLES FROM THE BRUNNENS OF NASSAU.
BY AN OLD MAN.

London. 1833. *8vo.*

This amusing volume was originally printed for private circulation, and reviewed in the " Quarterly Review ;"* the writer says,

---

* Vol. i. p. 308.

"We are able to bear witness to the fidelity with which it represents external nature—and its descriptions of social life will speak for themselves." The author is Sir Francis Head, Bart. Editions of this entertaining work will be found in all the towns adjacent to the Rhine, and the different German Brunnens.

———

IRENE, A POEM, IN SIX CANTOS.
MISCELLANEOUS POEMS.
London: Printed by Mills, Jowett, and Mills, Bolt-court, Fleet-street. M.DCCC.XXXIII. (Not published.) 8*vo.* pp. 206.

"The following selection from poems by the late Lady Northampton,* has been made, with the desire of preserving for her friends some—however inadequate—memorial.

"*Castle Ashby*, 1832." "NORTHAMPTON."

———

A DESCRIPTION OF THE CLOSE ROLLS IN THE TOWER OF LONDON;
With an Account of the early Courts of Law and Equity, and various Historical Illustrations.
BY THOMAS DUFFUS HARDY, F.S.A.,
of the Inner Temple.
Printed for private circulation. M.DCCC.XXXIII. 8*vo.* pp. 192.

This volume contains Mr. Hardy's Introduction prefixed to the Close Rolls, printed by order of his Majesty's Commissioners for Public Records.

———

* Margaret, wife of Spencer Joshua Alwyne Compton, second Marquis of Northampton.

The work itself, from its size and cost, was not likely to fall into the hands of general readers, to whom an account of those valuable and important documents, and the subjects incidentally connected with them, might be interesting : Mr. Hardy therefore printed a limited number of copies in this form, to induce a more extended acquaintance with the nature of the Close Rolls.

A Catalogue of the Printed Books and Manuscripts in the Library of the Inner Temple: Arranged in Classes.

London.   1833.   8vo.   pp. 239.

Compiled by the Rev. William Henry Rowlatt, M.A., Librarian.

These books (chiefly on juridical subjects) are alphabetically arranged, with reference to the presses and shelves in which they are deposited.

"The manuscripts in the Library of the Inner Temple are more than four hundred in number ; many of them are on subjects of divinity, general history, &c. &c. ; others are ancient MSS. of English historians ; and the remainder treat on parliamentary matters, statute and common law, and on ecclesiastical matters, or are copies and extracts from records, repertories to other repositories, and miscellaneous.   These MSS. were originally in part collected and partly composed by William Petyt, Esq., a learned antiquary of the seventeenth century, and keeper of the records in the Tower ; who bequeathed them to the Honourable Society of the Inner Temple. The MSS. are in good preservation, and easily accessible.   Particulars of their contents are in the First Report of the Public Records, pp. 375-378."—*Horne, Bibliogr.* vol. ii. p. 624.

"Selden left a most valuable library to his executors, Matthew Hale, John Vaughan, and Rowland Jewks, Esqrs., which they generously would have bestowed on the society of the Inner Temple, if a proper place should be provided to receive it : but, this being *neglected,* they gave it to the University of Oxford.   Selden, himself, had originally intended it for Oxford, and had left it so in his will, but was offended, because when he applied for a manuscript in the Bodleian Library, they asked, according to usual custom, a bond of 1000*l.* for its restitution. This made him declare, with some passion, that they should never have his collection. The executors, however, considered that they were executors of his will, and not of his passion, and therefore destined the books, amounting to eight thousand volumes, for Oxford, where a noble room was added to the library for their reception. Burnet says, this collection was valued at some thousands of pounds, and was believed to be one of the most curious in Europe. It is supposed that Sir Matthew Hale gave some of Selden's MSS. respecting law to Lincoln's Inn library, as there is nothing of that kind among what were sent to the Bodleian; and a few Mr. Selden gave to the Library of the College of Physicians."*

The following answer was returned to the Commissioners of Public Records, in their inquiries as to MSS. relative to English History. "There are not in the Inner Temple Library any of importance (alas! for the neglect of Selden's), except those of which there does exist a printed catalogue. The information furnished in 1800 (if any was furnished) related to those same manuscripts."

27th Nov., 1832.

———

TWO LECTURES

ON THE REMAINS OF ANCIENT PAGAN BRITAIN,

Illustrated with forty Lithographic Drawings of Druidical circles, barrows, cromlechs, sepulchral urns, celts, and other ancient memorials.

BY THOMAS STACKHOUSE.

London. 1833.   4*to.*   pp. iv. and 76.

Seventy-five copies printed for private distribution.

———

* Chalmers's Biographical Dictionary, vol. xxvii. p. 329.

GIUSTINA : A SPANISH TALE OF REAL LIFE.
A POEM, IN THREE CANTOS. BY E. S. L.
Not published.
[London.] 1833.   8*vo.* pp. 63.

By the Hon. Elizabeth Sophia Law, sister of Lord Ellenborough,
who also published, for private circulation, the following, viz.:—

MISCELLANEOUS POEMS ;
Dedicated to Joseph Jekyll, Esq., by E. S. L.
Not published.
[London.] 1832.   8*vo.* pp. 104.

IL VIAGGIATORE.
Dall' Inglese di Oliver Goldsmith. Ricato in Verso
Italiano, con altri Poemi ; e dedicato a sua Eccellenza il
Duca di Somerset.
Not published.
Printed for John Rodwell, New Bond-street. 1832.
12*mo.* pp. 57.

———

CATALOGUE OF THE LIBRARY COLLECTED BY MISS
RICHARDSON CURRER, AT ESHTON HALL, CRAVEN,
YORKSHIRE :
By C. J. STEWART, bookseller.
London : Printed for private circulation only.
M.DCCC.XXXIII. 8*vo.* pp. 501.

An improved and enlarged edition of the Catalogue mentioned at
page 267 : it contains the following plates :—

Eshton Hall : drawn by Mackenzie ; engraved by S. Rawle.

The Library, Eshton Hall : drawn by Mackenzie, from a sketch by
C. J. Stewart ; engraved by S. Rawle.

The Drawing Room, Eshton Hall : by the same artists.

View from the Library Window.

One hundred copies were printed.

A BRIEF ENQUIRY INTO THE ANTIQUITY, HONOUR,
AND ESTATE OF THE NAME AND FAMILY OF WAKE;
With a summary deduction of the lineal succession of
the chief branches of it, from its first rise down to this
present time.

BY WILLIAM WAKE, D.D., Rector of St. James's,
Westminster ; Chaplain in Ordinary to the King, and
afterwards Archbishop of Canterbury.

Warminster : Printed by J. L. Vardy. M.DCCC.XXXIII.
8vo. pp. 68.

"Only 100 copies printed."

Dedicated by Miss Etheldred Benett to the Rev. Henry Wake,
M.A., Rector of Over Wallop, Hants ; Vicar of Mere, Wilts ; and
Chaplain to the Marquess of Winchester.

FAUST ; A DRAMATIC POEM, BY GOETHE.
Translated into English Prose, with Remarks on former
Translations, and Notes ; by the Translator of Savigny's
" Of the Vocation of our Age for Legislature and Ju-
risprudence."

London. 1833. 8vo. pp. 279. [For private distribution ; not published.]

This translation is by Abraham Hayward, Esq., the translator of

"Savigny on Legislation," mentioned in page 408. It has since been reprinted for sale: in the preface to which edition the author states,—"I commenced this translation without the slightest idea of publishing it; and even when, by aid of preface and notes, I thought I had produced a book which might contribute something towards the promotion of German literature in this country, I still felt unwilling to cast it from me, beyond the power of alteration or recall. I therefore circulated the whole of the first impression amongst my acquaintance."

A CRUISE TO EGYPT, PALESTINE, AND GREECE, DURING FIVE MONTHS' LEAVE OF ABSENCE. BY the HON. W. E. FITZMAURICE, 2nd Life Guards. London: Printed by John Hill, Black-Horse-court, Fleet-street. 1834. 4*to.* pp. 75. Eight plates engraved in mezzotint.

"These notes were never intended for the press, and are not meant to be published. They were printed for private distribution only."

GURDON THORNHAUGH; ESSAY ON THE ANTIQUITY OF THE CASTEL OF NORWICH, ITS FOUNDERS AND GOVERNORS, FROM THE KINGS OF THE EAST ANGLES DOWN TO MODERN TIMES. Norwich. 1834. 8*vo.*

A private reprint by Hudson Gurney, Esq., of a very curious manuscript, originally published anonymously at Norwich in 1728. "Mr. Gurdon was an active magistrate and Receiver General of Norfolk, in the reign of Queen Anne. He published, in the year 1731, the 'History of the High Court of Parliament,' together with a 'History of the Court Baron and Court Leet.' 2 vols. 8vo."

DESCRIPTIVE CATALOGUE OF A
CABINET OF ROMAN IMPERIAL LARGE BRASS MEDALS.
BY CAPTAIN WILLIAM HENRY SMYTH, R.N.,
Member of the Royal Geographical Society, &c., &c.
Bedford: James Webb, Printer. M.DCCC.XXXIV. 4*to*.
pp. 352.

Two hundred copies printed. The author, now a retired Rear-Admiral, has also printed in the Transactions of the Bedfordshire Archæological Society, 1852, a catalogue of Bedford Tokens.

————

FRIENDLY CONTRIBUTIONS FOR THE BENEFIT OF
THREE INFANT SCHOOLS, IN THE PARISH OF KEN-
SINGTON.
Printed solely for the Right Honourable the Lady
Mary Fox. M.DCCC.XXXIV.
Kensington: Bournes, jun., Brothers, Church-street.
12*mo*. pp. 162.

Dedicated, by permission, to Lord Holland, by his affectionate daughter, Mary Fox.

————

THE PLAGUE OF MARSEILLES IN THE YEAR 1720.
From documents preserved in the Archives of the City,
and published by authority, in the Year 1820.
BY JOHN IRELAND, D.D., Dean of Westminster.
Read at the Royal College of Physicians, May 26,
1834.
London. M.DCCC.XXXIV.   *Small* 4*to*. pp. viii. 39.
London: Printed by William Clowes, Duke-street,
Lambeth.

INDICATION OF MEMORIALS, MONUMENTS, PAINT-
INGS, AND ENGRAVINGS OF PERSONS OF THE HOWARD
FAMILY, AND OF THEIR WIVES AND CHILDREN, AND OF
THOSE WHO HAVE MARRIED LADIES OF THE NAME, AND
OF THE REPRESENTATIVES OF SOME OF ITS BRANCHES
NOW EXTINCT, AS FAR AS THEY HAVE BEEN ASCER-
TAINED.
By HENRY HOWARD.
Corby Castle, December 10*th,* 1834.

The copy in Mr. Grenville's library is illustrated with numerous
additional drawings of Seals, Portraits, &c.

———

THE WIZARD PETER. A SONG OF THE SOLWAY.

" He'd muse upon old times, and try to weave
Traditions into Rhyme.--Oh vain attempt !
The verses, like himself, moved halting on
Disjointed all and pithless."—*Shelley*.

Edinburgh: Printed by Ballantyne and Co. 1834.
8*vo*. pp. 32. Title, Dedication to Miss Eliza Robertson, &c., pp. 6.

By the late C. K. Sharpe, Esq. Of extreme rarity.

———

POLYLOGIA, CONTAINING SPECIMENS OF
FOURTEEN LANGUAGES, WITH METRICAL TRANSLATIONS.
London: Printed by Munday, Threadneedle-street.
folio. 1834.

G G

A Sketch of the Case of John Lyndsay Crawfurd, Esq., now before the Lords Commissioners
of Privileges;

Comprising an exposure of the many extraordinary
circumstances, connected with the prosecution of his claim
to the titles and estates of Craufurd and Lindsay.

"The conviction of the Trial must be shown to be wrong."

Vide Brougham's Opinion, p. 22.

1834.   4*to.*   pp. 44, with a pedigree.

Mr. Dobie's refutation was most complete, and the title of Craufurd was some years afterwards adjudged to the Earl of Balcarres.

Nautical and Hydraulic Experiments, with
numerous Scientific Miscellanies.

By Colonel Mark Beaufoy, F.R.S., etc.

In Three Volumes, with Pl..tes.   Vol. I. (all as yet
published.)

London : Printed at the private press of Henry Beaufoy, F.R.S., South Lambeth, Surrey, under the superintendence of James Sparrow, Printer, South Lambeth.
Published May, 1834.   *Royal* 4*to.*

Description of Dropmore.
By Lord Grenville.

Printed by Woodfall, it is believed in the year mentioned. It
would appear to be excessively rare., for no copy has come under the
editor's notice.   It is inserted in the catalogue of Mr. Grenville's

library, but is not there, having, it is said, been claimed by the family after Mr. Grenville's death. The following notice of the work appeared in the *Morning Chronicle*, April 28, 1834:—

"Lord Grenville, at the time of his death, had far advanced in writing a history of Dropmore and its neighbourhood, which the noble Baron intended to illustrate with a variety of beautiful engravings, highly finished, from designs made purposely by distinguished artists. Nine sheets of the work are already printed, five copies upon vellum. The volume is in quarto, and was intended for private distribution only."

Documents of the Gunning Family.

Cheltenham: Printed by S. C. Harper, High-street. 1834. 8*vo.* pp. 68.

I write this principally for occupation, and to beguile an idle hour, and to establish my claim or right as next of kin to Peter Gunning, Bishop of Ely, who died in 1684; such having been assumed by others.

Geo. Gunning,
Lt. H. P. First Dragoon Guards,

Cheltenham, May, 1834.

The Argyle Papers.

Edinburgh: Thomas G. Stevenson. 1834. 4*to.* pp. 213.

This collection of papers relates principally to the Argyle family after their elevation to a dukedom; and many very curious memorials of the first Duke and Duchess are given from the Anderson MSS., preserved in the library of the Faculty of Advocates, Edinburgh. Fifty copies were printed; six on large paper, and one in vellum. This copy was sold in Mr. Eyton's library.

The Infant's Guide to Spelling and Reading.

"Undoubtedly the infant mind should be inured to labour ; but it can scarcely be denied, that it is better to bestow that labour upon what is within the comprehension of a child, than to cram its memory with what must be unintelligible. A child is taught to walk upon smooth ground, and no persons in their senses would put an infant on its legs for the first time on rugged rocks.

"It seems to be a very plain direction to a teacher, to proceed from what is known to the next step which is not known ; but there are pedagogues who choose the retrograde motion of going from what is little known to what is less known." — *Edgeworth's Address to Mothers.*

London : John Murray, Albemarle-street. 1834. *Square* 12*mo*. pp. 31.

Only six copies printed, and never sold. It was a compilation by Mr. and Mrs. Crofton Croker. as a first book for their son, who became an author at nine years old.

Memoir of George Granville, late Duke of Sutherland, K.G., By James Loch, Esq., M.P.

London : Woodfall, Printer. M.DCCC.XXXIV. [Not published.] 4*to*. pp. 83.

Prefixed, a Portrait of the Duke ; drawn by Corbould, from a bust by Francis : engraved by Scriven.

On page 29, a View of Ben Bhraggie, on which is erected an obelisk, in memory of the Duke.

> " And native accents shall his loss bewail,
> Who came a Saxon, and remained a Gael."
> Lord F. Egerton (*Earl of Ellesmere*).

LETTERS WRITTEN DURING A FOUR DAYS' TOUR
IN HOLLAND, IN THE SUMMER OF 1834.

Not published.

M.DCCC.XXXIV.   12*mo*.   pp. 127.   Title, Preface, &c.
pp. vii.

By Mrs. H. Gunn, daughter of Dawson Turner, Esq., the Editor,
to whom the letters were addressed.

Fifty copies printed.

———

A CATALOGUE OF THE LIBRARY
OF THE CORPORATION OF THE CITY OF LONDON.

Instituted in the Year 1824.

Printed for the use of the Members of the Corporation of the City of London.   1840.   8*vo*.   pp. 376.
Rules, &c., pp. 7.

SUPPLEMENT.

1842.   8*vo*.   pp. 1842.

ALPHABETICAL INDEX TO THE CATALOGUE.

1846.   8*vo*.   pp. 176.

A classed catalogue is said to be in preparation.

———

MEMOIRS OF THE PROFESSIONAL LIFE OF
AN ARCHITECT, BETWEEN THE YEARS 1768 AND 1833.

Not published.

London.   1834.   4*to*.   pp. 63.

The architect was the late Sir John Soane, R.A.

A CATALOGUE OF THE PROVINCIAL COPPER COINS, TOKENS, TICKETS, AND MEDALETS, ISSUED IN GREAT BRITAIN, IRELAND, AND THE COLONIES, DURING THE EIGHTEENTH AND NINETEENTH CENTURIES, ARRANGED ACCORDING TO COUNTIES, ETC.

With particulars of their fabrication, names of the Artists, and Miscellaneous Remarks illustrative of the rarity of particular specimens.

Described from the originals in the collection of Sir George Chetwynd, Bart., of Grendon Hall, in the County of Warwick. By THOMAS SHARP, author of Collections for a History of Coventry, a dissertation on the Coventry Pageants, and an Epitome of the County of Warwick.

London: Printed by J. B. Nichols and Son, 25, Parliament-street. 1834. 4to. pp. 280. Preface, &c., pp. xxi.

Sixty copies only are said to have been printed.

FRAGMENTS AND SCRAPS OF HISTORY.

London: Printed by William Clowes, 14, Charingcross. 1834. 2 vols. 4to.

Extract from "Preface and Dedication." "It may be satisfactory, if not even due, to those few friends for whom the private perusal of these pages is designed, &c."

COLLATION OF VOL. I.

Title, Half-Title, Quotation . . . . . . 8 pages.
Preface and Dedication . . . . 8 „

COLLATION OF VOL. II.

The author of this work is believed to be Mr. Harrison, who held a government appointment.

LETTERS FROM THE EARL OF PETERBOROUGH TO GENERAL STANHOPE, IN SPAIN.

From the originals, at Chevening.

Not published, and only fifty copies printed.

London: Printed by William Clowes, Duke-street, Stamford-street. 1834. 8vo. pp. 51.

Edited by Lord Viscount Mahon, lineal descendant of the gallant General.

REMAINS, IN VERSE AND PROSE, OF
ARTHUR HENRY HALLAM.
London: Printed by W. Nicol, Pall Mall. 1834.
pp. 363.

One hundred copies were printed.
Mr. Tenyson's poem, "In Memoriam," is inscribed to the memory
of this accomplished man.

MEMORABILIA OF THE CITY OF GLASGOW, SELECTED
FROM THE MINUTE-BOOKS OF THE BURGH.
M.DLXXXVIII–M.DCC.L.
Glasgow: Printed for private circulation. 1835. 4*to*.
pp. 110.

These extracts originally appeared in the *Glasgow Courier* Newspaper.

MEMOIR OF THE LATE FRANCIS COBB, ESQ.,
OF MARGATE.
Compiled from his Journals and Letters.
Maidstone: Printed by G. V. Hall and Son, Journal
Office, 1835. 8*vo*. Preface (signed W. F. Cobb) iv.
pages; Memoir 109 pages.

THE MAID OF ORLEANS, TRANSLATED FROM SCHILLER.
BY J. E. DRINKWATER BETHUNE.
London. 1835. 8*vo*.

Mr. Bethune was a member of council in India. He died in 1851.

A Catalogue of the Printed Books, to which is prefixed a Short Account of the Manuscripts, in the Library of Lincoln's Inn.

London: Printed by G. Davidson, Serle's-place, Carey-street. 1835. 8*vo.* pp. 215; Title and Advertisement 3 leaves.

Since 1835 the library has been greatly enlarged, the number of volumes being now at least threefold (about 28,000) ; a catalogue of which exists in manuscript, for the use of the readers in the library, and will probably be printed in the course of the ensuing year.

Sonetti e Canzone,
del Poeta Clarissimo Matteo Maria Boiardo,
Conte di Scandiano.

(London). 1835.   4*to.*

" Della Presente Editione sonosi tirate soli cinquanti esemplari da non esser porte in commercio."

Dedicated to Mr. Grenville, in whose catalogue it is stated that the text is, for the first time, presented in its original purity.

The Hubble Shue. By Miss Carstairs.

> " Harry-harry, hobillis schoue,
> Se quha is cummyn nowe."
> *The Crying of ane Playe.*

12*mo.*

No date, but printed in 1835 by Wm. H. Logan, Esq , Manager of the Northumberland and Durham District Bank at Berwick-on-Tweed.

A reprint of a very extraordinary Drama, by a Miss Carstairs ;

so remarkable for its absurdity, that the late Mr. C. K. Sharpe suggested a limited private reprint, and his idea was adopted by Mr. Logan. The ironical preface, in which the style of a learned antiquary and modern author is accurately imitated, is from the pen of Mr. Maidment. There were some half dozen copies on fine paper.

IoN; A TRAGEDY, IN FIVE ACTS; TO WHICH ARE ADDED A FEW SONNETS.

Second edition.

London: Printed by A. J. Valpy, for private circulation. Not published. 8vo. pp. 216; Title and prefaces, pp. xxi.

By Mr. Sergeant Talfourd, afterwards promoted to the bench. It is noticed in terms of high praise in the *Quarterly Review.**

Laoiḋe ċṅuiṫ áiṙa ṅa h-Eiṙeaṅ ḋo ṫiṫc aɜuṙ ḋ'iṅɜjoṅa ċiṙe ṅa ṅaṅ. Ṙe Ḋ. O' 2l).
"Eiṙiṅ ṁo ṁṙṙṅiṅ.

London: Printed by Robson, Levey and Franklyn, 46, St. Martin's-lane. 1835. 12mo. pp. 54.

It contains thirty-four religious songs, composed or collected by a poor fellow named David Murphy, a native of Kinsale, and who translated into Irish the preface written by "Charlotte Elizabeth" (the late Mrs. Tonna). Murphy meditated publishing an Irish Dictionary, of which some portion was printed, but failing to receive the necessary support, he emigrated to America. The last heard of him was that he was piously manufacturing cannon in the back woods.

---

* Vol. liv. p. 505.

Catalogue of the Works in Medicine and Natural History, contained in the Radclyffe Library.

Oxford : Printed by J. Collingwood, printer to the University. M.DCCC.XXXV. 8*vo*. pp. 330. Preface, pp. vii.

Compiled by J. Kidd, M.D.. Radclyffe librarian.

———

Two Essays, on the Sublime and Beautiful, and on Duelling.

By Charles Hay Cameron. Esq.

(Not for publication.) M.DCCC.XXXV.   8*vo*.

———

Extracts from the Literary and Scientific Correspondence of Richard Richardson, M.D., F.R.S., of Brierley, Yorkshire,

Illustrative of the State and Progress of Botany, and interspersed with information respecting the study of antiquities and general literature in Great Britain, during the first half of the eighteenth century.

Yarmouth : Printed by Charles Sloman, King-street. M.DCCC.XXXV. 8*vo*. pp. 451. Index, 6 leaves.

Plates.—Portrait of Richardson, lithograph, facing title.
North Brierley Hall,   ditto   p. xxv.
Cedar of Lebanon,   ditto   p. xxxi.

Edited by Dawson Turner, Esq., and printed at the expense of Miss Currer, the possessor of the correspondence from which this has been selected ; which, had it all been printed, Mr. Turner states would have formed eight volumes of the size of the present.

POETICAL DESCRIPTIONS OF ORKNEY. M.DC.LII.
(Edinburgh. 1835.) *small* 4*to.* pp. xxx.

A bitter satire on the inhabitants of Orkney, possessing great merit, and containing much curious information as to the manners and customs of the natives of that place in 1652. Printed from a MS. in the library of the Faculty of Advocates, Edinburgh.

On the back of the title-page, "thirty-five copies printed for presents."

———

SPECIMENS OF ANCIENT HYMNS OF THE
WESTERN CHURCH.
Norwich. 1835. pp. 36. 8*vo.*

The number printed was fifty-six.

A reprint of a very small collection of the above Hymns, privately printed by Mr. Mathias, in Rome, 1818, and preceded by a Latin preface from his pen. To these the Editor (the Rev. Frederick Martin) has added some popular Monkish Latin verses, with translations in English.

———

RECOLLECTIONS OF A FEW DAYS SPENT WITH THE
QUEEN'S ARMY IN SPAIN, IN SEPT. 1834.
London. 1835. 12*mo.*

By a Graduate of Cambridge. Noticed in the " Quarterly Review : "* " His details of what he saw," says the writer, " though he affects neither depth nor originality, are curious, as containing some sketches of the General Officers whose names have been trumpeted in England, and of those harrowing scenes, which are the necessary accompaniments of a civil war."

———

* Vol. liv. p. 186.

POEMS, BY ROBERT CHAMBERS.

" Nec cithara carente."

Edinburgh : Printed for private circulation, by T. Constable. M.DCCC.XXXV. *Small 4to.* pp. 48.

"In presenting this little volume to his friends," Mr. Chambers remarks, "the author deems it only necessary to state, that it contains nearly the whole of the versified compositions he has ever written."

———

A CATALOGUE OF THE LIBRARY OF THE LONDON INSTITUTION; SYSTEMATICALLY CLASSED.

Preceded by an Historical and Bibliographical Account of the Establishment.

VOL. I.—THE GENERAL LIBRARY.

(Not published.) 1835. *8vo.* pp. 669; Preface, pp. lxviii. Prefixed, a plan of the Library.

VOL. II.—THE TRACTS AND PAMPHLETS.

(Not published.) 1840. *8vo.* pp. 658; pp. xxxiii; Index. pp. xviii.

VOL. III.—THE GENERAL LIBRARY.

Additions and revisions. The index of Authors. The Index of Subjects.

(Not published.) 1842. pp. 667 ; Introduction, &c., pp. xcvi.

It is to be regretted that the catalogue of the pamphlets has been suspended, and is only carried down to the letter F.

WINCHESTER, AND A FEW OTHER COMPOSITIONS
IN PROSE AND VERSE.

Winchester: James Robbins, College-street. 1835.
4*to.* pp. 82.

By the Rev. Charles Townsend, Rector of Kingston-on-the-Sea
near Brighton. A volume, of which very few copies were printed
by the author for his friends. Our readers may see a notice of it,
written by Mr. Lockhart, in the "Quarterly Review" for July 1836,
"The Reverend Charles Townsend (best on the list of Sussex
parsons)."—*Preston.*

———

A GENEALOGICAL ACCOUNT OF THE FAMILY OF
DRUCE OF GOREING, IN THE COUNTY OF OXON, AND
THOSE OF KIN TO THE CHILDREN OF GEORGE DRUCE,
CITIZEN AND PAINTER STAINER, OF THE PARISH OF
ALL-SAINTS, BREAD-STREET, IN THE CITY OF LONDON,
BY WHOM THIS GENEALOGY WAS TAKEN, ANNO DOM.,
1735.

Together with the different families of kin, their marriages and issue, &c.

London: Printed in the Year M.DCCC.XXXV. pp. 30.
4*to.*

On the back of the title-page, "Reprinted from the edition of
1735, by E. Tucker, Perry's Place, Oxford Street. Fifty copies only
printed."

Privately printed by Charles Bridges, Esq., F.S.A.

POEMS ON SEVERAL OCCASIONS FROM 1793 TO 1816.
Edinburgh: Printed by Neil and Company. 1836.
8vo. pp. 124.

By John Dunlop, Esq., Collector of the Customs, Port-Glasgow.
They were collected by his son, the author of the "History of
Fiction."
Fifty copies printed. The poems are said to possess great merit.

NARRATIVE OF THE OPPRESSIVE LAW PROCEEDINGS,
AND OTHER MEASURES, RESORTED TO BY THE BRITISH
GOVERNMENT, AND NUMEROUS PRIVATE INDIVIDUALS,
TO OVERPOWER THE EARL OF STIRLING, AND SUBVERT
HIS LAWFUL RIGHTS;
Also a Genealogical Account of the Family of Alex-
ander, Earl of Stirling, &c., followed by an Historical
View of their Hereditary Possessions in Nova Scotia,
Canada, &c.
BY EPHRAIM LOCKHART.
Edinburgh. 1836.   4to.

Not printed for sale.

CATALOGUE OF THE LIBRARY OF ST. PAUL'S SCHOOL.
London: Printed 1836. (Not published.)   8vo.

From the perusal of "Vegetius de re Militari" in this library,
Marlborough, when a student in the school, is said to have imbibed
his taste for a military life. The copy is believed to be yet in
the library; but the disorder which prevails, prevented its being
identified. In the growing taste for reading, and the increase of

libraries to satisfy it, this library will most probably not long remain in its present neglected condition. The Mercers' Company possess ample funds to endow a librarian, and to render the library itself worthy the founder.

A GLOSSARY OF THE
PROVINCIALISMS IN USE IN THE COUNTY OF SUSSEX.
BY WILLIAM DURRANT COOPER.

"Juvat hæc sic obsoleta servari aliquando profitura."—*Wachter.*

Printed for private distribution, by W. Fleet, printer, Herald Office, Brighton. 1836. 8*vo.* pp. 34.

EXCERPTA.
SELECTIONS FROM THE CONTRIBUTIONS OF THE AMICI.

"Forsan et hæc olim meminisse juvabit."—*Virg.*

Maidstone: Printed for the Amici. M.DCCC.XXXVI. 8*vo.* pp. 151.

MEMOIR OF JOHN CARPENTER, TOWN CLERK OF LONDON IN THE REIGNS OF HENRY V. AND HENRY VI.
Compiled from original manuscripts and other authentic sources.
BY THOMAS BREWER, of the Town Clerk's Office.
London: Printed by Arthur Taylor, 39, Coleman-street. 8*vo.* 1836. pp. 62. Preface, pp. x.

Frontispiece, City of London School.

Reflections on the Genealogy of our Lord
and Saviour Jesus Christ as recorded by St.
Matthew and St. Luke.

By Daniel Benham.

London : John Cochran, Strand. M.DCCC.XXXVI. 4*to.*

Marculfus.

Read May 6, 1836, before the Leicestershire Literary
Society.

By T. Smith, Esq.

Printed at the request of the Society.

Leicester : Printed by J. Combe & Co. M.DCCC.XXXVI.
Royal 8vo. pp. 23. Preface and title, pp. xv.

A very able disquisition on Marculfus, a monk, of the diocese of
Paris, who lived in the reign of Clovis, about the year 660, and was
author of the " Formulæ," first published in 1613.

A Journal of a Tour in Italy.

" il bel paese,
Ch' Appenin parte e'l mar circonde e l'Alpe."
Petrarca : Sonnetto cxiv.

London. Privately printed. 5 vols. *crown 8vo.*

Vol. I. Title, Dedication to Mrs. C * * * * and Contents, xxiv
pages ; Journal, 356 pages. Vol. II. Title and Contents, xviii
pages ; Journal, 331 pages. Vol. III. Title and Contents, xxii
pages ; Journal, 336 pages. Vol. IV. Title and Contents, xxiii
pages ; Journal, 353 pages. Vol. V. Title and Contents, xxviii
pages ; Journal, 279 pages, which terminates on 26th May, 1836.

TRANSLATIONS FROM THE ITALIAN.
BY BARBARINA, LADY DACRE.
(London.) M.DCCC.XXXVI. 8vo.

Note on back of the title-page, " 150 copies printed for private distribution."
The translations are principally from Petrarch.

CLAIM OF MOLINEUX DISNEY, ESQ., TO THE BARONY
OF HUSSEY. M.DC.LXXX. WITH REMARKS
BY W. B. D. D. TURNBULL, ESQ., Advocate,
F.S.A. Scot.
Edinburgh. 1836. 8vo.

" The impression of this volume is strictly limited to forty copies, for private distribution."

ACCOUNT OF NAPOLEON BONAPARTE'S COMING ON
BOARD H.M.S. THE NORTHUMBERLAND, AUGUST 7TH,
1815.
With Notes of Two Conversations held with him.

Privately printed ; only fifty-two copies.
By the Hon. W. H. Lyttleton (fifth Lord Lyttleton), who died May 1, 1837. His Lordship is said to have also printed for private circulation, a "Catalogue of the Pictures at Hagley," and some "Prayers and Religious Meditations, for the use of his sons at college." *

---

* Gentleman's Magazine, New Series, vol. viii. p. 83.

Notices relating to Thomas Smith of Campden, and to Henry Smith, sometime Alderman of London.

By the late Charles Perkins Gwilt, B.A., of Christchurch, Oxford, and of the Middle Temple, London,

A descendant of the Family.

London: Printed by George Woodfall. M.DCCC.XXXVI. 8vo. pp. 80. Title, Preface, and Contents, pp. vii.

Monument of Thomas Smith, in Campden Church, page 1.
Two Views of the Elevation of ditto, page 6.
Monument of Henry Smith, at Wandsworth Church, page 48.

———

Some Notices of the Church of St. Patrick, Trim.

Collected from various authorities.

Trim: Printed by H. Griffith. 1837. *small 8vo.* pp. 38.

Collected by the Very Reverend the Dean of Clonmacnois, Vicar of Trim, who has also added the following :—

Some Notices of the Castle of Trim.

Collected from various authorities.

Second edition, enlarged.

Trim: Printed by H. Griffith. 1840. *small 8vo.* pp. 143.

The first edition was printed in 1835 ; and it is remarkable that these and the Annals, compiled by the same editor, the Very Reverend the Dean of Clonmacnois, are the first and only books

H H 2

that have been printed in this county, the largest and wealthiest in Ireland. The preservation of the ruins of Trim is chiefly to be ascribed to the energy and zeal of Dean Butler, the Vicar, who has taken immense pains, not only to collect a great body of information on the subject of Trim, but also to bring to light and preserve many of its antiquities. Few towns vie with Trim, in dirt, laziness, and apathy.*

RHYMES.
By William Stewart Rose.

"Stans pede in uno."—*Horat.*

Brighton. 1837. [Printed by Creasy and Baker.] 12*mo.* pp. 104. Title and last leaf with the printer's names.

The last work of that accomplished scholar, and most witty and agreeable companion, Mr. Stewart Rose. Printed, we believe, with the author's consent, by his friend, Mr. Townsend, of Kingston-on-the-Sea.

A Brief Descriptive Catalogue of the Medals struck in France and its Dependencies, between the Years 1789 and 1830, Contained in the Cabinet of the British Museum, with the Deficiencies noted.

By the editor of " The Napoleon Medals."

London: Printed by J. and C. Adlard. 1837. (Not printed for sale.) 8*vo.*

By Mr. Edward Edwards.

---

* " Beauties of the Boyne," by W. R. Wilde.

OWAIN MILES, AND OTHER INEDITED FRAGMENTS
OF ANCIENT ENGLISH POETRY.
(Small fac-simile vignette from the Auchinleck Manuscript.)
Edinburgh.   M.DCCC.XXXVII.   (1837.)   *post 8vo.*

Thirty-two copies printed for private distribution, at the joint expense of Mr. Turnbull, Advocate, and the Editor, Mr. Laing, of Edinburgh.

TRAGICAL TALES, AND OTHER POEMS,
BY GEORGE TURBERVILE.
Reprinted from the edition of 1587.
Edinburgh.   1837.   *4to.*

Printed for private circulation.   "This reprint is strictly limited to fifty copies."

ETCHINGS OF ANCIENT CAPITALS, ETC.
From drawings by WILLIAM TWOPENNY, ESQ.

"The world might stand amaz'd in this our age to see
Those goodly Fanes of theirs, which irreligious wee
Let every day decay."—*Drayton's Polyolbion.—Eleventh Day.*

London: Printed by W. Nicol, 51, Pall Mall.   1837.
folio.   Six plates, with descriptions.   Leaf, with dedication to the Marchioness of Lansdowne,   Preface one leaf.   A single leaf following the dedication.

" The following remarks are made merely with a view to give some kind of explanation of the etchings they accompany, and not with an intention to enter into any deep discussion, antiquarian or critical. The object in having the plates etched has been simply to place in the hands of those friends, who may care to possess them, representations of a few subjects remarkable either for beauty or curiosity."

A MEMOIR OF THE LIFE AND WORKS OF WILLIAM WYON, ESQ., A.R.A., CHIEF ENGRAVER OF THE ROYAL MINT.

"This glorious and still unrivalled country, to which all our hearts are bound by a thousand indissoluble ties."—*Bishop Porteus, Lect.* xxiv.

(London: Printed by W. Nicol.) 1837. 8*vo*. pp. 213. Postscript, pp. 63. Supplement, pp. 17.

Drawn up by the late Nicholas Carlisle, Esq.

A CATALOGUE BIBLIOGRAPHICAL AND CRITICAL OF EARLY ENGLISH LITERATURE, Forming a portion of the Library at Bridgewater House, the property of the Right Hon. Lord Francis Egerton, M.P. (Earl of Ellesmere).

BY J. PAYNE COLLIER, F.S.A.
London. 1837. 4*to*.

" The undertaking has been limited to early English Literature, because it is a department which, though less understood than some others, has of late years attracted much attention, both in this and foreign countries. Had a wider field been chosen, it would have been difficult to limit the work to any reasonable proportions ; and even now, not a few productions, particularly such as are of a graver cast and of larger dimensions, are not included. It was thought that the materials supplied by them would not accord with the lighter subjects of tracts in verse and prose, with which the library is peculiarly well furnished."—*Extract from Preface.*

Welcome and Farewell; a Tragedy.
(Privately printed.) 1837. *square* 12*mo.* pp. 119.

This tragedy is reviewed in the "Quarterly Review,"* at the end of which the reviewer says, "The author of this graceful work, printed, we may observe, with singular taste and elegance, is understood to be the Rev. William Harness, a clergyman, whose recent volume of Sermons, eloquent without art or affectation, and earnest without fanaticism, shows that he has not neglected the more serious duties of his profession, for an occasional holiday, enjoyed in the pleasant fields of poesy."

Mr. Harness was contemporary with Lord Byron at Harrow. Some of Lord Byron's letters to him are printed in Moore's Life of the noble poet.

Mr. Harness also printed

The First-born. A Drama.
London: Printed for private circulation. M.DCCC.XLIV. pp. 121 (*post* 8*vo.*), besides title-page, dedication, and Dramatis Personæ.

The Remedy.

The heading of a pamphlet, privately printed and circulated by Thomas Fowell Buxton, Esq., after the final act for emancipating

---

* Vol. lxi. p. 38.

slaves in the West Indies. The object of the essay is to promote the establishment of a settlement on the River Niger, and to encourage the cultivation of the soil by the natives, as a means of putting an end to the slave-trade.

There is no title-page, but it was printed by Clowes, circa 1837. 8vo. pp. 152.

———

CATALOGUE OF THEOLOGICAL BOOKS, FORMING A PART OF THE LIBRARY OF WILLIAM HARRISON, ESQ., OF CHESHUNT, HERTS.

1837.   *4to.*

Mr. Harrison was an eminent barrister, whose chief practice was parliamentary.

The catalogue was entirely restricted to private circulation.

———

POEMS AND POETICAL FRAGMENTS.

Wigan. 1838.   *8vo.*

By Lord Lindsay, who printed for private circulation one hundred copies, and twenty on large paper.

———

SUGGESTIONS FOR THE CLASSIFICATION OF THE LIBRARY NOW COLLECTING AT THE ATHENÆUM. BY SPENCER HALL.

London. 1838.   *8vo.*

These suggestions are by Mr. Hall, the intelligent librarian to the club. The library is a very good one ; but we regret to add, that permission to refer to it by a non-member is a difficult affair—a striking contrast to the Royal Institution, London Institution, and various other subscription libraries, to which a stranger may, with a proper introduction, obtain immediate access.

———

THE HISTORY AND ILLUSTRATIONS OF A HOUSE IN THE ELIZABETHAN STYLE OF ARCHITECTURE, THE PROPERTY OF JOHN DANBY PALMER, ESQ., AND SITU-ATED IN THE BOROUGH TOWN OF GREAT YARMOUTH, NORFOLK.
BY C. J. PALMER, ESQ., F.S.A., the drawings and engravings by H. SHAW, F.S.A.
London : Printed for private distribution only. 1838. 4*to*. pp. 25, and two leaves headed chapters iv. v. Forty-three Illustrations. Table of Contents, 2 leaves.

———

A CATALOGUE OF THE MANUSCRIPTS IN THE LI-BRARY OF THE HONOURABLE SOCIETY OF LINCOLN'S INN.
BY THE REV. JOSEPH HUNTER, F.S.A.
London. 1838. 8*vo*. pp. 157. Preface, pp. xvii.

"The want of an Index to the Catalogue of Manuscripts having been long felt, an Index has been compiled by the librarian, Mr. Spilsbury, and is bound at the end of the volume."

Mr. Spilsbury has also printed for sale an interesting volume on Lincoln's Inn and its Library. 12mo. Lond. 1850.

The Voluspa.

Read April 6th, 1838, before the Leicestershire Literary Society.

By T. Smith, Esq., F.S.A.

Printed at the request of the Society.
Leicester: Printed by Combe and Crossley.   1838.
8*vo.*   pp. 61.

Poems.

Not published.
London: Printed by Messrs. Clowes and Son.   1838.
pp. about 120.   8*vo.*

(By Alexander Cochrane.)   With a dedication to his father, Sir
Thomas Cochrane.   One hundred copies printed.

Semina Flammæ in Venis Silicis.
Memoir of the Flintshire Yeomanry Cavalry,
Commanded by Major the Earl Grosvenor.

Chester: Printed by T. Griffith, Grosvenor-street.
1838. 8*vo.*   pp. 97.

Graphidæ; or, Characteristics of Painters.

"Seyn, und du wirst eine.
"Jeder Character wird Dir ein eigenes Gemälde herrliche
Gallerie von Bildnessen zum Spiegel Deines Geistes um versammelt
haben.

"Tiecks Phantasien."

London.   1838.   8*vo.*

By Mr. H. Reeve.

ACCOUNT OF THE
FAMILIES OF BIRNIE AND HAMILTON OF BROOM HILL.
BY JOHN BIRNIE, ESQ.
Edited by W. B. D. D. TURNBULL, ESQ., Advocate,
F.S.A., Scotland.
Edinburgh: Printed for private distribution.
M.DCCC.XXXVIII. *4to.* pp. 82. Preface, &c., pp. xix.

"The impression of this volume is restricted to sixty copies."—
Preface.

ASCENT TO THE SUMMIT OF MONT BLANC, ON THE
22ND AND 23RD OF AUGUST, 1837.
Not published.
London. 1838. *8vo.* pp. 49, with a leaf of the
Ascents to Mont Blanc.

By Henry Martin Atkins; from Mr. Eyton's catalogue, No. 64.
It was a presentation copy to Southey, and had the Author's
autograph.

A BRIEF MEMOIR OF THE LIFE AND WRITINGS OF
THE LATE WILLIAM MARSDEN, D.C.L., F.R.S.
Written by himself, with notes from his correspon-
dence.
London: Printed by J. L. Cox and Sons, for private
circulation only. 1838. *4to.* pp. vii. and 101.

"He enjoyed to a very advanced age extraordinary vigour of mind
and body, equally respected and beloved for his learning, and very
varied acquirements; for his independent and disinterested character, and for his many social and domestic virtues."—*Address of
H.R.H. the Duke of Sussex, F.R.S.,* 30th November, 1831.

A Memoir of the Life of Edward,
third Baron Suffield.
By Richard Mackenzie Bacon.
Not published.
Norwich. 1838.   4*to.*   pp. 513.

Title; Lady Suffield's Dedication to her Children, 1 leaf; Editor's Preface, 1 leaf; Index, 5 leaves. Prefixed, a portrait of Lord Suffield. At page 139, a View of Gunton, lithograph, by Lynch.

———

Memoir of the late Dugald Stewart, Esq.,
Author of the " Philosophy of the Human Mind."
By Lieut.-Col. Mathew Stewart.
Edinburgh. M.DCCC.XXXVIII. *royal* 8*vo.* pp. [iv.] 16.

On the leaf following the above title,—" Originally published in the Annual Obituary for the year 1828. Longman and Co., London. Privately reprinted for the Author. (Twenty copies.) Edinburgh, 1838." An engraved portrait of Mr. Stewart is prefixed to these copies, and a notice of Mr. Stewart added pp. [viii.]. Mr. Stewart also printed privately the undermentioned :—

Some Remarks on a Passage of
Ammianus Marcellinus.
London : W. Nicol. 1848.

Half-sheet, number of copies, 5, small 8vo. ; and Title, and 5 large 4to.

Considerations on the State of France.
London : W. Nicol. 1848.   8*vo.*

One and a quarter sheet. Twenty copies printed.

Marbles, Bronzes and Fragments at Chatsworth.

M.DCCC.XXXVIII. 14 leaves. 4*to.*

The valuable collection of sculpture, in the possession of the Duke of Devonshire, consists of 382 specimens.

Journal of a Tour in Germany through the Tyrol, Salzkammergut, the Danube, Hungary, etc., during the Months of August, September, and October. (1839.)

Printed by W. H. Dalton, Cockspur-street, Charing-cross. (1839.) 12*mo.* pp. 230.

By Frederick John, fifth Baron Monson, who died Oct. 7, 1841.

Pinetum Woburnense;

Or, a Catalogue of Coniferous Plants, in the Collection of the Duke of Bedford, at Woburn Abbey; systematically arranged.

" Pinea sylva mihi, multos dilecta per annos."
Virgil. Æneid. ix. 85.

(London: Printed by James Moyes.) 1839. 8*vo.* pp. 226. Introduction by the Duke of Bedford, pp. vii; Preface by Mr. Forbes, pp. ix.–xvi. Sixty-seven plates, drawn and engraved by E. S. Weddell.

One hundred copies only were printed. The plates were, for the most part, coloured.

This was the last privately-printed work of the late Duke of Bedford, and was only completed a short time previous to his death. It may be permitted to the writer, to record his deep sense of gratitude to the memory of one from whom, during the period he held the office of his librarian, he received so many marks of indulgent kindness. The present and other works previously recorded are an illustration of the Duke's unwearied zeal in promoting the best interests of the fine arts, as well as his latest favourite pursuit—botany. Want of space prevents the editor indulging his wish of reprinting his admirable preface. All readers will receive pleasure from contemplating the grateful acknowledgment of the bounty of the Supreme Will, as well as the interesting account of the pleasure derived from the pursuits of Nature's works. The anecdote relative to the well-known "Evergreen" plantation, by his Grace's grandfather, in 1743, becomes peculiarly interesting at this time, since, not the "gardener," but the storm of December 26th, 1852, has "thinned" it most effectually. This storm destroyed 1030 trees in the park and its vicinity.

It would ill become the Editor to omit mentioning that the office he held under the late Duke has been continued to him by his present successor ; and the grateful leisure thus afforded him has enabled him to pursue this and other literary occupations.

The Meditation of a Gentleman.
Anno Domini, 1568.

Imprinted at London, in Flete Streete, nere unto Saint Dunstone's Church, by Thomas Marshe.

London : Reprinted by Charles Whittingham. 1839.
8vo.

Privately printed at the expense of George Soaper, Esq., Stoke, near Guildford.

A copy is in the Grenville library.

Memoranda relative to the Lines thrown up to cover Lisbon in 1810.
By Colonel John T. Jones (Corps of Royal Engineers), Aide-de-Camp to the King.
Printed for private circulation.
London. m.dccc.xxxix.   8*vo*. pp. 188.

" The following memoranda contain a portion of the ten sheets which the author deemed it right to withdraw from the second edition of the ' Journal of Sieges,' in consequence of a military force being sent to Lisbon."—*Preface*.

Prefixed is a map of the ground covered.

————

A Catalogue of Roman Silver Coins in the Library of Trinity College, Dublin.
Dublin: Printed by R. Graisberry, printer to the University. 1839. 8*vo*. pp. iv. and 96.

This catalogue was compiled by Mr. Malet, one of the Fellows of Trinity College, for private circulation only.

————

Appendix to the Court of Session Garland.
Edinburgh: Printed   for   private   circulation.
m.dccc.xxxix. 8*vo*. pp. 22.

A Parliament House Garland.
                                        8*vo*. pp. 8.

This last contains, among other things, two very clever songs by Andrew Skene, Esq., sometime Solicitor-General of Scotland, an able lawyer and excellent man, whose unexpected death alone prevented him from occupying a seat on the bench. Of the first, thirty copies were printed; of the second, twenty.

CATALOGUE OF THE SCIENTIFIC BOOKS IN THE LIBRARY OF THE ROYAL SOCIETY. London: R. & J. E. Taylor. 1839. *4to.*

Mr. Panizzi, in his evidence before the Committee of the House of Commons, on the British Museum, says, "This catalogue will beat anything for absurdity. Scientific men have obliged me to adopt a plan, that does not deserve the name of a classed catalogue."

CATALOGUE OF THE WORKS OF ART IN THE POS-SESSION OF SIR PETER PAUL RUBENS, AT THE TIME OF HIS DECEASE; Together with a fac-simile of the original unpublished Letter from himself; and with Two Letters from Sir Balthazar Gerbier. 1839. pp. 18. *8vo.*

One hundred copies, and two on vellum, were printed at the expense of Dawson Turner, Esq., of Yarmouth.

"Happy country, whose bankers and merchants are men of science and learning! Of the true application of this observation, a more illustrious instance does not occur than that of Mr. Turner. He is deeply versed in classical and general knowledge, and possesses an uncommon degree of literary taste and critical sagacity. Those who have access to his library, and to his unrivalled collections of autographic letters and documents, from the most celebrated characters in every age and country, will admire the extent of his researches, and the munificence of his spirit."* Since this was written, the larger portion of Mr. Turner's library has been sold by Messrs. Sotheby. 1853.

STATEMENT OF THE SERVICES OF MAJOR-GENERAL SIR ALEXANDER CALDWELL, G.C.B., SENIOR OFFICER OF THE BENGAL ARTILLERY.

(Without date, but about 1839.)   roy. 8vo.   pp. 19.

R. G. Durham, Printer, 9, Upper Berkeley-street, Portman-square.

A JOURNAL OF A VOYAGE TO, AND RESIDENCE IN, THE ISLAND OF JAMAICA, FROM 1801 TO 1805, AND OF SUBSEQUENT EVENTS IN ENGLAND, FROM 1805 TO 1811.

BY MARIA, LADY NUGENT.

London.   1839.   2 vols. 8vo.

With a portrait of the Lady.

A JOURNAL FROM THE YEAR 1811 TILL THE YEAR 1815, INCLUDING A VOYAGE TO, AND RESIDENCE IN, INDIA, WITH A TOUR TO THE NORTH-WESTERN PARTS OF THE BRITISH POSSESSIONS IN THAT COUNTRY, UNDER THE BENGAL GOVERNMENT.

BY MARIA, LADY NUGENT.

London.   1839.   2 vols. 8vo.

With a portrait of the Author.

Lady Nugent was the wife of General Sir George Nugent, Bart.;

---

* Dr. Valpy: Note in his own copy of Mr. Turner's Tour in Normandy.

I I

seventh daughter of Cortland Skinner, Esq., Attorney-General and Speaker of the House of Assembly of New Jersey, North America. She died in 1834. The Tour was not printed until several years after her death.

GLENCOE; OR, THE FATE OF THE MACDONALDS. A TRAGEDY, IN FIVE ACTS.

Not published.

(London. 1839.) 8vo. pp. 95. Title and Preface, pp. vi.

By Mr. Sergeant Talfourd, late one of the puisne judges of the Court of Common Pleas.

A REVIEW OF THE REFERENCES TO THE HORTUS MALABARICUS OF HENRY VAN RHEEDE VAN DRAA-KENSTEIN.

Not published.

Swansea: Printed at the Cambrian Office, by Murray and Rees. 8vo. pp. 70.

CATALOGUE OF THE LIBRARY OF THE ROYAL DUBLIN SOCIETY.

Dublin: Printed for the Society. 1839.   8vo.

This consisted of 279 pages, including an Index. In 1850 it was re-issued, with a Supplement of 195 pages (including Index of Pamphlets), containing books added since 1839. The collection now comprises about 21,000 volumes. The title, as it now stands is, " Catalogue of the Library of the Royal Dublin Society. Originally published 1839. Re-issued, with Supplement, 1850. Dublin: Printed by M. H. Gill, printer to the Royal Dublin Society. M.DCCC.L."

Il Trifoglio;
Ovvero scherzi metrici d'un Inglese non pubblicate, ma presentati a quei pochi amici cui piaque.

"Meas esse aliquid putare NUGAS."

Seconda impressione.

Londra: Wertheimer e Cia.   M.DCCC.XXXIX.   8vo. pp. 89.

Privately printed by Dr. Hawtrey, Head Master of Eton, recently elected Provost of the College.

Notes taken during Travels in Africa.
By the late JOHN DAVIDSON, F.R.S., F.S.A., ETC.
Printed for private distribution only.
London: Printed by J. L. Cox and Sons, 75, Great Queen-street, Lincoln's-inn-Fields. 1839. 4to. pp. 218.

Frontispiece: View of Wadnoon, lithograph, from a sketch by the Author.

Style of Buildings of Wadmoor, page 86.

This enterprising traveller was barbarously murdered by the savages, owing to his not heeding the caution he had received, to travel in more meagre costume than he indulged in. The following memoranda have been contributed, by a relative of the unfortunate traveller:—

"John Davidson, F.R.S., F.S.A., &c., born 3rd December, 1797, in London, was educated at an academy near London. Subsequently he entered the University of Edinburgh, with the intention of taking a degree, and practising as a physician. His health failing, he was recommended to pass a winter in Italy, and went to Naples in 1828 ; on his recovery, giving up all professional ideas. On his return to England, he set out for Egypt and India, intending, if possible, to proceed to China and Persia. Again his health failed, and, returning to Egypt, he made the tour of Palestine and Syria. From these journeys he obtained the matter that formed the substance of many interesting papers, which he read at the meetings of various scientific societies, particularly one on the ' Water of Well Zem-Zem,' at the Royal Society, in June, 1835. The papers on 'Jerusalem, the Pyramids, and Thebes,' were read at the Royal Institution. He travelled in the United States of America, Mexico, and Canada. His last journey, that to Africa, was in August 1835 : he arrived at the city of Morocco, February, 1836; there his knowledge of medicine was of great service to him ; not only the court, but all the city came for advice and medicine, which he gave, much to their surprise, gratis. In many instances presents were offered, but always refused. As he once feared he would not be allowed to leave, and had to plead at last that his stock of medicine was gone, a large medicine chest was, by his desire, sent to the Sultan from this country. About the end of November, 1836, he started for the Great Desert, and, when only fifteen days from the object of his journey, was waylaid at a watering place, called Swekeya, by the tribe El-Harib, by one of whom he was deliberately shot. This occurred in the early part of December, 1836."

NUGÆ METRICÆ ;
By Sir H. H. Bart. M.D.
Not published.
(London.) M.DCCC.XXXIX. Title, Preface and Contents, 3 leaves. 8vo. pp. 40.

By the late Sir Henry Halford, Bart.
" Written to beguile the tedium of many a long day spent

in my professional pursuits." This work is noticed in the "Quarterly Review."* The writer says, " Sir Henry was bred in a school, or at a time when the niceties of quantity were not enforced with proper regard."

CATALOGUE OF THE HOARE LIBRARY,
AT STOURHEAD, COUNTY WILTS;
With an Account of the Museum of Antiquities, a Catalogue of the Paintings and Drawings, and a Description of the Mansion.
BY J. B. NICHOLS.
London.   8vo.   1840.

LIVES OF THE LINDSAYS; OR, A MEMOIR
OF THE HOUSES OF CRAWFURD AND BALCARRES.
BY LORD LYNDSAY.
Wigan.   1840.   4 vols.   roy. 8vo.

One hundred and fifty copies, and six in quarto, privately printed. An edition of the work was published in 3 vols. 8vo. London, 1849.

A CATALOGUE OF THE LIBRARY OF THE
OXFORD AND CAMBRIDGE UNIVERSITY CLUB.
London: John Bohn, Henrietta-street, Covent-garden.
M.DCCC.XL.   8vo.   pp. 296.

A classed and alphabetical catalogue, printed solely for the use of the members.

---

* Vol. lxix. p. 462.

A FEW LETTERS CONCERNING THE
CHURCH GOVERNMENT IN SCOTLAND IN 1690,
From the Collection of the Earl of Leven and Melville.

Edinburgh : Printed for private circulation. 1840. 8*vo.* pp. 53.

By W. Leslie Melville ; from Mr. Eyton's Catalogue, 1064.

———

LITERARY CONGLOMERATE ;
OR, A COMBINATION OF VARIOUS THOUGHTS AND FACTS.
BY P. B. DUNCAN.

Oxford. 1840. 12*mo.*

———

OBSERVATIONS ON THE AURORA BOREALIS, FROM
SEPTEMBER, 1834, TO SEPTEMBER, 1839.
London: Printed by Moyes and Barclay. 8*vo.* 1842.

By Robert Snow, Esq.

———

COLLECTION OF STATUTES FOR THE UNIVERSITY
AND THE COLLEGES OF CAMBRIDGE ;
Including various early documents : and the Letters patent, for the Election of Two Members of Parliament for the University and Colleges.

London : William Clowes and Sons. 1840. 8*vo.* pp. 359. Preface, &c., pp. xv.

Privately printed by James Heywood, Esq., M.P. for North Lancashire.

The volume contains four "Codes of University Laws," which have been translated into English at the request of the editor. They are enumerated in the preface, with some notes upon them. It is a very interesting collection of documents, relative to the statutes of the university of Cambridge. Mr. Heywood has also printed for private circulation,

TRANSLATIONS FROM THE GERMAN.

1840.

_____

COPY OF A LETTER ADDRESSED TO DAWSON TURNER, ESQ., F.R.A., ETC., ON THE OCCASION OF THE DEATH OF THE LATE DUKE OF BEDFORD (JOHN, SIXTH DUKE, K.G.): PARTICULARLY IN REFERENCE TO THE SERVICES RENDERED BY HIS GRACE TO BOTANY AND HORTICULTURE.

> " Lord of every princely art,
> Liberal hand and open heart."

(Printed only for private distribution.)

Glasgow: Printed by George Richardson. 1840. 8*vo.* pp. 25; with an engraving of the Willow-leaved Bedfordia.

By Sir W. J. Hooker.

_____

DRAMATIC AND POETICAL WORKS.

Privately printed. Very rare.

1840.

This is inserted on the authority of a bookseller's catalogue. The editor has been unable to gain any information relative to the work.

Two Lectures read before the Essay Society
of Exeter College, Oxford.
Printed for private distribution. 1840. 8vo. pp.
100. Title and dedication, pp. v ; and *pax vobiscum qui
legitis*, two leaves.

Only thirty-three copies were printed.

———

Memoir of Mr. Sheridan.
Leeds : Printed for J. Cross, 2, Commercial-street.
1840. 12mo. pp. 74.

By the late Professor Smyth, of Cambridge.
In the dedication to Miss Cotton, he says, that he did not draw
up the Memoir with the intention to publish. It is said to have
been as much as possible withdrawn from circulation.

———

Case of Sir Colin Mackenzie, of Kilcoy, Baronet, on his Claims to the Title and Dignity
of Earl of Buchan and Lord Auchterhouse.
No date, but probably about 1840. *folio.* pp. 68,
and Pedigree.

This elaborate pleading, written by John Riddell, Esq., the
eminent peerage lawyer, was never presented to the House of
Peers, it having been discovered that Sir Colin was descended from
the younger, and not the elder, daughter of James, seventh Earl of
Buchan. The claim was to the old territorial earldom, and by no
means interfered with the more modern peerage, now held by a
younger branch of the ancient family of Mar. Mr. Douglas, of Brig-
ton, it is understood, is the heir of line of the old title of Buchan.

A Concise Account of the Principal Works in
Stained Glass that have been executed
By Thomas Willement,
of London, Fellow of the Society of Antiquaries.
[Printed for private distribution.]
London. 1840. 4*to.* pp. 75; a frontispiece, the
altar window of the Church of St. Peter, Hampton
Lucy, Warwickshire.

The works executed by Mr. Willement are arranged according to
the date of their execution. The subjects themselves are in general
marked with the monogram of the artist. The first work is dated
1812, and the last 1840. Eminently successful have been Mr. Willement's efforts in restoring this delightful decoration of our churches,
halls, and county mansions; in a great degree repairing the destruction that stained glass underwent from puritanic folly.

Primitiæ et Reliquiæ.

" *Valido mihi*
Latoë, dones ; et, precor, integrâ
Cum mente, nec turpem senectam
Degere, nec cithara carentem."

Hor. Ode xxxi. l. l.

Londini: Typis Gulielmi Nicol. 1840. 8*vo.* pp. 77.

Dedicated to " *Viro eximio Henrico Brougham,*" by the late Marquess Wellesley, known among his friends and contemporaries as a
distinguished and accomplished scholar.

These elegant lines are noticed in the " Quarterly Review." *

---

* Vols. lxv. and lxix.

REPORTS OF CLAIMS, PREFERRED TO THE HOUSE OF
LORDS, IN THE CASES OF THE CASSILIS, SUTHERLAND,
SPYNIE, AND GLENCAIRN PEERAGES,
BY JAMES MAIDMENT, ESQ., Advocate.
Edinburgh. M.DCCC.XL.

These cases were privately printed at different times, and then
collected into the present volume, with title-page and preface.
Their accuracy has been tested in the House of Peers, during the
long discussions on the Crawford and Montrose Peerages.

1. Cassilis' Peerage, with Appendix, pp. 72. Genealogical Tree.
Printed title and prefatory note, pp. 4.

2. Sutherland Peerage and Appendix, pp. 40, and title.

3. Spynie Peerage, pp. 12, and Title.

4. Glencairn Peerage, pp. 12, and Title.

General Title and Preface, pp. 4.

It was intended to have thrown off four copies on large paper ;
but, owing to an accident, one complete copy only, now in the
library of the Reporter, was taken. The impression was limited to
sixty copies.

STATUTES OF THE
MOST NOBLE ORDER OF THE GARTER.
London : Printed in the Year M.DCCC.XL. 4to. pp. 98.

These Statutes were first printed in 1766. 4to. pp. 58. They
were reprinted in 1786, with the addition of the Statute dated 31st
May, that year, pp. 60 ; but retaining the original date of 1766, on
the title-page. The Statutes of January and February, 1805, were
subsequently printed and added to many copies, making pp. 63.
Reprinted again in 1814, pp. 78, with a scheme of Stalls prefixed.
To this edition the Statute of 23rd May, 1816, was subsequently
added, making pp. 80. Reprinted again in 1825, pp. 84. In 1837,
the Statutes made from 1825 to 14th July in that year were added,

with a new title-page, bearing date 1837, and the scheme of Stalls prefixed. In 1840 the present edition, pp. 98, was printed, to which a table of contents was, for the first time, prefixed.

DESCRIPTIVE CATALOGUE OF THE GALLERY OF PICTURES COLLECTED BY EDMUND HIGGINSON, ESQ., of Saltmarsh, Herefordshire.

With Biographical Notices of the Painters, and Remarks on the distinguishing characters of their respective styles,

BY HENRY ARTARIA.

London: Printed for private distribution. M.DCCC.XLI. 4*to.* Advertisement, one page; Catalogue, pp. 84; Index, pp. 14.

CATALOGUE OF ENGRAVINGS, ETCHINGS, AND ORIGINAL DRAWINGS, DEEDS, ETC.,

Collected towards the Illustration of the Topography of Norfolk, and inserted in his copy of Blomefield's History of that County.

BY DAWSON TURNER.

Yarmouth. 1841. 8*vo.*

ESSAY AND TREATISES ON THE PRACTICE OF ARCHITECTURE.

BY WILLIAM HOSKING.

London. 1841. 8*vo.*

An Account of the Controversy between Reginald, Lord Grey of Ruthyn, and Sir Edward Hastings, in the Court of Chivalry, in the Reign of King Henry IV.

Introduction and Contents, pp. xix; the process in the Cause, pp. 36.

These sheets were edited by Sir Charles G. Young, Garter, then, 1841, York Herald; and were printed at the expense of the Right Hon. Jacob, Baron Hastings, for private distribution.

Order of Precedence, with Authorities and Remarks.

London. M.DCCC.XLI. 8vo. pp. 84.

Printed by Sir Charles G. Young, Garter, for private distribution: this tract exhibits all the known and recognised authorities which guide and regulate the order of Precedence in the civil order of society in this country.

Memoir of the Life and Services of Admiral Sir William Hargood, G.C.B., G.C.H. Compiled from authentic documents under the direction of Lady Hargood,

By Joseph Allen, Esq.,

Author of " England's Wooden Walls," &c.

Greenwich: Printed for private circulation only, by Henry S. Richardson. M.DCCC.XLI. 8vo. pp. 296. Title, Preface, pp. xii; Portrait, engraved by James Thomson.

POEMS,

BY ALEXANDER JAMES BEREFORD HOPE.

Privately printed.

W. Nicol, Shakespeare Press, Pall Mall. 1841. 8vo.

Two hundred copies were printed.

————

THE FOREIGN AFFAIRS OF GREAT BRITAIN AD-MINISTERED BY THE RIGHT HONOURABLE HENRY JOHN, VISCOUNT PALMERSTON.

Not published.

London: John Reid and Co. 1841. 8vo. pp. 276. With a portrait of the Noble Viscount.

————

HORÆ POETICÆ, IN THREE PARTS.

Part 1. The Spiritual application of the Classics.

Part 2. A Paraphrase of the Proserpine of Claudian.

Part 3. Lyrics on Various Subjects, to which is appended a Popular Epistle on the utility of the Classics.

London. 1841. Privately printed. 8vo. (pp. 242.)

————

SACRED AND MISCELLANEOUS POEMS.

BY JOHN BATTEN.

London: Printed by D. Batten, Clapham Common, for private circulation only. 1841. 12mo. pp. 309. Two leaves at end.

LETTERS TO A FRIEND.
BY JOHN STERLING.
Brighton.   1841.   8*vo*.

———

EXTRACTS FROM THE LETTERS OF JAMES BACKHOUSE, NOW ENGAGED IN A RELIGIOUS VISIT TO VAN DIE-MAN'S LAND AND NEW SOUTH WALES, ACCOMPANIED BY GEORGE WASHINGTON WALKER.

Part 1. 8*vo*. Lindfield. 1834. Second edition. 8*vo*. Lindfield. 1837. Third edition. 8*vo*. London. 1838.

Part 2. 8*vo*. 1837. Second edition. 8*vo*. 1838.

Part 3. 8*vo*. 1838.

Part 4. 8*vo*. 1838.

Extracts from the Letters of, when engaged in a Religious Visit to Australia, accompanied by George W. Walker;—Being

Part 5. 8*vo*. London. 1839.

Ditto, when engaged in a Religious Visit on the Island of Mauritius.

Part 6. 8*vo*. London. 1839.

Extracts from the Letters of, whilst engaged in a Religious Visit to South Africa.

Part 7. 8*vo*. London. 1840.

Part 8. 8*vo*. London. 1840.

Part 9. 8*vo*. London. 1841.

Part 10. 8*vo*. London. 1841.

The author is a native of York, and member of the Society of Friends. Being a Florist and Nurseryman, his books contain many descriptions of the plants and trees of the countries that he visited.

POEMS, UPON SEVERAL OCCASIONS,
BY PETER CUNNINGHAM, A PRENTICE IN THE
DIVINE ART OF POESY.

London: Printed for private circulation. 1841. *small* 4*to.* pp. 47.

"I have limited the number of copies, which are for private circulation only, to seventy-five."—*Preface.*

Twenty-six copies only were distributed, and the remainder have been destroyed.

———

SHIRLEY FAMILY. STEMMATA SHIRLEANA;
Or, the Annals of the Shirley Family, Lords of Nether and Eatington, in the County of Warwick, and of Shirley, in the County of Derby.

London. 1841. Plates. 4*to.*

One hundred copies were printed.

———

BALLADS, SONGS, AND POEMS.
Translated from the German.
BY LORD LINDSAY.

Wigan: Printed by P. S. Simms. 1841. 4*to.*

Dedication—" to Mr. James Lindsay, under whose roof, at whose selection, and with whose kind assistance, these translations are executed, they are now most affectionately inscribed.

"*Elysee, Lausanne,* 10*th September,* 1840."

One hundred and fifty-eight numbered leaves, preceded by half-title. Dedication, Preface, Contents, and Half-title repeated, occupying six leaves, and followed by one numbered leaf, containing "Note to the lost Church."

A JOURNEY IN NORTH AMERICA, DESCRIBED IN
FAMILIAR LETTERS TO AMELIA OPIE.
BY JOSEPH JOHN GURNEY.

" He is a freeman, whom the truth makes free,
And all are slaves besides."—*Cowper*.

Not to be reprinted in part or whole without the
Author's permission.

Norwich: Printed for private circulation by Josiah
Fletcher. 1841.

———

NOTES ON THE UNITED STATES.
BY the RIGHT HON. SIR AUGUSTUS J. FOSTER, BART.
London. 1841. Unpublished.

Sir Augustus Foster was Secretary of Legation at Washington,
in the years 1804–5–6. A review of these interesting notes will be
found in the " Quarterly," vol. lxviii. p. 20.

———

RECOLLECTIONS OF A FIRST VISIT TO THE ALPS,
IN AUGUST AND SEPTEMBER, 1841.
BY T. N. TALFOURD.
London : Printed for private circulation.

Since printed for sale, in 2 vols., 1845.

———

FOUR SERMONS.   BY A LAYMAN.
London. 1842.   8*vo*. pp. 74.

"The following Sermons were written at Paris, at the end of the year 1835. Composed without any view to publication, they are now printed solely for distribution among private friends."

By Frederick John, fifth Baron Monson.

————

NOTICES OF THE FAMILY OF WELBY,

Collected from Ancient Records, Monumental Inscriptions, Early Wills, Registers, Letters, and various other sources, by a member of the family.

For private circulation.

Grantham: Printed by J. Ridge, High-street. 1842. 8*vo.* pp. 97.

————

POETICAL PRODUCTIONS OF MY YOUTH.
BY J. C. B.

Birmingham: Printed for Charles Hawker, New-street. 1842. 12*mo.* pp. 38.

The author of this work is Mr. John Coxe Boyce, who privately printed these verses, at the early age of 15. He has since published for sale, "Bye Paths of Study," &c., 1852; and is said to be engaged on a poem on " The Pleasures of Adversity."

————

NOTICE REGARDING THE METRICAL VERSION OF THE PSALMS RECEIVED BY THE CHURCH OF SCOTLAND.
Edinburgh. 1842. 8*vo.* pp. 53.

From the Appendix to " Principal Baillie's Letters and Journals," vol. iii., privately and separately printed at the expense of the editor David Laing, Esq.

DEATH SCENES;

Extracted from Biographical and other works,

BY E. C. SHARPIN.

Yarmouth: Charles Sloman, King-street. M.DCCC.XLII.
On back of title, 'for private circulation.' 8vo. pp.
395. Title and Preface, pp. ix.

REMARKS ON THE HUSSEY PEERAGE, WITH PEDIGREES.
Edinburgh. 1842.

Privately printed, only forty copies taken off.
By Wm. B. D. D. Turnbull, Esq., and intended as a Supplement to
his very curious account of the Hussey Peerage.

OBSERVATIONS

ON THE STATE OF ARCHITECTURE IN LONDON.

By THOMAS GEORGE FONNEREAU.

London. 1842.　　　　　　　　　　　　　　8vo.

One hundred copies were printed.

Mr. Fonnereau was of a good family (French), which came to
England at the revocation of the Edict of Nantes. He was a posthumous child, and one of the two only children (sons) of his father,
whose profession or calling is unknown. Mr. Fonnereau's elder
brother died many years since, unmarried. He (Mr. F., the author)
was brought up as a solicitor, and practised in London for some
years. He then had considerable property left him by an uncle, a
brother of his father's, and retired; and after living some years in
London, he built a house at Bushey, Herts, and went to live in it.
This was the best-built house, and, for its size, the most expensive,

in England. He was a person of great taste and acquirements, considerable wit, and the most extraordinary sound common sense. He died 13th Nov. 1850, at Bushey, aged 61, unmarried. He wrote some of the Notes to Croker's edition of "Boswell's Life of Johnson." He also wrote and printed, privately, without his name, 100 copies of a small book called "The Diary of a Dutiful Son." It was reviewed or rather revised in the "Quarterly Review," vol. lxxxvi. p. 449.

COLLECTANEA GLOCESTRIENSIA :
Or, Catalogue of Books, Travels, Prints, Coins, &c., relating to the County of Gloucester.
In the possession of JOHN DELAFIELD PHELPS, Esq., of Chavenage House.
London : Printed by William Nicol, Shakespeare Press, Pall Mall. 1842. 8vo. pp. 284.

Ninety-four copies were printed in royal 8vo., and twelve imperial 8vo.

CORRESPONDENCE BETWEEN THE RIGHT HON. WILLIAM PITT AND CHARLES, DUKE OF RUTLAND, LORD LIEUTENANT OF IRELAND, 1781–1787.
Not published, and only one hundred copies printed.
London : Printed by A. Spottiswoode, New-street-square. 1842. 8vo. pp. 174. A single leaf of Introduction, signed "Mahon."

This correspondence forms an interesting paper in the "Quarterly Review;"* from the conclusion of which we borrow the following

---

* Vol. lxx. p. 289.

extract :—" We close this volume with the earnest hope that it may not be the only one of its class to come before us. Every succeeding day, as it bears us further from the era of Pitt and Fox, removes more and more of the few who yet lingered amongst us, the contemporaries and friends of these illustrious men. . . . . . The words ' private,' and ' most private,' on the cover, need be no longer spells to restrain us. We may, now, without any breach of public duty—without any wound to personal feelings—explore the hidden thoughts, the inward workings of those two great minds, which stood arrayed against each other during twenty-three stormy and eventful years. We may trace them in their boyhood, and inquire whether it was in part through careful training, or all by their endowments at birth, that each of them inherited his father's gift of genius — that rarest of all gifts to inherit from a parent — as if, according to the fine thought of Dante, the Great Giver had willed to show that it proceeds from Himself alone :—

> ' Rade volte risurge per li rami
> L' umana probitate : e questo vuole
> Quei che la da, perche da lui si chiami.' * "

Since this was written, the writer's wishes, as to the publication of the private correspondence of eminent statesmen, have been, in some degree, realised ; our readers are too well acquainted with them to require their enumeration. The time, it is to be hoped, is not very distant, when the world may look for the correspondence of the great statesman Sir Robert Peel, and his illustrious friend the Great Duke.

JOURNAL OF A STEAM VOYAGE
DOWN THE DANUBE TO CONSTANTINOPLE.
London : Printed by Moyes and Barclay. 1842. 8vo.

The author is Robert Snow, Esq.

---

* Purg. Lib. vii. verse 121.

MEMOIRS OF THE DISTINGUISHED NAVAL COMMAND-
ERS WHOSE PORTRAITS ARE EXHIBITED IN THE ROYAL
NAVAL GALLERY OF GREENWICH HOSPITAL.

Greenwich : Printed at H. Algernon Locker's private press. 1842. 8vo. pp. 120.

The editor is a son of the late Edward Hawke Locker, Esq., a Commissioner of Greenwich Hospital.

THE ORDERS IN COUNCIL AT PRESENT IN FORCE,
AND SOME OF THE ACTS OF PARLIAMENT FOR THE
REGULATION OF THE NAVAL SERVICE.

London : Printed by W. Clowes and Sons, for Her Majesty's Stationery Office. 1842. 8vo. pp. 628.

Compiled by C. P. Roney, Esq., and considered a valuable historical volume.

ALPHABETICAL CATALOGUE OF THE PRINTED BOOKS
IN THE LIBRARY OF THE INNER TEMPLE ;
With an Index to the Law Treatises and Reports.
London. 1843. pp. 300. 8vo.

BIBLIOTHECA HEARNIANA,
Excerpta from the Catalogue of the library of Thomas Hearne, A.M., printed from his own Manuscript.
London. 1843, with a Portrait of Thomas Hearne. 4to. pp. 48.

Seventy-five copies printed at the expense of Beriah Botfield, Esq.

SELECTED CENTURIES OF BOOKS, FROM THE LIBRARY
OF A PRIEST IN THE DIOCESE OF SALISBURY.
Printed by C. Whittingham. 1843. *sm. 8vo.* pp.
153, and a leaf at the end, with the colophon of Mr.
Pickering.

A Catalogue Raisonné of three hundred rare books in the library
of the Rev. William Maskell, who seceded from the Protestant
Church, in June, 1850.

STEMMATA BOTVILLEIANA.
Memorials of the family of Botfield, anciently De
Boteville, in the county of Salop.
Norton Hall. 1843. *8vo.* pp. 108, with plate of
arms and Pedigree.

Twenty-five copies printed.

ANNALS OF IRELAND,
FROM THE YEAR DCC.XCIII TO THE YEAR CM.XL.
From the " Scriptores Rerum Hibernicarum " of the
Rev. Dr. C. O'CONOR. Translated by the Rev. RICHARD
BUTLER (now Dean of Trim).
Trim: Printed by Henry Griffith. 1843. *12mo.*
pp. 194.

The intention of the reverend translator was "to bring some
knowledge of the times contained in Dr. O'Conor's volumes (see
page 216) within the reach of the public ; to give some notion of the
state of Ireland, as it was a thousand years ago, according to the
accounts furnished by the Latin historians."

LIST OF SOME OF THE EARLY PRINTED BOOKS IN THE
ARCHIEPISCOPAL LIBRARY AT LAMBETH;

With Bibliographical Notices and Indexes of places,
printers, and general matters.

By the REV. S. R. MAITLAND.

1843.   *8vo.*

HORTUS COLLINSONIANUS. AN ACCOUNT OF THE
PLANTS CULTIVATED BY THE LATE PETER COLLINSON,
ESQ., F.R.S.

Arranged Alphabetically, according to their modern
names, from the Catalogue of his garden, and other
Manuscripts.

Not published.

Swansea: Printed by W. C. Murray and D. Rees.
8vo.   pp. 64.

MEMOIRS AND RECOLLECTIONS OF THE LATE ABRA-
HAM RAIMBACH, ESQ., ENGRAVER, CORRESPONDING
MEMBER OF THE INSTITUTE OF FRANCE, AND HONO-
RARY MEMBER OF THE ACADEMIES OF ARTS OF ST.
PETERSBURGH, GENEVA, AND AMSTERDAM.

Including a Memoir of Sir David Wilkie, R.A.

Edited by M. T. S. RAIMBACH, M.A.

London: Frederic Shoberl, Jun., &c. 1843. (Not
published.) *4to.* pp. 203. Preface, &c., pp. viii.

"Raimbach rose to distinction at the beginning of the present
century—during the war—when book embellishment constituted
the principal employment of English engravers. The rare talent

and industry he displayed, combined with the dignity of mental independence to distinguish him above his professional contemporaries. Subsequently, when peace was restored, he engraved and published a series of large prints from pictures by Wilkie. In these works the painter and engraver were joint proprietors ; and, while the result helped to enrich Wilkie, it enabled Raimbach to bequeath to his family the comfort of pecuniary independence. The conditions of this partnership were, that Wilkie, in return for each of his paintings that he borrowed from their respective proprietors for Raimbach to engrave, became entitled to one-half share of the produce of the sale of the print engraved from it, after Raimbach had deducted the price agreed on as being the value of the plate, and all the expenses of publication. The following anecdote of the first of this series of important works was related, by Raimbach himself, to the author of this note. ' Wilkie painted for his friend and patron Lord Mansfield, for 35 guineas, the picture " Village Politicians ;" he afterwards borrowed it from his Lordship ; the plate was engraved and published, and,' said Raimbach, ' I have already paid to Wilkie 800l. on account of his share of the profit, and the print is still selling ! ' Raimbach's works have not merely spread over Europe, but throughout the civilized world, doing honour to Great Britain, to Wilkie, and to himself, by adding to the rational pleasures of civilized man.

" Thus it is, by engravings and casts of statuary, cherished by the mass of the people, the genius of great masters is spread abroad. Their conceptions are no longer pent up in galleries, open but to a few ; they meet us in our homes and are the household pleasures of millions. The various Academies of art of continental Europe do honour to engraving and its professors. They exhibited the works of Raimbach, and bestowed upon him academic honour, gold medals, &c. But at home, in London, the Royal Academy of Arts has put its ban alike upon engraving and its professors. Sir Robert Strange, who was knighted for the talent he displayed in the practice of that art, says, in his work on the Royal Academy, ' Care has been taken that the mode of admission shall effectually exclude from the establishment every engraver who has any of that conscious pride which the better artists always possess.' And Woollett, Sharp, and Raimbach having been of that opinion, they enjoyed no other distinction at home, as artists, than that which the public bestowed upon them by buying their works. Hence, engraving has never been fairly represented in the Royal Academy of Arts of London ; nor have the professors of that art, as yet, been deemed entitled to any place for the exhibition of their works more appropriate than print-shop windows, in which they are placed by the mercantile speculator, and constitute a material feature in the pleasures of the general public." *

HISTORICAL REMINISCENCES OF THE O'BYRNES, O'TOOLES, O'KAVANAGHS, AND OTHER IRISH CHIEFTAINS. BY O'BYRNE.

Printed for private circulation.

London : McGowan and Co. 1843. 8vo. pp. 94. Introductory notes, pp. x.

Dedicated to Thomas Wyse, Esq., M.P.

HISTORICAL NOTES
ON THE LENNOX OR DARNLEY JEWEL ;
The property of the Queen.
By PATRICK FRASER TYTTLER.
(London.) 1843. 4to.

Composed and printed by the command of the Queen. The impression did not exceed twenty-five copies.

---

* The Editor is indebted to his old friend the eminent engraver, John Pye, Esq., Honorary Member of the Imperial Academy of Arts, St. Petersburgh, for this interesting note.

JOURNAL OF A TOUR THROUGH THE UNITED STATES, AND IN CANADA, MADE DURING THE YEARS 1837–38. By CHARLES DAUBENY, M.D., F.R.S., ETC. With a motto from Warburton. Printed for private circulation only.

Oxford : Printed by T. Combe, printer to the University. 1843. 12*mo.* pp. 231.

"I have purposely confined the impression of this little volume to the number of one hundred copies."—*Preface.*

POEMS ON MISCELLANEOUS SUBJECTS. With a Preface and Notes.

London : Printed by Moyes and Barclay. 1843. 8*vo.*

MEMORANDA RELATIVE TO THE WORCESTERSHIRE YEOMANRY CAVALRY, NOW THE QUEEN'S OWN, Raised by Other Archer, 6th Earl of Plymouth, in 1831. Now under the command of Lieut.-Col. the Hon. Robert Henry Clive, M.P.

London : Printed by S. and J. Bentley, Wilson, and Fley. 1843. 8*vo.* pp. 124.

"An act of justice to the memory of that much-lamented nobleman, and to the gallant gentlemen and yeomen who so nobly responded to his patriotic appeal, to preserve some record of the first establishment and subsequent services of the Regiment.

"R. H. CLIVE."

The gallant and amiable commander of the Regiment has recently been removed from a circle of relatives and friends, to whom he was endeared by his excellent qualities. The Editor cannot let these memoranda pass without paying a humble tribute to his memory, and the deep regret he feels for the loss of a gentleman to whom he was indebted for many acts of kindness.

The memoranda were drawn up and revised by the Editor's son.

Arabiniana.

"*Duncan.* What bloody man is that?
Malcolm. This is the Serjeant."—*Macbeth*, Act I. Sc. 1.

For private distribution only.
London. M.DCCC.XLIII. Not published. *8vo.*

The Art of Hunting.
By William Twici, Huntsman to King Edward II.
With Preface, Translation, Notes and Illustrations,
By H. Dryden.
Daventry. 1843. *4to.*

A very few copies only, privately printed, by Sir H. Dryden, Bart.

Colloquies, Desultory and Diverse, but chiefly upon Poetry and Poets: between an Elder, Enthusiastic, and an Apostle of the Law.
From the Press of T. Lordan, Printer, Romsey. 1843.
8vo.

"From circumstances hereinafter adverted to, the sixty copies of

this original edition are not dispensed on customary 'considerations.'"

By C. L. Lordan, of Romsey, Printer.

"The Pen has been a stranger to the prose part of the composition
of this work; with the exception of quotations, I have been un-
aided by a line of 'copy,' and the 'composing stick' has been my
sole 'Help to Composition.'"—*Explanatory Dedication.*

———

A Collection of Documents expressive of Public opinion on the Utility and Importance of
the Ordnance Memoir of Ireland.
Dublin: Printed by M. H. Gill.   1844.   *royal 8vo.*
pp. 74.

———

An Olla Podrida;
or, Scraps, Numismatic, Antiquarian, and Literary.
By Richard Sainthill, of Topsham, Devon.
London: Printed (for private distribution only) by
Nichols and Son, 25, Parliament-street.   1844.   *8vo.*
pp. 388.

Contains Dedication and Preface, and Table of Contents, pp. xv.
Portrait of Sir Thomas Dyke Ackland, Bart. (to whom the book
is dedicated.)
Portrait of William Wyon, R.A.
Portrait of John E. Lindsay, Esq.
Portrait of Dr. Aguilla Smith.
Portrait of Rd. Sainthill, Esq. (father of the author.)
Portrait of the Author.
Portrait of Margaret O'Brien, the old Countess of Desmond.
Nineteen Plates of Medals and Coins.
Five Plates of Antiquities and Armorial Bearings.

Two Lithograph Fac-similes of writing, of Lord Nelson, and the Duke of Wellington.

Pedigree of Sainthill.

Two Wood Engravings of Coins, incorporated with the text.

Vol. II.
1853.   8vo.   pp. 444.

Preface, pp. xxx ; with a leaf containing a list of embellishments (27) mostly numismatic : prefixed to the volume is a portrait of Dr. Aguilla Smith ; and at page 270, one of the author, from a painting by D. McClise, R.A.

Two hundred copies were printed for private distribution.

PRIVATE AND CONFIDENTIAL. ON THE COLLECTION OF PRINTED BOOKS AT THE BRITISH MUSEUM, ITS IN-CREASE AND ARRANGEMENT.

London.   1844.   *folio.*   pp. 85.

This paper was presented by Mr. Panizzi to the chief officers of Government, and is an interesting account of what Mr. Panizzi felt necessary for the improvement of the valuable collection under his superintendence.   Nothing but his undaunted perseverance, insensible to the malignant attacks to which he has been exposed, could have enabled him to render the national library accessible to the student, and with facilities, we believe, no continental library can rival.

The editor has had access to several on the Continent, and he can readily bear witness to the infinite superiority, in all points, of our own large collection, for the purposes of consultation and the facilities of reference which the catalogues afford.   Having given considerable trouble to several of the gentlemen connected with the book and print department of the British Museum, he is bound to acknowledge, with gratitude, the unwearied care displayed in assisting him in the object of his inquiries.

MEETINGS OF THE NOVIOMINGIAN SOCIETY.
SESSION 1844–5.

Wednesday, November 20, 1844.

,,   December, 18, ,,

,,   January 15, 1845.

,,   February 19, ,,

,,   March 19,   ,,

,,   April 18,   ,,

Anniversary Meeting, Tuesday, 1st July, 1845.

Such is the title, if it can be so called, of a thin quarto volume, pp. 65. It is, apparently, a burlesque on Archæological Societies, more especially the British Archæological. At page 8, a separate leaf, "illustrations of the veritable effigy of Duke Humphrey," on wood : a few other vignettes are printed with the text.

————

PARLIAMENTARY DEBATES ON THE DISSENTERS' CHAPELS BILL, 7 & 8 VICT. c. 45., A.D. 1844. London. 1844. Introduction, &c., pp. xviii. pp. 1–492, including Appendix and Index. 8vo.

This copy was printed by the Nonconformists of Great Britain and Ireland, associated for promoting the Dissenters' Chapels Bill : for presentation to (the Temple Library.)

————

A NEW BOOK OF OLD BALLADS.
Edin. 1844. pp. 78.

Sixty copies.

" The volume is intended for private circulation, and the impression limited to sixty copies."

Edited by James Maidment, Esq. The more valuable portion of the contents is taken from a MS. belonging to Sir William Hamilton Bart., of Preston, which had been written about the beginning of last century by Mr. Hamilton of Airdie, an ancestor of Sir William.

Outlines of the History of Theology.
London. 1844.   8vo.

Hand-Book for Spain.
By Richard Ford.

An edition never published, and extending to 768 pages. It was cancelled ; under twenty copies only having been taken off ; one is in the British Museum.

Mr. Ford also printed,—

A Guide to the Diorama of the Campaigns of the Duke of Wellington,
By Richard Ford.
1852.

Large paper copies, a very limited number printed.

Hand-Book of Chatsworth and Hardwick.
London : Privately printed (1844).   4to.   pp. 233.

Written by the present Duke of Devonshire, in the form of a letter, to his sister, the Countess Granville.

The distribution of this interesting work is strictly confined to the relatives of the noble Duke, and a few of his personal friends.

SEVEN LETTERS
WRITTEN BY STERNE AND HIS FRIENDS.
Hitherto unpublished.

Edited by W. DURRANT COOPER, F.S.A.

London: Printed for private circulation by T. Richards, 100, St. Martin's Lane. 1844.

LITERARY REMAINS OF EDWARD LEWIS JOHNSON, ESQ. (Private circulation.)

Somer's Place, Hyde-park-square. 1844. *8vo.* pp. 72.

NOTICE ON THE SAVOY CHAPEL, BUILT BY KING HENRY VII., AND RECENTLY ENLARGED BY QUEEN VICTORIA, 1844.

(London: Printed by G. J. Palmer, in the Savoy.) *8vo.* pp. 20.

LEAVES FROM A JOURNAL.

M.DCCC.XLIV.   pp. 34. *royal 8vo.*

A very few copies privately printed, by Lord Robertson, one of the Senators of the College of Justice. These poetical lucubrations of the learned Judge were very favourably noticed in the " Quarterly Review."

Bibles, Testaments, Psalms, and other Books of the Holy Scriptures, in English, in the Collection of Lea Wilson, Esq., F.S.A., &c.

London.   1845.   4*to*.   pp. viii. and 352.

This book was not intended for public sale. Only a few copies were printed, for presents to the author's friends.

"I have much pleasure in testifying to the great accuracy and minuteness of many of the collations and descriptions in this Catalogue. Those of the earlier and more rare editions are given with a fulness and distinctness which leaves nothing to desire."—From the preface to the Venerable Archdeacon Cotton's most useful bibliographical work, "Editions of the Bible," &c., in English. Second edition. 8vo. Oxford. 1852.

A Garland for the New Royal Exchange: Composed of the Pieces of divers excellent Poets, made in memory of the First Opening thereof, on January the 23rd, Anno Dom., 1571: with the choice Verses and Devices of sundry fine wits of later time; depicting the same in the several Humours and Manners therein to be seen; or written in Honour of the Second Opening, on September the 28th, 1669.   Now first collected, and printed complete.

Colophon.   Imprinted at London, in Devonshire-square. Without Bishop's Gate, by John Dalrymple White: January the 23rd, Anno 1845.   Only fifty copies printed. *small* 4*to*.   pp. 98, with five leaves not paged.

A collection of twenty-four imitations of the older poets and prose-writers of England, descriptive of the first two edifices of the Royal Exchange; commencing with the time of Queen Elizabeth, and concluding with "The Author's Apology for this Book, attempted in the manner of J. B." (John Bunyan). The volume is printed in the style of the typography of the seventeenth century, with large initial letters, margins, and rules surrounding the pages. An account of this work, with some specimens, is given in "The Gentleman's Magazine," for July, 1846, page 45.

CATALOGUE OF ANCIENT ARMS AND ARMOUR AT UPLANDS, NEAR FAREHAM, HANTS. BY JOHN BEARDMORE, M.A. *Imp.* 4*to.* pp. 29, with 17 Lithographic Plates.

Fifty copies printed.

ON THE PORTRAITS OF MARY QUEEN OF SCOTS; With Remarks on an original picture of that Princess, recently discovered. London: Printed by Bentley, Wilson, and Fley. 1845. 4*to.* pp. 31.

By Patrick Fraser Tytler.

A CATALOGUE OF BOOKS USED IN, OR RELATING TO, THE PUBLIC SERVICES OF THE CHURCH OF ENGLAND DURING THE 16TH AND 17TH CENTURIES. (Chiswick: Printed by C. Whittingham.) 12*mo.* pp. 34.

Edited by the Rev. William Maskell; dated Broadleaze, near Devizes, May 17, 1845.

A SUPPLICACYON FOR THE BEGGARS;
Reprinted from the original edition of 1524, with a
preface.

London : Printed by C. Whittingham for W. Pickering. 12*mo.* 14 leaves unpaged, Title-page and Colophon. 1845.

One hundred copies, printed by the editor, the Rev. William Maskell, M.A.

BOB THIN ; OR, THE POOR-HOUSE FUGITIVE.
BY W. J. LINTON.
Illustrated by J. Sibson, W. B. Scott, E. Duncan,
W. J. Linton.
1845.   *Royal 8vo.*   pp. 39.

DECII JUNII JUVENALIS AQUINATIS SATIRÆ.
LATINE DECEM ET SEX.
AULI PERSII FLACCI SATIRÆ.   LATINE SEX.
Londini. 1845.   Sheets B to B B, printed by Whit-
tingham. 4*to.*

HISTORY OF THE SPECULATIVE SOCIETY OF EDIN-
BURGH, FROM ITS INSTITUTION IN 1764.
Edinburgh : Printed for the Society.   M.DCCC.XLV.
royal 8vo.   pp. 486.   Title and Preface, pp. 8.

Impression limited to fifty copies on large, and 250 on small
paper.

EPISTOLARIUM ; OR, FASCICULI OF CURIOUS LETTERS, TOGETHER WITH A FEW FAMILIAR POEMS, AND SOME ACCOUNT OF THE WRITERS, AS PRESERVED AMONG THE MSS. OF THE FORSTER FAMILY.

BY F.

Fasciculus I. Letters of particular Import.

Bruges. 1845. 8*vo.* pp. 268 (last page, in error, 168).

EPISTOLARIUM ; OR, THE CORRESPONDENCE OF THE FORSTER FAMILY.

Letters and Essays. Vol. II.

Bruges : Printed by C. de Moor, Philipstock-street. 1850. 8*vo.* pp. xxviii. 244 (last page, in error, 145.)

"The book is put together for private entertainment, and not for sale."—*Preface* to Vol. II.

It is the compilation of Thomas Ignatius Maria Forster, F.R.A.S., F.L.S.

The work above described is said to be a most extraordinary example of incorrect typography, the work of foreign compositors.

"The work is privately printed, only for a few friends, and was never intended for publication."—*Preface.*

————

LUTHER. KNOX. THE INQUISITION. NEW ENGLAND.

Papers from " The Teacher's Offering."

Not published.

Bungay : John Childs and Son. 1845. 12*mo.* pp. 224.

The production of the only daughter of Mr. Childs, who died in 1845. They were liberally distributed by the young authoress' father to those who will rightly appreciate them. Mr. Childs was well-known as a most eminent provincial printer, and active encourager of moral and religious improvement. He died in 1853.

LIVES OF THE CHRISTIAN HERMITS OF THE DESERT, FROM THE EARLIEST TIMES, TILL THE YEAR 600. BY ROBERT BLAKEY.

1845. 8*vo*.

Only forty copies printed for private circulation.

MEMOIR OF THE LATE HON. ALLAN MACONOCHIE, OF MEADOWBANK,

One of the Senators of the College of Justice in Scotland.

Edinburgh. M.DCCC.XLV. pp. 20. 8*vo*.

This tract was privately printed by his son Alex. Maconochie, Esq., of Meadowbank, formerly a Judge of the Court of Session; and is said, in the prefatory notice, "to have come from the pen of one who, during part of a long professional life, held the highest legal office under the Crown." No doubt Lord Brougham is the person meant.

A CATALOGUE OF THE LIBRARY OF THE HON. EAST-INDIA COMPANY.

London: Printed by J. and H. Cox, 1845. 8*vo*. pp. 324.

This Catalogue has that useful appendage, an Index.

A Descriptive Catalogue of the Pictures, forming that portion of Her Majesty's Collection
deposited in the Corridor of Windsor Castle.
1845.   4to.

Compiled by J. H. Glover, Esq., Librarian to the Queen. It is
only the first part of a work, which will, in all probability, consist of six. Mr. Glover hopes to proceed very soon with another
portion.

Catalogue of the Burghley-House Library :
Alphabetically and Classically arranged,
By J. F. Dove.
London : Printed by Alfred Sweeting, Bartlett's Build-
ings, Holborn, July 2, 1845.   8vo.   pp. 223.

The Charters of the Duchy of Lancaster.
Translated and edited by William Hardy, F.S.A.,
and printed by order of the Chancellor and Council of
the Duchy.
London.   1845.   8vo.   Preface and Contents, pp. xx.
pp. 385.

"This volume is printed by the authority, and under the direction, of the Chancellor and Council of the Duchy of Lancaster. It
contains the Charters granted by the Crown to the Earls and Dukes
of Lancaster, from the year 1342 to the accession of Henry of
Bolingbroke, Duke of Lancaster and Hereford, to the throne of
England, by the title of King Henry the Fourth, and the subsequent
Statutes and Acts of Parliament relating to the rule and manage-

ment of the Lancastrian possessions, as settled upon the King and his heirs for ever, separate from the Crown estates."—*Preface.*

CATALOGUE OF THE LIBRARY OF THE
MIDDLE TEMPLE.
Arranged according to Classes. Part I.
Arranged Alphabetically. Part II.
London. 1845.   pp. 1080.   8*vo.*

Compiled by the Rev. H. Rowlatt.

MEMOIR OF THE LIFE OF SIR CHARLES LUCAS.
Drawn up by THOMAS PHILIP, EARL DE GREY, K.G.
London. 1845. Privately printed. pp. 69.

Portrait in lithograph, from the original at Wrest Park. Forty copies were printed in 8vo., and ten in 4to.

OCCASIONAL VERSES:
To which are added, Extracts from Letters, &c., &c.
BY SOPHIA BAILLIE.
London: Printed, not published. 1846. 12*mo.* pp. 86.

Edited by the well-known Joanna Baillie,* and is the work of her sister-in-law, Mrs. Baillie (Miss Denman), wife of the physician Dr. Baillie.

---

* When more than eighty years old.

Songs of the Holy Land.
Edinburgh.　1846.　Printed by T. Constable.　pp. 70.
8vo.

On leaf facing title,—" Not published, only forty copies printed."

Songs of the Holy Land.
Second Series.
London.　1847.　Printed by T. Brettell.　pp. 33.　*8vo.*

On back of the title,—" Only twelve copies."
Of the first series a good many copies have been destroyed ; of
the second only three exist. The entire work was published, 8vo.
London. 1848. (J. Ollivier.) Ten copies were printed on large
paper. The author is William Stirling, Esq., M.P.

———

On the Elements of Picturesque Scenery, considered with reference to Landscape Painting.
London.　1846.　　　　　　*royal 8vo.*　pp. 375.

By Henry Twining, Esq., who has since printed a much-improved
edition for sale.

———

An Account of the Birds found in Norfolk, including Notices of some of the rarer Species which have occurred in the adjoining Counties;
With Remarks on Migration, and a Table showing the
numbers of the Resident and Migratory Species of each
Family.
By John Henry Gurney,
and William Richard Fisher.
1846.　　　　　　　　　　　　　　*8vo.*

DRAMAS FOR THE STAGE.
BY GEORGE STEPHENS,
Author of the " Manuscripts of Erdeley," &c.
In Two Volumes.
London: Ineditus. M.DCCC.XLVI. *8vo.*

The following notice is from the *Times* Journal:—

" Genius there is in George Stephens ; his ideas are vast, and he is really in earnest. His admirers have called him a true son of the Elizabethan age."

———

GENS SYLVESTRINA.
Memorials of some of my good and religious Ancestors, or Eleven Generations of a Puritan family.
BY JOSEPH HUNTER,
A Fellow of the Society of Antiquaries.

" That ye be not slothful, but followers of those who through faith and patience inherit the promises."

For private distribution only.
1846. *12mo.* pp. 189.

———

A HEBREW AND ENGLISH, AND ENGLISH AND HEBREW, DICTIONARY, WITH ROOTS AND ABBREVIATIONS.
BY ABIGAIL,
Third daughter of David Abarbanel Lindo, Esq.
Not published.
London: Printed by Samuel Meldola, 18, St. Mary Axe, City. *8vo.*

Prefixed is a portrait, in lithography, of the editor's father.

MEMORY, AND OTHER POEMS,
BY WILLIAM VENABLES, B.C.L.

"Concordiâ res parvæ crescunt."— *Sallust.*

(Not published.)

Oxford: Printed by J. Shrimpton. 1846. 8*vo.* pp. 60.

———

ANCIENT DOCUMENTS, IN THE POSSESSION OF THE REV. S. C. E. NEVILLE ROLFE, AT HEACHAM HALL, NORFOLK.

Yarmouth. 1846. 8*vo.*

Edited by Dawson Turner, Esq.

———

THE BISHOP OF CALCUTTA'S FAREWELL
TO ENGLAND.

Five Sermons, delivered on popular occasions, during a temporary Visit to England, together with the Address to the Propagation Society.

BY DANIEL,

Bishop of Calcutta, and Metropolitan of India.

For private circulation only.

Oxford: Printed by W. Baxter. 1846.

———

JOURNAL OF A RIDE POST THROUGH PORTUGAL
AND SPAIN, FROM LISBON TO BAYONNE.
BY CHARLES BEAUFOY, ESQ. 1820.

1846.

Three hundred copies were printed.

Cosas de España;
or, Scraps from the Portfolio of a Traveller.
London. 1847. *small 8vo.*

Fifteen woodcuts (afterwards used in "Annals of the Artists of Spain"), with a title page, and a leaf of contents : 17 leaves in all.

Twenty copies printed for the benefit of a charity bazaar at Perth.

Notes of an English Traveller, during a Two Days' sojourn at Ober-Wesel, on the Rhine.
1847. *8vo.* pp. 22.

By the Rev. Joseph Hunter, the historian of Hallamshire and South Yorkshire.

Count Alarcos. A Tragedy.
By B. D'Israeli, M.P. Author of "Tancred."

An edition of twenty-five copies only printed. Published by the Marchioness of Londonderry, at her Stall, in the Grand Bazaar, held for the relief of the distressed Irish, in the Regent's Park Barracks, May 26th, 1847. 8vo.

Memoirs of Charles Macintosh, F.R.S.
Printed by his son for private circulation in 1847.

"This little volume will not be overlooked by those curious as to the history of science; for the gentleman, whose name is popularly known only in connection with our water-proof capes and cloaks, was, in fact, a scientific chemist of great and varied accomplishments."*

---

* Quarterly Review, vol. lxxxiv. p. 70.

The Lay of the Purple Falcon.

A Metrical Romance, now first printed from the original manuscript, in the possession of the Hon. Robert Curzon.

London : Printed by William Nicol, Shakspeare Press, Pall Mall. 1847. 4*to.*

With four wood-cuts. The preface is in Roman letters, the romance in large black letter type.

Thirty-one copies were printed, and one on vellum, for distribution among Mr. Curzon's friends.

Lectures on the Church Catechism, delivered in Eton College Chapel.

Paris.   1845–7.   12*mo.*

By the Rev. Dr. Hawtrey, then Head Master of Eton College, since Provost ; who also printed privately, "Sermons and Lectures in Eton College Chapel, in the years 1848-9." Edinburgh. 12mo. 1849. "Continuation of Lectures." Edinburgh. 12mo. 1852.

Anglo-Saxon Calendar of the early part of the Eleventh Century.

From a Missal preserved in the Public Library of Rouen.

Edited by Benj. Williams, F.S.A.

London : Printed by Bentley and Co. 1847. 8*vo.* pp. 16.

A new prefatory note, with some Latin verses on the Calendar, were printed for a second edition in 1851.

SIGILLA ANTIQUA.

Engravings of Ancient Seals attached to Deeds and Charters in the Muniment room of Sir Thomas Hare, Bart.

1847. *folio.*

By the Rev. George Henry Dashwood, of Stowe, Bardolph. The production of his private press.

There is a copy in the library of the University of Cambridge, but, unfortunately, it could not be consulted by the author of this work, owing to some alterations going on at the time.

TALBOTYPE ILLUSTRATIONS TO THE ANNALS OF THE ARTISTS OF SPAIN.

London. 1847. *8vo.*

These illustrations consist of copies, on a reduced scale, of a variety of prints, pictures, drawings, and carvings, by Spanish artists, or representing Spanish subjects, executed according to the photographic process of Mr. Fox Talbot, by Mr. Nicolaas Heuneman, in Regent-street. There are seven preliminary leaves, including photographic title and dedication, and letter-press preface and contents, and sixty-six photographic impressions. All the copies were given away as presents along with the above-described copies of the Annals, to which they formed supplements.

The following note, which has been very kindly contributed by Mr. Stirling, will be very interesting to all who take an interest in Spanish Literature :

"Pacheco, Francisco. Arte de la Pintura. 4to. Seville. 1649.

"The *Prologo* to this very rare book, which was left by the author in his original MS., now or lately in the Prince of Auglona's library at Madrid, was, for some reason or other, omitted by him in printing the work. It was first printed by Cean Bermudez, in his

'Diccionario de los Bellos Artes en Españo,' 6 vols. 8vo., Madrid, 1800, vol. iv. p. 14. Being so fortunate as to possess two copies of Pacheco's book, I had the Prologo copied in MS., imitating the types of Faxardo Pacheco, printer, by Mr. Bishop, the well-known fac-simile maker at the British Museum, and afterwards caused twelve copies of it to be reproduced in litho-typography, together with a sketch from a portait of Pacheco in my posssesion. Of this *prologo* and portrait, I have placed impressions in the copies of Pacheco's book, in the libraries of the British Museum, Lord Ellesmere, Mr. Ford, and Sir Charles Eastlake."

———

CATALOGUE OF A SINGULARLY-INTERESTING COLLEC-
TION OF BOOKS, FORMED BY MR. S. LEIGH SOTHEBY,
FOR THE PUBLICATION OF HIS WORK ON THE AUTO-
GRAPH ANNOTATIONS BY THE GREAT THEOLOGICAL
REFORMERS, MELANCTHON AND LUTHER; AS FOUND
IN COPIES OF THEOLOGICAL AND CLASSICAL WORKS
FORMERLY IN THEIR POSSESSION.
London. 1848.   8vo. pp. 41.

———

MATERIALS FOR A FAUNA AND FLORA OF
SWANSEA AND THE NEIGHBOURHOOD.
By L. W. DILLWYN, F.R.S., &c., President of the Royal Institution of South Wales, and Vice-President of the British Association for the Advancement of Science.
Not published.
Swansea: Printed at the Cambrian Office, Wind-street, by David Rees. 8vo. 1848. pp. 44.

ANNALS OF THE ARTISTS OF SPAIN.
London: John Ollivier. 1848. *3 vols.* *8vo.*

Of this work, twenty-five copies were printed on large paper, with red lines round the pages; and twenty-five on ordinary paper, with proof impressions of the plates.

These fifty copies, which were given away as presents, had two extra plates, not found in the published work; a doorway at Toledo, serving as border to the dedication, and an etching of a picture at Keir: Virgin and child, by Alonso Cano, facing p. 795.

Although this can hardly be called privately printed, the peculiarity of the large paper copies of this interesting and valuable work appears to entitle it to a place in this catalogue.

CATALOGUE OF THE BOOKS IN THE LIBRARY OF THE
COLLEGE OF ADVOCATES IN DOCTORS' COMMONS.
London: Macintosh, Printer, Great New-street. 1848.
8vo.

A TESTIMONY: POEMS,
BY THE HONOURABLE HENRY SKEFFINGTON. 1834–46.

" Remember now thy Creator in the days of thy youth."
Eccles. xii. 1.

Published by W. D. Biden and Co., Kingston-upon-Thames. 1848. *4to.* pp. 167.

This volume was "the solacing occupation of compiling, and the happiness now of distributing amongst those who can so appreciate it."

CATALOGUE OF PICTURES IN THE POSSESSION OF
BERIAH BOTFIELD, ESQ., AT NORTON HALL.
London.   1848.   8*vo*.   pp. 78.   Two Plates.

Twenty-five copies printed.

———

SEPULCHRA EXPOSITA; OR, AN ACCOUNT OF OPEN-
ING SOME BARROWS IN THE NEIGHBOURHOOD OF
AUDLEY END.
1848.   8*vo*.

By the Hon. Richard Cornwallis Neville, eldest son of Lord Bray-
brooke.
" There is one noticeable fact in connection with the cemetery in
which Mr. Neville's researches have been made,—viz. that urns and
skeletons were found together : affording satisfactory evidence that
the two forms of burial were for some time co-existent."

———

CATALOGUE OF THE LIBRARY OF THE LITERARY AND
PHILOSOPHICAL SOCIETY OF NEWCASTLE-UPON-TYNE,
WITH THE LAWS, AND A LIST OF THE OFFICERS AND
MEMBERS.
                      " Vires acquirit eundo."

Newcastle : Printed by J. Blackwell and Co., Pilgrim-
street.   1848.

The catalogue is classified, with an index of authors and subjects.
Introductory matter and contents, pp. xlviii.   Catalogue and Index, pp. 838.

GUIDE TO THE HISTORIAN, BIOGRAPHER, THE AN-
TIQUARY, THE MAN OF LITERARY CURIOSITY, AND THE
COLLECTOR OF AUTOGRAPHS, TOWARDS THE VERIFI-
CATION OF MSS.

By DAWSON TURNER, F.R.S.

Yarmouth. 1848.   *8vo.*

A CATALOGUE OF THE LIBRARY OF THE LATE JOHN
BYROM, ESQ., M.A., F.R.S., formerly Fellow of Trinity
College, Cambridge, preserved at Kersall Cell, Lan-
cashire.

Printed for private circulation only.

London. M.DCCC.XLVIII.   *4to.*

"A catalogue of the library of the late John Byrom, whose poems
and system of short-hand have given a well-earned celebrity to his
name." It was prepared under the superintendence of the late
Mr. Rodd.

THE RECORD OF THE HOUSE OF GOURNAY, COM-
PILED FROM ORIGINAL DOCUMENTS BY DANIEL GUR-
NEY, F.S.A.

Printed (for private distribution only) by John Bowyer
Nichols. 1848. 4*to.*

A CATALOGUE OF THE BOOKS IN THE LIBRARY
OF THE DIOCESE OF DERRY.

Londonderry : Printed at the *Sentinel* Office. 1848.
8*vo.* pp. ii. and 47.

M M

A.D. 1316–1849. [*sic* in original.]
THE LAY OF THE TURINGS;
A Sketch of the Family History, feebly conceived and imperfectly executed : now dedicated to the Chief, with the sincerest respect and affection,
BY H. M. K.
4*to.* pp. 78, including the Notes.

Two hundred and fifty copies were printed, entirely for private circulation, by the Rev. Henry Mackenzie, vicar of St. Martin-in-the-Fields.

———

HISTORICAL ANECDOTES OF THE NOBLE FAMILY OF KENNEDY, MARQUESS OF AILSA AND EARL OF CASSILIS, WITH NOTICE OF SOME OF THE PRINCIPAL CADETS THEREOF.
Printed at Edinburgh. 1849. 4*to.* pp. 58. Appendix, containing Royal Letters, Commissions, and other papers of the Earls of Cassilis, pp. 40.

———

CATALOGUE OF BOOKS ON FOREIGN LAW, FOUNDED ON THE COLLECTION PRESENTED BY CHARLES PURTON COOPER, ESQ., TO THE SOCIETY OF LINCOLN'S INN.
LAWS AND JURISPRUDENCE OF FRANCE.
London : Printed by C. Roworth and Sons. 1849. 8*vo.* pp. 435.

At present this catalogue only comprises the ancient part of French jurisprudence.

"As this catalogue will point out all the books useful, historically or in legal practice, it is probable that no long time will elapse before the Library of Lincoln's Inn will, in the Foreign Law department, be equal, if not superior, to the Advocates' Library, Edinburgh."—*Preface.*

Mr. Cooper acknowledges the great aid he received from Mr. Spilsbury, the librarian. The Editor is glad to avail himself of this opportunity of bearing his tribute to the knowledge of that gentleman, and the kindness displayed in assisting him in the searches in the valuable library under his care.

CATALOGUE OF MATERIALS FOR WRITING, EARLY WRITINGS ON TABLETS AND STONES, ROLLED AND OTHER MANUSCRIPTS, AND ORIENTAL MANUSCRIPT BOOKS, IN THE LIBRARY OF THE HONOURABLE ROBERT CURZON, AT PARHAM, IN THE COUNTY OF SUSSEX.

London: Printed by William Nicol, Shakespeare Press, Pall Mall. 1849. *Folio.* With numerous woodcuts, and coloured fac-similes of early writings; and manuscript pages of books, titles, &c., printed in red.

Only fifty copies printed.

Most of the copies were distributed to the great public libraries of Italy, France, and England; a few were sold by Thorpe, others given to collectors of manuscripts.

WANDERINGS IN SEARCH OF HEALTH.
BY LORD ALBERT DENISON, R.C.H., F.S.A.

London: Printed for private circulation. 1849. *8vo.* pp. 319.

Vers de Société.
Historical Fragments, Sonnets, etc.

" Unpolished by art are the themes we have sung,
But they cheered our decline as they charmed us when young;
And when useful employment demanded our prime,
Our leisure they soothed without wasting our time."—*Grant.*

" Adolescens, pennam admovi;
Senex, dum perficerem, factus sum."

(Vignette.)
London: James Ridgway. 1849.   *2 vols. 8vo.*

By the late Joseph Denison, Esq., many years one of the representatives in Parliament for the county of Surrey; and whose large property is inherited by Lord Londesborough, author of the previous volume.

Catalogue of the Important Collection of Manuscripts from Stowe;
Which will be sold by Auction, by Messrs. S. Leigh Sotheby and Co., on Monday, 11th of June, 1849, and seven following days.
London: Davy and Son, Printers. 1849. *8vo.* pp. 252.

Facing the title page, fac-simile from the Gospel of St. John, " Inscriptiones Hibernicæ, &c.," a folding page, at the end, another folding plate " Inscriptiones Hibernicæ." Preface pp. vii., by the compiler, Mr. W. S. Smith, formerly librarian at Stowe.

The MSS. were purchased by the Earl of Ashburnham; and the catalogue having been withdrawn from circulation, it appeared desirable to record the contents of so valuable and interesting a collection.

Elementary Sketches of Moral Philosophy, delivered at the Royal Institution, in the Years
1804, 1805, and 1806.
By the late Rev. Sydney Smith, B.A.
London.   1849.   8vo.

One hundred copies printed for private distribution.

———

The Great Importance of a Religious Life
considered;
To which are added some Morning and Evening Prayers.

By William Melmoth, Esq., King's Counsel, and a
Bencher of Lincoln's Inn, in the Reigns of George I.
and George II.

A New Edition with a Memoir of the Author pre-
fixed, and four Appendices: — 1. Miscellaneous Notes.
II. Remarkable Persons buried in the Cloister under
Lincoln's Inn Chapel.   III. Short Notices of Prelates
and eminent Divines who have been Preachers to the
Society of Lincoln's Inn.   IV. Sermons Preached at the
Warburtonian Lecture in Lincoln's Inn Chapel, which
have been printed.

By Charles Purton Cooper, Esq., one of Her Majesty's Counsel, and a Bencher of Lincoln's Inn.

London : Printed by C. Roworth and Sons, Bell-yard,
Temple Bar.   1849.   8vo.   pp. 408.

This privately-printed volume was intended by Mr. Purton Cooper
for presents to the Benchers of Lincoln's Inn. It has never been

completed. In the copy under examination, is written—"This first sheet is the proof copy only." The leaf torn out contained a dedication, by permission, to the late Queen Dowager Adelaide. The index is carried no further than " Le Clerc."

_____

MELODIES OF SCOTLAND.

BY ARCHIBALD BELL, ESQ.

Edinburgh : Printed for private circulation.   1849. *post* 8*vo.*   pp. xix. 139.   On the last page, at the end of the Glossary, " Neill and Company, Printers, Edinburgh."

This is a collection of Songs in the Scottish dialect, being adapted to "airs of great beauty, which are unprovided with suitable words." The author, who passed Advocate in the year 1798, is Sheriff of the County of Ayr.

_____

STATUTA REGIA COLLEGII REGINALIS APUD CANTA-BRIDGIENSES, QUIBUS ACCEDUNT LITERÆ REGIÆ RE-GINÆ VICTORIÆ.

Cantab.   1850.   4*to.*   pp. 84.

_____

SIX WEEKS IN SOUTH AMERICA.

BY E. H. S.

Printed for private circulation.
(London.   1850.)   8*vo.* pp. 154.

By Lord Stanley, son of the present Earl of Derby, the result of a tour in the winter of 1849-50, on the Pacific coast of South America, and among the Cordilleras.

One hundred and fifty copies only were printed.

ECHYNGHAM OF ECHYNGHAM.
BY SPENCER HALL, Librarian to the Athenæum.
London: Printed by John Barclay. 8*vo.* 1850. pp. 22. Title and Preface, pp. viii.

———

CATALOGUE OF THE LIBRARY AT BICTON HOUSE, DEVON.
In Alphabetical arrangement. Compiled by the REV. W. D. MACRAY, M.A.
Oxford: Printed by T. Combe. 1850. 4*to.* pp. 402.

———

A CATALOGUE OF THE [LATE LORD ROLLE'S] LIBRARY AT STEVENSTONE, NORTH DEVON.
Alphabetically arranged.
Compiled by JOHN MACRAY.
Oxford: Printed by T. Combe. 1850. 4*to.* pp. 284.

———

REMARKS ON THE SUBJECT OF LANGUAGE, WITH NOTES ILLUSTRATIVE OF THE INFORMATION IT MAY AFFORD OF THE HISTORY AND OPINIONS OF MANKIND.
London: R. Taylor. 1850. 4*to.*

Only twenty-five copies printed.
By Colonel Matthew Stewart, who was in the Indian army, and many years ago brought despatches over land, performing the journey on horseback, with great speed. The fatigue incurred by this

journey, is believed to have seriously injured his health. He died in August 1851, and left his library to the United Service Club.

———

DUNBAR'S TWO MARRIED WOMEN,
AND THE WIDOW.
Translated into English Verse.
Edinburgh. 1850. 　　　　　　　　　 8*vo.* pp. 21.

Dedicated to James Maidment, Esq., Advocate.
By Robert Irving, Esq., eldest son of David Irving, LL.D., many years librarian to the Faculty of Advocates.

———

POETRY AND CRITICISM.
BY OUTIS.

"*Aut insanit homo, aut versus facit.*"—*Horace.*

Οὐκ ἄρα τὴν κεφαλὴν εἶχε, τοίαυτα γράφων.—*Anthol.*

Privately printed for the Author, by Bradbury and Evans, Whitefriars. 1850. 8*vo.* pp. 125.

———

A CATALOGUE OF THE LIBRARY OF THE DEVON
AND EXETER INSTITUTION.
With the Rules and Regulations.
Exeter: Printed by W. Balle, 56, High-street. 1850. 8*vo.* pp. 271.

A classed catalogue, with an index.

An Historical and Genealogical Account
of the Ancient Family
of Maunsell, Mansell, Mansel.
By William W. Mansell.

4*to.* pp. 88.

Printed for private circulation. The first part only of a work, which the reviewer in the "Gentleman's Magazine," September 1850, p. 301, desires to see continued, albeit he rather severely criticises it.

— —

A Private Memoir of the Life and Services of
the late William Barrow, Esq., (H.M.S. Rose,)
Commander Royal Navy.

For private circulation.

London.   1850.   8*vo.*   pp. 170.

This memoir was drawn up by his brother, Mr. John Barrow, second son of the late Sir John Barrow, Bart., Keeper of the Records in the Admiralty.

— —

Addresses presented to Lord Denman, and his
Lordship's Answers : with the proceedings on his
Accession to Office.

London : Printed by order of the Corporation of the City of London. 1850. 12*mo.* pp. 71. Preface, pp. iv.

A copy is in the library of the Inner Temple, presented by order of the Corporation of the City of London.

ANE BREVE CRONICLE OF THE EARLIS OF ROSS. INCLUDING NOTICES OF THE ABBOTS OF FEARN, AND OF THE FAMILY OF ROSS OF BALNAGOWN.
Edinburgh. M.DCCC.L. *small* 4*to.* Title, 3 leaves, and pp. 46.

Edited by W. R. B [aillie, Esq., Writer to the Signet], and printed "for private circulation among the friends of the family."

———

SOME NEW FACTS, AND A SUGGESTED NEW THEORY, AS TO THE AUTHORSHIP OF "JUNIUS:"
Contained in a familiar Letter addressed to J. P. Collier, Esq., V.P.S.A.
BY SIR FORTUNATUS DWARRIS, KNIGHT, B.A., F.R.S., F.S.A.
1850. (Privately printed.) 4*to.*

The author is a believer in Sir Philip Francis. The work has been noticed in the "Athenæum," in 1850, where will be found some interesting papers on the disputed authorship.

———

ON THE EARLY ENGLISH SETTLEMENTS IN SOUTH BRITAIN, BY EDW. GUEST, ESQ., M.A., F.R.S., Fellow of Caius College, (now Master.)
1850. 8*vo.* pp. 46, and a Map.

These remarks are extracted from the volume of Proceedings of the Archæological Institute at Salisbury, in 1849.

Early Writings of Robert Percy Smith, with a few Verses in later Years.

Edited by his surviving son, R.V.S.

Chiswick: Printed by C. Whittingham. M.DCCC.L.
4*to.* pp. 72.

Prefixed, is an article from the "Morning Chronicle," by Lord Morpeth (now Earl of Carlisle), March 1845.

Robert Smith was the eldest brother of the Rev. Sydney Smith, Canon of St. Paul's.

The editor is the Right Hon. R. Vernon Smith, M.P. for Northampton.

Recollections of Old Christmas: a Masque.

Performed at Grimston, Tuesday 24th December, 1850.

4*to.* pp. 22. Index, pp. x.

Written by Crofton Croker, Esq., at the request of Lady Londesborough: there are several woodcuts, and the notes are, as may be expected from Mr. Croker's knowledge, very interesting.

> " With the ivy dark and the glorious laurel,
> Say, where is the critic would like to quarrel,
> Crowned as they are, with sharp spear of holly!
> And what is more charming than Christmas folly?
> Only show me the man, who at Christmas time,
> Will not swallow nonsense if put into rhyme.
>> So rime—rime,
>> Christmas time ;
>> Let holly
>> Crown folly,
>> And make us jolly."—*Gesta Grimstononem.*

The prologue is by Barry Cornwall.

The number of plays, farces, burlettas, &c., printed privately, for performance at private theatres are too numerous and too unimportant to be inserted in this work ; it was thought desirable to mention this, to which may be added, " A Knock at the Door ; or, Worsted Works Wonders ;" acted at Castle Ashby, January 2, 1848. —Grantham.   Printed by J. Ridge.

An Essay towards a Collection of Books relating to the Arts of Design, being a Catalogue of those at Keir.

[Qui ubique est, nusquam est.]

London : Printed by A. Munro.   1850.   8vo.

On back of the title,
"Not published, only twenty-five copies printed."
A few copies have five leaves added at the end, with impressions of the binder's tools (of Mr. Stirling's arms and ciphers, &c.), which have been used on the bindings of the books.

Memoires d'un Voyageur qui se repose.
With Illustrations.

" Meminisse juvabit."—Æn. i. 203.

In Four Parts.

London.   1850.   (Privately printed.)   Fcp. 4to.

At back of title—
" Printed by T. Booker, 9, Rupert Street, Leicester Square."
Part I. pp. 1 to 188.
Part II. pp. 189. to 353. (354 blank.)
Part III. pp. 355. to 491. (492 blank.)

Part IV. pp. 493. to 551. (532 blank.)

Contents to each part, and titles, not paged. The author of this work is unknown ; it must not be mistaken for a work with a similar title, published many years ago, by M. Dutens.

Memoir of James Burnes, K.H., F.R.S., etc., etc., Physician-General, Bombay Army.

Compiled from the recent Indian periodicals.

Edinburgh. 1850. 16mo. pp. 31. Appendix, pp. xxiv.

Compiled by William Alexander Laurie, W.S., Grand Secretary to the Grand Lodge of Scotland.

Notes on his Name and Family, By James Burnes, K.H., F.R.S.

Edinburgh : Printed for private circulation. 1851. small 8vo. Notes on the name and Family of Burnes, pp. 42. Memoir of Sir Alexander Burnes, C.B., pp. 64. Memoir of James Burnes, K.H., F.R.S. (reprinted from the preceding work), pp. 16.

Descriptive Index of the Contents of Five Manuscript Volumes in his Library, illustrative of the History of Great Britain, in the Library of Dawson Turner, Esq., F.S.A., etc.

Never published.

Great Yarmouth. 1851.   8vo.

LEMMATA PROVERBIALIA.

London : Printed by T. Brettell. 1851.   *4to.*

On back of title page,

" Only ten copies printed :—nine on paper, one on vellum.'

Title, and twelve leaves printed in capitals, in red ink, and only on one side.

The tract is a selection of Proverbs in various languages, made for the purpose of being used as mottoes, for architectural and furniture decoration at Keir.

By William Stirling, Esq., M.P.

———

CRITICAL AND MISCELLANEOUS ESSAYS,
BY AN OCTOGENARIAN (JAMES ROCHE).

Cork : Printed by George Nash.   Vol. I., 1850.   Vol. II., 1851.

" They comprise my various contributions to the 'Gentleman's Magazine,' the 'Dublin Review,' and other periodicals, all composed from the seventieth to the eightieth years of my life, on a great diversity of subjects. Only one hundred copies were printed, and all distributed to my private friends, and a few public institutions."

" Mr. James Roche, well known as a most learned and copious contributor to the 'Gentleman's Magazine,' under the signature of 'J. R.' died last week, at Cork, in his eighty-third year, April 1853. In 'The Prout Papers,' he was happily called 'the Roscoe of Cork.' In early life he was a leading banker, but from commercial disaster he was compelled to part with a precious library. In literature, however, he found an unfailing source of enjoyment. His strongest mental faculty was, a memory of remarkable tenacity, joined to the talent of a linguist. He had stored up vast masses of erudition,— which he placed liberally at the service of his numerous literary correspondents. His reminiscences often went back to a time when the fathers of the present generation of literary men were at school, —so that his old world lore mixed itself up somewhat quaintly and pleasantly with the talk of his youth."—*Athenæum*, April, 1853.

Some Account of the Church of Cockayne, Hatley, Bedfordshire.

(1851.)

With seven plates of Views and details by Miss Cust.

The Gentlemen's Society at Spalding: its Origin and Progress.

London: William Pickering. 1851. pp. 61. 8vo.

DEDICATION.

" To the members of the Gentlemen's Society at Spalding, the earliest provincial association for the encouragement of Archæology, this brief sketch of the origin and progress of their Society, having been read before the Archæological Institute of Great Britain, at a meeting held at Lincoln in the year 1848, is respectfully inscribed by their friend and president, William Moore. Spalding, July 1, 1851."

The volume contains the sketch read at Lincoln, comprised in fifteen pages (that portion is printed in the Arch. Inst. Report, 1848); and " A List of Members of the Gentlemen's Society of Spalding," with occasional short biographical notices, occupies the remainder of the volume.

There are two engravings (which also appear in the Arch. Inst. Report) ; one, the Portrait and Arms of Maurice Johnson, founder of the Society ; the other, a sketch of the room in which the Society now holds its meetings.

The writer is the Rev. William Moore, D.D., Vicar of Spalding.

———

ANTIQUARIAN NOTICES OF LUPSET, THE HEATH, SHARLSTON AND ACKTON, IN THE COUNTY OF YORK. By the Author of the " Topography of Hallamshire and South Yorkshire." With a View of Lupset Hall. 1851. 8vo. pp. 107.

Written for the amusement of Mr. and Mrs. Daniel Gaskell, of Lupset Hall, near Wakefield, and printed at the request of Mr. Gaskell, for distribution among his family and friends.

There is a privately printed edition of this work, printed in 1848, square 12mo., pp. 86.

———

INTERNATIONAL MORALITY ; OR, THE TOUCHSTONE OF THE LAW OF NATIONS. BY GEORGE ATKINSON, Barrister-at-Law ; author of " The Sheriff Law," the " Worthies of Westmoreland," &c. London : G. Woodfall and Son. 1851. royal 8vo. pp. 156.

One hundred and fifty copies were printed.

———

A CATALOGUE OF THE BOOKS IN THE DIOCESAN LIBRARY OF LISMORE. Printed for the use of the Diocesan Clergy only. 1851. 8vo. pp. vii. and 56.

The Life of Diego Rodriguez de Silva y Velazquez, Painter to Philip IV., King of Spain.
By Richard Ford.

London. 1836. Reprinted by the anastatic process. 1851. *small 4to.* Title and pp. 11.

On back of title, under wood-cut, arms of Velazques, "only twenty-five copies printed."

Bachelor's Doubts.
A Commedietta, in Two Acts.
By Robert Guthrie, Esq.

Berwick-upon-Tweed: Printed at the "Warden" Office. M.DCCC.LI. *small 8vo.* pp. 43.

Written by Robert Guthrie, Esq., of the Helen Foundry Works, Spittal. Fifty copies privately printed after his demise, by Thomas Whyte, Esq., attorney, Berwick-on-Tweed. It was represented with success, at the theatres of York, Newcastle, and Berwick-on-Tweed.

Mr. Guthrie died in April or May, 1850, very much regretted by his friends.

The History and Topography of Ketteringham, in the County of Norfolk, the Seat of Sir J. P. Boileau, Bart.
By Joseph Hunter, F.S.A.,
An Assistant-Keeper of the Public Records.

Norwich: Printed by Charles Muskett, Old Haymarket. 1851. *4to.* pp. 70.

This was originally printed in the "Transactions of the Norfolk Archæological Society;" but Sir John Boileau had fifty copies struck off for private distribution, and to this edition Mr. Hunter prefixed a preface, not printed in the Transactions, which gave it the character of an original work.

ÆDES HARTWELLIANÆ; OR,
NOTICES OF THE MANOR AND MANSION OF HARTWELL.
BY CAPTAIN W. H. SMYTH, R.N., ETC.
Printed for private circulation. 1851. 4to.

A very ample account of this interesting work will be found in the "Gentleman's Magazine," November, 1851; together with several of the illustrations which adorn the volume.

CATALOGUE OF THE LIBRARY OF THE LAW SOCIETY
OF THE UNITED KINGDOM.
Incorporated by Charters, 2 Wm. IV., and 9 Vict.
London: Printed for the Society. 8vo. 1851. pp. 222.

The catalogue is arranged in classes; the library is in the Society's rooms, 103, Chancery Lane.

LEGAL LYRICS.
A Metrical Illustration of the Scotch Form of Process.
1851. 8vo. pp. 45.

One hundred copies printed for private distribution by George Outram, Esq., Advocate. The Lyrics are remarkable for their point and ability.

Notes of a Communication addressed to the
Fifeshire Literary, Scientific, and Antiquarian
Society.

By John Govan, Honorary Corresponding Secretary.

Published at the request of the Society.

Edinburgh: Printed by John Smellie. 1851. 4*to*.
pp. 34. With a view of Cupar, Fife, and a plan of the
town, 1642.

Fifty copies were printed for private distribution.

———

Canzone in lode di Bella Donna, aggiuntovi
un Sonetto "Fatto per uno ch'era in gran for-
tuna."

Componimenti Toscani del Secolo XIV., dati in
luce dal Dottore Enrico Wellesley, Superiore del Con-
vitto Ossoniense chiamato, New Inn Hall. Osford, Co'
tipi di I. Shrimpton. m.dccc.li. 8*vo*.

———

A Narrative of Military Transactions
in the Mediterranean, 1805–1810.

By Lieutenant-General Sir Henry Bunbury,
Bart., formerly Quartermaster-General of H.M. Forces
in the Mediterranean.

Privately printed.

1851.   8*vo*.   pp. 274.   Introduction, pp. xiii.

The term "Military Transactions" was too confined; for much of
the volume bears relation to the proceedings of the Neapolitan (or

Sicilian) Government, and to British diplomacy during that period. Sixty copies were printed. Sir Henry printed privately one hundred copies of a pamphlet in 1849, "A Narrative of the Campaign in North Holland in 1799," pp. 60.

MISCELLANEA PALATINA,

Consisting of Genealogical Essays illustrative of Cheshire and Lancashire Families.

BY GEORGE ORMEROD, D.C.L., F.R.S., &c., of Tyldesley and Ledbury Park, author of the "History of Cheshire."

1851. 8vo. Introduction, pp. iv. 1st and 2nd Part, pp. 116. 3rd Part (Domesday Roll), pp. 284.

[SYNOD OF THURLES.]

DECRETA SYNODI PLENARIÆ EPISCOPORUM HIBERNIÆ APUD THURLES HABITÆ, ANNO M.DCCC.L. Jussu Superiorum.

Dublinii: apud Jacobum Duffy, Ripa vulgo dicta, Wellington Quay. 1851. 8vo. pp. xvi. and 79.

It consists of preliminary matter, viz. the Pope's Brief, Instructions for the Synod, its Convocation, Prorogation, and Confirmation, &c., pp. i.–xvi.; the Decrees, 17 in number, pp. 1–63, signed by the Prelates in the following form: "Ego Paulus [Cullen], Archiepiscopus Armacanus, Totius Hiberniæ Primas, Sedis Apostolicæ delegatus, definiens subscripsi. Ego Daniel [Murray], Archiepiscopus Dubliniensis," &c. &c.

Appendix, consisting of four articles, pp. 65–79. One of these articles consists of Letters from the Propaganda College at Rome,

condemnatory of the Queen's Colleges ; recommending the bishops
to avoid dissensions, and in any case of doubt or diversity of opinion,
to refer the matter to the See of Rome.

These Statutes were sent to Rome for examination and approval;
and such alterations as were made in them by the College of Propaganda are marked by being printed in *Italics*. These are not many.
The tract is well printed. It is not sold to the public, but strictly
confined to Roman Catholic priests.

THE EARL AND THE DUCHESS.
A DIALOGUE.

Translated and adapted from De Musset's Proverbe,—
" Il faut qu'une porte soit ouverte ou fermée," expressly
for representation at Nuneham, in July, 1850; and dedicated to Frances, Countess of Waldegrave.

BY RICHARD MONCKTON MILNES, ESQ., M.P.

(London.) 1851. *8vo.*

This, although from its size it would, in ordinary cases, not be
styled a book, is introduced as a record for those who shall hereafter write a history of Private Theatricals, now in such favour
at Windsor, Woburn Abbey, Nuneham, Farming Woods, and other
distinguished residences, as a part of the amusements afforded to
their guests at Christmas, by the royal and distinguished owners of
these mansions.

" Where high-born courtesy and manners free
  Add grace to English hospitality,
  Where literature and art combine to please,
  Where social and historic memories,
  Where trouble flies from all, as night from morrow,
  And friendships live through time, and joy, and sorrow,
  Such charms as these meeting you where'er you turn,
  Long since have told you that our word is—WOBURN."

M.DCCC.LII.

TEN POEMS, VII., M., VII., C.,
LINES BY HENRY RIDLEY.

London. M., VIII., C., V. X., I. (1851.)

———

SELECTIONS FROM AN AUTOGRAPH COLLECTION.
Comprising Letters of Individuals Eminent in History
or Literature.

London : Printed for private circulation, by John
Gray Bell, Bedford-street, Covent-Garden. 1852. *roy.*
8*vo.* Advertisement, p. 1. pp. 25.

———

SPECIMEN OF A PROPOSED CATALOGUE OF A POR-
TION OF THE LIBRARY AT BRITWELL HOUSE, BUCK-
INGHAMSHIRE.
Collected by the late WILLIAM HENRY MILLER, ESQ.,
of Craigentinny.

Edinburgh. 1852.   4*to.* pp. 24.

" Thirty copies printed for private circulation."
With a portrait of Sir David Murray, Author of the " Tragical
Death of Sophonisba," 1611.
" The Library at Britwell House, collected with great taste and
judgment during a period of nearly forty years, by the late Mr.
Miller, of Craigentinny, contains, for rarity and condition, an unri-
valled collection of books belonging to the class of early English
Literature. It was his intention ultimately to prepare a Descriptive
Catalogue of his Library ; but no progress, not even a commence-
ment was made, in prosecution of this design. The books have

now been arranged in separate classes or divisions, to suit the different apartments; and it is proposed that a Catalogue of those portions of the Library in particular which embrace English Poetical and Miscellaneous Literature, be printed in successive parts or volumes, as these may be prepared so as to be at once serviceable for literary purposes, and a record of the Library in its chief departments."

———

PARENTALIA MEMORANDA.—LINEAGE AND ALLIANCES OF THE ALLANS OF STAFFORDSHIRE, AND BLACKWELL, CO. PAL. HYLTONS OF WESTMORELAND AND SOUTH DURHAM. CLERVAUX AND CHAYTOR FAMILIES OF CROFT IN RICHMONDSHIRE.

By W. HYLTON LONGSTAFFE, ESQ.

"And my God put into my heart to gather together the nobles, and the rulers, and the people, that they might be reckoned by genealogy."—*Neh.* vii. 5.

Newcastle-upon-Tyne : From the press of G. Bouchier Richardson, Clayton-street West. 1852. *royal 8vo.* Dedication, to Henry Chaytor, Esq., p. 1. pp. 46, unnumbered.

Profusely illustrated with cuts of arms and seals.

———

LEAVES FROM MY JOURNAL,
DURING THE SUMMER OF 1851.

[For private circulation.]
London. 1852.

By Lord Robert Grosvenor.

Secret Correspondence connected with
Mr. Pitt's return to Office in 1804.
Chiefly compiled from the MSS. at Melville Castle.
Not published.

London: Printed by Spottiswoodes and Shaw. 1852.
8vo. pp. 54.

" I may add, that although the letters of Mr. Pitt and Lord Melville in 1804 are here, as I have stated, confined to private circulation, I cannot, on now reviewing them in a collected form, see
much reason, beyond the smallness of the volume, and perhaps, it
may be thought, the inadequacy of my own share in it, why it might
not, even at present, or still more at some time hereafter, be
freely given to the world."—*Mahon.*

———

An Enquiry into the Authority for Echard's
Statement in his History of England — That
Lord Russell interfered to prevent the Miti-
gation of the Barbarous Part of the Punishment for High Treason, upon the Presentation
of the Petition of the Sheriffs Bethel and
Cornish, to the House of Commons, 23rd December, 1680.

" Swift affirms that no books or pamphlets appeared against the
Hanover succession ; and Lord Stair declares they were published
in great numbers.

" After this, be positive of historical facts !"
                    Lord John Russell, *Affairs of Europe*, vol. i. p. 284.

(London).   m.dccc.lii.   8vo. pp. 40.

By the Librarian to the Duke of Bedford. Fifty copies were

printed for private circulation by the Duke. It has since been reprinted in the appendix to the fourth edition of "Lord John Russell's Life of Lord Russell."

––––––

HISTORY OF THE MANOR AND ANCIENT BARONY OF CASTLE COMBE, IN THE COUNTY OF WILTS, CHIEFLY COMPILED FROM ORIGINAL MSS. AND CARTULARIES AT CASTLE COMBE, WITH MEMOIRS OF THE FAMILIES OF DUNSTANVILLE, BODLESMERE, SIPTOFT, SCROPE, FALSTAFF.

BY G. POULETT SCROPE, ESQ., M.P.

Printed for private circulation.

1852.   4to. pp. 404. Preface, pp. x.

There are four plates, but the map mentioned in the title-page was not inserted.

One hundred and fifty copies were printed.

––––––

CATALOGUE OF MANUSCRIPTS RELATING TO GENEALOGY AND HERALDRY, PRESERVED IN THE LIBRARY OF THE FACULTY OF ADVOCATES, AT EDINBURGH.

[Ten copies printed.]

London: Charles Dolman, 61, New Bond-street, and 22, Paternoster-row. 1852. 8vo. pp. 24.

Printed exclusively for the use of Sir Charles F. Young, Garter, and the Editor, by W. B. Turnbull, Esq.

CATALOGUE OF THE PICTURES IN HER MAJESTY'S GALLERY AT BUCKINGHAM PALACE, WITH AN APPENDIX, CONTAINING SHORT BIOGRAPHICAL NOTICES OF THE PAINTERS, AND OTHER INFORMATION RELATIVE TO THE PICTURES.

At page 58, end of the Catalogue, Thomas Uwins, R.A., Surveyor of Pictures in Ordinary to her Majesty. October, 1852. 8*vo.* pp. 118.

POEMS,

BY P. M. JAMES [PAUL MOON JAMES].

"Laborum dulce lenimen."

Manchester : Simms and Denham. 1853. pp. xvi. and 231.

Paul Moon James published a small volume of Poems in 1841. Some of the pieces from it are inserted in the above.

He is a magistrate of Manchester, and manager of the Manchester and Salford Bank.

IL TRIFOGLIO,

OVVERO SCHERZI METRICI D'UN INGLESE.

Londra. 1853. 8*vo.*

A LIST OF PRINTED SERVICE BOOKS ACCORDING TO THE ANCIENT USES OF THE ANGLICAN CHURCH.

BY F. H. DICKENSON, ESQ.

London : Printed by Joseph Masters. 1853. 8*vo.* pp. 30.

THE DIARY AND AUTOBIOGRAPHY OF EDMUND
BOHUN, ESQ., AUTHOR OF THE "HISTORY OF THE
DESERTION" OF THE THRONE BY KING JAMES II.,
ETC., ETC., LICENSER OF THE PRESS IN THE REIGN OF
WILLIAM AND MARY, AND SUBSEQUENTLY CHIEF JUS-
TICE OF SOUTH CAROLINA:
With an Introductory Memoir, Notes, and
Illustrations, by S. WILTON RIX.

" Vir justus, probus, innocens, timeris."—*Martial.*

Privately printed at Beccles, by Read Crisp.
M.DCCC.LIII.

Printed at the expense of Mr. Bohun, the possessor of the original
MS. Though it can be obtained from the Editor, the circulation is
so very limited, that it seemed to be entitled to be called private.

CATALOGUE OF A COLLECTION OF ANCIENT AND
MEDIÆVAL RINGS AND PERSONAL ORNAMENTS FORMED
FOR LADY LONDESBOROUGH.

" *Catalogues raisonnés* of Collections are very frequent in France
and Holland ; and it is no high degree of vanity to assume for an
existing collection an illustration that is allowed to many a temporary auction—an existing Collection—even that phrase is void of
vanity."—HORACE WALPOLE'S *Description of Strawberry Hill.*

Printed for private reference. M.DCCC.LIII. 4*to.* pp.
88. Prefatory letter to Lord Londesborough, pp. viii.

By T. Crofton Croker, Esq., who drew up the catalogue.
"That objects at the first sight so apparently trivial as rings
should engage the attention of the curious," says Mr. Croker, in
a pleasant prefatory letter addressed to Lady Londesborough, " is

not remarkable to any one who has examined the learned and instructive, though incomplete work of Licetus, on the subject, with the works of Gorlæus and Gorio ; although it must be acknowledged that they contain much more respecting the ancient gems which were set in rings, than respecting the ring itself. However, so important was this branch of goldsmithery considered in the middle ages, as to invest a body of artists with the distinctive title of *aneliers.*

"Nor should the claims that the ring has on our regard, through the vast cycle of ages over which its history extends, be forgotten,— its power and its poetry ; its alliance with religion and with love ; with chivalry and commerce ; with magic and the superstitious speculations of our forefathers ; its influence upon art and alchemy or chemistry, and their combined power upon the science of manufactures and medicine. Viewed under any of these several aspects, volumes might be written upon the ring, and the amount of thought or ingenuity of fabrication which,

> " 'Through climes and ages,'

have been bestowed upon personal decoration."

[The collection, purchased from Mr. Isaacs, by Mr. Croker, for Lord Londesborough, in 1850, and subsequently augmented by his Lordship, is now contained in the jewel-case of the Empress Marie-Louise.]

———

CATALOGUE OF MY ENGLISH LIBRARY, Collected and described by HENRY STEVENS, G.M.B., F.S.A., Literary Agent in London of the Smithsonian Institution.

"I will buy with you, sell with you."—*Shakespeare.*

London : Printed by C. Whittingham, Nov. 1853. For private distribution. 12*mo.* pp. 107 ; Preface, pp. xi.

VARIOUS PIECES OF FUGITIVE SCOTTISH POETRY;
PRINCIPALLY OF THE SEVENTEENTH CENTURY (1604–1707).
Second Series.
Edited with an Introductory Notice
By DAVID LAING, ESQ.
Edinburgh. 1853. *post 8vo.*

The impressions of this very interesting volume appear to be limited to SEVENTY COPIES, and, like the *first series* (printed in 1825), have, on the title-page, a Vignette, designed and etched by Charles Kirkpatrick Sharpe, Esq.

A DESCRIPTIVE CATALOGUE OF THE LONDON TRADERS, TAVERN, AND COFFEE-HOUSE TOKENS, CURRENT IN THE SEVENTEENTH CENTURY.

Presented to the Corporation Library by Henry Benjamin Hanbury Beaufoy, Citizen and Distiller, F.R.S., F.L.S., &c., &c.

"Though at present no high value be set upon English Town-pieces and Tradesmen's Tokens, by men of learning, a time will come when these coins will be as much esteemed in this country as the Town-pieces of the Greeks ; indeed, the use of the names of towns on the Anglo-Saxon and early English coins is now universally acknowledged."—*Dr. Combe.*

By JACOB HENRY BURN.

Printed for the use of the Members of the Corporation of the City of London. 1853. 8vo. pp. 237 ; Introductory Memoranda, pp. xlvii.

Prefixed is a portrait of Mr. Beaufoy, by H. W. Pickersgill, R.A., and at page 75, a View of the Devil Tavern, in Fleet Street, 1746, engraved by J. Cleghorn.

A Letter to the Right Honourable Robert Monsey Baron Cranworth, Lord High Chancellor of Great Britain, on the Constitution of the Ecclesiastical Courts:

With an Appendix, containing Proposed Bills for the Establishment of Ecclesiastical Courts throughout England, Ireland, and Wales, and to establish Courts of Probate and Administration throughout England and Wales.

By Archibald John Stephens, Barrister-at-Law.

London. [For private circulation only.] 1853. 8vo. pp. 198.

ADDENDA.

ANOTHER copy of Archbishop Parker's Work is in the Chetham Library. For this information, as well as the following collation, the Editor is indebted to Thomas Jones, Esq., Librarian of that valuable collection. It is said to be a very fine copy, and once contained the portrait, of which it has been robbed by some ruthless illustrator.

COLLATION.

There is no Title. It begins with an engraving, representing Justice, Mercy, Fortitude, Prudence, as that at the back of the woodcut of the public schools, except that Queen Elizabeth is not in the centre, which is here entirely blank. A Preface, consisting of four leaves unpaged, with a large illuminated capital on the first page Signatures ¶ j to ¶ iij, the fourth without a signature, finishing with fourteen lines on recto,—verso blank.

"De Vetustate Britannicæ Ecclesiæ Testimonia," 45 pages, of which page 15 is double, being marked 15 a, 15 b; and page 16 is quadruple, 16 a, 16 b, 16 c, 16 d. The reverse of page 45, blank. A leaf containing the arms of the bishoprics. Two Tables, the former consisting of one leaf, the latter of two leaves.

The Lives of the Archbishops, beginning with St. Augustine; 424 pages numbered, of which page 91 is blank, on the reverse; page 122, octuple from 122 a, to 122 h, (being the life of Thomas à Becket) page 254, repeated by mistake, there being no 255; page 294 followed by 294 a, 294 b; page 311 is printed 303, 312 is 304, 313 is 305, 314 is 306, 315 is 351.

The Life of the Archbishop, entitled "Matthæus." 12 leaves without numbers of pages, but the first nine numbered at the bottom from 1 to 18. Two leaves here have been cut out, evidently the blank leaf found in the Earl of Leicester's copy, and the Archbishop's portrait, as in the Eton College Library copy. Then three more leaves, the first two numbered in like manner from 19 to 22, the last without a number. The reverse blank. Two blank leaves. A list of books given by the Archbishop, 4 pages, all marked 25. Errata, 1 leaf. Index, 7 leaves. A blank leaf. Catalogus cancellariōū, &c. Title illuminated, with the arms of the University, of 14 Colleges, and the Chancellor's Seal. Another leaf giving, with two exceptions, the same arms. A leaf, containing a wood-cut of the public schools, at the back of which is a wood-cut of Queen Elizabeth, about to be crowned by Justice and Mercy, with Fortitude and Prudence beneath, below which is a person, probably the Archbishop, preaching to the Court; then the catalogue, 16 pages; "Episcopi ex Achademia Cantabrigiensi," &c., 1 leaf; "Hæc omnia Monumenta," &c., pp. 17 to 24; then follows a single leaf commencing— "Ac præter," and concluding "deincèps nominantur." "De Scholarum Collegiorumque," &c., 1 leaf. "Scholarum publicarum Extructio," 2 leaves. "Hospitiorum, &c., situs ac mutatio," pp. 31–48.

A BRIEFE DISCOURSE OF ROYELL MONARCHIE,

AS OF THE BEST COMMON WEALL :

Wherein the subject may beholde the Sacred Majestie of the Princes most Royall Estate.

Written by CHARLES MERBURY, gentleman, in duetifull reverence of her Maiesties most princely Highness.

Whereunto is added, by the same Gentleman,—A Collection of Italian Proverbs in benefitte of such as are studious of that Language.

Imprinted at London by Thomas Vautrollier, dwelling in the Blackefrieres, by Ludgate. 4to. 1581.

Dedicated to his especial good favourers, 4 leaves.
Henry Unton to the vertuous reader, 1 leaf, pp. 1–52.

"Proverbi vulgari raccolti in diversi luoghi d' Italia et la maggior parte delle proprie bocche de gl' Italiani, stessi per Carlo Merbury, gentil'huomo Inglese. Il quale ne fa presente di cosi fatta sua industria a gl' amici, et patroni suoi honorati, della lingua Italiana studiosi," (title) pp. 1–31.

" And though I have made these my writings to be printed, yet my meaning is not to put them into the hands of the Common People, not to send them to be soulde upon the Italioners shoppes : but to commende them onely unto some my especiall favourers and choisest friends : whereby, they, seeing my indeavour and disposition, my estate and condition, may be the more moved to afforde me their favourable and friendly helping hands unto the recovering of this wetherbeaten barque of mine, the which hath lost her sailes, masts and all her tacklinge."—*Extract from Dedication.*

A copy was in Reed's library, No. 5163.

THE LAMENTABLE ESTATE AND DISTRESSED CASE OF THE DECEASED SIR WILLIAM DICK, IN SCOTLAND, AND HIS NUMEROUS FAMILY AND CREDITORS FOR THE COMMONWEALTH.

London. 1656. *folio.* No separate Title. pp. 13, with three engravings, Rob. Vaughan, sculp., exhibiting his sufferings.

This very rare tract has produced large prices. There are two copies in the British Museum. The only copy in Scotland is in the possession of Mr. Laing; but unluckily, it has two leaves containing the 2nd and 3rd plates, supplied in fac-simile. Mr. Dent's copy produced 26*l.* 5*s.* ; and General Dowdeswell's 52*l.* 10*s.*

A Collection of Acts of Parliament, Charters, Trials at Law, and Judges' Opinions concerning those Grants to the Colledge of Physicians, London, taken from the Originals, Law
Books, and Annals, Commanded by Sir Edward
Alston, Kt., President, and the Elects and
Censors.

Made by Christopher Merrett, Fellow and Censor.

Anno Dom. 1660. 4*to*. Dedication, title, leaf of
Contents, and pp. 135.

Memoires,
By Sir John Hinton, Physician in Ordinary to
His Majesties person. 1679.

London. Bensley. 8*vo*. pp. 36.

At the back of the title-page in the copy in Mr. Twopenny's
library is a MS. note:—

"At the sale of Collins the bookseller, in Change Alley, I bought
the original MS. presented to Charles II., for three shillings, and
at my sale of books in 1814* it fetched nine guineas; it was
bought for the ———, but he refused to take it, and left it on the
hands of Calkin the bookseller in Pall Mall."

A Translation of Tully de Oratore.
By G. P.
(First part.)

London: Printed for the Author. 1723. 8*vo*. pp.
144.

---

* Mr. Hibbert.

CARMINA QUADRAGESIMALIA, AB ÆDIS CHRISTI OXON. ALUMNIS COMPOSITA ET AB EJUSDEM ÆDIS BACCALAUREIS DETERMINANTIBUS IN SCHOLA NATURALIS PHILOSOPHIÆ PUBLICE RECITATA.
Second part.
Oxonii : E Theatro Sheldoniano. 1723. pp. 168.

LIFE OF CHARLES O'CONOR (see page 36).
Dublin.   8vo.

"This curious and very scarce volume is particularly valuable for the information it affords of the incipient steps taken by the Roman Catholics for the repeal of the penal laws. The first volume only was published, and was suppressed soon after it appeared, in consequence, as is supposed, of apprehensions that its circulation might injure the family. The second was committed to the flames before publication, at the author's particular request, by the friend to whose care it had been entrusted. A copy of the first volume went off at a sale in Oxford, some years ago, for 14*l.* ; the present copy was lately purchased in Dublin for 4*l.*"—*Bibliotheca Hibernica*, (Sir R. Peel's collection, page 12.)

A LATIN GRAMMAR.
1730–32 (about).   No Title-page.   pp. 148.   4*to.*

This volume was drawn up by the Rev. Mr. Hunt, for the use of Thomas and George, sons of the second Earl of Macclesfield (whose names, and his own, occur at p. 17).

Dr. Richard Rawlinson wrote, in his copy of the work, now in the Bodleian Library, "Of this book were very few printed, it being drawn up for private use, by the Rev. Dr. Hunt, for Lord Maccles-field's sons, and therefore to be preserved among my MSS. R. R."

Archdeacon Cotton has a copy, which was procured from Lord Macclesfield's Library, in 1819. It contains some annotations in pencil, probably by Lord Macclesfield or Mr. Hunt. Dr. Cotton judges that the book was printed at the Clarendon Press, in Oxford, and probably about the year, 1730, -31, or -32. Thomas, the Earl's eldest son, was born in 1723 ; and George, whom Mr. Hunt calls "Littlie," in 1724, so that they may be supposed to have begun their study of Latin when about six or seven years of age.

[Roman-Catholic Statutes, etc.]

Constitutiones Ecclesiasticæ pro unitis Diœ-cesibus Ardfertensi et Aghadoensi, in duodecim Capita distributæ. In quibus tum Parochi, tum omnes curam animarum exercentes, ac etiam Con-fessarii omnes multa utilia ad munia sua rite et secure obeunda facile intueri possunt.

Sumptibus Cleri Kerriensis, ipsiusque impulsu nunc excusæ.

Waterfordiæ : Typis J. Calwell, in vico vulgo dicto Broad-street. [1748.] pp. 126. *large* 16*mo*.

This little book consists of twelve chapters ; at the end of it is the following authentication :—

" Lectæ, acceptatæ, & promulgatæ fuerunt hæ Constitutiones, in Conventu Cleri Sæcularis & Regularis *Kerriensis*, habito die 15 Mensis Julii, anno reparatæ salutis 1747, in oppido de *Listowel* sub Illmo & R^{mo} D.D. Gulielmo Episcopo *Kerriensi*. Laus Deo, et Virgini *Matri* sine labe originali conceptæ."

At p. 92, it states, that the Decrees of the Council of Trent were received in these two dioceses, without any restriction or limitation, except as to the decree concerning clandestine marriages, and a few others regarding discipline ; which, however holy and unexceptionable, could not be carried out, by reason of the unhappy state of the times in that country. The volume was not printed for general sale, but merely for the use of the Roman Catholic clergy. The "most illustrious" William, was William O'Meara, appointed titular Bishop of Kerry in 1747. Archdeacon Cotton has a copy.

JOHN WILKES'S ESSAY (page 58).
1763.

"The 'Essay on Woman' he calls an idle poem, in which he had ridiculed nothing, but a creed which the great Tillotson wished the Church of England fairly rid of."—*Corresp. of Fox*, by Lord John Russell, v. i. p. 14.

The Editor has never seen a copy of this volume; and his attention has been drawn to it by a friend who has made great inquiries into the political transactions of the time, especially as relating to Junius. He says, "there never was a perfect edition of the original work, or an edition at all. Only four sheets are said to have been printed." The work is hardly worthy of further investigation.

[ROMAN CATHOLIC STATUTES, ETC.]

MONITA PASTORALIA ET STATUTA ECCLESIASTICA, PRO UNITIS DIŒCESIBUS CLOYNENSI ET ROSSENSI. IN QUIBUS ETC. LECTA, ACCEPTATA, ET PROMULGATA IN CONVENTIBUS CLERI SÆCULARIS ET REGULARIS UTRIUSQUE DIŒCESIS, HABITIS ANNO DOMINI 1755.

Sub Illustrissimo et Reverendissimo D.D.

JOANNE O'BRIEN, Episcopo Cloynensi et Rossensi.

M.DCC.LVI. pp. 96. 16*mo.*

John O'Brien was titular Bishop of Cloyne and Ross, from 1748 to

1775. The book consists of seven chapters. The Decrees of the Council of Trent are declared to be received in the Diocese of *Cloyne*, with the same exceptions as previously noticed in the statutes of *Kerry*, 1748. And it is stated, that within the diocese of *Ross* the Decrees of Trent had been fully accepted from the first, having been promulgated by the Bishop, Thomas O'Herlihy, who himself was present at that Council.

The volume bears no printer's name, nor place. A copy is in Dr. Cotton's Library.

COPIES OF VARIOUS PAPERS, ETC., RELATING TO THE PEERAGES OF BRANDON AND DOVER.
No date (circa 1769,) or place.   *4to.*   pp. 30.

Printed privately at the expense of the Duke of Hamilton by John Davidson, the antiquary, his agent, to support his Grace's claim to the Dukedom, which was successful.

[ROMAN CATHOLIC STATUTES FOR THE PROVINCE OF DUBLIN.]
CONSTITUTIONES PROVINCIALES ET SYNODALES ECCLESIÆ METROPOLITANÆ ET PRIMATIALIS DUBLINIENSIS.
Anno 1770.   [pp. 148.]   *12mo.*

The volume consists of 46 chapters or sections. It contains,—

1. Statutes or Constitutions enacted for the Province of Dublin, at Kilkenny, in 1624, [at which time the Decrees of the Council of Trent were received in the Province, so far as they could be carried out.]

2. Acts passed at a Provincial Council at Tyrchogir, in the diocese of Kildare, in 1640.

3. A decree made by the Vicar-General of Dublin, in 1665.

4. Constitutions made by Abp. Peter Talbot, in 1670, and 1671.

5. Acts of a Provincial Council holden by Abp. Patrick Russell, in 1685.

6. Statutes for the Diocese of Dublin [only], made in 1686.

7. A Papal Bull, dated 1671.

8. A Letter from Rome, revoking a faculty of Dispensation, 1670.

9. Two Letters from the Vicar-General of Dublin, 1677.

10. Statutes for the Diocese of Dublin, enacted 1688.

11. Acts of a Provincial Council, holden in 1688.

12. Acts of a Diocesan Synod, holden at Dublin in 1689.

13. A Brief and Decree of Pope Alexander VII.

14. An Indulgence, for Oratories or Churches, by Pope Clement X., 1675.

15. Decrees of particular Congregations *de propagandâ fide*, on the affairs of the Irish Mission, 1751, 1761.

The volume bears no name of place or printer. Most probably it was printed in *Dublin ;* of course, for none but the clergy.

A copy is in Archdeacon Cotton's library.

An Account of Ireland (page 71).

" Written by Sir George, afterwards Earl Macartney. It is a masterly sketch of the political history of the country; and, when viewed as a continuation of Sir John Davies' work, both may be considered as forming an epitome of the political state of Ireland, from the landing of the English to Lord Townshend's administration, one of the striking epochs in the modern part of the history of the country."—*Shaw Mason. Sir R. Peel's Cat.*

1773.

[ROMAN CATHOLIC STATUTES, ETC.]

VADE MECUM PIORUM SACERDOTUM, SIVE EXERCITIA ET PRECES MATUTINÆ, VESPERTINÆ, ANTE ET POST MISSAM, ALIÆQUE SELECTÆ DEVOTIONES. AD COMMODITATEM SACERDOTUM TUM RELIGIOSORUM, TUM SÆCULARIUM. Prestoni : apud Gulielmum Stuart. M.DCC.LXXIV. 16mo.

The volume contains pp. 90, followed by one leaf of errata. It commences with a preface, in Monkish rhyme, supposed to be addressed by Jesus Christ to Priests and Clerks; beginning thus,—

> Piscatores hominum, Sacerdotes mei,
> Præcones veridici, lucerna diei,
> Charitatis radio fulgentes, et spei,
> Auribus percipite verba oris mei.
> &c., &c.

and concludes,

> Nam si sic gesseritis curam pastoralem,
> Vereque vixeritis vitam spiritalem,
> Postquam exueritis chlamydem carnalem,
> Ipse vobis conferam stolam immortalem.

The work was not intended for the public; but a copy was given by the Vicar Apostolic to each candidate whom he admitted to holy orders. The paper and print are good, and do credit to a small country town such as Preston at that time was.

A copy is in Archdeacon Cotton's library.

———

A SHORT TOUR MADE IN THE YEAR ONE THOUSAND SEVEN HUNDRED AND SEVENTY ONE. London : Printed in the Year 1775. 8vo. pp. 89.

By the Duchess of Northumberland.

A GENERAL DEFENCE OF THE PRINCIPLES OF THE REFORMATION, IN A LETTER TO THE REV. JOSEPH BERINGTON.

By the REV. JOHN HAWKINS.

Worcester: Printed by J. Tymbs, at the Cross. 1788. 8vo. pp. 212.

(Not published, only a few copies printed.)

Mr. Hawkins was a Roman Catholic Priest in Staffordshire, who conformed to the Church of England.

THE COMMERCIAL RESTRAINTS OF IRELAND CONSIDERED, IN A SERIES OF LETTERS TO A NOBLE LORD, WITH AN HISTORICAL ACCOUNT OF THE COMMERCIAL AFFAIRS OF THAT KINGDOM.

Dublin. 1779.

This volume was suppressed and burnt by the common hangman. Mr. Flood, the Irish orator, in his place in the House of Commons, shortly after its publication, said he would give a Thousand Pounds for one. ¡

"The libraries of the three branches of the Legislature cannot produce a copy of this work."—*Vide* Letter concerning it by Sir Valentine Blake to the Editor of the *Times*, and published in that Journal, Feb. 14, 1846.

It was written by John Hely Hutchinson, Provost of Trinity College, Dublin. A copy is in the Library of the late Sir Robert Peel.—*See Mason's Bibliotheca Hibernicana*, p. 50, No. 123.

GENEALOGICAL ACCOUNT OF THE FAMILY OF HOME
OF WEDDERBURNE, MADE OUT FROM THE PUBLIC RE-
CORDS.

4to. pp. 10.

There is no date, but, from internal evidence, printed anterior to
1791. It is of very rare occurrence.

COMMENTARY ON MEMOIRS OF MR. FOX.

(Lately written.)

London : Printed for the Author by T. Davison, Lom-
bard-street, Fleet-street, and sold by J. Murray, Fleet-
street. 1812.

By Walter Savage Landor.

This work was entirely wasted. One copy was sold at Mr.
Southey's sale, and is now in the possession of Mr. Monckton
Milnes.

[ROMAN CATHOLIC STATUTES.]

STATUTA SYNODALIA PRO UNITIS DIŒCESIBUS CASSEL.
ET IMELAC. LECTA, APPROBATA, EDITA ET PROMULGATA
IN SYNODO DIŒCESANA; CUI INTERFUIT CLERUS UTRI-
USQUE DIŒCESEOS, HABITA PRIMA HEBDOMADA MENSIS
SEPTEMBRIS, ANNO M.DCCC.X.

Ab Ili^{mo}. et Rev^{mo}. D.D. THOMA BRAY,
Archiepiscopo Cassel. et Imelac.

Vol. I.

Dublinii : Ex typographeo Hugonis Fitzpatrick, Typographi et Bibliop. Rom. Cath. Coll. de Maynooth.
M.DCCC.XIII. 12mo. pp. iv. and 132.

The first volume contains the *Statutes*, in 27 chapters ; a Bull of

Pope Benedict XIV., against the Free Masons, dated 1751 ; a Decree of the Council of Trent against Duellists, with an explanation of it *in English*, to be given by each priest to his flock ; a Pastoral, by Dr. Bray ; "Catholic Succession of the Archbishops of Cashel ; " "Short Memoirs of the Metropolitans of Cashel ; " "Catholic Succession of the Bishops of Emly ; " "Short Memoirs of the Bishops of Emly ;" "the names of the Dignitaries and Prebendaries of the Chapter of Cashel, in 1810." Parish Priests of the Archdiocese of Cashel and Diocese of Emly, in 1810. Regulations agreed on by the Roman Catholic Bishops of Munster, at a Provincial Meeting holden in *Limerick*, June 17th, 1808 : Regulations made and adopted by the Roman Catholic Prelates of Munster, at a Provincial Meeting holden in Cork, on 23rd August, 1808.

Second Volume.

Regulations, Instructions, Exhortations, and Prayers, etc., etc., in English and Irish: with the Manner of Absolving Heretics, in Latin and English: for the United Dioceses of Cashel and Emly.

By the Most Rev. Thomas Bray, D.D.,

Archbishop of Cashel, &c.

Vol. II.

Dublin: Printed by H. Fitzpatrick, printer and bookseller to the R. C. College, Maynooth. 1813. pp. 133–397.

This second volume contains a Latin Dedication to Dr. Bray, by Fitzpatrick, the printer : Two Exhortations, to be read at Mass four times a-year : Instructions on Confession, and on Communion : Dr. Bray's advice to Confessors : Instructions and Regulations on Matrimony : Instructions on Patrons [*i.e.* Feasts in Country places on the day of the Patron-Saint :] Instructions and Regulations on Stations : Instructions and Prayers for Communion : On the Confraternity of the Blessed Sacrament, established at Thurles ; Instructions and Regulations for Lent : Instructions on acts of Faith, Hope, and Charity : Acts of Contrition, Faith, Hope, and Charity : the manner of absolving Heretics (in Latin and English).

At the beginning of the first volume, Dr. Bray declares all previous Statutes and Decrees, "having the force of law in those Dioceses," to be revoked and abrogated : and that no Synodal Constitutions shall henceforth have any force or effect in law, unless sanctioned by the present Synod, or by similar ones in future.

In the next sentence he proclaims, that *the Bishop* is the sole judge and legislator in a Diocesan Synod : that he makes and promulgates decrees *in his own name;* and although he may sometimes ask the advice of those who stand near him, he is by no means compelled to follow it.

It is stated, at p. 216, that the Decree of the Council of Trent, against clandestine marriages, was duly published and received in the Dioceses of Cashel and Emly, in September, 1775, and since that period has been obligatory in both districts.

These volumes contain a variety of curious matter, some of which evidently was not intended for the general eye. The type and paper are not of the best quality. Archdeacon Cotton has a copy.

Tables containing an Alphabetical Arrangement of the Public Records, etc.

No title-page ; at the end, printed by Luke Hansard. 4*to.* pp. 155.

Poems.
By Sir W. T.

These poems were privately printed, and have neither date nor place. In the Grenville copy are some corrections, by Mr. Courtenay, who wrote the life of Sir William Temple.

12*mo.* pp. 89.

A Descriptive Catalogue of the Portraits in the Collection of John, Duke of Bedford, K.G., at Woburn Abbey.

> " Yes, here its warmest hues the pencil flings,
>   Lo ! here the Lost restores, the Absent brings ;
>   And still the Few best lived and most revered,
>   Rise round the board their social smile endeared."
>
> *Rogers.*

London : Printed by James Moyes, Castle-street, Leicester-square. 1834. 8*vo.* pp. 222. Contents, Introduction, &c., pp. viii.

On the half-title,—" Of this Catalogue, printed for private distribution, fifty copies only have been taken."

" A very imperfect account of the portraits at Woburn Abbey was, in 1782, given by Mr. Pennant, in his published ' Tour from Chester to London.' At the request of the late Duke of Bedford, in 1790, Horace Walpole engaged in a more correct specification of them,* an incorrect account of which, being surreptitiously obtained, was printed in the ' Annual Register ' for 1801 ; but there appears still to have been many portraits in the collection which even that intelligent connoisseur entirely omitted, some which he failed to identify, and a few which he has either mistaken or misnamed.

" The present descriptive Catalogue has, therefore, been prepared with entirely new materials, although with occasional reference to his caustic and acute remarks. Some sketch of the personal history or qualities of the personages depicted seemed desirable for the service of the visitant ; but those which are attached will be found very simple and succinct ; for a few incidental hints are generally all that is required to awaken our remembrance of departed characters, or to satisfy the natural inquiry,—

> " ' How lived, how loved, how died they ? ' "
>
> *Extract from the Introduction.*

---

* The original MS. is at Woburn Abbey.

Since this Catalogue appeared, several additions have been made to the collection, which have altered the arrangement. A new Catalogue is in contemplation, to include the valuable works of ancient and modern art, which adorn the walls of Woburn Abbey.

THE LIFE OF THOMAS DAY, ESQ.
Author of " Sandford and Merton."
Berwick: Printed by J. Weatherly, High-street. 12*mo.* pp. 8. 1836.

Privately printed by the late Mr. Wilkie, of Ladythorn, a gentleman of good estate in the north of England; but of somewhat eccentric habits.

GLENORMISTON.
First Paper.
[BY WILLIAM CHAMBERS.]
1849. Royal 8*vo.* Printed for private use. With Map and Plates.

This is a collection of "Private Memoranda, printed with a view to convenient preservation and reference," relative to the purchase of the estate of Glenormiston, in Inverleithen, Peeblesshire, by William Chambers, one of the publishers of "Chambers' Journal," in Edinburgh.

LETTER TO LORD MAHON ON THE MINISTERIAL CHANGES OF 1801 AND 1804.
For private circulation only.
(London.) 1852. James Ridgway, Piccadilly. 8*vo.* pp. 24.

Written by the Hon. Col. Grey, in consequence of the correspondence between Mr. Pitt and Lord Melville, mentioned in page 553.

In a postscript, Col. Grey says, "I cannot print the foregoing letter without adding a note to contrast the conduct of my father at this time towards Mr. Fox, with that of the Whig party towards himself at a later period, when in 1827 they left him to join Mr. Canning." After the letter was printed, Col. Grey added, in writing, the words "a large portion of." As the history of the political transactions of the period in question will, in all probability, not be written until a considerable period has elapsed, the Editor has been induced to add the following note, which has been contributed from the best authority, and has only to regret that he is not permitted to name it :—

"Before the period in question, Lord Grey contemplated retiring from public life, and recommended those political friends who regarded him as their leader, to place themselves under the guidance of the Marquess of Lansdowne. It is well known that noble Lord and 'a large portion' of the Whig party did support Mr. Canning, but a portion of the party equally large did not. Among the latter may be named the late Duke of Bedford, the late Lord Rosslyn, Lord Jersey, and others in the House of Lords. The present Duke of Bedford, Lord Althorpe, Lord George Cavendish, Mr. Coke, of Norfolk, and many others in the House of Commons.

"This portion of the party in the House of Commons were called the 'Charleys,' or Watchmen. Lord Althorpe, in writing to a friend, said he should observe a 'favourable neutrality.' "

ENGLISH AND LATIN POEMS, ORIGINAL AND TRANSLATED.
By the late JOHN LATHAM, D.C.L.,
of Bradwall, Cheshire.

"In memoriam."

Not published.
London : Printed by T. Richards. 1853. 12*mo*.

GENEALOGICAL HISTORY OF THE FAMILY OF BEATSON.
BY ALEX^{R.} JOHN BEATSON, ESQ.

Edinburgh.   1854.   Portrait.   4*to.*

Only fifty copies printed for private circulation.

SOME ACCOUNT OF A JOURNEY ACROSS THE ALPS,
IN A LETTER TO A FRIEND.

London: (Printed for private circulation.)   12*mo.*
pp. 44.

By Mr. A. Hayward.   ———

ENQUIRY INTO THE RATIONALE OF CHRISTIANITY.
(Attributed to Mr. Balguy.)
BY JOHN CLEAVER BANKS.

No title.   8*vo.*

" Liber rarissimus, never published, and given to Dr. Parr by his
friend, the author."

" This book has successively been in the possession of Jortin, M.
Lort, J. Cleaver Banks, and Dr. Parr, and has their autographs, and
the following MS. notices :—' This treatise hath not been published.
Jt is written by one whose name begins with B—.' So says Dr.
Jortin, out of whose collection of books this was purchased."—
Michael Lort. ' A very scarce book, never published ; and, in my
opinion, very unfit to be published.'—*S. Parr.* He calls himself
(*i. e.* Mr. Balguy) an able reasoner, see p. 206. ' Warburton had a
decisive instant for the power of Satan to torment the bodies of
men. (See *Divine Legation*, vol. 6, p. 254.) Balguy in this book,
assigns him a particular time to disturb the moral world.' "

Parr Catalogue, pp. 19 and 44.

INDEX.

Woodfall and Kinder, Printers, Angel Court, Skinner Street, London

AN ACCOUNT

OF

PRIVATE PRESSES AND BOOK CLUBS

Second Edition.

WITH CONSIDERABLE ADDITIONS.

LETTERS

OF THE

EARL OF CHATHAM TO HIS NEPHEW

A New Edition,

WITH A MEMOIR OF LORD CAMELFORD

A Sketch of the Character of the Noble Editor, LORD GRENVILLE, by permission of the Right Honourable Lord Brougham.

WITH NOTES

BY THE EDITOR OF THIS WORK.

.